"Scholarly yet eminently accessible to t[...]enlighten-
ing both as a historical introduction to the Bible and as an overview of how it
has been read from ecumenical, intercontinental, and thematic perspectives.
An invaluable tool for beginners as a way to situate themselves in the world
of the Scriptures and as a resource to set the convictions of the experienced
in a more inclusive context. A tour de force!"

—**Brother John**, Taizé Community, France

"Essays by an ecumenical and international team of scholars illustrate in a
vivid and effective way the complex composition of the Scriptures, the many-
faceted reception they have received over the centuries, and the rich variety
of methods of interpretation among those religious traditions that revere the
Bible. In a world where some fear diversity, this volume demonstrates that
authentic interpretation of the Bible champions both diversity and unity."

—**Donald Senior, CP**, Catholic Theological Union

"*Scripture and Its Interpretation* is unique, highly useful, clearly written, up-
to-date, and enlightening. It is written from a broader Christian perspective
and tone that virtually any self-identifying Christian can appreciate. Much
appreciation towards all who brought this wonderful book into existence.
Highly recommended."

—**Jamin Andreas Hübner**, *Canadian-American Theological Review*

"This finely produced volume will be highly useful for serious study groups
and introductory courses."

—**Peter J. Judge**, *Catholic Biblical Quarterly*

"Gorman has successfully and enjoyably brought together a group of diverse
scholars and topics to present a global, ecumenical introduction to the Bible.
The reader will not be disappointed at having spent the time investing in this
volume."

—**Chuck Sackett**, *Englewood Review of Books*

"This collective introduction to the Christian Bible results from the collaboration of twenty-two scholars representing a variety of faith traditions and
social contexts. . . . The volume is illustrated throughout with a variety of
tables, maps, photos, and reproductions of religious artwork."

—*Old Testament Abstracts*

"This is a substantive project, both in quantity and quality. In terms of quantity,
this volume serves, in many ways, as a 'one-stop-shop' textbook for biblical

interpretation. It provides significant discussion of introductory matters. . . . In terms of quality, this volume brings together some of the finest thinkers in Christian academia . . . while also providing voice to those who may not be as commonly known in Western circles. Each chapter is significantly researched and written well. Each chapter also ends with reflection questions, which can prove useful to a hermeneutics instructor, and with an annotated list of follow-up reading."

—Rob O'Lynn, *Stone-Campbell Journal*

"The originality of its design, its wealth of information, its breadth, and its accessible language make [*Scripture and Its Interpretation*] stand apart among the large number of general introductions to the Bible available to readers."

—John C. Endres, *America* magazine

"The contributors are diverse, and their selection of topics reveals a vital church with manifold ways of interacting with the Bible. . . . An excellent introduction to students, church members, and interested Christians who want to benefit from learning how other believers through time and space have interpreted Scripture."

—Abram Kielsmeier-Jones, *Bible Study Magazine*

"An impressive volume of biblical scholarship that is thoroughly 'reader friendly' in organization and presentation, *Scripture and Its Interpretation* is unreservedly recommended for church, seminary, community, and academic library Biblical Studies collections."

—*Midwest Book Review*

Scripture *and* Its Interpretation

A Global, Ecumenical Introduction to the Bible

Edited by Michael J. Gorman

B
Baker Academic
a division of Baker Publishing Group
Grand Rapids, Michigan

© 2017 by Michael J. Gorman

Published by Baker Academic
a division of Baker Publishing Group
P.O. Box 6287, Grand Rapids, MI 49516-6287
www.bakeracademic.com

Paperback edition published 2020
ISBN 978-1-5409-6419-9

Printed in the United States of America

The Library of Congress has cataloged the hardcover edition as follows:
Names: Gorman, Michael J., 1955– editor.
Title: Scripture and its interpretation : a global, ecumenical introduction to the Bible / edited by Michael J. Gorman.
Description: Grand Rapids : Baker Publishing Group, 2017. | Includes bibliographical references and index.
Identifiers: LCCN 2017000729 | ISBN 9780801098390 (cloth)
Subjects: LCSH: Bible—Criticism, interpretation, etc. | Bible—Introductions.
Classification: LCC BS511.3 .S368 2017 | DDC 220.6/1—dc23
LC record available at https://lccn.loc.gov/2017000729

In keeping with biblical principles of creation stewardship, Baker Publishing Group advocates the responsible use of our natural resources. As a member of the Green Press Initiative, our company uses recycled paper when possible. The text paper of this book is composed in part of post-consumer waste.

To our students:
past, present, and future,
in our classrooms and around the world

Contents

Illustrations

Acknowledgments

My greatest debt as editor is to the contributors to this book, all of whom are scholars with many commitments who made time for this project because they believed in it. They not only wrote their own articles with great precision and clarity, but they also helped one another (and the editor) as needed. Each author was amazingly dedicated to this project and its usefulness for students.

In addition, I am grateful to Emily Hicks, my friend, colleague, and occasional student, for helping to prepare much of the text for editing and revising; and to my first-rate research assistant and former student, Gary Staszak (now an MPhil/PhD student at the University of Wales), especially for preparing the first draft of the glossary, assisting with the bibliographies, and completing various other editorial tasks. I am grateful as well to Michelle Rader, my current research assistant, for her indexing and proofreading. Special thanks are due to two Old Testament colleagues, Christopher B. Hays at Fuller Seminary and Rebecca Hancock at St. Mary's Ecumenical Institute, for their input on specific issues. And many thanks are owed to Joel Green, also of Fuller Seminary and a contributor, for his input on the glossary.

I am grateful as well to the fine staff at Baker Academic, especially Bryan Dyer and Jim Kinney, for their strong support of this book from its inception. Tim West was an incredibly gracious, insightful, and flexible editor, and Brandy Scritchfield was enormously helpful in obtaining images.

Finally, I thank students and faculty who expressed appreciation for this book's forerunner and who saw the need for the sort of volume that has now come to fruition.

Specific authors of chapters (noted in parentheses) wish to voice their thanks to colleagues who read part or all of their work: John Kselman (Michael

Barré); Mark Gorman, Drew Strait, and Andy Johnson (Michael Gorman); Catherine Rowland (Christopher Rowland); and Melanie Baffes (K. K. Yeo).

I also acknowledge those who allowed us to reprint photos and other images and to adapt previously published work: Fondation Martin Bodmer in Cologny (Geneva), Switzerland, for the image in chapter 1; Claremont Colleges Library for assistance in obtaining access to the photo of Nag Hammadi codices in chapter 5; Oxford University Press for permission for Michael Holmes to adapt his essay "The Biblical Canon" from *The Oxford Handbook of Early Christian Studies*, edited by Susan Ashbrook Harvey and David G. Hunter (New York: Oxford University Press, 2008), for use in chapter 6; Art Resource for images in chapters 7 and 9; St. Johanniskirche, Lüneburg, Germany, for the photo in chapter 8; the Bavarian State Library in Munich, Germany, for the image of Origen in chapter 9; Ronald Witherup for the photo in chapter 13; Eerdmans Publishing for permission for Craig Keener to adapt portions of *Spirit Hermeneutics: Reading Scripture in Light of Pentecost* for chapter 15; the Flower Pentecostal Heritage Center for the photo in chapter 15; Lisa Hunt and Epworth Chapel United Methodist Church, Baltimore, Maryland, USA, for the photo in chapter 17; the Associated Press (AP) for one of the photos in chapter 18; and Wayne Healy for the image of his mural, also in chapter 18. In addition, the staff at Baker Academic provided several images and graphics, and Brother John of Taizé assisted in the selection of the photo in chapter 20.

Michael J. Gorman
Week of Prayer for Christian Unity
January 2017

Visit www.bakeracademic.com/professors
to access study aids
and instructor materials for this textbook.

Contributors

Michael L. Barré, PSS, was Professor of Sacred Scripture at St. Mary's Seminary & University in Baltimore, Maryland, USA, from 1992 to 2016. A translator for the New American Bible and a former president of the Catholic Biblical Association, he is the author of numerous articles on the text and translation of the Hebrew Bible / Old Testament. Fr. Barré is a Roman Catholic priest and a member of the Society of Priests of St. Sulpice.

Bungishabaku Katho is Professor of Old Testament at Shalom University of Bunia in the Democratic Republic of the Congo (DRC), where he was also previously the University President. He recently completed a commentary on the books of Jeremiah and Lamentations in the Africa Bible Commentary series (to be published by Zonder-van). His PhD is from the University of KwaZulu-Natal in South Africa. Katho is a minister of the Church of the Brethren of the DRC and president of the denomination.

Carole Monica C. Burnett is the editor of the Fathers of the Church series, published by the Catholic University of America Press. From 2000 to 2014 she taught courses in Christian history at St. Mary's Ecumenical Institute, Baltimore, Maryland, USA. She is the author of articles and book chapters on the era of Augustine, motherhood in ancient Christianity, and patristic interpretations of the promised land. She is a member of the Antiochian Orthodox Church.

M. Daniel Carroll R. (Rodas) holds the Blanchard Chair of Old Testament in the Graduate School of Wheaton College in Wheaton, Illinois, USA, and is adjunct professor at El Seminario Teológico Centroamericano in Guatemala City, Guatemala. He is the author or editor of thirteen books and has contributed to several one-volume commentaries, works on Old Testament studies, and both English- and Spanish-language journals. His research is primarily on the prophetic literature, Old Testament social ethics, and immigration. He is active in Anglo and Hispanic churches.

Patricia Fosarelli, MD, DMin, is the Associate Dean of St. Mary's Ecumenical Institute, Baltimore, Maryland, USA, where she also teaches in the areas of spirituality and practical theology. As a physician she worked with seriously ill and dying children, while as a Roman Catholic lay minister she worked as a pastoral associate and director of religious education at a Baltimore parish. She is the author of eleven books and numerous articles in both of her disciplines.

Stephen Fowl is Professor of Theology at Loyola University Maryland in Baltimore, Maryland, USA. He has written numerous books and articles on the interrelationships between scriptural interpretation and theology, including *Theological Interpretation of Scripture* (Cascade Companions) and *Engaging Scripture: A Model for Theological Interpretation*. He is an Episcopal layperson and serves on the Theology Committee of the Episcopal Church's House of Bishops. He lives in Baltimore and worships at the Cathedral of the Incarnation.

Michael J. Gorman holds the Raymond E. Brown Chair in Biblical Studies and Theology at St. Mary's Seminary & University in Baltimore, Maryland, USA. He is the author of a dozen books, including a companion to this volume, *Elements of Biblical Exegesis*, and works on Paul, Revelation, and related topics. He has taught in Cameroon and is an adjunct professor for doctoral students at Shalom University, Bunia, Democratic Republic of the Congo. He is a Methodist layperson with Anabaptist affinities.

Joel B. Green is Professor of New Testament Interpretation, Dean of the School of Theology, and Provost at Fuller Theological Seminary, Pasadena, California, USA. He has written or edited more than forty-five books, many related to the Gospel of Luke and the Acts of the Apostles, the theological interpretation of Christian Scripture, and theology and science. He is also the editor of the New International Commentary on the New Testament series (Eerdmans). Green is an elder in The United Methodist Church.

Michael W. Holmes is University Professor of Biblical Studies and Early Christianity at Bethel University in St. Paul, Minnesota, USA. He is the author or editor of ten volumes, including *The Greek New Testament: SBL Edition*; *The Apostolic Fathers: Greek Texts and English Translations*; *The Text of the New Testament in Contemporary Research* (with Bart Ehrman); and a commentary on the Thessalonian letters. He is a member of Trinity Baptist Church in St. Paul.

Edith M. Humphrey is the William F. Orr Professor of New Testament at Pittsburgh Theological Seminary, Pennsylvania, USA, and secretary of the Orthodox Theological Society in America. Her books concern biblical and other ancient vision-reports, Trinitarian spirituality, worship, Scripture and Tradition, contemporary ecclesial debates, and (forthcoming) C. S. Lewis. A pianist and oboist, she also directed music at St. George Anglican (Ottawa, Canada) and currently participates in the choir at St. George Antiochian Orthodox Cathedral (Pittsburgh).

C. Anthony Hunt is Professor of Systematic, Moral, and Practical Theology at St. Mary's Ecumenical Institute in Baltimore, Maryland, USA, and also teaches on the adjunct faculties at Wesley Theological Seminary in Washington, DC, and United Theological Seminary in Dayton, Ohio. He is the Senior Pastor of Epworth Chapel United Methodist Church in Baltimore. His publications include *Keep Looking Up: Sermons on the Psalms* and *Blessed Are the Peacemakers: A Theological Analysis of the Thought of Howard Thurman and Martin Luther King, Jr.*

Christine E. Joynes is Director of the Centre for Reception History of the Bible at the University of Oxford, UK. Her research focuses on the reception history of the New Testament, and she is currently writing a Wiley-Blackwell Bible Commentary, *Mark's Gospel through the Centuries*. She serves on the editorial board of the Bloomsbury journal *Biblical Reception* and has edited several volumes and written many articles exploring interpretations of the Bible in art, music, and literature. She is a member of Abingdon Baptist Church in Oxfordshire.

Craig S. Keener is F. M. and Ada Thompson Professor of Biblical Studies at Asbury Theological Seminary in Wilmore, Kentucky, USA. He has authored twenty books, including a work on Spirit hermeneutics, other works on the Spirit, and various commentaries—most notably on Matthew, a two-volume commentary on John, and four volumes on Acts. He is ordained as a minister in the National Baptist Convention, USA, and is also charismatic, identifying with the broad pentecostal tradition.

Brent Laytham is Professor of Theology at St. Mary's Seminary & University in Baltimore, Maryland, USA, and Dean of St. Mary's Ecumenical Institute. An ordained United Methodist with pastoral experience, he formerly taught at North Park Theological Seminary, has taught in Africa, and was the coordinator of The Ekklesia Project (2003–2015). The editor of two books and author of another, he is currently preparing a theological commentary on 2 Corinthians. He teaches and researches at the intersections of Scripture, liturgy, theology, ethics, and culture.

Claire Mathews McGinnis is a professor in the Department of Theology at Loyola University Maryland, in Baltimore, Maryland, USA, where she teaches both undergraduate and graduate courses. She has published two books on Isaiah, has written more than a dozen articles on the Hebrew Bible / Old Testament and its history of interpretation, and is currently writing a commentary on Exodus in the Reading the Old Testament series (Smyth & Helwys). She is a Roman Catholic layperson.

Christopher Rowland is Dean Ireland Professor of the Exegesis of Holy Scripture Emeritus at the University of Oxford, UK. He has written on the apocalyptic and eschatological traditions of the Bible, the influence of early Jewish mysticism on the New Testament, the reception history of the book of Revelation, political theology and the Bible, and liberation theology. His most recent book is on the biblical hermeneutics of the English visionary poet, artist, and engraver William Blake. Rowland is a lifelong member of the Church of England.

Christopher W. Skinner is Associate Professor of New Testament and Early Christianity at Loyola University Chicago in Chicago, Illinois, USA. In addition to several dozen articles and book chapters, he has written or edited seven books, including *Character Studies and the Gospel of Mark* (Bloomsbury/T&T Clark), *What Are They Saying about the Gospel of Thomas?* (Paulist Press), and *Reading John* (Cascade). In addition to teaching, he has more than a decade of pastoral experience.

Karen J. Wenell is a member of the Department of Theology and Religion at the University of Birmingham, UK, where she teaches New Testament. She has written about biblical sacred spaces, an interest that began with her book *Jesus and Land* (Continuum, 2007) and continues within her current work on the kingdom of God and its interpretation in the New Testament and beyond. She is an Anglican with a background in the Swedish Covenant Church, and was previously coeditor of the *Expository Times*.

Jonathan Wilson-Hartgrove is Director of the School for Conversion in Durham, North Carolina, USA. A cofounder of the Rutba House community in Durham, he is the author of numerous books on Christian spirituality and social action, including *New Monasticism: What It Has to Say to Today's Church* and, with Shane Claiborne, *Becoming the Answer to Our Prayers: Prayer for Ordinary Radicals*. Wilson-Hartgrove is a Baptist preacher and a popular speaker.

Ronald D. Witherup, PSS, is former Academic Dean and Professor of Sacred Scripture at St. Patrick's Seminary & University in Menlo Park, California, USA. The author of numerous books and articles on biblical and theological themes, including *Scripture: Dei Verbum*, in the Rediscovering Vatican II series, he holds a doctorate in biblical studies from Union Theological Seminary in Richmond, Virginia. He is a Roman Catholic priest and Superior General of the Society of Priests of St. Sulpice, residing in Paris, France.

N. T. Wright is Research Professor of New Testament and Early Christianity at St. Mary's College, University of St. Andrews in St. Andrews, Scotland. The former Bishop of Durham in the Church of England (2003–2010), he is the author of over eighty books and scores of articles on the Bible and its contemporary relevance. These include academic works such as the multivolume *Christian Origins and the Question of God* as well as the popular New Testament for Everyone commentary series. He has also published books on Christian belief, Christian virtue, the atonement, the authority of Scripture, and Christian hope and mission.

K. K. Yeo is Kendall Chair Professor of New Testament at Garrett-Evangelical Seminary and Affiliate Professor at the Department of Asian Languages and Cultures, Northwestern University, Evanston, Illinois, USA. He is also a Visiting Professor at Peking University and Co-director of the Center for Classical Greco-Roman Philosophy at Tsinghua University, China. He has authored and edited over thirty-five Chinese and English books on cross-cultural biblical interpretation, including *Musing with Confucius and Paul* (Wipf & Stock). He is a Methodist.

Paul P. Zilonka, CP, was Associate Professor of Biblical Studies at St. Mary's Seminary & University in Baltimore, Maryland, USA, from 1998 to 2009, where he taught in both the School of Theology and St. Mary's Ecumenical Institute. As a Passionist priest he also taught and did seminary formation work in New York, Chicago, Boston, and Jamaica, West Indies. Fr. Zilonka earned his SSL from the Pontifical Biblical Institute and his doctorate from the Gregorian University, both in Rome. He passed away in 2015.

Abbreviations

Biblical Books

Old Testament

Gen.	Genesis
Exod.	Exodus
Lev.	Leviticus
Num.	Numbers
Deut.	Deuteronomy
Josh.	Joshua
Judg.	Judges
Ruth	Ruth
1–2 Sam.	1–2 Samuel
1–2 Kings	1–2 Kings
1–2 Chron.	1–2 Chronicles
Ezra	Ezra
Neh.	Nehemiah
Esther	Esther
Job	Job
Ps(s).	Psalm(s)
Prov.	Proverbs
Eccles.	Ecclesiastes
Song	Song of Songs/Solomon
Isa.	Isaiah
Jer.	Jeremiah
Lam.	Lamentations
Ezek.	Ezekiel
Dan.	Daniel
Hosea	Hosea
Joel	Joel
Amos	Amos
Obad.	Obadiah
Jon.	Jonah
Mic.	Micah
Nah.	Nahum
Hab.	Habakkuk
Zeph.	Zephaniah
Hag.	Haggai
Zech.	Zechariah
Mal.	Malachi

New Testament

Matt.	Matthew
Mark	Mark
Luke	Luke
John	John
Acts	Acts
Rom.	Romans
1–2 Cor.	1–2 Corinthians
Gal.	Galatians
Eph.	Ephesians
Phil.	Philippians
Col.	Colossians
1–2 Thess.	1–2 Thessalonians
1–2 Tim.	1–2 Timothy
Titus	Titus
Philem.	Philemon
Heb.	Hebrews
James	James
1–2 Pet.	1–2 Peter
1–3 John	1–3 John
Jude	Jude
Rev.	Revelation

Old Testament Apocrypha (Deutero-canonical Books)

Add. Dan.	Additions to Daniel (= Bel and the Dragon, Prayer of Azariah, Song of the Three Jews, and Susanna)
Add. Esth.	Additions to Esther
Bar.	Baruch
Bel	Bel and the Dragon
1–2 Esd.	1–2 Esdras
Jdt.	Judith
Let. Jer.	Letter of Jeremiah (= Baruch 6)
1–4 Macc.	1–4 Maccabees
Pr. Azar.	Prayer of Azariah (often cited as part of the Song of the Three Jews)
Pr. Man.	Prayer of Manasseh
Ps. 151	Psalm 151
Sg. Three	Song of the Three Jews
Sir. (Ecclus.)	Sirach (Ecclesiasticus)
Sus.	Susanna
Tob.	Tobit
Wis.	Wisdom (of Solomon)

Bible Translations

AV	Authorized Version (= KJV)
CEB	Common English Bible
KJV	King James Version
NAB	New American Bible
NIV	New International Version
NJB	New Jerusalem Bible
NJPS	New Jewish Publication Society translation
NKJV	New King James Version
NRSV	New Revised Standard Version
RSV	Revised Standard Version

Other Abbreviations

AD	"in the year of our Lord" (Latin *Anno Domini*)
adj.	adjective
BCE	before the Common Era
ca.	approximately (Latin *circa*)
CE	Common Era (similar to AD)
cf.	compare (Latin *confer*)
ch(s).	chapter(s)
d.	died
DSS	Dead Sea Scrolls
ed(s).	edited by, editor(s), edition
e.g.	for example (Latin *exempli gratia*)
esp.	especially
exp.	expanded
i.e.	that is (Latin *id est*)
incl.	including
LXX	Septuagint (Greek translation of the Old Testament)
MT	Masoretic Text
n.	noun
NT	New Testament
OT	Old Testament
par.	parallels
PBC	Pontifical Biblical Commission
pl.	plural
rev.	revised
sing.	singular
trans.	translated by, translation

Introduction

MICHAEL J. GORMAN

Blessed Lord, who caused all holy Scriptures to be written for our learning:
Grant us so to hear them, read, mark, learn, and inwardly digest them, that we
may embrace and ever hold fast the blessed hope of everlasting life, which you
have given us in our Savior Jesus Christ; who lives and reigns with you and the
Holy Spirit, one God, for ever and ever. Amen.

—from the Anglican Book of Common Prayer

This book is a global, ecumenical introduction to the Christian Bible and its
interpretation across time and throughout various cultures. It has been prepared by a group of outstanding contributors from the four major streams of
Christianity in the world: Catholic, Orthodox, Protestant, and Pentecostal.
These contributors represent numerous countries and cultures: Britain, China,
the Democratic Republic of the Congo, France, Guatemala, and the United
States. The book is written in English, though that is not the mother tongue
of some of the contributors. Although more than half currently live in the
United States, several of these scholars have taught in other countries, and
many have lectured internationally—sometimes in other languages, including
Chinese, French, and Spanish.

Despite this broad range of contributors and their vast experience, it would
be impossible for any book to be a truly *comprehensive* global and ecumenical
text on Scripture and its interpretation because there are so many tributaries

within the various Christian streams and so many subcultures within the various cultures Christians inhabit. This reality means that there are very different approaches to the Bible within those streams and their tributaries, and within those cultures and their subcultures. For instance, when I asked a fellow biblical scholar in India to recommend some books on Indian or South Asian interpretation of the Bible (hermeneutics), he replied, "There is *dalit* ["oppressed," "untouchables"] hermeneutics, tribal hermeneutics, eco-hermeneutics, feminist hermeneutics, and postcolonial hermeneutics from the Indian point of view. And there is North India hermeneutics, South India, etc."

While acknowledging these sorts of unavoidable limitations, we think this book is a unique and significant approach to Scripture and its interpretation, a critically important way to begin the study of Scripture in our contemporary global context. It is particularly significant for Western readers (and perhaps especially for Americans) to realize how the Bible is read elsewhere—and how it is read in many different ways in the multicultural contexts of their own countries. We encourage readers to look at the chapters on scriptural interpretation within various traditions and cultures as significant but also as *representative* rather than comprehensive.

The first part of the book deals with the Bible itself, including its character as both library and single book, its historical and geographical contexts, surveys of both Testaments, the formation of the canon, associated books that did not make it into the Bible, and the history of Bible translations. The second part of the book considers the reception and interpretation of Scripture in various traditions. After a chapter introducing the topic of the Bible's reception, there are chapters devoted to biblical interpretation from premodern to postmodern times and also to the recent return to theological interpretation. There follow chapters on Protestant, Roman Catholic, Orthodox, and Pentecostal interpretation, as well as chapters on African, African American, Latino/Latina, and Asian and Asian American interpretation. The chapters in the third part of the book look at the relationship between Scripture and spirituality, Christian ethics, politics, Christian community, and Christian mission.

I am privileged to count many of the contributors to this book as good friends. More importantly, however, they are all first-rate scholars who have a shared passion for responsible, informed, contextualized reading of the Bible as Scripture—as a word of divine address. As the editor, I hope that readers will benefit immensely from this unique global and ecumenical collaborative effort.

This volume is the sequel to an earlier book I edited, which was called *Scripture: An Ecumenical Introduction to the Bible and Its Interpretation.* The chapters of that book were all written by current or former members of the faculty of St. Mary's Ecumenical Institute, an academic division of St. Mary's Seminary & University in Baltimore, Maryland. Established in 1791, St. Mary's is the oldest Roman Catholic seminary in the United States and, as far as we know, the only one in the world with an ecumenical division. It was founded by, and is still owned by, what is now called the Society of Priests of St. Sulpice, based in Paris. The Sulpicians are dedicated to theological education around the world, so it makes complete sense that the current book follows one that emerged from a context of global and ecumenical commitments. All contributors were chosen because of their own global and ecumenical concerns.

Some of the chapters in this book appeared also in the earlier volume. Those essays have all been revised and updated, with special attention to developments in their particular areas of study, especially new publications.

As we will see in the first chapter, one way to think of the Bible is as a library. Libraries are so vast and specialized that we would be foolish to think we could navigate one easily. That is why we often need the assistance of a librarian to locate quickly the information we are seeking. The contributors to this book are, in part, like librarians who have some significant familiarity with what you can discover in the Bible and in its varied interpretations over the centuries and across cultures. (For there is also a library of books—literal and figurative—*about* the Bible.) We do so, not as disinterested, neutral parties, but as committed interpreters of Scripture ourselves. Our goal is to help you find your own way, and to show you how others have found their way, through and in the pages of Scripture.

You may have many questions as you begin your study of the Bible, and we will provide answers to some of them. But, like spending time in any library, reading Scripture carefully will also raise questions you have not yet formulated. And like a good library, in fact like any good book, Scripture also invites all of us into a world that we could not imagine on our own. In addition, there are approaches to reading and interpreting the Bible that you have probably never heard of or considered. We hope to point you in the direction of some of these interesting questions, answers, and perspectives.

When all is said and done, we aim to help you discover the breadth and depth of Sacred Scripture by taking the time to read through its many books carefully and reflectively in the company of others—people from familiar surroundings as well as those from other centuries and locations.

A Note to the Reader

Boldfaced terms are words or phrases included in the glossary. Such terms are generally boldfaced the first time they appear in the book, and sometimes in later chapters as well. Students are advised to consult the glossary as necessary while they read.

Full publication information for works cited parenthetically or in footnotes is found in the bibliography at the end of each chapter.

The Bible

In part 1 of this book, we orient you to the Bible as a whole, its geographical and historical contexts, and the contents of the two Testaments. We also introduce you to some important nonbiblical writings, the formation of the Bible (the canon of Scripture), and the transmission and translation of the Bible over the centuries.

In addition to this book, a good study Bible prepared by a team of scholars is a helpful resource. Some options for readers of English include the following:

Attridge, Harold W., ed. *The Harper Collins Study Bible*. Rev. ed. New York: HarperOne, 2006. New Revised Standard Version (NRSV).

Berlin, Adele, and Mark Zvi Brettler, eds. *The Jewish Study Bible*. 2nd ed. New York: Oxford University Press, 2014. New Jewish Publication Society translation (NJPS) of the Hebrew Bible (Christian Old Testament).

Carson, D. A., ed. *NIV Zondervan Study Bible*. Grand Rapids: Zondervan, 2015. New International Version (NIV).

Green, Joel B., ed. *The CEB Study Bible*. Nashville: Abingdon, 2013. Common English Bible translation (CEB).

Harrelson, Walter, ed. *The New Interpreter's Study Bible*. Nashville: Abingdon, 2003. New Revised Standard Version (NRSV).

Levine, Amy-Jill, and Marc Zvi Brettler, eds. *The Jewish Annotated New Testament*. New York: Oxford University Press, 2011.

Senior, Donald, John Collins, and Mary Ann Getty, eds. *The Catholic Study Bible*. 3rd ed. New York: Oxford University Press, 2016. New American Bible translation (NAB).

Each chapter in this book concludes with a list of recommended reading for further study. Other general recommended resources for serious biblical study include the following.

One-Volume Resources

Freedman, David Noel, ed. *Eerdmans Dictionary of the Bible*. Grand Rapids: Eerdmans, 2000. A one-volume Bible dictionary with almost 5,000 contributions from more than 600 scholars.

Muddiman, John, and John Barton, eds. *The Oxford Bible Commentary*. Oxford: Oxford University Press, 2001. A one-volume collection of commentaries on all the biblical books.

Patte, Daniel, ed. *Global Bible Commentary*. Nashville: Abingdon, 2004. A one-volume commentary on both Testaments, with contributions from scholars around the world.

Vanhoozer, Kevin J., ed. *Dictionary for Theological Interpretation of the Bible*. Grand Rapids: Baker Academic, 2005. Biblical, theological, and interpretive articles.

Multivolume Resources

Keck, Leander E., ed. *The New Interpreter's Bible*. 12 vols. plus an index volume. Nashville: Abingdon, 1994–2004. General articles on various aspects of the Bible precede extensive commentaries for each biblical book that include theological reflection on every passage.

Sakenfeld, Katherine Doob, ed. *New Interpreter's Dictionary of the Bible*. 5 vols. Nashville: Abingdon, 2006–2009. In-depth articles on everything related to the Bible and biblical study.

Electronic Resources

Among the most sophisticated programs for biblical studies, the following generally come in various packages: Accordance, BibleWorks, Gramcord, and Logos.

1

The Bible: A Book, a Library, a Story, an Invitation

Paul P. Zilonka and Michael J. Gorman

The title of this book contains within it two ways of referring to its subject matter: **Scripture** and the **Bible**. The first, Scripture, sometimes used in the plural (the Scriptures), comes from the Latin for "writings" (*scriptura*); this in turn corresponds to a common way of referring to sacred writings in **Greek**: *hai graphai* (the writings). The second, Bible, comes from the Greek word for "book," *biblion*. What we are about to explore, then, is a book, or collection, of sacred writings. For this reason, people of faith sometimes call this book the Sacred Scriptures or the Holy Bible.

Although many people use the terms "Bible" and "Scripture" interchangeably, as we will here, the two terms can suggest different nuances of meaning. For instance, many religious traditions have sacred texts, or scriptures, but only Judaism and Christianity refer to their scriptures as "the Bible." Ironically, however, some people feel that the term "Bible" is more religiously neutral, and perhaps more academic, than the term "Scripture," with its connotation of holiness or divine inspiration. In fact, this situation is now so commonplace that some biblical scholars, including many contributors to this book, insist

Paul Zilonka wrote the original version of this chapter and, when faced with an illness that would soon take his life, asked the book's editor to update and expand it.

that when we interpret the Bible from the perspective of faith, even from an academic point of view, we are treating it as Scripture, as sacred text—not merely as ancient literature.

In this and the following chapters, we will attempt to look at the Bible, or Scripture, from both an academic perspective and a faith perspective. That is to say, we want to understand it, simultaneously, as both human book and sacred text.

Our investigation begins with a consideration of the Bible as both book and library, and then, more briefly, as both story and invitation.

The Bible as Book

As we have just explained, the English word "Bible" originated from the Greek term for book (*biblion*), which is derived in turn from the Greek words for the **papyrus** plant (*byblos*) and its inner bark (*biblos*). Egyptian craftsmen produced an ancient version of paper by matting together strips of this marshland plant. The dried sheets of papyrus were then glued together in rolls to become a **scroll**. Jeremiah, especially in its ancient Greek version (the **Septuagint**, abbreviated **LXX**), gives a colorful example of how the invention of these materials contributed greatly to the development of the Bible:

> In the fourth year of King Jehoiakim son of Josiah of Judah, this word came to Jeremiah from the LORD: Take a scroll [Greek *chartion bibliou*] and write on it all the words that I have spoken to you against Israel and Judah and all the nations, from the day I spoke to you, from the days of Josiah until today. (Jer. 36:1–2 [43:1–2 LXX])[1]

Baruch, Jeremiah's secretary, refers to the process: "He dictated all these words to me, and I wrote them with ink on the scroll [Greek *en bibliō*]" (v. 18). Even though the angry king burned the document "until the entire scroll was consumed in the fire" (v. 23), Jeremiah dictated another with "all the words of the scroll that King Jehoiakim of Judah had burned in the fire, and many similar words were added to them" (v. 32). From this biblical passage, it is relatively easy to understand the transition from writing on *papyrus* (Greek *biblos*) to naming the finished product, a scroll or a *book* (Greek *biblion*).

---

1. Two notes for the reader: (1) When the word "**Lord**" appears in most translations of the **Old Testament** (**OT**) in small caps (LORD), it translates God's personal name, **YHWH**. (2) For a variety of reasons, the division of the OT into chapters and verses sometimes varies from the original Hebrew to the LXX.

Ordinarily, only one side of a papyrus scroll contained writing. (The heavenly visions in Ezekiel and Revelation specifically mention writing on both sides of the papyrus as a sign of an extraordinary, supernatural message: Ezek. 2:10; Rev. 5:1.) Scrolls were the ordinary instrument for preserving and reading the sacred texts in synagogues; locating a particular passage required some dexterity with large scrolls. The Gospel of Luke describes the scene in the Nazareth synagogue when "the scroll of the prophet Isaiah was given to [Jesus]. He unrolled the scroll and found the passage where it was written: 'The Spirit of the Lord is upon me . . .'" (4:16–17).

Papyrus was not the only material on which ancient writers inscribed texts. After animal skins were thoroughly cleaned, stretched, dried, and stitched together, they served the same purpose as the more costly papyrus, which grew only in certain lowland regions (e.g., Egypt, Galilee) and thus often had to be imported. The abundance of sheep and goats in Palestine provided a steady source of durable scrolls called **parchment** (Greek *membrana*). Scribes who produced the collection of Jewish manuscripts (from around the time of Jesus) that scholars today call the **Dead Sea Scrolls** (**DSS**) used these animal skins, which were durable enough to survive after more than 1,900 years in clay jars.

In Roman times, writing tablets with wax surfaces were framed and hinged together along one edge. Since the frames were made of wood (Latin *caudex*), the set of writing tablets was called a **codex**. This arrangement allowed for writing on both sides. Soon sheets of papyrus or parchment were sewn together at the spine. The result was the precursor of the modern book. By the second century **CE**,[2] the emerging books of the Christian **canon** (a collection of authoritative sacred texts) were inscribed in this kind of codex, while the Jewish community generally retained the scroll format. The practicality and economy of a portable document with writing on both sides were eminently suited to the rugged missionary lifestyle of Christian evangelists, and the codex helped Christians to think of their various sacred texts as constituting one book.

The Bible as One Book

Most people come to the reading of the Scriptures with some preconceptions about what they are. Since they are often described by one, singular title—"the Bible"—and since, like most other books, the Bible has a front and a back cover, it is understandable that so many people think of the Bible simply as

2. CE, the abbreviation for "**Common Era**" (i.e., the shared Christian and Jewish era), is an alternative to AD.

Figure 1.1. The first page of the Gospel of John from P⁶⁶ (Papyrus Bodmer II), the earliest relatively complete manuscript of that Gospel, dating from ca. 200 CE.

one book. A quick glance at the titles in a Bible's table of contents might give the impression that it is one book with many chapters. Likewise, believers confidently speak of the whole Bible as the "Word of God." This familiar heartfelt expression of faith significantly reinforces the idea that God is the one author of everything contained in its unified pages. And to be sure, the Bible does tell one grand story of God's love for humankind, which theologians have tried to summarize in such biblical words as grace, salvation, the kingdom of God, or **covenant**. (We shall return to this story toward the end of the chapter.)

However, even after spending only a little time paging through the dozens of individual sections of the Bible, we discover great diversity in writing style and content, suggesting many different human authors and objectives. In addition, the dates implied in these texts range from the beginning of the world to what seems like its end in the not-too-distant future. This variety of historical epochs suggests long periods of use and reinterpretation of earlier documents.

Honestly recognizing the complexity of the Bible as a diverse collection prepares us to experience both why it is a treasure of great spiritual value and why it also requires careful study. In fact, the Bible attests to its own diversity.

The Bible as Many Books

The Bible clearly indicates that it contains other books within itself. Frequently, the Bible refers to the "book of the law of Moses" (2 Kings 14:6) or the "book of Moses" (Mark 12:26). Mention is also made of other specific documents, such as the "book of the words of the prophet Isaiah" (Luke 3:4; cf. 4:17), the "book of the prophets" (Acts 7:42), the book of "Hosea" (Rom. 9:25), and the "book of Psalms" (Acts 1:20).[3]

The Gospel of John also refers to itself as a "book" (John 20:30; Greek *biblion*). Likewise, the author of the Acts of the Apostles tightly knits that document to the story about Jesus that the same person had presented "in the first book" (or "account"; Greek *logon*)—namely, the Gospel according to Luke (Acts 1:1; cf. Luke 1:1–4).

This little journey of discovery alerts us to the truth that the Bible is not really just one book. In fact, we can speak quite appropriately of it as a library of books.

The Bible as Library

In a library, individual books are usually organized according to particular topics. There are sections for science, philosophy, religion, history, art, music,

3. The Bible also refers to other books that, though not included in the Bible itself, were apparently used as sources for the composition of some biblical texts. This phenomenon is mostly associated with descriptions of the deeds of the Israelite monarchy. For example, there is the "Book of the Acts of Solomon" (1 Kings 11:41), the "Books of the Annals of the Kings of Israel" (1 Kings 14:19), and the "Book of the Annals of the Kings of Judah" (1 Kings 14:29). There is a similar phenomenon in the **New Testament** (**NT**). Luke 1:1–4 mentions more than one previous narrative of what Luke also intends to write as an "orderly account" (v. 3).

biography, fiction, and so on. An educated person has certain expectations about what information would be contained in the books grouped in these various sections of the library. Since library books are not generally organized by the dates they were written, two books by two authors who lived twenty centuries apart can stand side by side. For example, we might find a philosophical work by Plato (430–347 BCE) on the same shelf as a commentary on that work by a modern philosopher and published just last year. Despite the vast difference in time, both books focus on the same literature of Plato. We benefit greatly when we read both works together, even though they were written more than two millennia apart.

In the Bible, individual books containing material spanning many decades (in the case of the **New Testament**, abbreviated **NT**) or even many centuries (in the case of the **Old Testament**, abbreviated **OT**) are joined together in collections. For example, the first five books in the Jewish collection (the Christian Old Testament) are usually associated with Moses, whose story links four of them (all but Genesis) together, yet the books were not written at the same time. Other books from different periods are grouped together because of their association with the ministry of individual Hebrew prophets. A smaller group of writings from various centuries concerns itself with provocative topics of a general nature, such as the challenge of belief in a God of love and justice while believers live in a world where innocent people suffer and their oppressors prosper. The book of Psalms gathers together 150 hymns written over many centuries. **Gospels** attributed to four different Christian authors stand side by side, even though many factors, including date of composition, distinguish them from one another. The same is true of letters by various Christian missionaries. The profound religious relationship among all of these writings from various time periods is not always immediately evident.

The diversity in the Bible with respect not only to date but also to literary **genre** (type) is thus quite remarkable. As the previous paragraph suggests, the Bible contains historical works, prophetic books, quasi-philosophical writings, hymns, biographies (the Gospels),[4] and letters. There are also legal documents, short stories, collections of proverbs, sermons, records of visions, and other kinds of literature. Within each of these kinds of books, we find numerous additional literary forms, such as the well-known parables.

Having all the books of the Bible gathered together between two covers of one book makes them all available to us at the same time. Even though they have much in common with one another, we should never forget that

---

4. In some respects the Gospels may be understood as ancient, though not modern, biographies. See further discussion in ch. 4.

each book has its own history of development and its own unique perspective. Despite some strong literary ties among them, most of the books in the Bible are quite independent of one another, just like the books in any other kind of library.

In Search of a Name

What's in a name? We are all sensitive to people who misspell or mispronounce our personal names. Thus, people of Jewish and Christian faith who cherish these collections of religious books are justifiably sensitive to the names other people use to designate their sacred writings. For example, **Jews** organize their twenty-four books (thirty-nine as counted in the Christian Bible) into three collections that they call **Torah** (tradition/instruction/law), **Nevi'im** (prophets), and **Ketuvim** (writings). Together, this library of Jewish sacred texts is often called TaNaK, or **Tanak**, which is an acronym formed from the initial **Hebrew** letter of each collection—the equivalent of the English letters T, N, and K.[5] Jews may also call this collection simply "the Bible" or "the Scriptures." Christians usually refer to it as "the Old Testament" or "the Christian Old Testament" (see further discussion below). Some Christians and biblical scholars who prefer a more neutral or nuanced term than "Old Testament" designate these same documents as the Scriptures of Israel or the **Hebrew Bible** (abbreviated **HB**), since most of the collection was originally written in Hebrew, though there are several portions in **Aramaic**, the **lingua franca** of the Persian Empire and the language that gradually replaced spoken Hebrew after the **Babylonian exile** (586–539 BCE).[6]

The cessation of Hebrew as a spoken language and the rise of the empire under Alexander the Great (356–323 BCE)—which spread Greek culture, religion, and language—threatened the religious and cultural heritage of Jews scattered around the Mediterranean and further East.[7] Under these circumstances, Jews had to find a way to preserve their sacred texts for a new cultural and linguistic reality.

5. Alternate transliterations for the second and third divisions are Nebi'im and Ketubim, Kethuvim, or Kethubim; for the whole, Tanakh.

6. Dan. 2:4b–7:28; Ezra 4:8–6:18; 7:12–26; Jer. 10:11. BCE means "before the Common Era," a scholarly alternative to "BC," meaning "before Christ," and used in conjunction with CE.

7. While we today take for granted that the Bible should be translated into every language of the earth so that its message might be accessible to all, this was a new idea two millennia ago. Indeed, even today the Qur'an in its original Arabic is the sole norm for Muslim worship and scriptural study, no matter what the nationality or ethnic background of those who embrace Islam. Only recently has the Roman Catholic Church authorized its worship in vernacular languages after Latin prevailed generally for 1,500 years in the Latin Rite churches.

The Septuagint

About 250 BCE, Greek-speaking Jewish inhabitants of Alexandria in Egypt took the bold step of translating their Hebrew scriptures into Greek. The Letter of Aristeas (written around 120 BCE)[8] offers a defense for the evolution of the Greek translation that came to be known as the Septuagint (a Latin expression for "seventy"). This name and its customary abbreviation, LXX (the Roman numerals for 70), stem from the sacred legend, recorded in the Letter of Aristeas, that seventy Jewish scholars produced the translation independently of one another under the inspiration of God and without any error or confusion. Although scholars today provide a more nuanced theory for the growth of the Septuagint as a long-term process, the existence of this Greek translation facilitated the popular acceptance of other inspirational Jewish books written in Greek rather than in Hebrew. These include the Wisdom of Solomon, Judith, Baruch, the Letter of Jeremiah, 1–2 Maccabees, and some short Greek additions to Esther and Daniel. (Today these books are included in some Christian Bibles, but not in the Jewish Bible; see the tables in figs. 1.2–5 below and the discussion in chs. 3 and 6.) In addition to what we call the Septuagint, other translations of the OT into Greek were made.

Jesus read from the Hebrew Scriptures in the synagogue of Nazareth, but soon after his death and resurrection disciples like Paul of Tarsus evangelized Jews, converts to Judaism (proselytes), and non-Jews in many Greek-speaking cities of the Mediterranean world. The Christian church was born with a Bible in its cradle—namely, the Greek Septuagint. The twenty-seven Christian documents that came out of that period of growth of the early church are treasured today as the New Testament. They were originally written in Greek, and when those documents quote from the Jewish Scriptures, they clearly demonstrate a preference for the LXX version, the wording of which sometimes differs from the original Hebrew text.

Old Testament, New Testament

The Christian Bible has two divisions, or **Testaments**. As noted above, Christian tradition designates the books of the Tanak with the term "Old Testament" in light of the customary name of its own collection of twenty-seven documents: the "New Testament," from a Latin word, *testamentum*, that can mean "covenant."[9] The literary and theological relationship between

8. This second-century BCE Jewish document is considered to be one of the OT **Pseudepigrapha** (see ch. 5).
9. Henceforth in this book, Old Testament and New Testament are often abbreviated OT and NT.

the Jewish and Christian collections—the two parts of the Christian Bible—explains both the origin and the significance of these related titles.

"Covenant" (Hebrew *berît*; Greek *diathēkē*) is one of the most significant concepts in the experience of Jewish and Christian faith. This important term links together the salvation stories associated with Noah, Abraham, Moses, David, and Jesus. Indeed, the collections of Jewish and Christian writings arose over centuries as the respective communities described, commented upon, and propagated the realities of successive covenants. When Jeremiah 31:31 speaks of God establishing a "new covenant with the house of Israel and the house of Judah," the foundation was laid in the minds of later generations for some new revelation that would add to what was not yet present in the former experiences of covenant. Thus, the Christian writings characteristically refer to the "Scripture(s)" (Tanak) as being "fulfilled"—that is, brought to completion in some new way by Jesus or by a person or event in Christian experience (e.g., John 19:24, 36; cf. Luke 24:27, 44–45).

As if to echo the words of Jeremiah, in the Gospel tradition Jesus explicitly refers to the "new covenant in my blood" (Luke 22:20; cf. 1 Cor. 11:25). Paul speaks of old and new covenants (2 Cor. 3:6, 14). Even more explicitly alluding to Jeremiah 31:31, the Letter to the Hebrews contrasts the former covenant with Israel with the Christian experience of Jesus as mediator of a "better" (7:22; 8:6), and "new" (9:15) covenant.

So as to address a perceived disparaging tone in the comparison of "old" and "new" covenants, various scholars, as well as some lay Christians concerned about Jewish-Christian relations, have suggested more neutral terms such as Two Testaments, though this still involves speaking of the **First Testament** and the **Second Testament**. In reality, the Christian Bible shares the Tanak (the first of the two Christian Testaments) with the continuing religious community of Judaism today. For Christians, then, the Scriptures of Israel are also Christian Scripture. (It is therefore erroneous, factually and theologically, to refer to the NT alone as "the Christian Scriptures.") Even Augustine's assertion, centuries ago, that the New Testament lies hidden in the Old and the Old is made manifest in the New, supports this shared understanding of the Hebrew Scriptures. One Christian scholar, Philip Cunningham, suggests rewording Augustine's formula in this way: "In the Shared Testament, the **rabbinic** texts and the Christian Testament find their perpetual foundations; in the Christian Testament, the Shared Testament is intensely read anew in Christ" (*Sharing the Scriptures*, 18).

Perhaps sensitivity is best exercised by taking into account the religious context of discussion. Differing Jewish and Christian titles such as Tanak, Old Testament, and New Testament make eminent sense within their respective faith communities. These terms do have a biblical basis for their origin and usage. The use of these tradition-specific terms, even in scholarly discussion, acknowledges how the diverse faith groups have traditionally thought of their own documents. In this book we will use terms such as "New Testament" and "the writings of the New Covenant" interchangeably, as we will also do with terms such as "the Old Testament," "the Hebrew Bible," and "the Scriptures of Israel."

Canons

A collection of sacred texts forms a standard or norm for a particular religious community. The Jewish and Christian communities use the term "canon" (Greek *kanōn*) for their respective official lists of individual books they consider inspired and sacred. The root meaning of this term is "measuring stick"; hence, the canon is the standard, or norm, that guides a tradition's belief and behavior. (Though a *canon* of biblical books is quite different from a *cannon* used in military combat, biblical canons have led to a lot of heated debate over the centuries.) Chapter 6 of this book considers the formation of the biblical canons.

Figure 1.2. The Jewish Scriptures / Tanak (24 Books)

Torah (Instruction)	Nevi'im (Prophets)	Ketuvim (Writings)
Genesis	Former	Psalms
Exodus	Joshua	Proverbs
Leviticus	Judges	Job
Numbers	Samuel	Song of Songs (Song of Solomon)
Deuteronomy	Kings	Ruth
	Latter	Lamentations
	Isaiah	Ecclesiastes
	Jeremiah	Esther
	Ezekiel	Daniel
	The Book of the Twelve*	Ezra–Nehemiah
	Hosea	Chronicles
	Joel	
	Amos	
	Obadiah	
	Jonah	
	Micah	
	Nahum	
	Habakkuk	
	Zephaniah	
	Haggai	
	Zechariah	
	Malachi	

* The Book of the Twelve is considered one book.

Figure 1.3. The Protestant Old Testament
(= the Jewish Bible counted as 39 books)

Pentateuch	Historical and Poetic Books	Prophetic Books
Genesis	Joshua	Isaiah
Exodus	Judges	Jeremiah
Leviticus	Ruth	Lamentations
Numbers	1–2 Samuel	Ezekiel
Deuteronomy	1–2 Kings	Daniel
	1–2 Chronicles	Hosea
	Ezra	Joel
	Nehemiah	Amos
	Esther	Obadiah
	Job	Jonah
	Psalms	Micah
	Proverbs	Nahum
	Ecclesiastes	Habakkuk
	Song of Songs (Song of Solomon)	Zephaniah
		Haggai
		Zechariah
		Malachi

Since at least the rabbinic era, Jewish practice includes twenty-four books in the Tanak, while Christian practice since the late fourth century includes twenty-seven books in the NT.[10] But Christian Bibles contain different numbers of books in their OTs. Students who come to the Bible for the first time often ask why the Protestant, Catholic, and Orthodox Bibles do not agree on the number of books in the OT. A glance at the various canons in the lists provided in the tables in figures 1.2–5 clarifies the matter. While the Orthodox Church and the Roman Catholic Church follow the (longer) Septuagint list as the basis for their OT, churches that follow the Protestant reformations of the sixteenth century have opted to use the (shorter) Hebrew canon as the basis for their translations. They designate the additional Septuagint books written in Greek as the **Apocrypha**, from the Greek word for "concealed" or "hidden." Catholics acknowledge the inspired status of these books but designate them as **deuterocanonical** (secondarily canonized) books because they were not originally included in Jerome's Latin **Vulgate** translation of OT books that had been the official Bible of the church from the fourth to the sixteenth centuries. Many **ecumenical** editions of the Christian Bible contain the apocryphal/deuterocanonical books in recognition of their canonical status for Catholic and Orthodox Christians, and in order that others may consult

10. There are minor exceptions. A small part of the Syrian Orthodox tradition (the Nestorian Church) has never accepted the books of 2 Peter, 2–3 John, Jude, and Revelation, and the Ethiopic Church's broader NT canon has 35 books (compared to the narrower 27-book canon).

Figure 1.4. The Roman Catholic Old Testament
(the Jewish Bible [plus minor additions]
+ 7 deuterocanonical books [in italics] = 46 books)

Pentateuch	Historical and Wisdom Books	Prophetic Books
Genesis	Joshua	Isaiah
Exodus	Judges	Jeremiah
Leviticus	Ruth	Lamentations
Numbers	1–2 Samuel	*Baruch* (incl. *Letter of Jeremiah*)
Deuteronomy	1–2 Kings	Ezekiel
	1–2 Chronicles	Daniel*
	Ezra	Hosea
	Nehemiah	Joel
	Tobit	Amos
	Judith	Obadiah
	Esther (incl. the six additions)	Jonah
	1–2 Maccabees	Micah
	Job	Nahum
	Psalms	Habakkuk
	Proverbs	Zephaniah
	Ecclesiastes	Haggai
	Song of Songs (Song of Solomon)	Zechariah
	Wisdom of Solomon	Malachi
	Sirach (Ecclesiasticus)	

* Including the Prayer of Azariah and the Song of the Three Jews, Susanna, and Bel and the Dragon.

and study them. Figures 1.2, 1.3, 1.4, and 1.5 exhibit the various canons of the Jewish Scriptures / Tanak / Christian OT.

Names and Contents of Books

While most traditional names or titles of biblical books may offer some limited information about the contents of the book, many do not. The names arose in various ways.

Sometimes the titles of individual books of the Bible come from the first word of the book. For instance, the name of the first book in the Tanak is *Bereshit,* from the first word in Hebrew (meaning "In the beginning" or "When [God] began"). Christians usually refer to this same book with the Septuagint title "Genesis," which is not a translation of *Bereshit* but a reference to the initial story of the *"generations* of the heavens and earth when they were created" (Gen. 2:4, emphasis added). The last book in the NT begins with the Greek word *apokalypsis,* giving rise to the naming of the book as **Apocalypse** when transliterated, or as "Revelation" when translated into English.

Figure 1.5. The Orthodox Old Testament
(= the Jewish Bible in the LXX + ca. 10 additional LXX books [in italics])

Historical Books	Poetic and Didactic Books	Prophetic Books
Genesis	Psalms (incl. Ps. 151)	Hosea
Exodus	Job	Amos
Leviticus	Proverbs	Micah
Numbers	Ecclesiastes	Joel
Deuteronomy	Song of Songs (Song of	Obadiah
Joshua	Solomon)	Jonah
Judges	*Wisdom of Solomon*	Nahum
Ruth	*(Wisdom of) Sirach*	Habakkuk
1–2 Kingdoms		Zephaniah
(1–2 Samuel)		Haggai
3–4 Kingdoms		Zechariah
(1–2 Kings)		Malachi
1–2 Chronicles		Isaiah
1 Esdras		Jeremiah
2 Esdras (Ezra, some-		*Baruch*
times also Nehemiah)		Lamentations
Nehemiah		*Letter of Jeremiah*
Tobit		Ezekiel
Judith		Daniel*
Esther (with the six		
additions)		Also:
1–3 Maccabees		*4 Maccabees*, in an appendix
		Prayer of Manasseh, in an appendix
		3 Esdras in Slavonic Bibles of Rus-
		sian Orthodox Church, in an
		appendix

* Including the Prayer of Azariah and the Song of the Three Jews, Susanna, and Bel and the Dragon.

At other times, the title of a biblical book designates a collection of similar items, such as the book titled Psalms, which contains 150 examples of the same basic type of literature. While there is a variety of psalms (e.g., praise, lament, thanksgiving), they all follow the general format of a hymn written in poetic **parallelism,** or "thought rhyme."

Often the name of a biblical book bears relation to the principal charac- ter in the book, such as Hosea or Amos, or to the traditional author of the work, such as Matthew, Mark, Luke, and John. However, a name does not immediately settle the question of authorship or of content. Names can be misleading in a number of ways. For instance, the Acts of the Apostles is not really about the twelve apostles. Rather, it focuses principally on Peter, one of the original Twelve, and Paul, the apostle to the **gentiles,** who was not part of the original group of Twelve with Jesus.

The content of individual books ranges from the words and ministry of in- dividual prophets, such as Jeremiah, to the grand panorama of Israelite history sketched in 1–2 Kings. The apostolic letters attributed to Paul, James, Peter, and John give insight into the early decades of the Christian community. On the other hand, Ecclesiastes deals with issues of good and evil that transcend any particular century of human history and even the limited boundaries of specific religious groups.

It is obvious that a book's title is not always the key to understanding the full scope of what may lie between its covers. For instance, the Song of Songs does not discuss music, nor is it a hymn (though it may have been composed from the lyrics of some local wedding songs). Rather, the repetition of the word "song" in the title expresses the superlative degree in Hebrew. A more accurate translation of the title would be "The Greatest Song."

The titles of groups of biblical books may also be somewhat misleading. For example, the first five books of the Hebrew Bible are grouped under the Hebrew term *torah*, which may be best translated as "tradition" or "instruction." In Christian writings, under the influence of the LXX translation of *torah* into Greek as *nomos* (law), this same group of books is referred to as "law" or "the Law." We would expect a modern library with a section devoted to "law" to be stocked with materials on legal matters for the sake of lawyers, judges, and other interested persons. While at least four of the five books of the Torah do contain some laws, much more is present there, making it inaccurate to think of those books as if they were simply legal codes. Rather, the Torah begins by reflecting on the origins of the earth and the human family before extolling the family traditions of Israel's ancestors, all bearing witness to the main character, God.

Finally, a word about the section subheadings that appear in many Bibles within the text itself. Apart from the brief letter that Paul the apostle wrote to Philemon, and some of the other letters in the NT, most books in the Bible today cover many pages in length. We are accustomed to using the editorial headings that divide each book into smaller, more manageable portions to help us follow the development of the story, or to call our attention to significant topics, such as "The Ten Commandments" or "The Baptism of Jesus." However, these headings are not part of the biblical text, and it is important to realize that these good efforts to help readers may reflect modern concerns or the perceptions of translators and editors more than the intentions of the original authors.

Chapters and Verses

When we write a letter to a friend, we do not usually group the paragraphs into chapters. Nor do we number the sentences as verses. If we did so, people might think us a bit pretentious or odd. But that is precisely what we find when we open our Bible to read Paul's letters to the Romans or Galatians. Paul would most certainly have considered that behavior as unusual as we do today. He wrote in a straightforward fashion with passion and powerful rhetorical skill. But hundreds of years later, practically every sentence of his letters, and the rest of the Bible, had become so important in church debates that it became convenient to number them in order to keep straight which verse the debaters were talking about.

Historical Development

Divisions in biblical manuscripts had a rich history even before the rise of the current system that has held sway for the past five hundred years. Early Jewish and Christian religious leaders and scholars divided the books of the Bible into sections according to various methods. Our modern system of chapter divisions dates back to the Middle Ages with Stephen Langton (d. 1228), a lecturer at the University of Paris working with the Latin Bible, or Vulgate. His system was diffused more widely through a **concordance** (alphabetical index) to the Latin Vulgate that was produced by Cardinal Hugo of St. Cher (d. 1263). Gradually the same system was used with Bibles in other languages.

But it would be another two hundred years before the further subdivision of the text into verses started appearing in various ways. In 1440, Rabbi Isaac Nathan numbered verses in the Hebrew Bible for his Hebrew concordance. However, Robert Stephanus (Estienne) was the first person to issue the whole Bible (including the Apocrypha) with the current system of verses in his edition of the Latin Vulgate at Geneva in 1555. (In scholarly usage, verses may be further subdivided by the use of lowercase letters, such as Rom. 5:1a and 5:1b, the first and the second part of Rom. 5:1, respectively.)

The use of punctuation to separate chapters and verses in biblical references has varied over time and still varies around the world. The standard form in the United States (used in this book) is to divide chapter and verse by means of a colon (e.g., Gen. 1:1, referring to the first verse of the first chapter of Genesis [Gen. 1]), though occasionally a period is used (e.g., Gen. 1.1). The period, rather than the colon, is standard in British English, in European usage, and thus in most of the rest of the world. It is a universal practice to indicate a continuous passage (set of verses) with a hyphen or dash (e.g., Gen. 1:1–3, referring to the first three verses of Gen. 1). It is customary to separate a list of noncontinuous verses with commas (e.g., Gen. 1:1, 3, 5, referring to verses 1, 3, and 5 of Gen. 1), while lists of verses from different chapters of the same biblical book are generally separated by semicolons (e.g., Gen. 1:1; 2:1; 3:1).[11]

Modern Uses and Cautions

Some people familiar with the Bible can quote chapter and verse. This is an advantage for locating a familiar or beloved text quickly, such as Psalm 23, which begins, "The LORD is my shepherd." In the case of a psalm, dividing a short section of Scripture into verses is not a great problem because a psalm is generally a short unit unto itself with a clear beginning and ending. The parallelism, or "thought rhyme," characteristic of Hebrew poetry often quite naturally divides the thoughts from one another. But when a letter of Paul with a complicated theological discussion (such as Rom. 9–11 or 1 Cor. 12–14) is chopped into chapters and verses, the modern divisions often do not respect Paul's original line of thought. (See, for example, 1 Cor. 11:1, which is actually the conclusion to chs. 8–10!) Such inappropriate divisions of the text may significantly interfere with our correct comprehension and interpretation of a biblical text.

The medieval chapter divisions occasionally correspond appropriately to movement within the biblical text, such as Matthew 5:1, when Jesus goes up the mountain to teach. But the subsequent division of this "Sermon on the Mount" into chapters two more times (as Matt. 6 and 7) makes it clear that the traditional system is primarily of utilitarian value and should not dissuade us from searching out the more intrinsic points of division within each biblical document in the course of our study.

Modern attention to the narrative and rhetorical quality of biblical documents enhances our appreciation of the literary skill of the original authors. The study of the narrative character of biblical documents gives attention to the natural progression of the story line in the document and may clearly indicate divisions in the text that do not coincide with traditional chapter and verse divisions. Modern commentators emphasize literary elements within the text, such as movement from place to place, repetition of the same idea at a later time, and shifts in content and tone. Consequently, outlines in modern commentaries (and even in study Bibles) regularly disagree with traditional chapter and verse divisions.[12]

11. There is also a variety of abbreviations for the biblical books; one set of scholarly standards is provided in the front of this book.

12. Readers who can access an electronic version of the Bible (such as via BibleGateway.com) may test their own ability in analyzing the structure of biblical texts. They can print out a few chapters of Exodus or Romans or Matthew, deleting the customary chapter and verse numbers, then try to discover the inner dynamic of the biblical passages without the distraction of later

The Bible as Story

We have already noted that although the Bible consists of many books that constitute a library, there is still a grand narrative to the Bible as a single book. Some have described the Bible's dramatic narrative in terms of "acts," as in a play. One popular version of this, building on the suggestion of N. T. Wright (*Scripture and the Authority of God* and elsewhere), is to see the drama's acts in terms of creation, fall, Israel, Jesus, church, and consummation (new creation). While there is a natural appeal and validity to this construal of the Bible's story from a Christian perspective, it has a potential weakness: it may cause us to underestimate the importance of Israel's story—something Wright himself vigorously decries. That story occupies about three-fourths of the biblical text, and it includes major events such as the exodus, kingship, **exile**, and restoration (see ch. 3) that should not be neglected. Furthermore, a grand-narrative perspective may cause us to overlook the twists and turns in the biblical accounts. Richard Bauckham therefore urges us to see the Bible as a "plurality of *narratives*," all of which together constitute a "single coherent *story*," but none of which tells the whole story ("Reading Scripture as a Coherent Story," 6; emphasis added).

The scriptural story, as Bauckham also points out, has a variety of significant and sometimes surprising themes—such as God's repeated choice of the powerless. Perhaps one motif that is especially significant to notice is indicated by the Bible's "bookends" of Genesis and Revelation: the story of creation (Gen. 1–3) to new creation (Rev. 21–22). Theologically speaking, this grand story from the first to the last pages of the Bible is sometimes referred to as testimony to the "mission of God," or, using the Latin phrase, the *missio Dei*. Certain prophets and apostles bore witness to this hope of a new creation (e.g., Isa. 65:17–25; 2 Cor. 5:17; Gal. 6:15; 2 Pet. 3:13). Although the phrase "from creation to new creation" does not tell the entire biblical story, it does say something significant about the movement of the biblical drama as a whole, and about the hope of salvation for humanity—and for the entire cosmos—to which Scripture bears testimony for both Jews and Christians.

At the end of the day, however, even naming the important theme of creation and new creation does not tell the whole of the biblical story. Why? Because the words "creation" and "new creation" assume a creator—a creative person—and a *re*-creator, a redeemer. Indeed, the Bible is first of all, and last of all, a book about God (see, e.g., Feldmeier and Spieckermann, *God of the*

---

editorial divisions. This experiment often gives new insight into familiar passages, as well as others that are less widely known.

Living; Goldingay, *Biblical Theology*). Surprisingly, perhaps, it is sometimes easy for people to forget that truth as they study the Bible.

The Bible as Invitation

As we have hinted in this chapter and will see in more depth in later chapters, the Bible is a varied and complex library/book, and its interpretation has been, and remains, equally and appropriately varied and complex. At the same time, the contributors to this volume also find the Bible to be an *inviting* book, even though it is at times strange (which can actually be a good thing) and sometimes confusing. In fact, we might picture the Bible as an invitation into a journey with others and—from the perspective of faith—with the God to whom the biblical texts bear witness. According to Scripture itself and both the Jewish and Christian traditions, this journey is also a journey with, and even into, the Reality—the Person—to whom it testifies. "Give me life, O Lord, according to your Word," writes the psalmist (Ps. 119:107), and "I wait for the Lord, my soul waits, and in his word I hope" (Ps. 130:5). In the words of Jesus according to the Gospel of John, "When the Spirit of truth comes, he will guide you into all the truth" (John 16:13). These affirmations of relationship and assistance are ultimately grounded, theologically, in the conviction that God has spoken in, and continues to speak through, this library/book: "All scripture is inspired by God and is useful for teaching, for reproof, for correction, and for training in righteousness, so that everyone who belongs to God may be proficient, equipped for every good work" (2 Tim. 3:16–17). This conviction does not rule out the need for careful, diligent study, but such effort may be exercised in confidence that there is help to be found in the community of fellow interpreters and, ultimately, in God.[13]

Because of this divine inspiration and assistance in interpretation, we might even think of the Bible more specifically as an invitation to a surprise party—a party at which *we* are the ones surprised: surprised by what we find in its pages, surprised by what others have found and how they have understood those findings, and even surprised at what happens to us as we read the Bible in the company of others, whether living or dead, whether like us or very different from us. We suspect (and, frankly, hope) that many readers of this book will be transformed in very interesting ways as they read both it and the Bible itself.

---

13. The technical term for careful historical, literary, and theological engagement with Scripture is **exegesis**; the technical term for interpretation more generally is **hermeneutics**.

QUESTIONS FOR REFLECTION AND DISCUSSION

1. What were some of the new facts about, and perspectives on, the Bible that you encountered in this chapter?

2. Do you think it is important to be aware of the various biblical canons and of the issues involved in the name(s) we give to the Bible and its two main divisions? Why or why not?

3. Do you think it is important to think of the Bible as both a single book with a grand story and a library that includes various types of literature and diverse contents? Why or why not?

4. What, in your mind, is the relationship between a faith perspective and serious academic study of Scripture?

FOR FURTHER READING AND STUDY

Alexander, T. Desmond. *From Eden to the New Jerusalem: An Introduction to Biblical Theology*. Nottingham, Eng.: Inter-Varsity, 2008. An account of the Bible's story of creation to new creation, beginning with Revelation.

Bartholomew, Craig G., and Michael W. Goheen. *The Drama of Scripture: Finding Our Place in the Biblical Story*. 2nd ed. Grand Rapids: Baker Academic, 2014. A biblical scholar and a missiologist recount the biblical drama in six acts, focusing on the theme of God's kingship.

Bauckham, Richard. "Reading Scripture as a Coherent Story." In *The Bible in the Contemporary World: Hermeneutical Ventures*, 1–16. Grand Rapids: Eerdmans, 2015. How the plurality of biblical narratives yields a single coherent story.

Brown, Michael Joseph. *What They Don't Tell You: A Survivor's Guide to Biblical Studies*. 2nd ed. Louisville: Westminster John Knox, 2015. Popular introduction to the academic approach to Scripture and to the integration of that approach with the Christian faith by means of twenty-nine rules of thumb.

Brown, William P., ed. *Engaging Biblical Authority: Perspectives on the Bible as Scripture*. Louisville: Westminster John Knox, 2007. Biblical scholars from various religious traditions and ethnicities reflect on the significance of the Bible for them.

Childs, Brevard S. *Biblical Theology of the Old and New Testaments: Theological Reflection on the Christian Bible*. 1992. Reprint, Minneapolis: Fortress, 2011. Classic canonical study of the discrete witness of each Testament and the major theological themes of the Bible as a whole.

Cunningham, Philip. *Sharing the Scriptures*. Mahwah, NJ: Paulist Press, 2003. A booklet on the role of the Bible in Jewish-Catholic relations.

Feldmeier, Reinhard, and Hermann Spieckermann. *God of the Living: A Biblical Theology*. Translated by Mark E. Biddle. Waco: Baylor University Press, 2011. A

NT scholar and an OT scholar collaborate to represent the character and activity of God throughout the Bible.

Goldingay, John. *Biblical Theology: The God of the Christian Scriptures*. Downers Grove, IL: IVP Academic, 2016. Examines the common-core understanding of God, creation, the people of God, God's reign and triumph, and so forth in the two Testaments together.

Hurtado, Larry W. *The Earliest Christian Artifacts: Manuscripts and Christian Origins*. Grand Rapids: Eerdmans, 2006. Fascinating study of the codex and related topics.

Jenkins, Philip. *The New Faces of Christianity: Believing the Bible in the Global South*. New York: Oxford University Press, 2006. Appreciative study of the role of Scripture and belief in supernatural activity among Christians in Africa, Asia, and Latin America.

Laytham, D. Brent. "The Narrative Shape of Scriptural Authority: Plotting Pentecost." *Ex Auditu* 19 (2003): 97–119. Uses Acts 2 to argue that God's story in Scripture is also our story, which gives us both our identity and the story to tell others.

Levering, Matthew D. *Participatory Biblical Exegesis: A Theology of Biblical Interpretation*. Notre Dame, IN: University of Notre Dame Press, 2008. Significant account of biblical interpretation by Christians and Jews as transformative participation in the divine life that also takes careful historical study seriously.

Metzger, Bruce, and Michael Coogan, eds. *The Oxford Companion to the Bible*. New York: Oxford University Press, 1993. Useful, encyclopedia-like, one-volume reference work with articles on such topics as books and bookmaking in antiquity, chapter and verse divisions, the canon, covenant, and much more.

Rogerson, J. [John] W. *An Introduction to the Bible*. 3rd ed. New York: Routledge, 2014. Survey of the history and composition of the OT and NT books, including contemporary issues of the Bible's relationship to matters such as science, the life of Jesus, and fundamentalism.

———, ed. *The Oxford Illustrated History of the Bible*. Oxford: Oxford University Press, 2001. Beautifully crafted history of the composition and interpretation of the Bible.

Sumney, Jerry L. *The Bible: An Introduction*. 2nd ed. Minneapolis: Fortress, 2014. Basic text, nicely illustrated, about how we received the Bible and about the form and contents of the various books.

Wright, N. T. *Scripture and the Authority of God: How to Read the Bible Today*. New York: HarperCollins, 2011. A guide to reading the Bible as Scripture, including its dramatic character divisible into acts, by a leading biblical scholar.

2

The Setting: Biblical Geography, History, and Archaeology

KAREN J. WENELL

This chapter deals not so much with biblical texts and their *content*, but rather with their *context*, the world in which they may be situated. The biblical texts we now have were written over the course of hundreds of years and come from a certain part of the world—the ancient Near East and the Mediterranean Basin. Our goal in this chapter is to introduce the relationship between the texts of the OT and NT and the contexts of the biblical world to which they belong. The focus is on Palestine, since that is the locus of almost all events associated with the OT and the NT Gospels. We also briefly consider areas west of Palestine (Asia Minor, Greece, and Italy) to which emerging Christianity spread.

One way to illustrate the connections between geography, history, and archaeology is to propose *land* as an important element for all. That is, geography deals with how *land* may be mapped, identifying different regions, topography, and climate. In terms of history, *land* may be designated as the particular area where certain events are known to have taken place. Archaeology partially entails excavating the *land* itself in order to find traces of past societies—material culture—showing how different peoples lived in the past. In terms of biblical texts, when God first promises a *land* to the descendants of Abram (Gen. 12:1–7), this is not a scientific description (verifiable in light

23

of geographical, historical, or archaeological evidence) but rather symbolizes the beginning of a relationship among God, people, and land. Here, *land* is a "promised land" and part of a **covenant**.

The example of the **promised land** reminds us that the Bible is full of symbolic meanings and descriptions even though it is also concerned with **Israel's** (and the Christian church's) past. It is perhaps best to think of an ongoing dialogue among the disciplines of geography, history, archaeology, and biblical studies. In different ways, these fields inform one another as scholars from each discipline gather new information, increasing their knowledge of the ancient world in which the biblical texts are situated and in which the biblical authors accomplished their (primarily religious) purposes.

A Note on Terminology: Land and People, Then and Now

There is some potential confusion when it comes to distinguishing the ancient world from modern entities, such as Israel and Palestine. Related to this is the question of how to refer to the people who belong to that part of the world, both then and now. The following definitions correspond to their use in this chapter and throughout the book:

- *The ancient Near East*—Mesopotamia (the land between the Tigris and Euphrates Rivers), Egypt, Syria, and Israel of the ancient world. The kingdom of Assyria was in the north of Mesopotamia, Babylonia in the south.
- *Mediterranean Basin*—the lands surrounding the Mediterranean Sea— parts of Asia, Africa, and Europe—where **Greco-Roman** cultures thrived in antiquity.
- *Roman Empire*—the military, political, and legislative entity that grew out of the Roman Republic (governed by an oligarchy, the Senate) and began with the establishment of the first emperor, Octavian (Caesar Augustus), in 27 BCE.
- *Asia Minor*—the peninsula (roughly equivalent to modern Turkey) that has as its northern border the Black Sea, on its western side the Aegean Sea, and to the south the Mediterranean Sea.
- *Palestine*—the name of the territory from the Mediterranean Sea to the Jordan Valley and from Galilee in the north to the Negev (or Negeb) in the south; it is derived from the Hebrew word for "land of the Philistines" and dates from the fifth century BCE. Generally, this is the preferred scholarly designation since it encompasses a broad definition.

- *Israel*—the "promised land" of the Hebrew Bible; in biblical texts the name refers to both a geographical region (the extent and meaning of which varies from era to era) and the nation/people residing there.
- *Hebrews*—the ancestors of the Israelite nation (Abraham and Sarah to Moses).
- *Israelites*—the people of God from Moses to the **Babylonian exile** (586 BCE).
- *Jews*—the descendants of the Israelites after the exile; derived from the Hebrew and Greek words for **Judah** and Judean.
- *Israelis, Palestinians*—modern peoples living within the region of ancient Palestine.[1]

Maps and Geography of the Ancient Near East and the Mediterranean Basin

We could draw many maps to illustrate the lands that relate to the Bible. For instance, within Palestine itself we could show a map of the twelve tribes, David's kingdom, the divided kingdom (Israel and Judah), the **Hasmonean** conquests, or political boundaries (e.g., **Judea**, Samaria, Galilee) at the time of Jesus. In addition to this, we could depict the areas of Egypt, the Sinai Peninsula, and Babylonia that relate to Israel's **exodus** and exile, or of Asia Minor and Europe, which relate to the missionary journeys of Paul. Each of these would relate to a different historical era and to different biblical texts. The list could go on, suggesting maps for different areas and different eras of history, such as may be found in a Bible atlas. For purposes of simplification, we will include just three maps that show some of the places relevant to the Bible across historical eras. Places change, as do their names, but the purpose of the maps is to give a relative picture of certain places in relationship to wider geographical regions (which have even different names today).

Palestine

Ancient Palestine is located within the **Fertile Crescent,** the area of arable land stretching from the Nile Valley at the southeast coast of the Mediterranean Sea to the Persian Gulf, making a curve or crescent shape around the Syrian Desert along the way. Within Palestine itself, there are five main

1. Adapted in part from Bandstra, *Reading the Old Testament.*

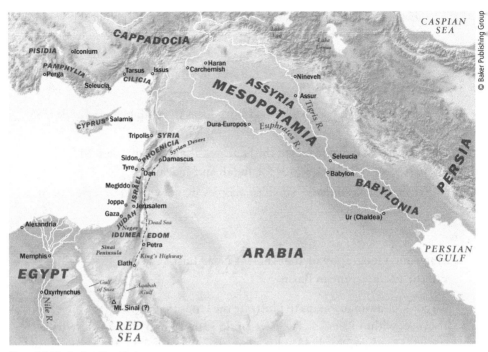

Figure 2.1. The Ancient Near East

geographical regions, from west to east:[2] the coastal plain along the Mediterranean, the central hills, the Jordan Valley, the plateau of Jordan, and the deserts. The Sea of Galilee and the Dead Sea are the major bodies of water within Palestine. Starting just north of Lake Huleh (itself just north of the Sea of Galilee, though now largely drained), the Jordan River winds southward between the two seas. There are other rivers in Palestine, many of which are seasonal, existing only when there is sufficient rain or melting of snow. Since our aim is to discuss both text and context, we will include some relevant biblical examples as we describe each region.

The Coastal Plain

The coastal plain includes an ancient international highway known as the *Via Maris* (Way of the Sea). This road extended from Egypt through Palestine along the Mediterranean Sea through the Megiddo pass toward Damascus and

2. Five regions will be discussed, though another region is also discernible: the Shephelah (Hebrew for "lowlands"). This is a small lowland area separating the coastal plain and the central hills in the southern region of Palestine. Lachish is the major city of the Shephelah region (see map and table of major events in figs. 2.2; 2.7).

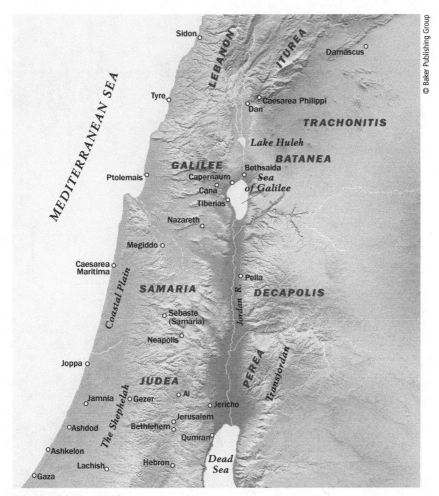

Figure 2.2. Palestine / Israel

Mesopotamia. Isaiah 9:1 mentions the *Via Maris* and the time when it will be made "glorious." The coastal plain in Palestine extends 125 miles from Gaza in the south to Lebanon in the north. The Philistines, who were enemies of the Israelites, were located in the southern part of the coastal plain area, in the Negev (a semi-desert region) on the southern border.

The Central Hills

This area is probably the most important geographic region of Palestine. Generally speaking, it is located to the east of the coastal plain and runs about 180 miles from Galilee in the north to Sinai in the south. It includes highlands

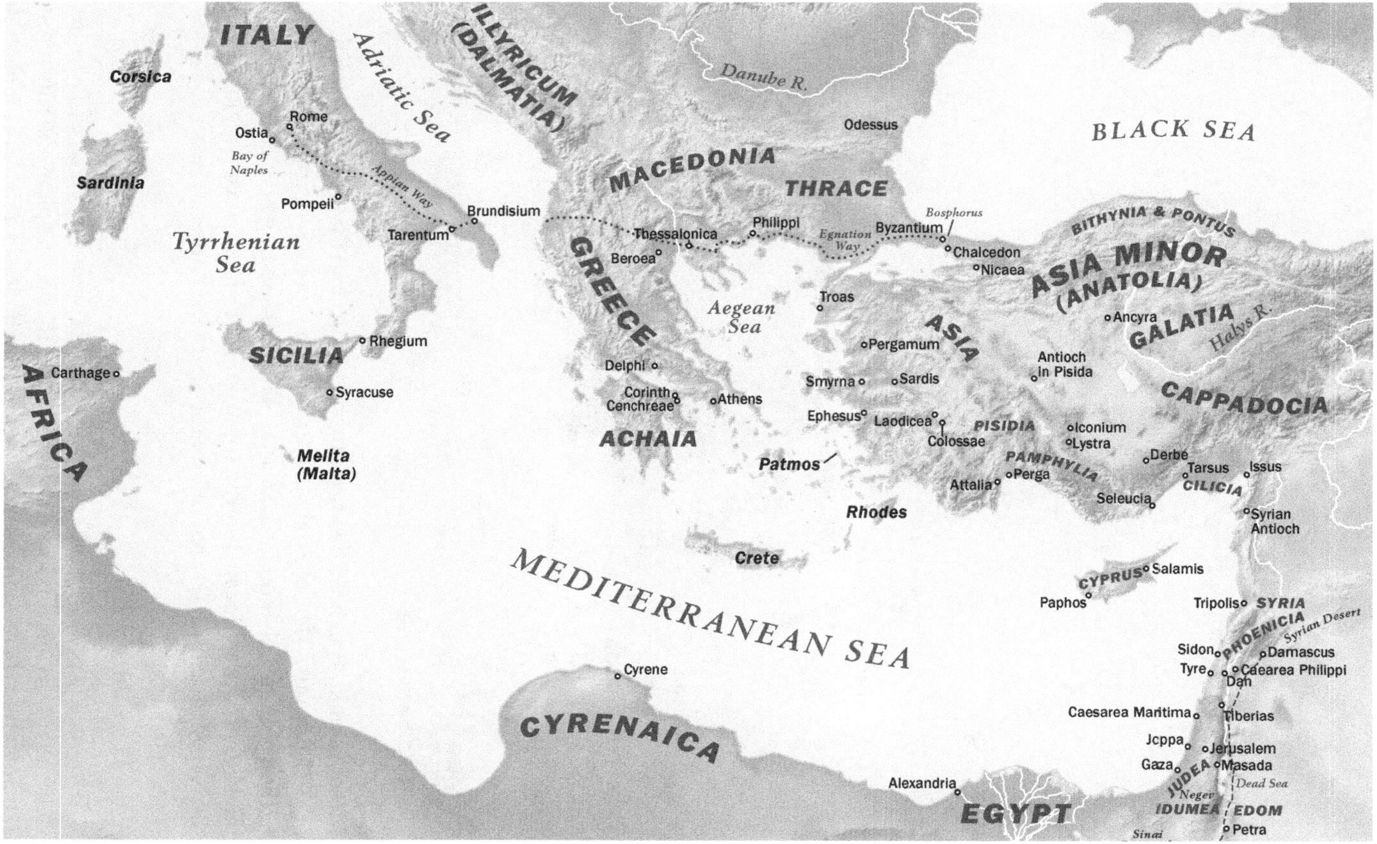

Figure 2.3. The Mediterranean Basin

(in Judea, Samaria, and Galilee), valleys, and plains. In Galilee, for instance, a valley (east-west) divides Lower Galilee from Upper Galilee, whose elevations differ by approximately one thousand feet. Locations in Lower Galilee are mentioned frequently in the Gospels (e.g., Nazareth, Capernaum, Cana). After the Second Jewish Revolt (132–135 CE), the areas of Upper and Lower Galilee were important for both Jews and the early Christians. Also within this region, about twenty miles west of the northernmost tip of the Dead Sea, is the city of Jerusalem, in which the temple was located.

The Jordan (or Rift) Valley

As we move east again from the Central Hills, there is a dividing feature of the landscape—a depression in the land that runs for about 260 miles between Dan in the north and Elath in the south. Between Lake Huleh and the Dead Sea, the Jordan River flows along the Rift Valley. At 1,300 feet below sea level, the point where the Jordan River ends at the Dead Sea is the lowest place on the surface of the earth. In the NT, John's ministry and baptism of forgiveness took place in and around the Jordan River in Judea (see, e.g., Matt. 3:5–6).

The Plateau of Jordan

To the east of the Jordan River, a level plateau running north-south from Damascus to the Gulf of Aqaba is appropriately termed the Jordan Plateau. Another major international route called the King's Highway passes through the Plateau of Jordan. In Numbers 20:17 the King's Highway is mentioned in a message from Moses to the king of Edom. In the story of Joshua's division of the land (Josh. 13), the land east of the Jordan River (the Transjordan, east of the Jordan and west of the Syrian Desert) features in the tribal divisions.

Desert

The most easterly region is that of the Syrian Desert, which borders on the Plateau of Jordan and reaches north toward Syria as well as eastward into present-day Saudi Arabia. This mostly uninhabited region shapes the arc of the Fertile Crescent to the north and forms a natural barrier, since the desert was not suitable to be traversed by traders or armies.

As we are able to see, the geography of Palestine is highly diverse, so it makes sense that the climate also varies from region to region. For instance, Jerusalem in the Central Hills region gets approximately twenty-five inches of rain per year, while the Dead Sea in the Jordan Valley gets only about four inches of rainfall. Generally speaking, there are only two seasons in Palestine.

Summer lasts from May to October, while winter falls between November and April. The first-century CE Jewish historian Josephus reports that agriculture was the basis of the economy of Palestine in ancient times (*Against Apion* 1.60). This was also true for many surrounding regions.

Asia Minor, Greece, and Italy

Moving westward, we will give a brief overview of some of the areas of the Roman Empire most important to the biblical (NT) context: Asia Minor / Anatolia (modern Turkey), Greece, and Italy. These regions were part of the Mediterranean Basin, which was divided into provinces during the Roman Period. One such province, Galatia, is familiar from Paul's Letter to the Galatians. Networks of well-built paved roads made it possible to move throughout the empire, whether for military or for trading purposes. The sea itself may also be considered a highway of sorts, and transport by ship would at times have been less expensive than travel by land. As in Palestine, the climate of the Mediterranean Basin has two seasons, summer and winter, and agriculture was central to its economy.

Asia Minor

The peninsula of Asia Minor (roughly equivalent to modern Turkey), also known as Anatolia ("land of the East"), has as its northern border the Black Sea, on its western side the Aegean Sea, and to the South the Mediterranean Sea. It is about 720 miles in length. Some of the provinces of Asia Minor mentioned in the NT (e.g., Acts 2:9; 1 Pet. 1:1) are Cappadocia, Bithynia, Pontus, and **Asia** (the westernmost Roman province of Asia Minor—not to be confused with the continent of Asia). Galatia is also one of the provinces of Asia Minor, located roughly at the center of the peninsula and containing mountainous regions (in the southern part of the province). The well-known city of Ephesus, a port on the Aegean Sea, was the capital of the Roman province of Asia and also the first of the seven cities (all located in Asia) mentioned in the book of Revelation (chs. 1–3).

Greece

The famous Egnatian Way (*Via Egnatia*) was a major Roman road linking Italy to Asia. It extended from the western coast of Greece (Adriatic Sea) to the Byzantium straits in the east. In Macedonia, a key province in northern Greece, the Egnatian Way passed through the cities of Thessalonica and Philippi. Paul would have traveled along this road on his second missionary journey (Acts 15–18). The cities of Athens and Corinth, both visited by Paul, were located in the province of Achaia, in southern Greece.

Italy

The city of Rome, founded in 753 BCE (traditional dating), became the capital of the Roman Empire and a major center for its administration. Most of the land of Italy is peninsular (separated from mainland Europe in the north by the Alps), and therefore the seas were essential for transportation to and from Italy during the period of Roman rule. On land, the Appian Way (*Via Appia*) extended across Italy from the Bay of Naples to the Adriatic Sea. It is likely that Paul traveled along the Appian Way on his journey to Rome (Acts 28:11–15).

Major Biblical Events from ca. 1800 BCE to ca. 100 CE

We are not able to go into any great detail in describing almost two thousand years of history, but it is nonetheless possible to give a broad overview, taking into account major occurrences that are essential for understanding the world of the Bible—its context. We will proceed in summary fashion, following the table of major periods and biblical events found at the end of this chapter (fig. 2.7, pp. 41–42) and including references to some of the important archaeological discoveries relating to each period of history.

The Ancestral Period, the Exodus, and the Settlement of Palestine (ca. 2200–1025 BCE)

Genesis 1–11 contains fascinating accounts of the origins of the world from creation to the spread of people and language over the earth in the story of the Tower of Babel. The rest of Genesis (chs. 12–50) focuses on Abraham and Sarah and their descendants, the ancestors of the Israelite nation. Because there is no evidence outside the Bible to aid scholars in dating the **Ancestral Period**[3] (the time from Abraham and Sarah to Moses), there has been much debate over historical placement. For many scholars, finding the best fit between the Genesis narratives and what is known historically means placing the time of the Hebrews in the Middle Bronze Age (2200–1550 BCE). Notably, writing was developed in the ancient Near East during the Middle Bronze Age. The

---

3. It is common to refer to this time as the **Patriarchal Period**, but the more inclusive term "Ancestral Period" takes into account not only Abraham, Isaac, Jacob, and his twelve sons, but also the important **matriarchal** figures: Sarah, Rebekah, Rachel, and Leah.

famous Law Code of Hammurabi, which dates to the eighteenth century BCE, when Hammurabi was king of Babylonia, has parallels with the laws contained in the **Pentateuch (Torah)**.

The next phase of biblical history includes the exodus from Egypt and **conquest** or **settlement** in Israel. This corresponds to the Late Bronze Age through the beginning of the Iron Age (1550–1000 BCE). The earliest mention of Israel from any material source occurs in the Merenptah Stela—a ten-foot-tall black stone slab with an inscribed surface—dating to 1209 BCE. This granite stela, found in western Thebes (the ancient capital of Egypt) among the remains of the pharaoh Merenptah's funerary temple, is an account of some of the military victories of his rule, which lasted from approximately 1213 to 1203 BCE. It is interesting that among defeated Canaanite peoples such as Ashkelon and Gezer, which are designated as city-states by an Egyptian hieroglyph on the stela, the name "Israel" is written along with the hieroglyph used for nomadic peoples. If the end of the thirteenth century BCE were to be fixed as the beginning of Israelite presence in Palestine, this would date the exodus to sometime around the middle of that century, perhaps about 1250–1240 BCE. However, there are many scholarly debates over the historicity and date of the exodus.

Related to this issue are the dating and history of Israelite settlement in Palestine. Basically, there are two biblical portrayals of the settlement—one in the book of Joshua and one in Judges—and several scholarly theories that attempt to reconcile the portrayals with historical and archaeological evidence. The traditional theory about the settlement follows the accounts in Joshua and argues for decisive military campaigns against various cities and peoples within Palestine. There are, however, difficulties when it comes to correlating this with nonbiblical archaeological evidence. For instance, extensive excavations at Jericho and Ai have not revealed evidence of destruction and occupation to corroborate the biblical accounts. Alternative theories have been offered to explain Israel's origins in Palestine, including the peaceful-infiltration model, which holds that nomadic peoples gradually settled within the land, and the peasant-revolt model, which posits that social unrest led to a revolution that promoted Yahwism (the worship of **YHWH**).

Regardless of the manner in which the entity "Israel" came to exist in Palestine, the end result was that a tribal people accepted the leadership of various dynamic figures called judges and gradually moved toward centralization. Archaeological evidence indicates that the population of Palestine increased at the beginning of the Iron Age. Excavations have uncovered houses that had two to four rooms on their lower levels (the four-room house). These served as home to family groups and were sometimes arranged in clusters or villages.

Figure 2.4. A portion of the archaeological excavations at Jericho, revealing remains of the famous Canaanite walls that surrounded the city.

The Monarchy, Exile, and Return (ca. 1025–332 BCE)

The Monarchy

During the period of the monarchy (1025–586 BCE), centralization of the tribal people was brought about through the institution of kingship. The stories of Saul (the first king), David, and then Solomon are found in 1–2 Samuel, 1 Kings, and 1–2 Chronicles. Under the leadership of these three important figures, Israelites from north and south were joined together under a **united monarchy** (ca. 1025–928 BCE). During this time Jerusalem came to be an important city, both religiously and politically. It became the capital of the kingdom under David and the center of Israelite worship when David's son Solomon built the temple there. The temple housed the formerly mobile entity, the ark of the covenant, the locus of YHWH's presence with the people. Solomon also organized the construction of a large and lavish palace complex adjacent to the temple site. Unfortunately, because Israel's conquerors later destroyed the temple and other public buildings in the city, there are very few remains that can be positively identified with the Jerusalem of the time of the early monarchy.

After the demise of Solomon, Israel and Judah continued as separate entities with their own kings. This period is therefore known as the **divided monarchy**

(928–722 BCE). By the eighth century BCE, Israel (in the north) was the weaker of the two kingdoms and was defeated when Samaria (which belonged to the northern kingdom) fell to the Assyrian king Sargon II in 722 BCE (2 Kings 18–25). Some of the inhabitants of the fallen kingdom of Israel migrated to Judah (in the south), and at this time the population of Jerusalem expanded. Hezekiah, who was king of Judah from 715 to 687 BCE, took measures to reform cultic practice, thereby bolstering public worship in Jerusalem.

Archaeology confirms some of the biblical history of this period, particularly references to places and topography. To give one example, 2 Chronicles 32:9 mentions that forces of the Assyrian king Sennacherib were at Lachish during the time of Hezekiah. The Lachish Reliefs from Sennacherib's palace in Nineveh confirm an Assyrian victory at Lachish in 701 BCE and depict Israelite prisoners being led away from the battle.

In 612 BCE the Babylonians defeated the Assyrians and took over the former kingdom of Israel. The relatively small kingdom of Judah was in a precarious position between Egypt and Babylonia and was attacked by Babylonian forces. The last Israelite king to rule Judah was Zedekiah, who came into conflict with Nebuchadnezzar, king of Babylon. Nebuchadnezzar's defeat of Judah is mentioned on a tablet called the Babylonian Chronicle as occurring in the seventh year of his reign. Jerusalem and the temple were destroyed during this attack. Zedekiah and many of the inhabitants of Judah were deported to Babylon in two phases, marking the beginning of the Babylonian exile in 586 BCE.

Exile and Return

The Babylonian exile (586–539 BCE) was a major catastrophe in Israelite/Jewish history, and the resulting sense of loss is reflected in many biblical texts, particularly Psalms and Lamentations. Nonetheless, a number of the inhabitants of Judah appear to have remained in their land and were not sent into exile in Babylon. Among those Jews who were exiled, many were afforded economic opportunities, and it is likely that many of them prospered. The prophets of the exile (e.g., Jeremiah, Ezekiel, and Second Isaiah [see discussion in ch. 3]) issued warnings of judgment but also proclaimed a message of hope for God's people.

The period of the exile came to an end in 539 BCE when Cyrus, king of the Persian Empire, defeated the Babylonians and issued a decree freeing the Jews from their captivity. The Cyrus Cylinder—a nine-inch cylinder inscribed in Babylonian cuneiform and made of baked clay—is an account of military ventures of the Persian king in Babylonia. Though it does not mention

Judah or Judea in particular,[4] it shows Cyrus's general policy of restoring the religious practices of conquered people and allowing them to return to their homelands. Thus, as described in Ezra 6, Cyrus allowed for the return of Jews to Judah/Judea and for the rebuilding of their temple, granting them considerable autonomy under his rule.

The temple built in Jerusalem after the return from exile is called the **Second Temple** because it was constructed on the foundations of the First Temple, or Solomon's Temple (Ezra 5:15; 6:7). The beliefs and practices of Jews (Judahites, later Judeans) during the period of the Second Temple (including Herod the Great's reconstruction of that temple) came to be known as **Judaism**. During this time, called **Second Temple Judaism** (and sometimes "**early Judaism**"), the temple was of central significance for Jews in Palestine as well as for Jews of the **diaspora** (dispersion).[5] This period of Judaism, which extends into the Hellenistic and Roman Periods (see below), was characterized by diversity, as evidenced by the appearance of groups such as Pharisees, Sadducees, Essenes, and Zealots. Its end may be marked by the destruction of the Second Temple in 70 CE and the subsequent emergence of **rabbinic** Judaism.

The Hellenistic and Roman Periods (ca. 332 BCE–100 CE)

The Hellenistic Period

Yet another change for land and people in Palestine occurred in 333 BCE, when the Greeks under Alexander the Great defeated the Persian Empire at the Battle of Issus (in southeastern Asia Minor) and marched in to take control of the Near East. This marks the beginning of Greek rule and the influence of **Hellenism**, or Greek culture, in Palestine. An example of this influence is the building of the Xystos center in Jerusalem. This structure, known from archaeology, was the site of a famous Hellenistic gymnasium (a center for education and physical activity). Another example is the translation of the Hebrew Bible into Greek (the **Septuagint**), begun around 250 BCE.

After Alexander's death in 323 BCE, this **Hellenistic Period** continued under his generals Ptolemy (who ruled Egypt, Phoenicia, and Palestine from 323 to 282 BCE) and Seleucus (who ruled Syria and Mesopotamia from 312 to 281 BCE). The dynastic successors of Ptolemy and Seleucus fought over Palestine, which bordered their territories. The **Seleucid** Empire gained the upper hand in 198 BCE, when Antiochus III the Great (223–187 BCE) took control of Palestine from Ptolemy V (successor to Ptolemy I). His infamous

---

4. Judea is the Greek term for Judah used after the exile.

5. Because of their distance from the temple, their attachment to it was different from that of their counterparts in Palestine, particularly in relation to cultic practice and festivals.

son, Antiochus IV Epiphanes, ruled from 175 to 164 BCE and was called "an evil root" (my translation) in the book of 1 Maccabees (1 Macc. 1:10) because he forbade Jewish religious practices and defiled the Jerusalem temple by sacrificing a pig (an offense to biblical law) and building an altar to Zeus. These actions of Antiochus sparked the Hasmonean revolt, in which Judas Maccabeus ("the Hammerer") liberated Jerusalem in 164 BCE and rededicated the temple. (The feast of Hanukkah derives from this event.)

The Hasmonean and Herodian Periods

The Hasmonean family eventually became a dynasty, expanding their kingdom and establishing Jewish dominance throughout Palestine. The Hasmonean period lasted from 164 to 63 BCE. Among other Hasmonean leaders, Aristobulus (104–103 BCE) and Alexander Jannaeus (103–76 BCE) extended Jewish rule to the boundaries of the Davidic kingdom, once more including Galilee. This period of independence—finally achieved in ca. 142 BCE—and expansion constituted a remarkable achievement in light of the foregoing history of foreign empires' domination of the land, though it was not without conflict and pressures, both internal and external.

It was during the Hasmonean era that the Pharisees and Sadducees emerged as two groups concerned with interpretation of the law. Recent archaeological excavations in Galilee, Samaria, and Judea have uncovered structures called *miqwa'ot*, which were ritual baths used to maintain purity, an important issue for Pharisees and Sadducees as well as the Jewish population in general. Stone vessels (which could not contract impurity) and ossuaries—stone boxes for burial of bones—are also important archaeological discoveries relating to this time period. Yet another set of highly significant discoveries from this era are the remains of the community at **Qumran**, established on the upper western shore of the Dead Sea between 166 and 150 BCE and continuing in use until its destruction in 68 CE. The most important of these remains are the famous **Dead Sea Scrolls** (see ch. 5).

The nearly eighty years of Jewish independence ended when the Roman general Pompey conquered Judea in 63 BCE, making it part of the Roman province of Syria. The territories won by the Hasmoneans now all paid tribute to Rome. Rome's expansive power, known to much of the Mediterranean Basin already during the latter part of the Roman Republic (509–27 BCE), grew still further in the imperial era. Augustus, the grandnephew and adopted son of Julius Caesar, became the first Roman emperor and reigned from 27 BCE to 14 CE. Augustus extended the empire to include additional regions of Europe and Asia Minor, as well as Egypt. Thus began the so-called **Pax Romana**, a period of relative peace and stability throughout the conquered lands that lasted until the early fifth century CE.

The **Herodian Period** (37 BCE–66 CE) is a kind of sub-era of the Roman Period in Palestine. All of the Herodian rulers from Herod the Great to his great-grandson (Herod) Agrippa II owed their political power to Rome. Herod the Great, well known from the opening of Matthew's Gospel (Matt. 2), ruled Judea, Idumaea (south of Judea), Perea (east of the Jordan), Samaria, and Galilee from 37 BCE to his death in 4 BCE. He is known for his many building projects, most notably the reconstruction of the Jerusalem temple in Hellenistic style. This magnificent building project begun by Herod and completed by Agrippa II in 64 CE was admired widely in the Greco-Roman world. Some of Herod the Great's other building projects included fortresses, palaces, and a city named in honor of the emperor—Caesarea.[6]

The New Testament Period

The New Testament Period is also a sort of sub-era of the Roman Period (though not technically a historical period defined by rulers or other normal markers). It may be said to begin around the time of Herod's death in 4 BCE. (Scholars estimate that Jesus was born in approximately 6 BCE.) In his will, Herod indicated a three-way split of his kingdom among his sons Archelaus, Antipas, and Philip.[7] The reign of Archelaus over Judea, Idumaea, and Samaria was very brief, lasting only from 4 BCE to 6 CE. Thereafter, Rome ruled Judea directly by prefects (or procurators) who lived in Caesarea on the coast; Pilate, who is portrayed in the Gospels, held this title from 26 to 36 CE. In Galilee, Herodian rule lasted longer than it did in Judea. Herod Antipas, simply called "Herod" in the NT, ruled over Galilee from 4 BCE to 39 CE. He is the Herodian ruler most frequently referred to in the NT (see, e.g., Luke 3:1; Matt. 14; Mark 6; Luke 23; Acts 12).

After the crucifixion of Jesus in about 30 CE, the message of his life, death, and resurrection—the gospel, or good news—spread from Jerusalem (the location of the Pentecost experience described in Acts 2) into the surrounding Greco-Roman world. The writings of Paul, the "apostle to the Gentiles" (Rom. 11:13), are dated to the 50s of the first century CE and give insight into

---

6. Located 25 miles north of modern Tel Aviv, on the Mediterranean, the city is also known as Caesarea Maritima ("seaside"), distinguishing it from the inland city of Caesarea Philippi.

7. Archelaus (named ethnarch of Judea, Idumea, and Samaria, ruling 4 BCE–6 CE), Antipas (tetrarch of Galilee and Perea 4 BCE–39 CE), and Philip (tetrarch of Batanea, Trachonitis, and Iturea, 6–41 CE).

EFBM / Wikimedia Commons

Figure 2.5. The Western Wall (also known as the "Wailing Wall") of the Jerusalem temple, part of the temple's retaining wall built by Herod the Great and now a sacred place of prayer.

some of the places or communities where emerging Christianity was gaining acceptance in the gentile world.

When Paul wrote his letters, he was sometimes in prison or perhaps under house arrest. Suffering was a reality for early Christians (see ch. 4). Paul himself had been a persecutor of the church before his conversion (Phil. 3:6). The last Herodian rulers, Agrippa I (41–44 CE) and Agrippa II (48–66), probably persecuted Christians (Acts 12:1–2), and the NT tells us that communities in provinces and cities outside Palestine, such as Galatia, Asia (e.g., Pergamum), and Macedonia (e.g., Thessalonica, Philippi), were also under persecution.[8]

Tensions rising over Roman rule in Judea and Galilee led to the start of the **First Jewish Revolt**, which began in 66 CE and ended with the fall of Masada in 73–74 CE. The devastating blow to this uprising was the Roman army's destruction of the Jerusalem temple in 70 CE. (The Western Wall, or Wailing Wall, of today's Jerusalem is part of the remains of the great Herodian temple, completed a mere six years before its destruction.) In about 90 CE the heirs of the Pharisees, the rabbis, formed a council at Jamnia (or Yavneh), where there was a rabbinic school. From Jamnia and other locations, they worked to develop their traditions, the oral law (e.g., Mark 7:3). The realm of the rabbis was the synagogue, and many of the first Christians were Jews who participated in synagogue worship. Over time tensions arose in synagogues in which Christians (or Jewish-Christians) and Jews were both active (as can be seen in the Gospel of John, dated to around 90–95 CE; e.g., John 9:22).

8. See, e.g., Acts 16:16–24; 17:1–15; Phil. 1:29; 1 Thess. 1:6; 2:2, 14–16; 1 Pet. 1:1–9; and Rev. 2:12–13. This persecution was not systematic but sporadic, often instigated by mobs rather than Roman officials.

By the end of the first century CE, Judaism and emerging Christianity had begun a gradual process of separating into distinct entities.

External Evidence of Emerging Christianity

The most important evidence we have for the spread and development of emerging Christianity in the first century CE is found within the NT itself, but these texts are subject to various interpretations (e.g., regarding the controversies at churches mentioned or alluded to in Paul's Letters). Among the sparse external evidence is an inscription that helps to date some of the work of Paul and his colleagues. This inscription was found at Delphi in Greece and dates to ca. 52 CE. It mentions Gallio, who held the title of proconsul of the Roman province of Achaia (southern Greece), of which Corinth was the capital. Acts 18:12–17 also refers to Gallio, allowing scholars to place Paul's stay at Corinth during his second missionary journey (Acts 18:11) in the early 50s CE.

At this time Jews living in communities outside Palestine, in the Jewish diaspora, actually outnumbered those living within the land of Israel. An inscription (partially deteriorated) found at Corinth reads "Synagogue of the Hebrews"; though probably dating from later than the NT period, it provides evidence of a Jewish community located there. Movement throughout the empire was vitally important to the spread of the Christian gospel and the formation of Christian communities. Paul and his coworkers would have traveled along sea routes and imperial roads to visit cities where there were diaspora communities. In this way their message gained acceptance among Jews and **gentiles** (non-Jews), especially in Asia Minor and Greece. Key centers of emerging Christianity outside Palestine included Syrian Antioch (north of Palestine), Ephesus, Corinth, and of course Rome.

Archaeologists and historians have learned much about the social world of the NT, including its customs and moral attitudes, that illuminates the NT texts themselves. But there is relatively little material evidence that sheds light on the early Christian communities. For example, in many areas where Christianity was spreading throughout the first century, groups of Christians are believed to have met in homes, as house churches, or perhaps other buildings such as insulae (apartment blocks) in urban environments such as Ephesus. Since no early examples of these meeting places have yet been found by archaeologists, we must study various kinds of actual houses and other buildings that have been excavated so as to learn something about possible gathering places. We may also observe the development of the house church in later examples, such as a third-century CE chapel within a domestic

Figure 2.6. The ruins of the agora (forum) and temple of Apollo in Corinth, one of the most important cross-roads of the Roman Empire and a focal point of the Pauline mission.

residence excavated at Dura-Europos on the Euphrates River. The only other significant archaeological evidence for the presence and beliefs of Christians around this time (third and fourth centuries CE) is the remaining Christian graffiti, which includes signs such as crosses and the Christogram Chi-Rho (the first two letters of the word "Christ," *Christos* in Greek, superimposed as ☧). The NT remains the largest deposit of evidence for the development of Christianity in the first century.

Texts in Contexts: Final Remarks

In the space of a brief discussion of the geography, history, and archaeology of the Bible, we have not achieved the goals some people may have in pursuing these fields: we have not "proved" that the Bible is true or even that it is always necessarily accurate. Rather, we have explored some of the different contexts in which biblical texts are situated. For any detailed and serious study of the Bible, it is important to be aware of the physical setting, significant events, and material culture relating to the world of the texts. This knowledge is invaluable since it allows us to gain insights into the way biblical texts emerged out of particular historical situations and were shaped by them. Even so, we must always keep in mind the purpose of the texts as mentioned at the beginning

Figure 2.7. Major Periods and Biblical Events*

Archaeological Periods and Finds		Major Events and Associated Biblical Books†		Years
Middle Bronze Age	Hammurabi's laws (1792 BCE)	Ancestral Period (Abraham and Sarah)	Genesis (12–50)	ca. 2200–1550 BCE
Late Bronze Age I & II	Merenptah Stela— first mention of Israel (1209 BCE)	Egypt and exodus (Moses)	Exodus, Leviticus, Numbers, Deuteronomy	ca. 1550–1200 BCE
Iron Age I	The four-room house	Settlement/conquest (to 1025)	Joshua, Judges, 1 Samuel	ca. 1200–1025 BCE
Iron Age II	• Sennacherib (Assyrian king) • Reliefs showing Israelite prisoners captured at Lachish (701 BCE) • Babylonian Chronicle	• United monarchy (1025–928) • Divided monarchy: Israel and Judah (928–722) • Judah alone (722–586) • Death of Josiah, king of Judah (609) • Destruction of Jerusalem (586)	1–2 Samuel, 1–2 Kings, 1–2 Chronicles, First Isaiah (Isa. 1–39), Jeremiah, Amos, Hosea, Micah, Nahum, Zephaniah, Habakkuk	ca. 1025–586 BCE
Babylonian and Persian Periods	• Cyrus Cylinder • Darius I Inscription	• Babylonian exile (586–539) • Return and restoration (538–333) • Second Temple construction (520–515) • Battle of Issus (333) • Conquest of Palestine by Alexander the Great (332–331)	1–2 Chronicles, Ezra, Nehemiah, Esther, Second and Third Isaiah (Isa. 40–66), Jeremiah, Lamentations, Ezekiel, Joel, Obadiah, Haggai, Zechariah	586–330 BCE
Hellenistic Period I	• Hellenistic gymnasia • Xystos in Jerusalem • Qumran caves	• Septuagint begun (ca. 250) • Profanation of the temple by Antiochus IV Epiphanes (167) • Maccabean (Hasmonean) revolt (167–142) • Liberation of the temple (164) • Foundation of the community at Qumran (ca. 166–150)	Daniel, Ecclesiastes, Sirach, 1–2 Maccabees	332–164 BCE
Hellenistic Period II (Hasmonean)	• Miqwa'ot • Ossuaries • Stone vessels • Jerusalem temple	• Jewish political independence (142) • Galilee added to the Jewish kingdom under Aristobulus (103)	1–4 Maccabees	164–63 BCE

Archaeological Periods and Finds	Major Events and Associated Biblical Books†		Years
	• Pompey conquers Judea, makes it part of the Roman province of Syria; Hasmonean kingdom becomes client state (63)		
Roman Period • Synagogues	• Herod the Great rules under Roman authority (37–4 BCE)	New Testament	63 BCE–
• House churches			ca. 100 CE
• Early Christian symbols	• Octavian (Caesar Augustus), first Roman emperor (27 BCE–14 CE)		(last NT writings)‡
	• Jesus born (ca. 6 BCE)		
	• Jesus crucified (ca. 30 CE)		
	Letters of Paul (50s CE)		
	Destruction of Jerusalem (70 CE)		
	Fall of Masada (73–74 CE)		
	Council at Jamnia (ca. 90 CE)		

* Adapted in part from Coogan, *Oxford History of the Biblical World*, 447–51.

† The inclusion of a biblical book in the "Major Events and Associated Biblical Books" column indicates that the book has some relevance to that period, not that its authorship dates to that era; all the NT books were written during the Roman Period. Discussion of the dating of some OT writings appears in ch. 3.

‡ The actual end of the Roman Empire, and therefore the Roman Period, is variously dated to the fourth or (more often) fifth century.

of the chapter. That is, they are primarily written not to inform us of history but to show history in terms of the relationship between God and humanity. Nonetheless, they contain messages and meanings that still speak to the unique contexts of readers and hearers today.

QUESTIONS FOR REFLECTION AND DISCUSSION

1. If the Bible was not written to be "history" in the sense that we might understand that term today, do you think it is fair to evaluate it for its historical content? Does it matter whether or not things happened in the way they are described? Why or why not?

2. What do you think is the value of archaeological data from the ancient world in relation to the biblical texts? Is this value different with respect to the Bible's two Testaments (OT, NT)?

3. What difference do you think the climate and geographical features of the land (Palestine and surrounding areas of the Mediterranean Basin) made to the authors of the biblical text and to their hearers/readers? Think, for instance, of rain, snow, wind, and such, on the one hand, and seas, mountains, deserts, and such, on the other.

FOR FURTHER READING AND STUDY

Arnold, Bill T., and Bryan E. Beyer, eds. *Readings from the Ancient Near East: Primary Sources for Old Testament Study*. Grand Rapids: Baker Academic, 2002. Primary-source readings from the ancient Near East related to each OT book, especially for students.

Bandstra, Barry. *Reading the Old Testament: An Introduction to the Hebrew Bible*. 4th ed. Belmont, CA: Wadsworth, 2009. Thorough introductory text containing numerous maps, tables, time lines, charts, and pictures, plus a CD-ROM.

Barclay, John M. G. *Jews in the Mediterranean Diaspora: From Alexander to Trajan (323 B.C.E–117 C.E.)*. 2nd rev. ed. London: T&T Clark Continuum, 2016. Detailed description and evaluation of diaspora Judaism in the Hellenistic-Roman era.

Barrett, C. K., ed. *The New Testament Background: Writings from Ancient Greece and the Roman Empire That Illuminate Christian Origins*. Rev. and exp. ed. New York: HarperCollins, 1995. Hundreds of excerpts illustrating political, philosophical, and religious aspects of the NT era.

Bartlett, J. R., ed. *Archaeology and Biblical Interpretation*. London: Routledge, 1997. Essays on topics that explore how biblical texts (OT and NT) and archaeological discoveries may illuminate one another.

Carter, Warren. *The Roman Empire and the New Testament: An Essential Guide*. Nashville: Abingdon, 2006. Overview of imperial officials, spaces, theology, economics, and more.

———. *Seven Events That Shaped the New Testament World*. Grand Rapids: Baker Academic, 2013. Key events from Alexander the Great's death to the canonization of the NT.

Cline, Eric. *Biblical Archaeology: A Very Short Introduction*. New York: Oxford University Press, 2009. A survey of the discipline and some of its findings.

Collins, John J., and Daniel C. Harlow, eds. *The Eerdmans Dictionary of Early Judaism*. Grand Rapids: Eerdmans, 2010. Treats major aspects of the period.

Coogan, Michael D., ed. *The Oxford History of the Biblical World*. New York: Oxford University Press, 1998. Invaluable reference work for biblical history (and archaeology), with chapters relating to historical eras from the ancestral period to the spread of Christianity in the Roman world.

Crossan, John Dominic, and Jonathan L. Reed. *Excavating Jesus: Beneath the Stones, behind the Texts*. San Francisco: HarperCollins, 2001. Historical Jesus scholar John Dominic Crossan and Galilean archaeologist Jonathan Reed shed light on the life and social world of Jesus.

———. *In Search of Paul: How Jesus' Apostle Opposed Rome's Empire with God's Kingdom*. New York: HarperCollins, 2004. Crossan and Reed elucidate the life and social world of Paul.

Davies, Philip R., and John Rogerson. *The Old Testament World*. 2nd ed. Louisville: Westminster John Knox, 2005. The background of the OT, focusing on setting, history, religious beliefs, types of literature, and the formation of the OT.

Ehrman, Bart D. *The New Testament: A Historical Introduction to the Early Christian Writings*. 6th ed. New York: Oxford University Press, 2015. A text that is historical in orientation, containing numerous pictures and useful supplementary material.

Fant, Clyde E., and Mitchell G. Reddish. *A Guide to Biblical Sites in Greece and Turkey*. New York: Oxford University Press, 2003. A reference guidebook on significant sites in Greece and Turkey (mostly NT, but some OT, too).

Green, Joel B., and Lee Martin McDonald, eds. *The World of the New Testament: Cultural, Social, and Historical Contexts*. Grand Rapids: Baker Academic, 2013. Nearly fifty topics, plus tables and photos.

Hayes, John H., and J. Maxwell Miller, eds. *Israelite and Judaean History*. 2nd ed. London: SCM, 2012. Classic volume containing chapters on periods up to the Roman era, including discussion of archaeological and written sources.

Laughlin, John C. H. *Archaeology and the Bible*. London: Routledge, 2000. Detailed discussion of the archaeology of the ancient Near East from the Early Bronze Age to Iron Age II.

Longenecker, Bruce W. *The Crosses of Pompeii: Jesus-Devotion in a Vesuvian Town*. Minneapolis: Fortress, 2016. Finds material evidence of first-century devotion to Jesus in the ruins of Pompeii.

Mitchell, T. C. *The Bible in the British Museum: Interpreting the Evidence*. 2nd ed. London: British Museum, 2004. The extraordinarily rich collection of antiquities relating to biblical archaeology held by the British Museum.

Moore, Megan Bishop, and B. E. Kelle. *Biblical History and Israel's Past: The Changing Study of the Bible and History*. Grand Rapids: Eerdmans, 2011. Authoritative guide to the issues, with the authors' perspectives on the questions.

Pritchard, James B., ed. *HarperCollins Atlas of Bible History*. New York: HarperOne, 2008. Maps, time lines, and narrative text.

———, ed. *The HarperCollins Concise Atlas of the Bible*. San Francisco: Harper-Collins, 1997 (orig. 1991). Maps with historical, archaeological, and literary background as well as helpful charts and tables.

3

The Scriptures of Israel
(The Christian Old Testament)

CLAIRE MATHEWS McGINNIS

This chapter discusses the first and larger part of the Christian Bible. It begins with a consideration of several introductory topics before examining the story told in each of the three major divisions of Israel's Scriptures, the Christian **Old Testament**. In addition, at the end of the chapter there is a table of dates of key events and periods in the history of Israel.

Introductory Matters

Israel's Scripture as Christian Scripture

The first generations of Christians did not yet have any distinctively *Christian* Scripture; for them, as for Jesus, what functioned as Scripture were the Scriptures of Israel. These Scriptures were read aloud in the synagogue, prayed by the faithful, and studied carefully to discern God's past, present, and future actions. Thus, when the apostle Paul wrote to the earliest Christian communities, or when the four evangelists crafted their Gospels, it was only natural that they would appeal to Israel's Scriptures in order to interpret and explain the new thing that they understood God to be doing in Christ. They did so through direct quotation as well as through allusion, borrowing the language, imagery, concepts, and hopes expressed in Israel's Scriptures. Over time, early Christian writings, saturated with the thought and language of Israel's Scriptures, were recognized by the Christian community as also having their own status as Scripture, resulting in a Christian Bible that consists of two parts, organically related to each other: Israel's Scriptures (what Christians have long referred to as the Old Testament, abbreviated OT) and the Scriptures of the New **Covenant** (what Christians have long referred to as the New Testament). From a Christian perspective, neither **Testament** is fully intelligible apart from the other.

Israel's Scriptures have always been something that the Jewish and Christian communities have in common. However, as noted in chapter 1, there are differences in the order in which the books appear in each community's Bible, and even in the number of books in each. These differences are the result of two historical phenomena: first, the collection, or **canon**, of Israel's Scripture was not fully solidified at the time Christianity emerged; and second, the scriptural books existed not only in their original **Hebrew** forms (with some **Aramaic**) but also as Greek translations of those books. (The Greek translations of the Hebrew were made for the benefit of the Jewish communities living in the Greek-speaking **diaspora** [dispersion]). The order of the books in the Christian OT follows that of the Greek version, known as the **Septuagint** (**LXX**), rather than that of the **Hebrew** (or Jewish) **Bible**. To complicate matters further, the Catholic, Protestant, and Christian Orthodox canons of the OT all differ slightly from one another. As we saw in chapter 1, the Catholic and Orthodox canons are longer, containing books from the Septuagint (the **deuterocanonical** books) not found in the Hebrew canon. Various Orthodox canons also differ slightly among themselves.

Despite these differences, the amount of material *not* shared among the Jewish and Christian versions of Israel's Scripture is minimal in comparison to that which *is* shared (see figs. 1.2–5 in ch. 1). A number of figures known from the OT are also spoken of in the Qur'an, the sacred book of Islam. Like Judaism and Christianity, Islam claims its place as an Abrahamic faith, particularly through the lineage of Abraham's son Ishmael.

Structure and Development

The Jewish way of referring to Scripture, **Tanak**, is an acronym for its three major divisions, the *Torah* (Hebrew for "instruction" or "law," also called the **Pentateuch**), the **Prophets** (*Nevi'im* in Hebrew), and the **Writings** (*Ketuvim*), as discussed in chapter 1. The term "TaNaK" (i.e., Tanak) is formed by taking the first letter of each division (*T*, *N*, *K*), and adding in vowels.

This threefold division reflects something of each section's content and historical development.[1]

In terms of content, the Torah (the first five books, Genesis through Deuteronomy) traces the narrative of Israel's history from creation to the moment before its entry into the **promised land**, and includes the body of law handed down to Moses on **Mount Sinai**. The Prophets (Joshua through Kings, plus

Figure 3.1. Thirteenth-century Torah scroll rescued from the Karlsruhe synagogue in southwest Germany on or just after Kristallnacht in 1938; now in the Sir Isaac and Lady Edith Wolfson Museum in Jerusalem.

Isaiah, Jeremiah, Ezekiel, and the **Book of the Twelve** [the **Minor Prophets**, in Christian terminology], as well as Baruch in the longer canons) contain narrative accounts of life in the land up to the **Babylonian exile** (586 BCE), as well as collections of prophetic oracles and narratives about the prophets delivering them. These historical narratives, like those in the Torah, were thought to have been penned by prophetic figures, which is why both kinds of material bear the designation "Prophets." The section known as the Writings is composed of a variety of **genres** (e.g., prayers, love poems, dialogues, proverbs) on a variety of topics.[2]

In terms of historical development, the evidence suggests that the books of the Torah were solidified as an authoritative collection first, followed by the Prophets, then finally by the collection of Writings, even if some material in the Prophets and Writings was much older than the final form of the collections as a whole. These stages in the canon's development are reflected,

1. For the issue of naming the Scriptures of Israel / the first part of the Christian Bible, see also ch. 1.

2. The division known as "Writings" in the Jewish canon includes Psalms, Proverbs, and Job; the Song of Songs (or Song of Solomon); Ruth, Lamentations, Ecclesiastes, and Esther (known collectively as the Scrolls); and Daniel, Ezra, Nehemiah, and 1–2 Chronicles. In the Christian canons, groupings of "Historical" and "Wisdom" (or "Poetic" or "Didactic") books appear in place of the section "Writings." For example, Historical books include Ruth, Chronicles, Ezra, Nehemiah, and Esther, along with Tobit, Judith, and Maccabees in the longer canons. The Wisdom, Poetic, or Didactic books include Job, Psalms, Proverbs, Ecclesiastes, and Song of Songs, along with Wisdom of Solomon (Wisdom) and Sirach in the longer canons. Daniel and Lamentations appear among the prophets in the Christian canons. See figs. 1.2–5 in ch. 1.

for example, in the fact that NT texts variously refer to "the Law and the Prophets" or "Moses and the Prophets," without specifically mentioning "the Writings" (e.g., Matt. 7:12; Luke 16:16, 29; cf. Acts 28:33). Reference is also made to "the Law of Moses and the Prophets *and Psalms*," the last of the three being found in the division now known as the Writings (Luke 24:44, emphasis added).[3] Such references suggest that the canon of the Torah and Prophets was largely solidified by time of Jesus, but that the canonical collection of Writings was still in flux.

Taken together, the books of the OT recount a narrative of God's dealings with Israel from the call of Abraham to the period of the **Second Temple** after the Babylonian exile, setting this story in a larger context of the story of humanity, beginning with creation. This story of Israel is supplemented by nonnarrative material that engages and comments on the story line in various ways: by means of thanksgiving, prayer, and lament; by prophetic critique of Israel at various stages along the way; by setting forth the ways of living wisely garnered through observation and experience, and by exploring the limits of this conventional wisdom; by reflecting on the problem of unjust suffering; by musing on the deep and satisfying relationship of divine-human love; and by affirming one's hope in God and God's justice even in the darkest hours.

Historical and Critical Issues

Out of the many stories and multiple books that compose the OT, it is possible to discern an overarching story line of God's dealings with Israel, and with the other nations. However, when one looks at those books closely, it becomes apparent that this story line emerges out of a variety of complementary and sometimes competing perspectives on Israel's story, and that these diverse perspectives exist side by side. Many different voices are heard within the OT's pages from multiple moments in its history, some speaking with foresight, others from hindsight.

Traditionally, prophetic authorship of the narrative biblical books was assumed; for example, Moses was thought to be the author of the Torah, or Pentateuch. However, careful attention to the structure and specific wording of biblical texts, in a context in which greater emphasis was being placed on historical questions about the texts' origins, changed the ways in which scholars thought about the development of the biblical literature and how to date its component parts. To the degree that one may speak of a consensus view among biblical scholars, it recognizes the following:

3. Some translations (e.g., NIV, NJB) use initial uppercase letters for these divisions (e.g., "Prophets"), while others, including the NRSV, do not.

1. Much of the material found in biblical books circulated in oral form before, and along with, their written form.

2. Not all of this material, therefore, was put into writing contemporaneously, or nearly so, with the events described.

3. The biblical books that became part of the scriptural canon themselves may have been the end product of successive additions to shorter texts. That is, many biblical books had multiple authors over a relatively long period of time.[4]

Such historical investigations and conclusions are not equipped to address questions of divine inspiration and revelation, however. Claiming that Moses did not write the Pentateuch does not negate a claim to divine inspiration; it simply asks us to reconsider how that inspiration occurred within the dynamics of a human community. So, for instance, in trying to articulate how these texts can both be divinely inspired *and* bear the marks of the time and place in which they were written, the Roman Catholic *Dogmatic Constitution on Divine Revelation (Dei Verbum)*[5] asserts that while the books of the Bible were "written under the inspiration of the Holy Spirit [and so] have God as their author," their human writers still made use of their own powers and abilities, acting as true authors. But because God was "acting in them and through them, they, as true authors, consigned to writing everything and only those things which He wanted" (*DV*, §11). Many Protestant and Orthodox Christians would agree in large measure with these claims. *Dei Verbum* draws an analogy between the divine and human natures of the Scriptures and those of Christ, the Word: "For the words of God, expressed in human language, have been made like human discourse, just as the word of the eternal Father, when He took to Himself the flesh of human weakness, was in every way made like [humans]" (*DV*, §13).

The implications of this position are, on the one hand, that in reading the Bible one ought to pay attention to the characteristic literary forms and modes of discourse of the Bible's human authors. As a written document, the Bible exhibits certain literary features, as do all written texts, and in order to understand biblical texts one must in some way make sense of those features. On the other hand, in order to read the Bible *as Scripture*, and not simply as an ancient literary artifact, one must read and interpret it "in the sacred spirit in which it was written," particularly giving serious attention "to the

4. For a brief overview of what is called "**source criticism**" of the OT, see ch. 10.

5. Abbreviated *DV* here. See the discussion of this 1965 document from the Second Vatican Council in ch. 13.

content and unity of the whole of Scripture" (*DV*, §12). In other words, while acknowledging the seemingly complex development of the biblical texts at the hands of human authors, *Dei Verbum* also affirms what Christians have always done, interpreting any part of Scripture in relation to the whole of Scripture, seeking to do so under the guidance of the Holy Spirit.

Because many readers have relatively little acquaintance with Israel's Scriptures, the Christian OT, the remainder of this chapter offers a synopsis of the story found in those texts, with a focus on major theological claims that emerge in the narrative, as well as some attention to critical issues such as dating, sources, and development.[6]

The Story of Israel's Scriptures: The Torah (Genesis–Deuteronomy)

Creation, Sin, and the Patriarchal Promise (Genesis)

The story line of the Old Testament is given coherence through the chronological shape of its narrative. It begins in Genesis with creation and what is known as the **primeval history** (Gen. 1–11). These stories set the stage for Israel's story, which begins with the call of Abraham and the subsequent generations of Israel's **patriarchs** (Abraham, Isaac, and Jacob) and **matriarchs** (Sarah, Rebekah, Rachel, and Leah), or ancestors.

Genesis opens with two, complementary accounts of creation (Gen. 1:1–2:3; 2:4–25). Each has its own flavor. For example, in Genesis 1 God creates simply by calling things into being, whereas in Genesis 2, God forms the first human from the earth almost as a potter would. Also, the order of the created elements in the two stories differs. Moreover, in Genesis 1 the Creator is referred to with the more generic Hebrew term *Elohim*, or "God," whereas Genesis 2 uses both this term and God's personal name **YHWH** (rendered as "Lord" in most English translations), hence "The Lord God." Such observations have led to the conclusion that the two stories derive from different human authors, likely from different periods in Israel's history. The first story functions as a preface to the book, while the second functions as the first episode in a story that develops in subsequent chapters. Despite their differences, the two creation stories make similar points about the Creator, humanity, and the rest of creation, and relationships among them. In so doing, they set the stage for the material that follows in the book of Genesis, and beyond.

---

6. A table displaying dates of events and periods of Israel's history appears at the end of this chapter in fig. 3.5 (pp. 69–70); also see fig. 2.7 in ch. 2 (pp. 41–42).

The first creation account emphasizes God's complete command of the creation. This is noteworthy when compared, for example, to Mesopotamian creation myths, where the created order results in part from divine battles. In Genesis, "the deep," or primeval waters, is not a hostile force that God must contend with, as in the Babylonian story *Enuma Elish*. Part of the creation's goodness is exhibited in its order; each part of creation—the waters, the land, the sky, and those creatures that inhabit them—is given its proper boundaries and place within the whole. Humanity is honored by the declaration that men and women are created "in the image of God" (Gen. 1:26–27). However, human life is itself ultimately to be ordered toward God. This is signaled by the fact that the story ends not with the creation of humans, but with the seventh day on which God rests and which God sanctifies. This ending implicitly points ahead to the commandment to observe and sanctify the Sabbath day, first given in Exodus. In this way the first creation narrative signals that humans find the fullest expression of their humanity in worship of, and in obedience to, God their creator.

The second creation account, which begins at Genesis 2:4, focuses more narrowly on relationships among humans and with God. Once again the uniqueness of human creatures is affirmed, this time in the search for a "suitable partner," who is not found in the animal kingdom but only in another human. But again, the man and woman as a human community also exist in relation to God, who places them in the garden, where their life together may flourish, and who sets boundaries in the form of a commandment not to eat of the tree of the knowledge of good and evil (Gen. 2:15–16). The continuation of this story in Genesis 3 demonstrates what happens when humans overstep the boundaries God has set—that is, when they sin. The effects are felt within the human community (i.e., between humans), between humans and God, and even in humanity's relationship to the rest of creation.

All of these effects of sin will resound throughout the rest of the Bible's story. In subsequent chapters humanity descends into a spiral of violence, so that, by the time of the flood, the earth is filled with it, and the wickedness of humankind is deemed to be great (Gen. 6:5, 11; 8:21). This portrait of the seemingly disproportionate effects of Adam and Eve's sin (along with human experience of sin's effects) has led, in the Christian tradition, to various forms of reflection on the sources and effects of sin. St. Augustine argued that Adam and Eve's sin occasioned an ontological defect in our originally good natures; he said that it is not just human society that needs restoration but also the human will itself. Another way of looking at the seeming inevitability of human sin has been to observe the way in which each of us is formed since birth in a community and a society that are already marked by distortions of God's intentions for humankind.

The authors of Genesis appear to have woven the primeval history (Gen. 1–11) out of distinct smaller pieces, many likely from **oral tradition**. Those pieces include the story of Cain and Abel, a list of the descendants of Cain, a poetic snippet presented as words of Lamech, a genealogy from Adam to Noah, and a curious tale about "the sons of gods" mating with "the daughters of men" (Gen. 6:1–4). This small section of narrative is a good example of how the biblical writers combined a variety of traditions in order to create a whole that is greater than the sum of its parts. When stitched together, these smaller units present the rise of human civilization. But the portrait of human civilization provided shows some ambivalence about it, for, as we have seen, its rise is also accompanied by an explosion of sin, particularly violence. This may explain why the story of quasi-divine beings and women was included even though it runs counter to the wholly monotheistic presentation of Genesis 1. It seems to serve as an extreme example of crossing the proper boundaries established at creation.

God responds to the explosion of sin by sending the flood (Gen. 6–9). In this story a beacon of hope is first found in Noah, who is described as "a righteous man, blameless in his generation" (Gen. 6:9). From this point forward the quality of **righteousness** will serve as the standard for those who maintain right relationships with their fellow humans and with God. Additionally, Noah's story testifies to the power of the righteous to benefit the rest of the world. Also introduced in the flood story is the first of a series of covenants (binding relations between God and humans), in this case with all of humankind. Noah's deliverance and the covenant inspired by his offering to God begin the story of God's redemptive activity on behalf of humankind. The story quickly narrows, however, in Genesis 11–12, when God calls Abraham, and it is here that Israel's story properly begins. By setting the story of Israel in the larger context of creation, the OT affirms not only that Israel's God is the God of the whole earth but also that the arena for God's redemptive activity will be among Abraham and his descendants. The creative tension between the particularity of the story of God and Israel, on the one hand, and the recognition that Israel's God is the creator of all peoples (or **"the nations"**), on the other, will resurface over and over in the biblical literature.

God makes a covenant with Abraham and promises him numerous descendants, blessing, and the land of **Canaan** for his offspring. The ambiguity of God's statement to Abraham in Genesis 12:3 becomes important: the phrase *"by you* all the families of the earth *will bless themselves"* (cf. NJB) can also be rendered *"in you* all the families of the earth *shall be blessed"* (NRSV; cf. 22:18, which uses the term "peoples" or "nations" rather than "families"). This

Figure 3.2. The traditional site of Mount Sinai (Jebel Musa in Arabic), overlooking St. Catherine's Monastery, where the important fourth-century CE Codex Sinaiticus was found in the nineteenth century.

ambiguity has led to debate about whether God's calling Abraham and his descendants is instrumental (for the sake of the rest of the world—the latter reading) or whether God's choice of Abraham and love of Israel is ultimately inexplicable, following what Walter Moberly calls "the particularizing logic of love" (*Old Testament Theology*, 20). In the NT, Paul opts for the latter reading, "all the 'peoples/nations' shall be blessed in you" (cf. all translations) to explain how it is that **gentiles** (non-Jews) might be considered descendants of Abraham through faith (Gal. 3:6–9).

The remainder of Genesis traces the transmission of the Abrahamic promises to subsequent generations, and their partial fulfillment. By the end of the book, Abraham's descendants are on their way to becoming a numerous people; the twelve sons of his grandson, Jacob, are represented as the forebears of what will become the twelve tribes of Israel (Gen. 49:3–28). However, possession of the land of Canaan, as foretold in Genesis 15:13, will have to wait.

Liberation, the Law, and Sacrificial Worship (Exodus–Deuteronomy)

Exodus

At the center of the book of Exodus is the **theophany** (Exod. 3), or appearance of God to Moses and the **Israelites** on Mount Sinai (also known as

Mount Horeb). On the one hand, this theophany is the culmination of events recounted in the first eighteen chapters of the book. On the other hand, it serves as the basis for Israel's relationship with God going forward and indeed as the basis for religious observance for classical (or **rabbinic**) Judaism beyond the biblical period.

Exodus begins with the ruthless enslavement of the Israelites by Pharaoh and the Egyptians and the attempt to limit the Israelite population, particularly the males. Moses' deliverance as a baby sets the stage for his later call to serve as God's prophet and agent of deliverance. This leads to a series of signs and wonders by which God convinces Pharaoh to let the people go. After the Israelites depart, though, Pharaoh changes his mind and pursues them with his army to the Red Sea. The Israelites are delivered by the miraculous parting of the waters, enabling them to walk through the seabed on dry ground. Throughout the series of signs and wonders leading up to this event, Moses delivers God's imperative to Pharaoh over and over: "Let my people go, that they might worship me." In this way the confrontation repeatedly underscores the underlying issue: that the Israelites' "service" (Hebrew *avodah*) rightly belongs to the LORD, not to Pharaoh. (The word *avodah* can connote both worship and servitude.)

After delivering them from the harsh taskmaster, God enacts a covenant with the Israelites as a whole, claiming them as a treasured people among all nations, and asking for their complete obedience. A central feature of this obedience entails observance of the covenant laws that God hands down on the mountain, beginning with the **Decalogue**, or **Ten Commandments**. God also delivers detailed instructions for construction of a portable tent shrine, the **tabernacle**, that will serve as the locus for the divine presence in Israel's midst. These instructions are carried out in the latter part of Exodus, and the book culminates with the arrival of the divine **"glory"** (manifestation of God's presence, Exod. 40:34) in the appearance of a cloud over the tabernacle.

Many of the commandments given on Mount Sinai (Exod. 20:1–17) pertain to things that ordinarily might be considered civil practices, such as the administration of justice and restitution for damage done to another's property. Others govern what might more strictly be considered religious observance, such as festivals to the LORD, and the building of altars for sacrifice. However, because both sorts of actions are characterized as part of the covenant with Israel, both serve as a means of responding to God's gracious deliverance and loving embrace. The scope of matters governed by the law demonstrates that Israel's response to God engages the totality of one's life.

Following the Ten Commandments is a compact code of law (Exod. 20:22–23:19) often referred to as the Covenant Code. Further exposition of law is given in subsequent books, however, particularly in Leviticus and in Deuteronomy. Each has a distinct vocabulary, perspective, and set of concerns, which suggests that these three law codes derive from different periods in Israel's history. But in the overall narrative all three are granted an authoritative status as having been given at Sinai.

Leviticus

Leviticus picks up where Exodus left off, first with instructions for the sacrifices to be offered at the tabernacle (and which will later be offered at the temple in Jerusalem), and then with directives for the ordination of priests and for other priestly duties. These commandments are then fulfilled, as the ordination of Aaron and his sons as priests is recounted and sacrifices begin. The book's primary concern is with **holiness** (the quality of being set apart for divine use) and **ritual purity**. In this, it is consistent with the latter parts of Exodus that describe the tabernacle and its contents. The tabernacle, like its successor, the temple in Jerusalem, consists of successive, gradated realms of holiness, moving from the innermost room, the most holy place (the "holy of holies"), to the outer room where lights and the tables of "showbread" are placed; then to the courtyard with its altar for sacrifice; and finally to the space outside of the tabernacle and its court. This geography is indicative of Israel's understanding of the important distinction between what is holy, set apart for God's use, and what is common. If Israel does not treat these holy spaces and holy things appropriately, and if Israel itself does not maintain holiness among its people and habitation, then the Holy One will no longer choose to dwell in their midst.

Leviticus does not explain as explicitly as we might like its understanding of sacrifice, why it is necessary, and how it achieves what it does. One theory, propounded by Jacob Milgrom, is that sin causes defilement, which functions as a contagion that then defiles the sanctuary (the tabernacle or the temple), and even the land (*Leviticus: A Book of Ritual and Ethics*). The effects of this contagion are repaired through sacrifice. In addition, an individual can acquire a state of **ritual impurity**, which prevents one from having contact with sacred things, and which can be rectified by ritual purification. Leviticus uses the terms "clean" and "unclean" to describe states of ritual purity and impurity. But these terms are also applied in the **kosher laws** (Lev. 11:47) to foods that are and are not allowed to be consumed by the Israelites. In terms of ritual impurity, various degrees of uncleanness come about through contact with carcasses, the emission of certain bodily fluids, and the presence of leprous-like skin diseases. This way of thinking about things that make one ritually clean or unclean seems foreign to those who think of God caring mostly about the moral intention of our actions rather than our physical state. However, as Milgrom has observed, the rationale for identifying these particular substances as those that make one unclean is that all are indicative of the forces of life and death. While some uncleanness is removed simply through time and ritual bathing, other forms call for sacrifice. In addition to sacrifices for the reparation of ritual impurity, sacrifices are also offered for thanksgiving, upon the completion of vows and other spontaneous occasions, and, of course, as atonement for sin.

The contents of Leviticus pertain most directly to the concerns and actions of Israel's priestly circles, which is why it (together with material in other biblical books that share its perspectives and concerns) is referred to by scholars as "Priestly," or "P," material. The dating of this material is complicated by the fact that, while some of it may reflect practices as late as the Second Temple period (from 516/515 BCE onward), other parts derive from earlier periods. The sense among biblical scholars is that Priestly writers also had a hand in editing and giving shape to the final, canonical versions of certain biblical texts, such as Genesis. The flood story in Genesis serves as a classic example of a text in which multiple perspectives or sources can be identified because it contains much duplication and even contrasting enumerations within the narrative. For example, Genesis 7 indicates that the flood lasted for 40 days, but also for 150 days (Gen. 7:17, 24). Noah is told to take two of every kind of animal on the ark (6:19) and then told to take seven pairs of "clean" animals and one pair of those that are "unclean" (7:2–3). According to the standard theory about the dual origins of the flood story, it is the priestly (P) version of the story that has Noah taking only two of every animal, since from a priestly perspective, clean animals would not be needed for sacrifice until the institution of Israel's official sacrificial cult in Leviticus. Genesis 1 is also identified as originating from priestly circles.

Numbers and Deuteronomy

In addition to the Covenant Code in Exodus and the book of Leviticus, an equally distinct law code is presented in Deuteronomy, which follows the book of Numbers, an account of events in the wilderness between Sinai and the land of Canaan. Deuteronomy is presented as Moses' concluding speech, given as the Israelites are poised on the edge of the promised land, ready to enter and take it after forty years in the wilderness. Deuteronomy opens with an exhortation by Moses, who then offers a second iteration of the Ten Commandments and further law (hence the name for the book from the Greek *deuteronomium*, or "second" law; see Deut. 17:18). In the lengthy introduction, Moses encourages fidelity to "the statutes and ordinances" propounded and warns against the dangers of being seduced by other gods, particularly the gods of the people living in the land that the LORD is giving to the Israelites. Moses' speech enjoins Israel to love the LORD with all of their heart, soul (or being), and might (strength). The fruitfulness of the land and the Israelites' ability to remain in it are depicted as dependent on the people's faithfulness. Thus, Moses' prefatory speech ends by setting forth blessings for obedience and curses for turning from the commandments to follow other gods. This motif is picked up near the end of the book, in chapter 28, where the consequences for disobedience are described as conquest by a foreign nation and exile, as well as subjection to the diseases of Egypt and a return thereto (Deut. 28:47–68). Interestingly, description of fidelity as a kind of love, and the use of blessings and curses, reflect the language of ancient Near Eastern political treaties, suggesting the borrowing of a familiar literary genre for the structure of the book.

Certain features of Deuteronomy's contents have been correlated with the religious reforms conducted under King Josiah in the late seventh century BCE, as recounted in 2 Kings 22–23, particularly the centralization of worship at the one temple, in Jerusalem. (Until Josiah's centralization efforts, there had been other sanctuaries in addition to Jerusalem's temple, and the Israelites had offered sacrifices throughout the land, for instance, at various "high places.") Although Deuteronomy legislates that sacrifice is to take place at one central sanctuary, it does not name the Jerusalem temple specifically, which would have been an anachronism in the context of Moses' speech. Instead, it speaks of the place that the LORD will choose to make his name dwell (Deut. 12:11). Some of Deuteronomy's laws address the ramifications of this centralized worship. The correlation of the book's concerns with the religious reform of King Josiah has led to the conclusion that an early form of Deuteronomy was the book that was found in the temple when it was undergoing renovation (2 Kings 22). Deuteronomy's law code is often described as programmatic— that is, as laying out an ideal for Israelite society rather than reflecting actual long-standing practices. In comparing the laws of Deuteronomy to the Covenant Code of Exodus, some scholars have seen Deuteronomy as revising and updating the laws in Exodus in the light of new circumstances.

Just as scholars have discerned material designated as "Priestly" outside of the book of Leviticus, so, similarly, material that shares the particular concerns and speech patterns of Deuteronomy has been discerned in the historical narratives that follow it. As a result, some scholars have referred to the stretch of narrative from Joshua through 2 Kings (omitting Ruth) as the **Deuteronomic History**. This appellation is not meant to suggest that all of Joshua through

2 Kings was written by the same hand, for even in these books one finds quite disparate material. Rather, the notion of a Deuteronomic History arises from the perception of a unifying thread reflecting the perspectives and language of Deuteronomy. This unifying thread is found in comments added to older material or to early versions of these books, as well as in the way the telling of the history of the monarchy was shaped by these Deuteronomic perspectives. In the division of the Jewish and Christian canons, however, Deuteronomy is placed with the Torah, or Pentateuch (five books), while the books of the so-called Deuteronomic History are found in the Prophets.

The Story of Israel's Scriptures: The Prophets

The division known as Prophets in the *Tanak* contains books with historical narratives as well as collections of prophetic oracles. As noted earlier, the rationale for this combination seems to have been that the historical books were thought to have been written by prophetic figures; they also contain stories about prophets. Those books containing historical narratives are frequently referred to as the **Former Prophets**, while those primarily containing prophetic oracles as the **Latter Prophets.**

The Former Prophets

Joshua and Judges

The books of Joshua and Judges recount entry into the promised land under the leadership of Moses' successor, Joshua, and the period of early **settlement**. The picture of those events is a mixed one. On the one hand, there is a handful of battles in which God quickly gives the victory, suggesting that conquest of the land was swift and complete. On the other, it is also clear that the Israelites fail to take over the land completely, so that they exist in the promised land alongside other peoples. The book of Judges also portrays a pattern of the Israelites' faithlessness and the resulting oppression by enemies, followed by their deliverance under the leadership of a charismatic "judge" whom God raises up for that purpose. Stories toward the end of the book portray life in the land as somewhat chaotic, with Israelites even warring against one another, opening the possibility of the need for a different form of governance: kingship.

1–2 Samuel

Israel's early experiment with kingship is recounted in the books of 1–2 Samuel. Israel's request for a king is initially portrayed as a rejection of God's rule over Israel. But God also assures the people that all will be well if they and their king are obedient to God and to the voice of God's prophet. Saul is anointed as Israel's first king, commencing a period known as the **united monarchy** (ca. 1025–928 BCE), but his disobedience results in God's rejection of him. Upon Saul's death the kingship is given to David, son of Jesse. The narratives about David's reign are some of the most gripping and realistic in the Bible. David is portrayed as deeply flawed but also as devout and able to find God's favor—and forgiveness. David establishes Jerusalem as his capital, to which he moves the ark of the covenant after it had resided first in the tabernacle and later at a shrine at Shiloh. The ark, a gold-covered box with cherubim on top, is variously described as God's throne or God's footstool; it was placed in the holy of holies in the tabernacle and, later, in the temple. According to 1 Samuel, the ark also went out before the Israelite armies at war.

David places the ark in a tentlike shrine. According to the narrative, David expresses the desire to build a permanent temple for the ark, but it is his son Solomon who actually achieves this. The Jerusalem temple was part of a royal complex, sitting alongside Solomon's palace. But until King Josiah's later (seventh century BCE) program of centralizing worship in Jerusalem (following his great-grandfather Hezekiah's less enduring attempts), the existence of the temple did not exclude the possibility of other shrines or sites of religious activity throughout the land. The Jerusalem temple was a place where daily animal sacrifices took place as part of worship of YHWH, along with sacrifices for annual pilgrimage festivals and sacrifices for other occasions.

In 2 Samuel 7 the prophet Nathan relays an oracle to David, promising that God will not reject David's kingship as he had Saul's, but will establish a Davidic descendant on the throne in Jerusalem in perpetuity. This is indeed the case throughout the period of the monarchy. Even when the kingdom splits into northern and southern realms (ca. 928 BCE), each with its own king (the **divided monarchy**), a Davidic descendant sits on the throne in Jerusalem until the time of the Babylonian exile (586 BCE). The hope for the restoration of a Davidic kingship remains for a time after the return from exile, but is not realized. Yet the hope for a restored era of peace and prosperity in the land is projected into the future in various ways. For example, although early in the book of Isaiah the prophet speaks of a coming righteous king (Isa. 9:1–7), the latter part speaks more generally about the important role of Israel's servant, who suffers on behalf of the many (Isa. 42:1–4; 49:1–6; 52:13–53:12). The identity of this servant is ambiguous. At times it seems to be the prophet, at other times Israel itself. In the NT, hopes for God's reign under the leadership of a Davidic king become attached to the person and mission of Jesus, as does the role of the suffering servant. For example, the genealogies of the Gospels of Matthew and Luke identify Jesus as a descendant of David and associate him with the term "**messiah**," from the Hebrew *mashiach*, or "anointed one." The term originally was a designation for the Israelite king, who was anointed with oil for that role. A story in Acts associates Jesus, as the Messiah, or **Christ** (from Greek *christos*, "anointed"), with the suffering servant of Isaiah (Acts 8:32–35).

1–2 Kings

The books of 1–2 Kings chronicle the reign of David's son Solomon over the united monarchy and, after the Israelite tribes divide into two kingdoms upon Solomon's death, chronicle the reigns of the northern kings of **Israel** and the southern kings of **Judah**. The history of the divided monarchy is particularly concerned with two major crises that form the historical backdrop for a good deal of the prophetic writings and necessitated considerable theological reflection: (1) the demise of the northern kingdom, Israel, at the hand of the Assyrians (722 BCE), followed, more than a century later, by (2) the conquest of Judah by the Babylonians and the exile of most of its citizenry (the Babylonian exile).

The books of Kings assess Israelite rulers on the basis of their degree of devotion to YHWH, and the northern kings fare particularly poorly because of their violent coups and allowance of illicit worship practices. In 722 BCE the northern kingdom is conquered by the Assyrians. Many of its citizens are exiled, and its capital, Samaria, is repopulated with other peoples. The book of 2 Kings explains the northern kingdom's demise as

David Jastrow / Wikimedia Commons

Figure 3.3. Statue of King David by Nicolas Cordier in the Borghese Chapel of the Basilica di Santa Maria Maggiore in Rome.

Andrew Shiva / Wikimedia Commons

Figure 3.4. Southern aerial view of the Temple Mount, where both the first and the second temples were located.

God's judgment for worshiping other gods, including the Canaanite deity Baal and the host of heaven; for sacrificing on high places; and for setting up pillars and sacred poles, among other illicit worship practices (2 Kings 17:7–18).

The southern kingdom of Judah also suffers at the hand of the Assyrian armies, but is mercifully spared the fate of the north when, in 701 BCE, the Assyrian king Sennacherib fails to complete his siege of Jerusalem. Judah confronts similar circumstances again in the sixth century after the demise of the Assyrian Empire and the rise of the Babylonian. In 597 BCE, when the Judean king withholds tribute, the Babylonian king, Nebuchadnezzar II, takes him into exile along with the upper echelons of Judean society, placing the Judean king's uncle on the throne instead (2 Kings 24:8–17). This **first deportation** of 597 is followed, in 586, by a second Judean rebellion, in response to which the Davidic monarchy is brought to an end. Jerusalem is conquered, the temple is burned, and all but a small number of the very poorest of the land are taken into exile in Babylon (2 Kings 25:1–12). Second Kings explains the Babylonian exile in light of the leadership and religious devotion of Judah's kings, just as it had for the north. Some kings in Judah, such as Hezekiah and Josiah, show marked devotion to YHWH; other rulers there lead the people astray, particularly Manasseh (2 Kings 21:1–17), and it is the accumulated evil that leads to Judah's exile.

The books of 1–2 Kings also attest to the important role that prophets played, particularly during the period of the monarchy, in announcing God's intentions and in serving as a check on the king's power. Stories about the great prophets Elijah and Elisha, as well as stories about lesser-known prophets and even anonymous ones, are woven into the narrative of Kings. Some prophets are depicted as serving a professional role as the king's advisers, while others are portrayed as functioning more independently. Thus, 1–2 Kings illuminates the tension between "professional" prophets, those in the king's employ who feel the pressure to speak what the king would like to hear, and those not specifically in the king's employ, who are willing to speak the word of the LORD given them no matter what the consequences might be.

The Latter Prophets

The collection of prophetic sayings includes three relatively large books, Isaiah, Jeremiah, and Ezekiel, and a dozen shorter ones, known in Judaism as "the Book of the Twelve" (see fig. 1.2, p. 12). While some of the prophets recount visions, more frequently they deliver their words using the messenger formula "Thus says the LORD. . . ." On occasion they also use prophetic "sign acts," actions that provide visual metaphors for their prophetic messages. While the term "prophecy" has taken on "prediction" as its primary connotation, the prophets did much more than speak about future events. They addressed the injustices and wrongdoings in the community, providing a divine perspective on them and warning of God's punishment should the people not turn from their sinful ways. The prophets' many indictments include abuses by the privileged and powerful; oppression of the poor; violent behavior and crimes against humanity; worship of other gods, even while also worshiping YHWH; sexual improprieties; transgression of the covenant law; and failure to recognize that ritual worship of the LORD through sacrifice must be accompanied by moral action toward one's neighbor—that is, by practicing justice and righteousness.

Isaiah, Jeremiah, and Ezekiel

A good deal of the preaching of Isaiah, Jeremiah, and Ezekiel centers on the political and military crises brought on by the vying of Egypt, Assyria, and Babylon for control over the territory east of the Mediterranean Sea in the eighth and sixth centuries BCE. Generally, the prophets argue against military alliances for protection in lieu of dependence on God, but in certain circumstances they also counsel submission to foreign rulers as part of God's plan. Isaiah of Jerusalem, who prophesied in the eighth century, counseled King Ahaz to stand firm and trust in God when the kings of Israel and Aram sought to depose him in order to form a unified front against Assyria. Instead, rejecting the prophet's counsel, Ahaz appealed to the Assyrian king for help, paying tribute with gold and silver from the temple and the king's treasury (2 Kings 16). Subsequently the prophet describes the Assyrian king with his army as "the rod of [God's] anger" that the LORD wields in order to punish Judah for its sin—but that, when he is finished doing God's bidding, God will in turn punish for his arrogance (Isa. 10:5–19; cf. 7:18–25; 8:5–8). Isaiah's book also includes a vision of **the glory of the LORD** filling the temple (Isa. 6); oracles about a coming king who will rule with justice and righteousness (9:1–7); and a depiction of a time when nations will stream to **Zion** to learn God's ways, enabling a world where swords, instruments of war, will be beaten into plowshares, instruments of agriculture (2:1–4).

The collection of prophetic sayings in Isaiah points to an issue of great interest to scholars: How did oracles that were delivered orally end up as a book? This question is particularly pressing with regard to Isaiah because Isaiah of Jerusalem spoke in the eighth century, but the latter half of the book (chs. 40–66) addresses in some detail issues pertaining to the end of the Babylonian exile (sixth century) and the return of the exiles to Judah during the time of Cyrus, ruler of the Persian Empire (ca. 539 BCE). It appears that an unnamed prophet in the late sixth century was seen as Isaiah's successor, building on the earlier prophet's words, images, and ideas, and that the book as a whole was formed by joining the sayings of Isaiah of Jerusalem to those of this successor. Thus, Isaiah 40–55 is often referred to as **Second Isaiah** (or **Deutero-Isaiah**).[7] Second Isaiah contains some of the most purely monotheistic passages in the OT, recognizing that other gods are not only no competition for YHWH, but in fact are illusory; the God of Israel is also the God who controls all the nations, indeed, is God over all the earth. Additionally, some theorize that Isaiah 50–66 is from the hand of yet a third prophet, known as **Third Isaiah** (or Trito-Isaiah).

The book of Jeremiah is equally complex because of the diversity of its contents. It includes oracles in poetic form as well as passages often described as sermonic prose, prophetic laments, narratives about the prophet himself, and, as with Isaiah, a collection of oracles against the (other) nations. Jeremiah's service as a prophet may have begun as early as 627 BCE, and his

---

7. Hence, Isa. 1–39, largely the work of Isaiah of Jerusalem, is sometimes referred to as **First Isaiah**.

early oracles of judgment speak more generally about a disaster that will come at the hands of "the kingdoms of the north" (Jer. 1:14–15). His later prophetic activity is largely directed toward Judah's specific response to the threat of the Babylonians, particularly leading up to the first deportation in 597, and the fall of Jerusalem in 586. The deliverance of Jerusalem in 701 had led some to the opinion that Jerusalem, or Zion, the place of God's abode, was inviolable. Jeremiah warns against this view (Jer. 7, esp. vv. 1–4) and is threatened with death for having spoken of Jerusalem's impending destruction (Jer. 26). In the period between the first deportation and the fall of Jerusalem, Jeremiah advocates submission to the king of Babylon rather than rebellion. He illustrates his position that God has given Judah and surrounding lands into King Nebuchadnezzar's hand by appearing in a wooden yoke: "Bring your necks under the yoke of the king of Babylon, and serve him and his people, and live," he announces (Jer. 27:12). When his advice is not heeded and the city is besieged, his message turns to hope. Beyond the inevitable destruction of the city and the temple, he foretells restoration, and a new covenant beyond the one made at Sinai, a law written on the people's hearts (Jer. 31:31–34; 32:1–15).

The prophetic book of Ezekiel opens with the prophet among the exiles in Babylon after the first deportation in 597. Ezekiel, like Jeremiah (and likely Isaiah), is of a priestly family, and this identity is perhaps most central to his message. As told at the beginning of the book, while he is in exile, Ezekiel has a vision of the glory of the LORD on a chariot throne, which seems to signal that God is with the exiles in Babylon and has abandoned the temple. The counterpart for this vision is another in chapters 8–10 in which Ezekiel is led through the temple, witnessing the accumulated abominations that had been performed in it. The vision culminates with the glory of the LORD leaving the temple's holy of holies and passing out of the city, a sign that God has now abandoned it to its destroyers for judgment. Like Jeremiah, Ezekiel also speaks of hope beyond the disaster, which includes the promise of a new, everlasting covenant (Ezek. 16:59–63) and a vision of the dry bones of Israel being brought back to life (Ezek. 37:1–14). Most striking, however, is Ezekiel's final vision of a rebuilt temple. The tribes of Israel are once again settled in their newly apportioned territories around it, and a river flows from beneath the temple, bringing all things to life and lined with fruit-bearing trees whose leaves are for healing.

The prophetic orations leading up to the disaster of the exile, and the prophetic words of hope even as disaster was upon them, helped the Judean people perceive how God was in control of history, even as other, larger nations seemed to have such sway. This acknowledgment of YHWH's action behind the movement of the more powerful nations, and the prophetic affirmation that the exile was not a complete abandonment of Israel, enabled the Israelites to move beyond disaster to perceive a future in their land. In addition to their counsel about whether or not to submit to foreign conquerors, Isaiah, Jeremiah, and Ezekiel offered guidance about what attitudes and actions were called for in order to walk in the way of the LORD. Thus, the words of these prophets were preserved not only because they were seen to have spoken rightly about events surrounding the exile, but also because they offered guidance for the returning exiles on how to live life in such a way as to avoid such future disasters.

The Book of the Twelve

Other prophets, whose words are contained in the Book of the Twelve, made their own contributions to Israelite theological reflection before, during, and after the Babylonian exile. For example, three eighth-century (BCE) prophets (Amos, Hosea, and Micah) spoke out against injustice in the legal, social, and economic spheres and declared Israel's worship to be meaningless in the face of such injustices. They also condemned religious pluralism, including worship of the Canaanite god Baal, particularly in the northern kingdom. In contrast, three prophets of the late sixth and early fifth centuries (Haggai, Zechariah, and Malachi) concerned themselves with the reconstruction of the Second Temple in Jerusalem and the piety of the reconstituted Jewish community around it. The **postexilic** book of Jonah, in many ways unique among the Twelve, is a satirical story that reflects on the very serious matter of the possibility of forgiveness and God's relationship to the nations (particularly those considered to be Israel's enemies), as well as on the dilemma of the prophetic task itself.

The Story of Israel's Scriptures: The Writings

The collection of books known as the Writings represents a variety of genres and topics. These include historical narratives, poetry, **wisdom literature**, and more.

Ruth, Ezra, Nehemiah, and 1–2 Chronicles

Akin to the historical narratives of the Former Prophets are the books of Ruth, Ezra, Nehemiah, and 1–2 Chronicles. (Indeed, in Christian Bibles these appear along with the Former Prophets as "historical books.") Ruth, set in the time of the judges, recounts the story of an Israelite's Moabite wife who returns to Bethlehem as a widow, with her widowed mother-in-law. Through marriage and childbearing she is able to restore a family that had been bereft. As the story of King David's great-grandmother (Ruth 4:18–22), Ruth also serves as a commentary on the incorporation of non-Israelites into the people of God. First and Second Chronicles retell the history found in the books of Samuel and Kings, but with special emphasis on the role of David and Solomon in building the temple and installing those who served various functions there. Likely written in the fourth century BCE, its interests lie in the legitimacy of the Second Temple and its rituals. The books of Ezra and Nehemiah, which bear the names of a priest and a governor in the early postexilic period (539 to ca. 430 BCE), recount the restoration of the exiles to the Jewish homeland, the building of the Second Temple and of Jerusalem's wall, and the attempts to create a community with strict observance of Jewish law.

Daniel and Esther

Daniel contains stories about the figure whose name the book bears, along with his companions. These are set in Babylon during the exile and explore the difficulties of maintaining Jewish practice in a non-Jewish and sometimes hostile setting, in this case, in the royal administration. The latter half of the book contains **apocalyptic** visions (revelations given through a heavenly intermediary that are symbolic representations of events in the near future). The events to which the visions pertain are the persecutions of Jews, including the desecration of the temple in 167 BCE by the **Seleucid** ruler Antiochus IV. Greek versions of the book (in the LXX) include additional stories, a prayer, and a song. Esther, like Daniel, tells the story of a Jewish individual with a role in a foreign royal house, but notably in this case the hero is a woman who, with the help of her cousin, saves the Jewish people from slaughter and turns the enemy's plot on its (and his) head. Esther also exists in a shorter Hebrew version and a longer Greek version.

Psalms, Lamentations, and Song of Songs

The other books of the Writings are much less tied to the particularities of narrative; they engage the experience of life in communion with God and the experience of God's seeming absence. The book of Psalms is a collection of 150 poetic compositions, some of which indicate use in temple liturgy in sung form. Often called the "prayer book of Israel," the **Psalter** exhibits a number of recurring genres such as prayers of thanksgiving, praise, and reminiscence on God's great acts, as well as collective and individual laments. There are also

psalms that celebrate the king, and others that reflect Israel's wisdom traditions (e.g., Ps. 1; see further below). A number of the Psalms are attributed
to David and pegged to particular events in his life (e.g., Pss. 51; 54; 56–59;
60). Both Jonah in the OT (Jon. 2:1–9) and Jesus in the NT (e.g., Matt. 27:46;
cf. Ps. 22:1) are depicted as having prayed psalms, and the psalms are used in
Jewish and Christian liturgical worship to this day. The book of Lamentations, traditionally ascribed to Jeremiah because of the laments contained
within his prophetic book, consists of laments over the condition of fallen
Jerusalem. The Song of Songs, or Song of Solomon, is a collection of love
poems in the voices of two characters, a male and a female, attesting to the
beauty of the beloved and the longing to be united. Its inclusion in the biblical canon derives from the recognition that this appreciation and longing for
the beloved expresses an important aspect of the divine-human relationship.
Indeed, marriage is a frequent metaphor used by the prophets in reflecting
on God's relationship to Israel.

Wisdom Literature

The remaining books of the Writings that are common to all canons—
Proverbs, Job, and Ecclesiastes—are often spoken of together as examples
of Israel's "wisdom" traditions. The term is most relevant to the book of
Proverbs, which is largely a collection of proverbial sayings, but prefaced by
a reflection on the rewards of embracing wisdom and a depiction of wisdom
personified as a female figure. While the book enjoins the fear of the LORD
and staying on a pathway that avoids sin, much of the proverbial wisdom
provided is of the sort derived from observing nature and the outcome of
various courses of action.

The suggestion one may derive from Proverbs that prosperity, health, and
long life are necessarily the results of a given set of actions is called into
question, however, in the book of Job. A narrative introduction to the book,
which otherwise consists largely of dialogues between Job and others, presents
Job's many trials as the result of a wager between God and "the *satan*" (or
"the accuser") about whether Job's fear of God is dependent on the many
rewards Job enjoys. Would Job continue to fear God if his blessings were taken
away, or would he then curse God to God's face, as the accuser claims (Job
1:9–11)? Job does not curse God, but after a period of silence, he engages in
dialogues with his friends. These dialogues are wide-ranging, but they engage
the questions of whether there is a direct relationship between sin and suffering
and whether the world is ordered in a way that is just and makes sense. The
presence of wickedness, suffering, and disaster seems to call into question the

goodness of creation. In the end, God responds to Job out of the whirlwind, and Job's righteousness is affirmed by the restoration of all that he had lost. But many of the questions raised in the book, particularly regarding the justness of the suffering of the righteous and the seeming prosperity of the wicked, are never fully resolved.

Ecclesiastes, presented as the reflection of the very wise King Solomon, reflects on the apparent vanity and ultimate meaninglessness of life's pursuits and includes the sort of reflection through observation also found in Proverbs. The book's epilogue enjoins one to fear God, the judge of all deeds, whether good or evil.

Deuterocanonical Books (the Apocrypha)

Finally, the deuterocanonical books (the **Apocrypha**)—the books not in the Jewish or Protestant canons—use many of the same literary forms as the rest of the canon: narratives pertaining to historical events (1–2 Maccabees, 1 Esdras); letters, prayers, and other liturgical texts (Baruch, additions to Esther and Daniel, Ps. 151); practical advice for the pious, or wisdom texts (Sirach, Wisdom of Solomon); polemic against idols (Letter of Jeremiah); and legendary stories about the trials and heroics of the righteous (Tobit and Judith). Most of these books originated in the second and first centuries BCE, likely in the three major centers of Jewish life: Judea, Alexandria, and Babylon. They exhibit a deep engagement with the earlier books of Scripture, and, since the period in which they were written largely coincides with the spread of Hellenistic (Greek) culture and dominance over Palestine, their overarching concern is with how to preserve Jewish identity and live faithfully in a largely gentile context. Various NT books show familiarity with the teachings found in these texts, particularly Wisdom and Sirach, and a number of early Christian authors quote or refer to their contents.

Conclusion

Israel's Scripture, the Christian OT, traces the story of God's relationship to the people of Israel, beginning with the call of Abraham. The story of Israel is the story of God's love for the Israelites, which can be compared to the way a bridegroom loves his bride. At the same time, Israel as God's people is called to be a holy nation and as such serves as a light to the (other) peoples and nations who, in Isaiah's vision, will one day stream to Zion to learn the ways of the LORD (Isa. 2:1–4). In the late Second Temple period, when the classical expressions of Judaism were being formed, the Scriptures served as a guide for Jewish readers on how to live a prayerful life of covenant faithfulness that was pleasing to God. Readers also searched the Scriptures in order to understand how God was acting in their own day. For them the words of the prophets were not just addressed to previous generations, but to their own era as well. The first Christian writers appealed to Israel's Scriptures in similar ways. Ultimately, the path of nascent Christianity diverged from its Jewish roots. Nonetheless, Christian faith and practice has been shaped in numerous ways by its Jewish antecedents and is forever rooted in its Jewish origins.

From a Christian perspective, if the words of the Bible are to address the reader as a word of God, they are to be read with the guidance of that same Spirit under whose inspiration they were written. Moreover, a Christian approach to Scripture involves reading any one part of Scripture in light of the whole. Thus, the texts of the Christian Old Testament are not simply a prelude to the texts of the New; instead, they offer their own important testimony to the God of Israel, who is both the Creator and God of all the earth.

Figure 3.5. Major Periods and Events in Israel's History*

Period by Regional Power	Event	Approximate Dates (all BCE unless marked CE)
	Exodus from Egypt	13th century (?)
	Israel in Canaan prior to monarchy	1250–1025
	United monarchy: Reigns of Saul, David, Solomon Solomon builds temple in Jerusalem	1025–928
Assyrian	Divided monarchy: Northern Kingdom = Israel Southern Kingdom = Judah	928–722
	Assyria captures Samaria Deportation of inhabitants of northern kingdom (Israel)	722
Babylonian	First deportation of Judean citizens to Babylon	597
	Second deportation; destruction of temple	586
Persian	Cyrus, king of Persia, captures Babylon Return of exiles begins	539 538
	Rebuilding of Second Temple in Jerusalem	520–515
Hellenistic	Conquest of Syria/Palestine by Alexander the Great Hellenistic (Greek) culture introduced	332
	Antiochus IV desecrates temple	167
	Maccabean revolt	167–164 (142)
	Hasmonean (Maccabean) rule of Judea	ca. 160–37†

Period by Re-gional Power	Event	Approximate Dates (all BCE unless marked CE)
Roman	Hasmonean kingdom becomes Roman client state	63
	Herod the Great is king of Judea	37–4
	Judea becomes a Roman province	6 CE
	First Jewish Revolt against Rome	66–74 CE
	Second Temple destroyed	70 CE

* Adapted from Michael D. Coogan, ed., *The Oxford History of the Biblical World* (New York: Oxford University Press, 1998), 447–51. See previous chapter for more detail.
† Political independence began ca. 142 BCE and ended in 63 BCE, when the Hasmonean kingdom became a client state of Rome.

QUESTIONS FOR REFLECTION AND DISCUSSION

1. What ties together the various books of Israel's Scriptures / the Christian Old Testament as one Scripture?

2. How are the human features of Scripture (language, characteristic forms of discourse, imagery, and so forth) related to the divine aspects (to the claim that it is divinely inspired)? Do you see these two things as being mutually exclusive or as working hand in hand with each other? Why?

3. What issues and questions raised by the OT are particularly relevant to the questions and concerns of contemporary readers? What issues and questions seem the least relevant?

4. How are the ways that contemporary readers and writers think about history and historical events different from those of the biblical writers? How are they similar?

FOR FURTHER READING AND STUDY

Arnold, Bill T., and Brent A. Strawn, eds. *The World around the Old Testament: The People and Places of the Ancient Near East*. Grand Rapids: Baker Academic, 2016. Articles, with illustrations, on people and places surrounding ancient Israel.

Birch, Bruce C., Walter Brueggemann, Terence E. Fretheim, and David L. Petersen. *A Theological Introduction to the Old Testament*. 2nd ed. Nashville: Abingdon, 2005. Discusses OT texts chronologically, with attention to theological issues.

Boadt, Lawrence. *Reading the Old Testament: An Introduction*. 2nd ed. Revised and edited by Richard Clifford and Daniel Harrington. Mahwah, NJ: Paulist Press, 2012. Comprehensive introduction to OT texts in their historical and cultural environment.

Brueggemann, Walter. *Theology of the Old Testament: Testimony, Dispute, Advocacy.* Minneapolis: Augsburg Fortress, 1997. A modern classic on Israel's core testimony, countertestimony, unsolicited testimony, and embodied testimony in the OT, and the enduring power of that witness.

Cohen, Shaye J. D. *From the Maccabees to the Mishnah.* 3rd ed. Louisville: Westminster John Knox, 2014. Helpful examination of late Second Temple Judaism, the emergence of classical or rabbinic Judaism, and the parting of ways with Christianity.

deSilva, David A. *Introducing the Apocrypha.* 2nd ed. Grand Rapids: Baker Academic, 2018. Discusses the historical context for the deuterocanonical books, summarizes their content, and describes their significance in the Christian traditions.

King, Philip J., and Lawrence E. Stager. *Life in Biblical Israel.* Library of Ancient Israel. Louisville: Westminster John Knox, 2001. Provides concrete details about Israelite life, drawing on biblical texts and the archaeological record.

Matthews, Victor H. *A Brief History of Ancient Israel.* Louisville: Westminster John Knox, 2002. Relatively concise history of Israel in the biblical period.

Moberly, Walter R. W. L. *Old Testament Theology: Reading the Hebrew Bible as Christian Scripture.* Grand Rapids: Baker Academic, 2013. Engages a series of texts and issues to demonstrate approaches and challenges to Christian theological appropriation of the OT.

Murphy, Roland. *Tree of Life: An Exploration of Biblical Wisdom Literature.* Grand Rapids: Eerdmans, 2002. Introduction to the OT genre of wisdom literature, including canonical and deuterocanonical books.

Page, Hugh R., Jr., ed. *The Africana Bible: Reading Israel's Scriptures from Africa and the African Diaspora.* Minneapolis: Fortress, 2010. Essays on OT books and topics by scholars from Africa and its diasporas, especially the United States.

Petersen, David L. *The Prophetic Literature: An Introduction.* Louisville: Westminster John Knox, 2002. Overview of texts and issues in the study of the Latter Prophets.

Reynolds, Gabriel Said. "The Qur'an and the Bible." In *The Emergence of Islam: Classical Traditions in Contemporary Perspective,* 121–53. Minneapolis: Fortress, 2012. Discusses the nature of the Qur'an and its relationship to OT and NT traditions.

Routledge, Robin. *Old Testament Theology: A Thematic Approach.* Downers Grove, IL: InterVarsity, 2008. Covers major themes in OT literature.

Ska, Jean-Louis. *An Introduction to Reading the Pentateuch.* Winona Lake, IN: Eisenbrauns, 2006. Comprehensive introduction to academic study of the first five OT books.

Walton, John H. *Ancient Near Eastern Thought and the Old Testament: Introducing the Conceptual World of the Hebrew Bible.* Grand Rapids: Baker Academic, 2006. Sets OT perspectives in the larger context of ancient Near Eastern thought.

4

The Writings of the New Covenant
(The New Testament)

MICHAEL J. GORMAN

Like their counterparts in the Old Testament, the writings of the **New Testament** constitute a small library of sorts. Yet just as the OT is unified in its affirmation of the one God who has chosen to be in **covenant** relationship with Israel in the context of God's love for all humanity, there is also a unity to the NT. Its diverse documents all bear witness to Jesus of Nazareth, known by experience to be the resurrected Lord, as the one sent by the same God to be Israel's **Messiah** and Savior of all. This chapter briefly considers the nature of the books that make up the NT, how they came to be, and the basic story and theology they convey, both separately and together.

An Overview

The twenty-seven NT writings—the same twenty-seven for Catholics, Protestants, and Orthodox[1]—represent four basic **genres** (literary types), grouped together according to their type:

1. Actually, as noted in ch. 1, there are minor exceptions: a small part of the Syriac church has a twenty-two-book NT canon, and the Ethiopic church's broader NT canon contains thirty-five books.

72

- Gospels (4)—The Gospels according to Matthew, Mark, Luke, and John, comprising about half of the NT text;
- Acts (1)—The Acts of the Apostles;
- Letters (21)—thirteen attributed to Paul (Romans through Philemon) and eight attributed to other writers or anonymous (Hebrews through Jude), comprising about one-third of the NT text; and
- Apocalypse, or Revelation (1)—The Revelation to John.

Each of these types of literature has much in common with similar kinds of Jewish and non-Jewish writings of the first century. At the same time, by virtue of the unusual subject matter and purpose of these writings, each genre is unique and is, in some sense, a new literary type. For example, it is sometimes said that Paul created the "pastoral letter," while someone (probably the author of Mark) fashioned a new entity that told the story of the central figure in the Christian good news (Greek *euangelion*), or **gospel** (Middle English for "good news").

Like the OT, the NT includes writings from various times and places. While the chronological span is shorter than that of the OT, the geographical breadth is wider. The earliest NT writing, either 1 Thessalonians or Galatians, dates from about 50 CE, approximately two decades after the death of Jesus (ca. 30–33 CE). The dates of the latest books are more disputed (ca. 95 to ca. 150 CE), but the span is only about fifty years for the majority, if not all, of the documents. Yet these documents were written by and for people not only in Palestine and Syria but also in other parts of the Roman Empire, including Asia Minor (modern Turkey) and Europe (modern Greece and Italy). Since the **lingua franca**, or "common tongue," of the Roman Empire was **Greek**, all of the NT documents were written in Greek, not Hebrew, **Aramaic**, or Latin, though some of the sources for the Gospels may have been in Aramaic.

In many respects, the NT is both a narrative continuation of, and an extended commentary on, the OT in light of Jesus **Christ**—that is, Jesus the Jewish Messiah. The NT contains more than three hundred direct OT quotations and perhaps several thousand additional allusions to the OT, generally drawing from the **Septuagint** (**LXX**). Of particular importance to the NT writers are Genesis, Exodus, Deuteronomy, the Psalms, Isaiah, Jeremiah, and Daniel. Commonly heard OT texts range from legal-ethical material (e.g., Lev. 19:18, "Love your neighbor as yourself") to royal-messianic poetry (e.g., Ps. 2:7: "You are my son; today I have begotten you") to prophetic and **apocalyptic** promises and visions (e.g., Jer. 31:31–34, the "new covenant"; Isa. 65:17, "new heavens and a new earth"). Such texts reverberate throughout all NT genres and writings, though the most OT quotes are found in Matthew, Romans, and Hebrews.

This extended scriptural commentary that we call the NT conveys the significance of God's gift of the one whom these writings call Son of God, Messiah, Savior, and Lord. This Jesus is the one who has embodied and inaugurated the prophetically promised new age: the kingdom (or reign) of God, the age of the Messiah, the era of God's Spirit. As a body, these writings sequentially narrate and interpret the story of Jesus (the Gospels), the story of the Spirit's work in spreading the gospel (Acts), the stories of early communities of Christ-believers being guided from afar by their spiritual leaders (the Letters), and the promise of Jesus' return to complete God's saving work as the **canon** closes, appropriately, with the new heaven and earth (Revelation)—the goal of the NT story and of the entire biblical story.

We consider now each of the four NT genres in turn. As we do so, we must keep in mind that biblical scholarship is constantly evolving and that the "majority opinions" of today are not the "final answer."

The Gospels

Scholars have scoured antiquity for genres, such as ancient biographies or "lives" of the famous or holy, into which they might place the four canonical Gospels. While comparing the Gospels to other ancient texts such as biographies is useful and not incorrect, there is a uniqueness to these four writings that calls for a discrete classification. Our working definition of a Gospel is as follows:

> An intertextual, interpretive narrative of the saving event of the appearance, ministry, teaching, death, and resurrection of Jesus the Messiah and Lord, and of the significance that event has for those who hear or read it.

That is, a Gospel does not just present a string of events and reports of Jesus' teaching. It is a story that interprets Jesus by means of structure, plot, character development, and so on. Gospels are **intertextual** writings,[2] deeply connected to the Scriptures and the God of Israel. Moreover, they are fundamentally about **Christology**—who Jesus is and what he did—and about discipleship—following in the way and mission of Jesus. They portray Jesus not as a figure who has arrived on his own initiative but as a fully human being who is also the saving presence of the God of Israel, empowered by God's Spirit. Moreover, following Jesus in the Gospels is not merely an individual

2. The phenomenon of a text using and reshaping other texts as resources is called **intertextuality**.

vocation but is also a communal experience: the Gospels seek to shape both personal and group identity.

Along with these shared features, however, each Gospel has its own literary and theological character, owing to the varied authors, communities, and circumstances that helped produce them. Most recent scholars have believed that each Gospel was also written to address the needs of a particular community, though some experts think that the Gospels were designed instead, or also, for more universal Christian usage. In any case, having four Gospels means having four perspectives on Jesus and on discipleship.

None of the Gospels bears the name of an author (the "titles" were added later), and early-church traditions associating each Gospel with a particular apostle or his associate may be oversimplifications of the actual situations. The Gospels are not merely the records of eyewitnesses. Instead, a complex process of transmission seems to have occurred (see Luke 1:1–4) in several "stages," of which all but the first are overlapping:

- *The words and deeds of Jesus (late 20s? to early 30s)*—These were observed, remembered, and passed on, especially by Jesus' closest disciples. His oral Jewish culture encouraged both the careful preservation and the interpretation of these memories.

- *Corporate memory and oral transmission (30s to 60s and beyond)*—After their experience of Jesus' death and resurrection, the disciples and others increased the volume of oral recitation (and interpretation) of Jesus' words and deeds as they proclaimed Jesus to prospective and recent converts.[3] This process continued even after written sources emerged.

- *Early written sources (40s? and beyond)*—The Gospels seem to incorporate earlier written documents, such as short collections of miracle stories or parables, and perhaps accounts of Jesus' **passion** (suffering and death). Most importantly, many scholars believe that a significant collection of Jesus' teachings (in the form of sayings or discourses) was produced around the 50s and was used by both Matthew and Luke. It is designated **Q** as an abbreviation for *Quelle*, the German word for "source" (see further below).

- *The canonical Gospels themselves (late 60s? to 90s?)*—Beginning just before or after the destruction of the Second Temple in 70 CE, the four

---

3. Some scholars believe that teachings and stories were not only *adapted*, but also regularly *invented*—and attributed to Jesus—during this period. But this view, especially in its most radical (and sometimes vocal) forms, is not the position of most NT scholars. More promising is the recent application of theories of **social memory** to the process of remembering Jesus (see further in ch. 10).

canonical Gospels (and possibly others) were produced. Most scholars date Mark to the late 60s or early 70s, Matthew and Luke to the 70s or 80s, and John to the 90s. (A few scholars date Matthew and Luke before 70, and some put John earlier than the 90s.) The individual responsible for a written Gospel is called an **evangelist**, but because a Gospel tells a story, the evangelist is sometimes called the narrator.

Scholars refer to the Gospels of Matthew, Mark, and Luke as the **Synoptic Gospels,** or simply "the Synoptics" ("seeing together" or "seen together"), since they tell their stories of Jesus in a similar way and can be fairly easily compared side by side, whereas John is rather different. Scholars have tried to explain the similarities and differences among the Synoptics (the so-called **Synoptic Problem**).[4] Especially striking are two phenomena: (1) the teachings of Jesus common to Matthew and Luke but absent from Mark (generally designated "Q," for the German word *Quelle*, "source") and (2) the similarities and differences in wording and arrangement among all three.

For some time the majority opinion has been that Mark is the earliest Gospel (**Markan priority**) and that Matthew and Luke each used and adapted Mark and the source Q. This is referred to as the **Two Document Hypothesis** or **Two Source Hypothesis.** In addition, according to this proposal, Matthew and Luke each added his own special material (from written and/or oral sources), abbreviated by scholars as **M** and **L**, respectively. Thus, this sort of hypothesis is also sometimes called the **Four Document Hypothesis** (if M and L are considered written sources, which is unlikely) or the **Four Source Hypothesis.** This majority view can be illustrated as follows:[5]

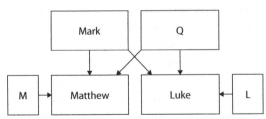

Figure 4.1. The Four Document or Four Source Hypothesis

4. Scholars use various descriptive phrases for the basic theories described here; students should attend primarily to the content of the theories rather than to the labels. For further discussion of **source criticism** of the Gospels, see ch. 10. Mark Allan Powell (*Introducing the New Testament*, 92–99) calls the Synoptic Problem simply the Synoptic Puzzle.

5. The abbreviations "M" and "L" should be used to refer to the unique Matthean and Lukan material, regardless of whether it is from written sources, from oral sources, or from both.

A growing number of scholars (a significant minority) question whether the document Q ever existed, arguing that Matthew and Luke each used Mark and that Luke also used Matthew (the **Farrer** or **Farrer-Goodacre Hypothesis**). This theory may be illustrated simply as follows:

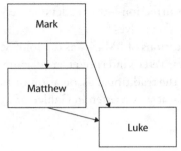

Figure 4.2. The Farrer-Goodacre Hypothesis

In this approach, Matthew and Luke still added unique sayings and stories (M and L, respectively). A much smaller number of scholars believe that Matthew is the earliest Synoptic Gospel, used by both Mark and Luke (the **Griesbach-Farmer hypothesis**, developed in the modern period, though the idea actually dates at least to Augustine in the late fourth to early fifth century). Whatever their convictions about Gospel origins, however, most scholars today are committed to the interpretation of the final form of the text (each Gospel as it appears in the NT canon).

Mark

According to most scholars, the Gospel of Mark is the earliest of the four Gospels and dates from just before or after 70 CE. It is the shortest, lacking much of the teaching material found in the other Gospels, and it contains no birth or postresurrection appearance narratives. Rather, Mark is an action-packed story about the advent of the kingdom of God, a story that falls into two main sections. The first half reveals the *power* of Jesus in bringing the kingdom as healer and exorcist. The second half (beginning at 8:27–30, Peter's confession of Jesus as Messiah at Caesarea Philippi) paradoxically stresses the *death* of Jesus, who takes on the role of Suffering Servant as the ultimate purpose of his own coming, the paradigm of discipleship, and the counterintuitive manifestation of divine power.

Mark's audience should therefore expect to suffer like Jesus and to serve others, including the marginalized, such as children. It must reject the imperial values of power and domination. In addition, those who encounter this Gospel will likely find themselves mirrored in the descriptions of the disciples, who constantly do not "get it," for a suffering Messiah and costly discipleship are not easily accepted. Nevertheless, the disciples are explicitly commissioned early in the Gospel to share Jesus' mission, and they are encouraged to persevere. Moreover, when the Gospel ends surprisingly—without any public testimony to Jesus' resurrection—the readers/hearers are implicitly invited to bear that testimony themselves.[6]

Traditional identifications of "Mark" as the John Mark of Acts (and a few Pauline letters), who was Peter's interpreter, are disputed today. Most scholars, however, find credible the traditional association of this Gospel with Rome, though some argue that it was written in Galilee or Syria.

Matthew

The Gospel of Matthew appears to have been written in the 70s or 80s, though perhaps earlier, primarily for a Jewish-Christian audience (Jews who believed Jesus was the Jewish Messiah). Many scholars believe the Gospel originated in Syria. Its principal christological theme is that Jesus fulfills the Scriptures of Israel and is, in fact, "Emmanuel," or "God with us" (1:23, citing Isa. 7:14; cf. Matt. 28:20).

Mathew's probable use of several sources (Mark, Q, and M) does not produce a hodgepodge of material but an artfully designed literary whole. Unlike Mark, Matthew begins the story of Jesus with a birth narrative and concludes with resurrection appearances. The main part of the Gospel is structured, like Mark, in two parts (see 4:17 and 16:21), the first focusing on Jesus' preaching and healing, the second on his suffering and death. It also contains five distinct blocks of teaching material (e.g., the so-called Sermon on the Mount, chs. 5–7)—parallel to the five books of Moses (the **Torah**, or **Pentateuch**)—that alternate with miracle stories and other narratives. The evangelist thereby asserts that Jesus is now the Teacher for both Jews and gentiles to follow.

To follow this Teacher means to pursue a "greater **righteousness**": to take up the yoke of a new law of compassion and mercy rather than sacrifice. It is also, as in Mark, to expect suffering and to attend to the needs of the marginalized, such as the hungry and those in prison. Furthermore, it is explicitly to make disciples of all nations (28:16–20).

6. The best manuscripts of the Gospel of Mark end at 16:8 with an empty tomb but no appearances of the resurrected Jesus. The longer endings printed in some Bibles come from inferior manuscripts and were almost certainly added to the text of the Gospel to supplement the unusual ending (whether deliberate or accidental) at 16:8.

Figure 4.3. The northwestern area of the Sea of Galilee from the Mount of Beatitudes, between Capernaum and Gennesaret, where tradition says Jesus delivered the Sermon on the Mount (Matt. 5–7).

Luke

The Gospel of Luke is the first volume of a two-volume narrative (Luke-Acts) of God bringing salvation to the whole world through the ministry of God's Son, Jesus, and his followers, empowered by the Spirit. The salvation and "peace on earth" (2:14) offered by God surpass the salvation and the **Pax Romana** (Roman peace) offered by the emperor.

In addition to its emphasis on the Spirit and on universal salvation, Luke's Gospel highlights Jesus' ministry to the poor and oppressed, the role of women, and prayer. The special L material includes some of the Synoptics' best-known texts, such as the parables of the good Samaritan (10:25–37) and of the prodigal son (15:11–32). Like the other Synoptics, Luke also assumes that Jesus' followers, who must share his mission of compassion and liberation (4:16–30), will be persecuted, and it encourages faithful witness in spite of such suffering.

The authorship and provenance of this Gospel cannot be determined with surety. The audience is almost certainly gentile and probably urban; the evangelist may have been Paul's traveling companion, but many scholars question that traditional identification. Luke's Gospel is usually dated to the 70s or 80s, though it may be earlier.

John

Known for centuries as the "spiritual" Gospel, the **Fourth Gospel** is decidedly different from the Synoptics. Nonetheless, it is of the same basic genre. It narrates the story of Jesus as the incarnation, or enfleshment, of the divine Word (cf. 1:14).

In John, Jesus delivers long discourses, not short parables. Rather than healing multitudes and exorcising demons, he performs seven signs (none of which involves demons), many interpreted by a discourse. "I am" statements (e.g., "I am the bread of life") tersely summarize these discourses in OT-rich symbolic language. Rather than speaking only implicitly about his divinity, Jesus repeatedly affirms his unity with the Father. In this Gospel, Jesus seldom uses the idiom of the kingdom of God, but he does speak of eternal life, the life of the promised age-to-come already present now.[7] And in this Gospel, Jesus dies, not on Passover itself (as in the Synoptics), but on the Day of Preparation, just as the Passover lambs are being slain.

The origins of the Fourth Gospel are disputed, but its current form— perhaps the last of several redactions, or editions—probably emerged in Ephesus (a chief city of the Roman province of **Asia**, in the western part of modern Turkey), perhaps from within a community that originated in Palestine. Some scholars find hints in the Gospel that the community was persecuted and had been excluded or expelled from a synagogue. Most scholars believe that John is the latest canonical Gospel (ca. 95). It is likely that **oral traditions** such as those lying behind the Synoptic Gospels, and perhaps also one or more of the Synoptics themselves, served as sources for John.

Whatever John's relationship to the Synoptics, there is little doubt that the Johannine discourses and accounts of signs have evolved over time. Some have suggested that this development is the creative or inspired work of the evangelist or of prophets in his community. The Gospel's narratives and discourses may well have been shaped to reflect the community's experiences, both good and bad, as they remembered Jesus. The evangelist would undoubtedly attribute this activity to the promised work of the Paraclete (meaning "Advocate"), or Spirit (14:26).

John's Gospel can be divided into four parts: a prologue or opening (1:1–18: "In the beginning was the Word . . ."); a narrative of Jesus' life-giving "signs" (through ch. 12); Jesus' farewell instructions for discipleship and mission after his departure, and the account of his death (chs. 13–19); and an account of his resurrection appearances (chs. 20–21). Jesus has "descended" from God

7. In John, Jesus' own style of speaking is remarkably similar to that of the Gospel narrator and is therefore similar to the style of 1 John as well.

to bring true, abundant life to humanity, as the signs indicate, and will return to God. Jesus' death is interpreted as part of his glorification and as the means of healing and salvation for the world. Knowing Jesus means being attached to him as branches to a vine; continuing the sort of humble, loving service seen in Jesus' washing of the disciples' feet, itself a foreshadowing of his death; and bearing witness as a unified community to God's love before an often hostile world.

Acts

Together with Luke's Gospel, what we now call the Acts of the Apostles constitutes a history of the origins of the Christian faith and the mission of the early church. The narrative of Acts begins in Jerusalem, with the ascension of Jesus and the coming of the Spirit at Pentecost, and ends in Rome, the heart of the empire, with Paul preaching there in chains. There are literally dozens of stops in between, some briefly noted and others extensively chronicled. In addition to narratives, Acts contains numerous speeches, the main evidence of early Christian preaching we have from the first century.[8]

Acts (like the Gospel of Luke) is a *theological* history in which God, especially the Spirit of God, is the primary actor. The movements and miracles of human actors, and thus the spread of the gospel, are explicitly attributed to divine activity. Acts is also a *selective* history. Despite its canonical title, it does not recount the deeds of all the apostles. Early on, Peter (with James and a few others) is the focus of attention, while Saul/Paul, the apostle to the gentiles, dominates the second half of the book. Nevertheless, Luke's literary aim is not to crystallize the legacy of early Christian missionary-heroes. Rather, his emphasis is on the Spirit-empowered spread of the gospel from Jerusalem to Rome. As the abrupt ending to Acts indicates, the "hero" of Acts is not the incarcerated Paul; it is, rather, the unhindered proclamation of Jesus and the kingdom of God (Acts 28:31), and thus ultimately the Spirit.

Traditionally, Luke was thought to be Paul's traveling companion who composed the so-called we-sections of Acts.[9] Much twentieth-century critical scholarship questioned the authenticity of these passages and the historical

---

8. There are missionary sermons to Jews (Acts 2:14–36, 38–39; 3:12–26; 4:8–12, 19–20; 5:29–32; 10:34–43; 13:16–41) and to gentiles (14:15–17; 17:22–31), as well as Paul's apologetic (defense) speeches (22:1–21; 23:1–6; 24:10–21; 25:6–12; 26:2–32; 28:25–28).

9. Acts 16:10–17; 20:5–8, 13–15; 21:1–18; and 27:1–28:16, in which the text is narrated in the first-person plural ("we").

reliability of Luke's other accounts, such as the many speeches he reports and the additional apostolic activity he recounts. Emphasis was placed on the evangelist's theological agenda and literary artistry, and "Luke" was not equated with the companion of Paul. Recently, however, there has been renewed interest in the historical value of Acts in its first-century context without discounting Luke's theological interests.

The Letters (Epistles)

The twenty-one NT documents called "letters" (sometimes "epistles")[10] can be divided into two main categories, the thirteen attributed to Paul and the eight others attributed to others or to no one (in the case of Hebrews). All twenty-one (except perhaps Hebrews and 1 John), by various writers, are examples of actual letters to real people. There are various kinds of letters, but for the most part they follow the standard format of ancient correspondence:

- Salutation (writer to recipient)
- Greeting
- Prayer/wish
- Body of the letter
- Closing exhortations
- Greetings
- Final prayer/wish

The NT Letters are also specimens of ancient **rhetoric**; that is, they resemble speeches or discourses—intended to appeal to the mind, will, and emotions of the hearers/readers—that have been put into written form. Furthermore, letters made it possible for community identity formation and relationships between leaders and communities to continue from a distance.[11] The combined epistolary, rhetorical, and formational aspects of these letters were normally

10. After earlier scholarly debates about the differences between a letter (more personal) and an epistle (more formal), today the terms are often interchangeable, though the preferred generic term is "letter." Certain conventions remain: 1–2 Timothy and Titus are usually called the "**Pastoral Epistles**," not the "Pastoral Letters," and the non-Pauline letters are generally called the "Catholic Epistles." The whole collection is sometimes called "the Epistles."

11. In this sense, the early Christian letter was an ancient form of social media, permitting relationships to exist across great distances by means of sharing narratives and images (in antiquity, word-images).

experienced by the recipients as the letters were read aloud in the early Christian assemblies gathered for worship and instruction.

The question of the dating and authorship of the Letters is a difficult one, for we have few pieces of hard evidence. Although many of the letters bear the names of apostles or were associated with apostles, scholars study the evidence they can muster to determine whether the person to whom a letter is attributed is genuinely the author, or whether a later disciple or admirer could have written in the apostle's name. The phenomenon of such **pseudonymous** writings may have been regarded in antiquity not as dishonest, but as a way of honoring a teacher and continuing his tradition after his death. Though some scholars think that more than half of the NT Letters are pseudonymous, there are still debates about the issues and about specific letters.

The Pauline Letters

Paul, the onetime persecutor turned apostle, dominates the pages of the NT once we move past the Gospels.[12] Sometimes with the assistance of companions and secretaries, he was apparently earliest Christianity's most prolific writer of pastoral letters. Drawing on the Scriptures, early Christian traditions, the teachings of Jesus, Jewish and non-Jewish wisdom of his day, and his own experience of the risen Lord, he corresponded with congregations, or "churches," and individuals.[13]

Of the thirteen letters attributed to Paul, the first nine in the canon are written to congregations, the last four to individuals, with each group ordered (more or less) from longest to shortest. There is no serious dispute about the authorship of seven of the thirteen letters, known as the **undisputed letters**: Romans, 1–2 Corinthians, Galatians, Philippians, 1 Thessalonians, and Philemon. The remaining six—2 Thessalonians, Ephesians, Colossians, 1–2 Timothy, and Titus—are called the **disputed letters**. Their authorship is contested on the basis of three main criteria: their style (vocabulary, sentence construction, and so forth), their theology and ethics, and the historical situations reflected within them.

The undisputed letters, despite certain differences among them, appear to reveal the mind of one man (Paul) writing in the 50s. The others vary sufficiently in style, content, and possible historical circumstances to make many

12. It is also possible that Paul's Letters exercised some influence on Mark (and thereby indirectly on Matthew and Luke) and/or on John.

13. As noted in ch. 2, the earliest Christians did not own buildings for worship but rather met in houses and elsewhere. The NT term for an early Christian community, or congregation ("church" in that sense), is *ekklēsia*.

scholars think that disciples or admirers of Paul, who adapted his gospel for a later generation, actually wrote them. (Those who are convinced of these letters' pseudonymity call them the **deutero-Pauline** letters, or the deutero-Paulines.) If some or all of these letters are in fact pseudonymous, they were written at various times after Paul's death in the 60s, but probably none later than about 100 CE.

The following table shows two (of several) ways to group the thirteen Pauline Letters:

Figure 4.4. Ways of Grouping the Thirteen Pauline Letters

Canonical Order	Authorship
Letters to Churches	*Undisputed*
Romans	Romans
1 Corinthians	1 Corinthians
2 Corinthians	2 Corinthians
Galatians	Galatians
Ephesians	Philippians
Philippians	1 Thessalonians
Colossians	Philemon
1 Thessalonians	
2 Thessalonians	
Letters to Individuals	*Disputed*
1 Timothy	1 Timothy
2 Timothy	2 Timothy
Titus	Titus
Philemon	Ephesians
	Colossians
	2 Thessalonians

Undisputed Letters: Romans and 1–2 Corinthians

Romans, Paul's longest letter and the most influential on Christian theology, has often been understood as a kind of miniature textbook on doctrine, a "compendium of the Christian religion," as Martin Luther's assistant Melanchthon called it. More popularly, it has often been read as a guide to how an individual can find salvation in Christ. Recent studies of Romans, however, have stressed that the document is truly a letter, not a systematic theology, and that its chief theological theme is not the salvation of individuals. Rather, Romans is about the gospel of God's shocking yet faithful act of justifying, or reconciling, both Jews and gentiles in Christ so that all persons may be restored to the glory, righteousness, community, and true worship that God originally intended for humanity.

Written in the mid- to late 50s from Corinth, Romans has a systematic feel to it because Paul is explaining his gospel in full, to a church he has neither founded nor visited, in order to help the multiethnic Roman church(es) live a harmonious, Christlike life together according to the gospel. Paul may have also wished to explain his message fully to win support for upcoming mission endeavors.

According to Romans, both Jews and gentiles need the gospel because both groups are under the power of Sin, which rules them like a master. Only God's faithfulness to Israel and to all, manifested in the faithful, self-giving death of Jesus and accepted by people in faith, can liberate and redeem enslaved humanity. Although most who have responded to Paul's gospel are gentiles, and Paul is distressed that most of his fellow Jews have not believed, he stresses that God's covenant with Israel cannot be broken and that all Israel will be saved. In anticipation of that time, the church must be a hospitable place for both Jewish and gentile believers in the gospel, in all their cultural diversity.

First and Second Corinthians, unlike Romans, are addressed to a church that Paul *has* founded—in the capital of the province of Achaia (southern Greece)—but where his gospel was somewhat misunderstood and his apostleship frequently questioned. Both letters were written in the mid-50s, before Romans.

In 1 Corinthians, a rhetorically skillful discourse, Paul seeks to unify a fractious and chaotic church by urging them to embody the gospel in purity and especially in Christlike, selfless love. Some of Paul's most well-known texts appear in this letter as part of his response, including his discussion of sex and marriage (chs. 5–7), the Lord's Supper (11:17–34), the church as the body of Christ (ch. 12), love that is patient and kind (ch. 13), and the final resurrection of the dead and destruction of death (ch. 15).

In 2 Corinthians (which some scholars think is actually a compilation of two or more letters), we see Paul explaining and defending his apostleship. He has committed some faux pas in his relationship with the Corinthians, which he seeks to fully rectify early in the letter. He uses this as a bridge to explain the reconciling work of God in Christ, which yields one of his most succinct and profound expositions of what would later be called the incarnation and atonement and their transformative effects (5:11–21).[14] In rebutting his critics and those he labels "false" and "super-" apostles (chs. 10–13), Paul asserts that the true mark of an apostle is Christlike self-giving, suffering, and weakness, for that is the way of the cross (**cruciformity**).

14. "Incarnation" refers to the Son of God becoming flesh (human); "atonement" ("at-one-ment," or reconciliation) refers to his saving activity, especially in his death.

Undisputed Letters: Galatians, Philippians, 1 Thessalonians, and Philemon

Sometimes called the Christian's Magna Carta, Galatians is, for many, Paul's exposition of the doctrine of justification by faith. It has often been interpreted as Paul's rejection of keeping the Jewish law, or performing any good deeds, in order to merit salvation; all that is needed is faith. While there is some truth in this view, Paul's argument is subtler, and the traditional view can be misinterpreted to make Paul less Jewish and less concerned about good works—what he calls the "law of Christ" and the "fruit of the Spirit"—than he really is.

The relatively short letter, which could have been written in the late 40s or (more likely) the 50s, but before Romans, is addressed to some of the churches of ancient Galatia, in central Turkey. Paul wishes to convince his readers that gentile believers do not need to be circumcised in order to be full members of God's covenant community, as some interlopers have been telling the Galatians. Rather, their response of faith to Paul's gospel—that is, their identification ("co-crucifixion," 2:19–20) with Christ's faithful, loving, and self-giving death—has brought them the gift of the Spirit and thus made them all (Jew and gentile, slave and free, male and female; 3:28) children of Abraham.

Philippians, written sometime in the mid- to late 50s while Paul was imprisoned, is a short but rhetorically powerful letter to a church in the Roman colony of Philippi. The letter is an expression of friendship and thanks to a community in Macedonia (northern Greece) that has generously supported Paul. It also seeks to inspire unity in the midst of persecution from external opponents as well as certain tensions within the community.

Paul accomplishes these goals through an extended exposition of the central and most famous text in the letter, 2:6–11, which is about Christ's self-emptying incarnation and death, and which many scholars believe to be an early Christian poem or hymn that Paul cites and interprets (and perhaps supplements). The theme of the poetic text becomes the theme of the letter and the pattern of Christian humility and love. The Christian community is portrayed in political language as a kind of alternative to the Roman colony, with its own "lord" and "savior" (Jesus, not the emperor).

First Thessalonians, probably Paul's earliest surviving letter (ca. 51), expresses Paul's thanksgiving that the tiny, beleaguered church in Macedonia has survived persecution. Paul first rehearses his own parent-like apostolic ministry with the believers there. He then encourages them to live together in holiness, faithfulness, love, and hope in anticipation of the **parousia** (appearance, second coming) of Jesus and their reunion with deceased fellow believers, possibly martyrs.

Paul's short but powerful letter to Philemon concerns their relationship to Philemon's slave Onesimus. Onesimus has somehow wronged his master but then becomes a Christian through the ministry of Paul, who is also responsible for Philemon's conversion. Paul urges Philemon to recognize Onesimus as his brother, forgive his "debt" (v. 18), and (probably) release Onesimus (v. 16).

Disputed Letters: 2 Thessalonians, Colossians, and Ephesians

Second Thessalonians is a brief letter with verbal similarities to, but also theological differences from, 1 Thessalonians. This combination divides scholars on the issue of Pauline authorship. The letter addresses a situation in which certain teachers are announcing that the "day of the Lord" has already arrived. The response, a rehearsal of events that must precede that day, is thought by some to contradict Paul's alleged belief in an imminent parousia as expressed in 1 Thessalonians. The differences, however, may be generated by differing pastoral needs and may in fact be mutually compatible.

Two Pauline letters are addressed to communities of believers in the province of Asia. Colossians (referring to the modest city of Colossae) and Ephesians (referring to Ephesus) are similar to each other in style and theology. Many scholars believe that Ephesians is a deutero-Pauline letter (perhaps from the 80s) that actually borrows from Colossians, whose Pauline authorship is more often, though not universally, accepted. Both letters present a cosmic Christ, who is the head of the church, seated in the heavenly places above the cosmic powers he has defeated. Believers are already seated with him in some sense even as they are required to live lives of love and purity here on earth. Both letters also contain texts known as "household codes," or "household tables" (*Haustafeln*): directions for relationships between Christian husbands and wives, fathers and children, and slaves and masters.

There are also differences between the letters. Colossians clearly addresses a concrete situation that has arisen in the church at Colossae. It seeks to warn its addressees against a movement combining Jewish asceticism and mysticism with interest in angels and other cosmic powers (often called the "Colossian heresy" or the "Colossian error") by stressing the supremacy and sufficiency of the cosmic crucified Christ. Ephesians, on the other hand, addresses no obvious burning issue and appears to many scholars to be more of a general or circular letter about life in the church, which is made up of gentiles and

Figure 4.5. The majestic theater at Ephesus (see Acts 19), the prominent city of western Asia Minor (modern Turkey) that served as an important base for Paul and a center of early Christianity.

Jews reconciled in Christ.[15] Its rich spirituality, **ecclesiology** (theology of the church), and ethics have been very important throughout the centuries.

Disputed Letters: 1–2 Timothy and Titus

The First and Second Letters to Timothy and the Letter to Titus have been collectively known as the **Pastoral Epistles** for several hundred years. The addressees are two of Paul's close colleagues in their capacity as church leaders, or pastors, continuing the Pauline tradition.

The three writings share a common, distinctive vocabulary and style that differ from the undisputed letters. Nevertheless, scholars today increasingly insist that 2 Timothy, which has the form of a testament as Paul prepares to die, and is intensely personal, be distinguished from the other two. First Timothy and Titus focus on the ordering of church life and the responsibilities of various kinds of ministers: bishops/overseers, deacons, elders, and perhaps widows.

Many scholars consider the Pastoral Epistles to be pseudonymous and date them to the late first, or even early second, century, when the churches were

15. The general or circular character of Ephesians is further suggested by the absence of the phrase "in Ephesus" from the opening of the letter in the best manuscripts.

developing more standardized forms of ministry and **creed** to combat **heresy** or **heterodoxy**. However, a growing number of scholars question this late date, especially for 2 Timothy, and a case can still be made for Pauline authorship.

The Catholic (General) Epistles

The non-Pauline letters of the NT are often called the **Catholic Epistles** or the **General Epistles**. However, although the intended recipients of these letters are sometimes unnamed in the text of the letter, or spread throughout a wide geographical area, it is doubtful that any NT letter was written for all the churches of its time ("**catholic**" in the sense of "universal"). The Catholic Epistles as a part of the canon originally numbered seven, bearing the names of James, Peter (two), John (three), and Jude, in part because that was an appropriate number and in part because Hebrews was thought to be Pauline. Today Hebrews is sometimes grouped with the Catholic Epistles, and the Johannine Letters are sometimes separated out and connected with the Fourth Gospel. In general, these documents (with perhaps one or two exceptions) appear to be later than the undisputed Pauline writings.

Hebrews and James

The anonymous "letter" to (the) "Hebrews" calls itself a "word of exhortation" (13:22)—what we would call a **homily** or sermon. It does not begin like a letter, though it ends like one, suggesting perhaps that final exhortations and greetings were added to a homily and then sent off to a church. Although Hebrews has some similarities to the Pauline Epistles, its style and method of argumentation differ markedly from them. Thus, it is likely that the judgment of the third-century theologian Origen is correct: only God knows who wrote Hebrews.

Hebrews focuses on Jesus as Son of God and great High Priest, his sacrificial death, and the covenant his death inaugurates—and their superiority to Moses, the high priest/sacrificial system, and the covenant associated with them. This theme is presented as an argument *against* turning away from the new faith (apostasy) in the face of pressure and persecution, and *for* covenant faithfulness. It is joined with several strong warnings about the consequences of abandoning the faith as well as promises of reward for the faithful.

Both the content and the rhetorical style of Hebrews—written in superb Greek—reveal a blend of Jewish biblical interpretation with the use and transformation of images and motifs from **Greco-Roman** culture, religion, and philosophy. Some critics have found in Hebrews an anti-Jewish attitude, but that judgment may be both anachronistic and inappropriate, since the author is likely Jewish. (Nonetheless, Christians must be careful not to misuse Hebrews for anti-Jewish purposes.) One conspicuous feature of the argument is the absence of a reference to the temple; scholars debate whether that provides a hint to the date of Hebrews (before or after the destruction of the temple in 70 CE), but there is no consensus. Hebrews may have appeared as early as the 60s or as late as the 80s.

"A right strawy letter" is what Martin Luther called the Letter of James, because it supposedly contradicted Paul's teaching on justification and did not preach Christ or the gospel. In recent decades, however, the "epistle of straw" has been rehabilitated as a major part of the NT's social conscience. This brief example of Jewish-Christian **wisdom literature** offers moral counsel in the tradition of the prophets and Jesus, as well as the wisdom writers. Topics treated include God-given wisdom, the necessity of "works" as a demonstration of faith, the dangers of wealth and the need for practical concern for the poor, and control of the tongue. Addressed to "the twelve tribes in the Dispersion [**diaspora**]" (probably a reference to mainly Jewish believers in Jesus living outside Judea), the letter suggests an audience of poor and mistreated people located in more than one place. As to authorship and date, there are several possibilities: James the (step-?) brother of Jesus, or James the son of Alphaeus, each of whom would have written in the 40s or 50s; or an unknown writer, probably decades later, creating a pseudonymous letter. Scholars are divided on these issues.

1–2 Peter and Jude

Addressees similar in description to those of James—"exiles of the Dispersion"—are named in 1 Peter, indicating a significant aspect of early Christian self-understanding. This audience, however, is a group of gentile churches located throughout the provinces of central and western Asia Minor, and they are suffering various forms of (probably non-state-sponsored) persecution. Although Peter is the named author, possibly located in Rome (referred to as "Babylon," 5:13), from what we know from other NT sources, the concerns of the book are more Pauline than Petrine. If Peter is the author, it probably dates from the 60s, but if it is pseudonymous, as most scholars think, it is likely from the last quarter of the first century.

Using the language of the Scriptures, early Christian confessions of Jesus, and possibly an early baptismal liturgy or set of instructions for converts, 1 Peter urges the letter's recipients to remain God's holy people in a pagan context; to imitate Jesus in innocent, nonretaliatory suffering; and to give outsiders no reason to mistreat them.

The short letter called 2 Peter is thought by many scholars to be pseudony-mous, and perhaps the latest NT writing, though both issues are debated. It is generally characterized as a testament (or farewell address) in letter form, the purpose of which is the correction of misunderstandings of Christian **eschatology**, the theology of the "last things." Some think it is a revision of the very brief letter of Jude (brother of James and of Jesus), which was written to discourage apostasy and is similarly debated with respect to its authorship and date.

1–3 John

Of the three Johannine Letters, the second and third have the standard letter format while 1 John lacks it, perhaps because of its broad theological and ethical appeal. First John, a sort of interpretation of the Fourth Gospel, deals with two basic problems related to the community it addresses: the failure of some to live in imitation of the love of God/Christ, and the denial by others (who have left the church and whom the letter calls "antichrists") of the reality of Christ's incarnation and death. It eloquently presents a series of basic tests of authentic faith and life in response to these issues. Second and Third John, probably by the same author, continue some of 1 John's themes and concerns.

Revelation / The Apocalypse

The inspiration for woodcuts by Albrecht Dürer, choruses in *Messiah* by G. F. Handel, colorful paintings by William Blake, and countless other works of art, the book of Revelation, or the Apocalypse, is the only example of a full-length apocalyptic work in the NT.[16] It has been the subject of immense debate almost since the visions given to John were first recorded. Some have suspected that the author of the book's fantastic images was insane or on drugs, while countless literal-minded believers, especially in recent Western Christianity (witness the Left Behind series of books and the flood of "apoca-lypse" movies), have become obsessed by those images and the future realities they are believed to reveal. Scholars today insist that it is best to read the im-ages, symbols, numbers, and rhetoric not as if they are literal reports but as dimensions of visionary, symbolic literature similar to political cartoons, with culturally understood symbols, codes, and exaggerated images drawn from other Jewish apocalyptic literature, such as the books of Ezekiel and Daniel.

16. Apocalyptic passages may also be found in portions of the Gospels and in various letters.

As with other **apocalypses**, the NT apocalypse communicates visions about the unseen world of heaven and about future eschatological events in order to depict the cosmic struggle between God and God's enemies. This apocalypse, however, also begins and ends as a letter, even as it contains seven messages to specific churches in Western Asia Minor within it (chs. 2–3). Thus, it has a pastoral function, like other NT letters; the burden of Revelation is not merely the future but also, even especially, the present. Some of the churches are being persecuted in various ways, and all appear to be tempted to accommodate to the Roman political, economic, religious, and cultural system, represented by the infamous beasts of Revelation 13. Drawing on Jewish apocalyptic and early Christian traditions, and alluding to the OT hundreds of times (without directly quoting it), John writes about the present and future reign of God and "the Lamb who was slaughtered" (Christ)[17] in order to strengthen, challenge, and reassure the churches in this dangerous situation.

Revelation begins with a graphic vision of the central character, the exalted Jesus, which leads to the collection of letters to the seven churches. These are followed by a long series of visions culminating in the fall of "Babylon" (Rome—as in 1 Peter—and, by extension, all powers opposed to God) and the descent of the new Jerusalem to earth—what some scholars have called a "**rapture** in reverse." (Despite popular interpretations, there is no rapture, or escape of believers to heaven, in Revelation.)

Scholars are divided over the identity of John, which was a common name in early Christianity, and the date of his writing. His style differs markedly from that of the fourth evangelist, but he is clearly a respected church leader whose ministry in and around Ephesus has resulted in his exile to the nearby island of Patmos. Most scholars date John's work to the mid-90s under the emperor Domitian, though some think that all or part of it comes from the 60s and alludes to the emperor Nero.

Conclusion: Unity in Diversity

Despite the diversity among the NT documents, seven basic commonalities may be briefly mentioned in conclusion:

- *Centered on Jesus*: The NT writers, in all their diversity, are primarily focused on proclaiming Jesus (as Messiah/Christ, Lord, Son of God, and so forth) and his significance for them and the world.

17. See, e.g., Rev. 5:6–14; 7:9–12; 11:15–17; 22:1–5.

- *Eschatologically conscious*: Eschatology, as noted above, concerns itself with the "last things." The NT documents, however, do not describe a people waiting around for the end of the world. Rather, they are aware of living in a new age—the "last days," the age of the Spirit promised by the prophets and inaugurated by the life, death, and resurrection of Jesus.
- *Scripturally defined*: The NT writers universally quote and echo the Scriptures (the OT) as they understand both Jesus and themselves in light of those texts.
- *Narratively shaped*: Whether in the form of narrative or built upon such a narrative, the NT writings present the story of Jesus in continuity with the story of Israel, inviting hearers and readers of that story to participate in it.
- *Focused on discipleship*: The purpose of the various NT writings is not merely to recount a story or to teach doctrine, but above all to encourage communities to follow Jesus faithfully.
- *Counterimperial*: Many scholars are convinced that most if not all of the NT documents are either implicitly or explicitly counterimperial in the sense of proposing a different Lord, Savior, gospel, and polity (community lifestyle) from that offered by Rome (as seen in its worship of the emperor, the traditional gods, and deified Roman "virtues" such as Victory; its devotion to accumulating honor; and its imperial power).
- *Expectant of suffering*: Almost all of the NT writings give indication of a persecuted writer, community, or both. This phenomenon has prompted some to speak of the NT as the "martyrs' canon"—the collection of texts that were, and are, able to inspire and sustain those suffering for the faith.

These twenty-seven writings, in their diversity and unity, have shaped the Christian church and inspired believers and nonbelievers alike for two thousand years; they continue to do so.

QUESTIONS FOR REFLECTION AND DISCUSSION

1. How has this chapter challenged your understanding of the NT?
2. How might the understanding of the Gospels presented in this chapter affect the way you read and engage them individually and collectively?
3. Is it important to know something about the specific situation, including the author and community, that occasioned a NT writing, such as

a letter? Why or why not? Does it matter that we cannot always know the author and audience? Why or why not?

4. Which one or two of the proposed unifying factors in the NT writings do you find most significant? Why?

FOR FURTHER READING AND STUDY

Bird, Michael F. *The Gospel of the Lord: How the Early Church Wrote the Story of Jesus.* Grand Rapids: Eerdmans, 2014. A helpful guide to the formation and nature of the canonical Gospels, dealing with oral tradition, source criticism, social memory, and so forth.

Blount, Brian K. *Then the Whisper Put on Flesh: New Testament Ethics in an African American Context.* Nashville: Abingdon, 2001. Looks at the ethical contributions of various NT writings from an African American perspective.

Brown, Raymond E. *An Introduction to the New Testament.* New York: Doubleday, 1998. A massive, semitechnical introduction summarizing the results of twentieth-century critical scholarship and respectful of faith-based perspectives; available in several languages.

Downs, David, Joel B. Green, and Marianne Meye Thompson. *Introducing the New Testament.* 2nd ed. Grand Rapids: Eerdmans, forthcoming (orig. 2001). A basic but solid introduction emphasizing the theological content of the NT texts, as well as literary and historical matters, with helpful maps and illustrations.

Ehrman, Bart D. *The New Testament: A Historical Introduction to the Early Christian Writings.* 6th ed. New York: Oxford University Press, 2015. A popular and significant introduction written from a nontheological perspective.

Flemming, Dean. *Why Mission?* Reframing New Testament Theology. Nashville: Abingdon, 2015. A brief but rich examination of several NT writings with respect to their witness to the mission of God and the church's participation in it.

Gooder, Paula. *Searching for Meaning: An Introduction to Interpreting the New Testament.* London: SPCK, 2008; Louisville: Westminster John Knox, 2009. Gooder and various scholars discuss the application of various modern and postmodern criticisms (see ch. 10) to NT study.

Gorman, Michael J. *Apostle of the Crucified Lord: A Theological Introduction to Paul and His Letters.* 2nd ed. Grand Rapids: Eerdmans, 2017. An introduction to and commentary on all thirteen of the Pauline Letters in their original contexts that also raises questions about their contemporary relevance; first edition also in Korean.

Hays, Richard B. *Echoes of Scripture in the Gospels.* Waco: Baylor University Press, 2016. Argues that, through their interpretation of Israel's Scriptures, the four Gospels present Jesus as Israel's Messiah and the embodiment of Israel's God, and call the church to participate in Jesus' mission.

————. *The Moral Vision of the New Testament: Community, Cross, New Creation; A Contemporary Introduction to New Testament Ethics.* San Francisco: Harper-Collins, 1996. A classic, influential consideration of most of the NT writings from the perspective of their theological ethics.

————. *Reading Backwards: Figural Christology and the Fourfold Gospel Witness.* Waco: Baylor University Press, 2014. A shorter forerunner of *Echoes of Scripture in the Gospels* (see above).

Hooker, Morna D. *Beginnings: Keys That Open the Gospels.* Eugene, OR: Wipf & Stock, 2009 (orig. Trinity, 1997). The significance of the beginning of each Gospel.

————. *Endings: Invitations to Discipleship.* London: SCM; Peabody, MA: Hendrickson, 2003. The significance of the ending of each Gospel.

Howard-Brook, Wes, and Sharon H. Ringe, eds. *The New Testament: Introducing the Way of Discipleship.* Maryknoll, NY: Orbis, 2002. A brief but insightful overview of most of the NT writings and their call for radical devotion to Jesus and his way.

Johnson, Luke Timothy, and Todd Penner. *The Writings of the New Testament: An Interpretation.* 3rd ed. Minneapolis: Fortress, 2010. A brilliant engagement with the NT texts, emphasizing their literary and religious dimensions; CD included.

Levine, Amy-Jill, and Marc Zvi Brettler, eds. *The Jewish Annotated New Testament.* New York: Oxford University Press, 2011. A first-rate study edition of the NT by Jewish scholars, with introductions, notes, short essays, maps, and tables.

Matera, Frank J. *New Testament Theology: Exploring Diversity and Unity.* Louisville: Westminster John Knox, 2007. The theological content of each writing, plus consideration of the NT's "diverse unity."

Patzia, Arthur D. *The Making of the New Testament: Origin, Collection, Text and Canon.* 2nd ed. Downers Grove, IL: InterVarsity, 2011. A helpful guide to the process by which the NT books and canon came into being.

Porter, Stanley E., and Cynthia Long Westfall. *Empire in the New Testament.* Eugene, OR: Wipf & Stock, 2011. Treats the way various NT books engage and critique the Roman Empire.

Powell, Mark Allan. *Introducing the New Testament: A Historical, Literary, and Theological Survey.* Grand Rapids: Baker Academic, 2009. A succinct but engaging guide, lavishly illustrated and with many accompanying online materials.

Wright, N. T. *How God Became King: The Forgotten Story of the Gospels.* New York: HarperOne, 2012. Argues that the Gospels present Jesus as the one in and by whom God established his rule.

————. *Paul: In Fresh Perspective.* Minneapolis: Fortress, 2005. Presents Paul in light of his imperial context and as a Jew reworking themes of God, God's people, and God's future in light of Jesus and the Spirit.

There are, of course, many commentaries on the various NT writings. Of particular interest to those with global concerns are those written from within non-Western contexts, such as the India Commentary on the New Testament series (Primalogue Press); the Africa Bible Commentary series (HippoBooks and Zondervan); the one-volume *Africa Bible Commentary*, edited by Tokunboh Adeyemo (Nairobi: WordAlive; Grand Rapids: Zondervan, 2006); and *The New African Bible* (Nairobi: Paulines Africa, 2011), from the Roman Catholic Church in Africa. These basic resources are available in many countries.

5

Significant Noncanonical Writings

Christopher W. Skinner

The writings of the Hebrew Bible (the Christian Old Testament) and the New Testament did not emerge in a vacuum. They share a rich cultural, philosophical, and religious heritage with many other texts that did not find their way into the Jewish and Christian **canons**. Numerous writings from outside the Bible have proved useful for helping us understand some of the different theological trajectories within Judaism, especially of the **Second Temple** period, as well as the various shapes that devotion to Jesus took in the first four Christian centuries. In this chapter we consider five different groups of literature: the Old Testament **Pseudepigrapha**, the **Dead Sea Scrolls**, the **Nag Hammadi** library, the New Testament **Apocrypha**, and the **Apostolic Fathers**. Our primary aim in examining these writings is to consider their contributions to our knowledge about and study of the Bible. For each corpus (body of literature) introduced below, there is a discussion of pertinent background information, a description of its writings, and a representative text.

The Old Testament Pseudepigrapha

The term "pseudepigrapha" derives from two Greek roots meaning "falsely attributed" and refers to a diverse group of Jewish and Jewish-Christian writings that appeared between 200 BCE and 200 CE. These writings were originally composed in Hebrew, Aramaic, and Greek. However, the spread of Judaism and Christianity throughout the ancient world also meant the translation of their respective sacred writings into other languages. Since we possess no original texts from this period, some pseudepigrapha have survived only as translations. As with some of the other literature covered in this chapter, there is no officially recognized list of pseudepigrapha, and it is probably the case that most of these writings were never formally associated with one another. Rather, the grouping of these writings into a larger corpus is a modern task undertaken by scholars.

The standard reference work on the OT Pseudepigrapha outlines the commonly accepted criteria used in classifying these documents: (1) they are Jewish or Christian; (2) they are attributed to ideal figures in Israel's past; (3) they claim to contain a message from God; (4) they often claim to build upon ideas found in the OT; and (5) with a few exceptions, they appeared between the late second century BCE and the early third century CE.[1] Thus, the Pseudepigrapha are writings falsely attributed to important biblical characters, such as Abraham, Moses, Job, David, and Elijah, as well as nonbiblical figures venerated within Judaism, as a means of establishing **authority** with the specific aim of relaying a message from God. Several common themes run throughout the Pseudepigrapha, most of which will be familiar to readers of the Bible. These themes include the fall and redemption of humanity, the triumph of God over evil, the existence of angels, the end of the world, and the resurrection of the dead. In addition, the identity and characteristics of a coming messiah form a particularly prominent theme in the Pseudepigrapha.

Numerous **genres** of literature make up the OT Pseudepigrapha. Here is an abbreviated list of works that fall under those genres:

(1) Apocalyptic literature: 1 Enoch, Sibylline Oracles, 4 Ezra

(2) Testamentary literature: Testaments of the Twelve Patriarchs, Testament of Moses

(3) Expanded OT legends: Letter of Aristeas, Joseph and Aseneth, Life of Adam and Eve, Jubilees

(4) Wisdom literature: 3–4 Maccabees, Pseudo-Phocylides

(5) Prayers, Psalms, and Odes: Other Psalms of David, Psalms of Solomon

The OT Pseudepigrapha are important to our study of the Bible for several reasons. First, they exercised religious authority and social influence among

---

1. James H. Charlesworth, ed., *The Old Testament Pseudepigrapha*, 2 vols. (1983–1985; repr., Peabody, MA: Hendrickson, 2010), 1:xxiv–xxv.

Jews and especially among Christians even though, with rare exceptions, they did not ultimately make their way into either tradition's canon.[2] Also, some Christians continued to use these texts even after their canon was considered more or less closed. Thus, twenty-first-century Christian understandings of biblical authority and its relationship to a closed canon were foreign to the experience of many early Christians. Furthermore, these texts often reflect developments in theological thought that provide insights into how conversations were taking place among people of faith. The road to **orthodoxy** for both Jews and Christians was ultimately a long one, and these writings give us a glimpse into various stops and detours along the way. The Pseudepigrapha provide a wide context for helping us come to grips with how certain theological ideas were developed and articulated in the centuries between the writing of the Hebrew Bible and the canonization of the New Testament.

Excerpt: 1 Enoch

Enoch, a character described in Genesis as the seventh descendant from Adam, inexplicably developed an important status within the religious culture of Judaism. He is the enigmatic figure about whom it is written, "Enoch walked with God; then he was no more, because God took him" (Gen. 5:24). Three different writings are attributed to him, the most important of which is 1 Enoch. First Enoch was written sometime between the second century BCE and the first century CE and was widely used; it is even cited in the NT letter of Jude (vv. 14–15).

In this largely **apocalyptic** work, Enoch is the protagonist who tours heaven, earth, and **Sheol** (the place of the dead) as the eschatological age unfolds and gives way to the final judgment of humanity. First Enoch reveals the complexity of Jewish thinking during this period of history, and it contains a cluster of the themes that often appear in isolation throughout the Pseudepigrapha. The text below is an excerpt from 1 Enoch that contains language and imagery strikingly similar to that found in the NT teachings of Jesus, as well as in the book of Revelation:

> Then there came to them a great joy. And they blessed, glorified, and extolled the Lord on account of the fact that the name of that Son of Man was revealed to them. He shall never pass away or perish from before the face of the earth. But those who have led the world astray shall be bound with chains; and their ruinous congregation shall be imprisoned; all their deeds shall vanish from before

2. 1 Enoch and Jubilees appear in the Ethiopian Christian canon, 3 Maccabees and Psalm 151 in the Greek and Russian Orthodox canons, and 4 Maccabees in the Greek Orthodox canon.

the face of the earth. Thenceforth nothing that is corruptible shall be found; for that Son of Man has appeared and has seated himself upon the throne of his glory; and all evil shall disappear from before his face; he shall go and tell to that Son of Man, and he shall be strong before the Lord of the Spirits. Here ends the third parable of Enoch. (69.27–29)[3]

The Dead Sea Scrolls

In the winter of 1947, a young Bedouin shepherd named Muhammed edh-Dhib and several of his friends were searching for a lost goat on the cliffs of the northwest shore of the Dead Sea, near an area called **Qumran**. Approaching one cave in which he presumed his goat might have wandered, Muhammed tossed a stone, hoping to startle the animal. Instead, he heard a crashing sound. Upon entering the cave (known today as Cave 1), Muhammed and his friends found ten oddly shaped clay jars. After investigating the jars further, they discovered seven ancient scrolls wrapped in linen cloths. They could not read the ancient script but presumed the scrolls were valuable, so they tucked them away with the intent of selling them on the antiquities market. This initial discovery set about a series of events as Bedouin trea-sure hunters and archaeologists feverishly scoured the surrounding caves for more scrolls—a search that eventually culminated in the discovery of nearly nine hundred scrolls or fragments in eleven different caves, dating from around 200 BCE to 68 CE. Because of the proximity of the discoveries to the Dead Sea, these writings were dubbed the **Dead Sea Scrolls** (DSS). They are sometimes also called the Qumran writings, the Qumran library, or simply the Scrolls.

The Dead Sea Scrolls were primarily written in Hebrew, though there are numerous texts in both Aramaic and Greek. Most scholars believe that a group known as the **Essenes** was responsible for copying, composing, and preserving these documents.[4] The Essenes were a separatist Jewish group that rejected the legitimacy of the temple leadership in Jerusalem. It appears that some Essenes moved into the Judean desert to form an ascetically oriented community at Qumran. Among their distinctive practices were ritual baptisms and communal meals, and they believed in an apocalyptic end of the world. They referred to themselves as "sons of light" and to their enemies as "sons of darkness," and they followed the instruction of a figure known as the

3. From the translation by E. Isaac in Charlesworth, *Old Testament Pseudepigrapha*, 1:49.
4. For more on the Essenes and their presumed association with the Dead Sea Scrolls, see VanderKam, *Dead Sea Scrolls Today*, 97–156.

Figure 5.1. Some of the caves near the Qumran community on the edge of the Dead Sea, where the community hid its scrolls from the world until their accidental discovery in 1947.

"Teacher of Righteousness." Scholars believe the documents were deposited in the various caves near the end of the **First Jewish Revolt** (ca. 66–74 CE).

The writings discovered at and near Qumran can be divided into two groups: biblical texts and nonbiblical texts. With the exception of the book of Esther, every book from the Hebrew canon appears at least once among the Dead Sea Scrolls; some appear numerous times, including twenty-five copies of Deuteronomy, thirty copies of the Psalms, and nineteen copies of Isaiah. What is perhaps even more significant is that some of the biblical texts found at Qumran predate our earliest previously known manuscripts of the Hebrew Bible by nearly one thousand years!

By and large, the nonbiblical writings discovered at Qumran reflect the sectarian theological emphases of the Essene community. Among these non-biblical writings is the Temple Scroll, which contains a revelation given to Moses by God and describes an ideal Jewish temple, along with regulations for those worshiping there. Another important text is the War Scroll, which outlines a seven-stage confrontation between the "sons of light" and the "sons of darkness" culminating in the defeat of darkness and the restoration of the Jewish temple. Yet another is the so-called Thanksgiving Scroll, containing psalms in which the author speaks (in the first person) of his persecution by those opposed to his ministry.

The Dead Sea Scrolls are important to our study of the Bible for the large amount of comparative material they provide. Most of the Jewish writings known to us from the time of Jesus or shortly thereafter reflect a rabbinic or **proto-rabbinic** form of Judaism. However, the Dead Sea Scrolls reflect a nonrabbinic, apocalyptic, and separatist worldview that unveils a very different theological trajectory within Judaism. Also, although the Essenes are never mentioned in the NT, our awareness of their connection to the Dead Sea Scrolls provides us with evidence of another sectarian Jewish group contemporaneous with John the Baptist, Jesus, and Paul.

Excerpt: The Rule of the Community

The Rule of the Community (sometimes called the Manual of Discipline) was one of the original scrolls discovered in the winter of 1947. It is largely concerned with outlining communal practices such as **ritual purity** by immersion and protocol for common meals. This text, like others among the scrolls, sheds light on developments within Judaism that can help us situate important ideas in the NT. For example, for decades scholars assumed that dualistic categories found in the NT (e.g., light vs. dark; truth vs. lie, and so forth), arose from the influence of Greek philosophy. However, both the Rule of the Community and the War Scroll reveal an explicit emphasis on these very dichotomies, which has immediate implications for our study of the Bible, and notably for the Gospel of John. Practically, it means that some NT writings could have been influenced by these seemingly Hellenistic ideas that actually arose within a contemporary Jewish setting rather than a Greek philosophical framework.

Here is an excerpt from the Rule of the Community:

> Those born of truth spring from a fountain of light, but those born of injustice spring from a source of darkness. All the children of righteousness are ruled by the Prince of Light and walk in the ways of light, but all the children of injustice are ruled by the Angel of Darkness and walk in the ways of darkness. The Angel of Darkness leads all the children of righteousness astray, and until his end, all their sin, iniquities, wickedness, and all their unlawful deeds are caused by his dominion in accordance with the mysteries of God. Every one of their chastisements, and every one of the seasons of their distress, shall be brought about by the rule of his persecution; for all his allotted spirits seek the overthrow of the sons of light. But the God of Israel and His Angel of Truth will succour all the sons of light. (3.19–24)[5]

5. From Geza Vermes, *The Complete Dead Sea Scrolls in English*, rev. ed. (London: Penguin, 2004), 101.

Institute for Antiquity and Christianity

Figure 5.2. Some of the leather-bound codices of gnostic texts in Coptic that were discovered at Nag Hammadi in Egypt in 1945.

The Nag Hammadi Library

In December 1945, two brothers searching for fertilizer in the **Nag Hammadi** region of the Egyptian desert (on the west bank of the Nile, north of Luxor) inadvertently uncovered an earthenware jar containing twelve leather-bound codices. The books contained fifty-two ancient texts, all of which were written in **Coptic**, and most of which were previously unknown to scholars of early Christianity. The majority of these texts were written between the mid-second and the mid-fourth centuries CE, though there are a few exceptions. Some of the texts were most likely composed in Greek and later translated into Coptic. Because of the location of their discovery, these writings are often referred to as the Nag Hammadi library.

While we cannot paint this entire corpus with a broad brush, most of the writings found at Nag Hammadi reflect a **gnostic** theological outlook, stressing the reception of specially revealed knowledge for salvation. Among the documents discovered at Nag Hammadi were previously unknown gospels, including the Gospel of Truth, the Gospel of the Egyptians, and the Gospel of Philip, along with enigmatic works such as the Hypostasis of the Archons, Trimorphic Protennoia, Pistis Sophia, and Eugnostos the Blessed. In a number of Nag Hammadi texts, Jesus is the central character, though the picture of him that emerges is quite different from what we see in the NT. He appears as a divinized, quasi-mystical being who dispenses esoteric teaching. Numerous other Nag Hammadi writings feature characters from the Bible; these include texts about NT figures such as Jesus' disciples, his brother James, and Paul, along with texts about OT figures like Adam, Shem, Seth, and Melchizedek. Other writings from this collection, such as Plato's *Republic* and the Sentences of Sextus, while not gnostic in origin, were probably included because their ideas were appealing to early gnostic Christians.

In 367 CE, Athanasius, the bishop of Alexandria, used the occasion of his Thirty-Ninth Festal letter, or Easter letter, to provide an authoritative list of the twenty-seven books of the NT (see ch. 6). He did this with the intention of both ending discussions over the authority of certain disputed books and with a view to forbidding their use. Scholars have speculated that the Christians who regarded these gnostic writings as authoritative hid the collection sometime in the late fourth century in order to avoid complying with the edict of Athanasius.

The Nag Hammadi library is important to our study of the Bible for numerous reasons. First, it shows us that many of the early christological disputes reflected in the NT were still not resolved even into the fourth century. Rather, interpretations of the significance of Jesus' life continued to evolve in the teaching and preaching of various early Christian groups. Second, this collection also shows us some of the different ways gnostic expressions of Christianity diverged from what eventually became known as orthodoxy. Finally, the history behind this collection helps us better appreciate some of the struggles that emerged during the process of NT canonization as well as some of the early attempts to resist that formalization process.

Excerpt: The Gospel of Thomas

One of the most important texts discovered at Nag Hammadi for our study of the Bible is the Gospel of Thomas (not to be confused with the Infancy Gospel of Thomas noted below under "The New Testament Apocrypha"). This writing was previously known to scholars only by name because it was mentioned by Hippolytus of Rome and condemned by Origen of Alexandria, both of whom were writing in the early part of the third century. Three Greek fragments of the Gospel of Thomas had previously been discovered in 1897 and 1903 in another area of the Egyptian desert known as Oxyrhynchus. The Coptic version discovered at Nag Hammadi represents the only complete version of this ancient text that we possess. The Gospel of Thomas was of immediate interest to researchers because of its many parallels to passages from the Synoptic Gospels. These similarities have led to seemingly endless speculation about the date of the Gospel of Thomas, with some concluding that it appeared before our earliest written Gospels and others arguing that it was dependent on them.

The Gospel of Thomas is not a "gospel" in the purest sense. It has no overarching narrative structure, no birth story, and no passion or resurrection narratives. Instead, it is a list of 114 independent sayings of Jesus, most of which begin with the phrase "Jesus said" or "he said." Below are examples of both familiar and unfamiliar sayings of Jesus found in the Gospel of Thomas:

Familiar Sayings

9. Jesus said, "Look, the sower went out, took a handful (of seeds), and scattered (them). Some fell on the road, and the birds came and gathered them. Others fell on rock, and they didn't take root in the soil and didn't produce heads of grain. Others fell on thorns, and they choked the seeds and worms ate them. And others fell on good soil, and it produced a good crop: it yielded sixty per measure and one hundred twenty per measure." [see Mark 4:1–8; Matt. 13:4–8; Luke 8:5–8]

31. Jesus said, "No prophet is welcome on his home turf; doctors don't cure those who know them." [see Mark 6:4; Matt. 13:57; Luke 4:24]

34. Jesus said, "If a blind person leads a blind person, both of them will fall into a hole." [see Matt. 15:14; Luke 6:39]

Unfamiliar Sayings

7. Jesus said, "Lucky is the lion that the human will eat, so that the lion becomes human. And foul is the human that the lion will eat, and the lion still will become human."

42. Jesus said, "Be passersby."

77. Jesus said, "I am the light that is over all things. I am all: from me all came forth, and to me all attained. Split a piece of wood; I am there. Lift up the stone, and you will find me there."

82. Jesus said, "Whoever is near me is near the fire, and whoever is far from me is far from the kingdom."[6]

6. From the translation by Stephen J. Patterson and Marvin Meyer in *The Complete Gospels*, ed. Robert J. Miller, 4th ed. (Salem, OR: Polebridge, 2010).

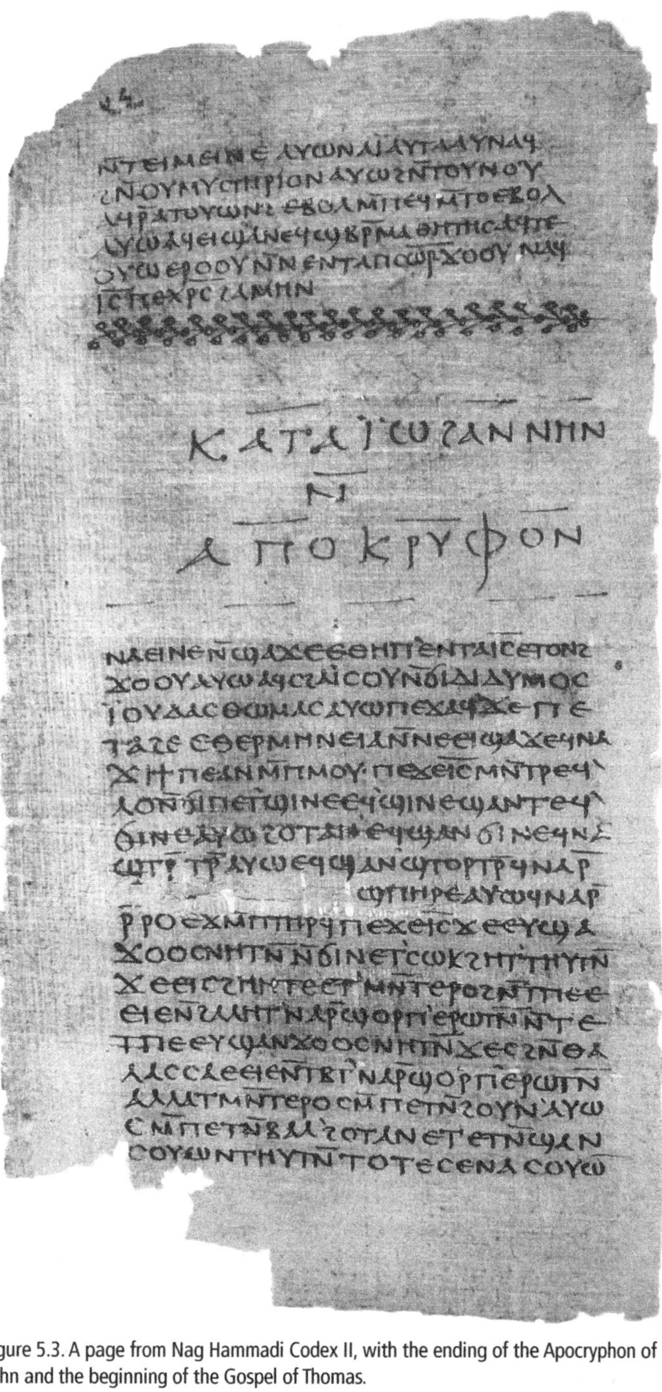

Figure 5.3. A page from Nag Hammadi Codex II, with the ending of the Apocryphon of John and the beginning of the Gospel of Thomas.

The New Testament Apocrypha

The term "Apocrypha" is an English **transliteration** of a Greek word meaning "hidden" or "secret." When preceded by "New Testament," it designates nonbiblical Christian literature about Jesus, his disciples, his family members, or other associates. (Thus, the NT Apocrypha should not be confused with the OT Apocrypha, or **deuterocanonical** books, discussed in ch. 3 and included in some Christian canons.) These books themselves were not necessarily hidden—many were widespread—though some may have been composed as part of a corpus of writings for smaller "secret" Christian groups. As with the Pseudepigrapha, there is no officially recognized list of NT apocryphal writings, and the texts commonly identified as apocryphal likely had no organic relationship to one another outside the work of modern scholars.

The various NT Apocrypha were composed in Greek, Latin, **Syriac**, and Coptic, the four major languages of the Roman Empire's eastern provinces. With a few exceptions, these writings appeared between 100 and 400 CE—later than most, if not all, of the canonical NT documents. In certain respects they are similar to much of our NT material and were often used alongside the writings of the NT. However, they were excluded from the canon because they did not attain widespread use or approval in the churches, because those in charge of deliberating about what was included in the NT found them objectionable on theological or historical grounds, or because they were composed after the process of selection.

One goal of many apocryphal texts was to supplement beliefs that had become foundational to the experience of early Christians, though the texts often appear to rival their canonical counterparts. In particular, the virginal conception of Jesus, the bodily resurrection of Jesus, and the **parousia** (or second coming) are ideas that appear frequently in the NT Apocrypha. Special attention is also paid to Jesus' birth and crucifixion. Apocryphal texts expand upon what the NT has to say about these and other theological concerns, sometimes filling in perceived lacunae (gaps) in the NT documents. Some apocryphal texts appear to have been written with the goal of solidifying the historical nature of various biblical stories—especially those concerning Jesus—and others focus on helping the reader develop Christian virtues.

The apocryphal writings appear in various genres, many of which are similar to those found within the NT. Below is an abbreviated list:

- Infancy gospels: Protoevangelium of James, Infancy Gospel of Thomas, Tales of the Magi

- Gospels of Jesus' ministry: Gospel of Peter, Gospel of Bartholomew, Gospel of the Savior
- Apocryphal acts: Acts of John, Acts of Andrew, Acts of Barnabas, Acts of Peter, Acts of Paul and Thecla, Acts of Thomas
- Apocalypses: Apocalypse of Paul, Apocalypse of Peter
- Stories of people associated with Jesus: History of Joseph the Carpenter, Dormition of Mary, Life of John the Baptist

The NT Apocrypha provide an important historical window into the growth of Christianity within the four or five centuries of the church after the first century CE. We see what virtues Christians cherished, what doctrines they valued, and even the ways they envisioned Jesus as present in their world. We also see the veneration of other figures from the life of Jesus. Early Christianity continued to develop as various groups sought to articulate their understanding of the faith. One of the most important concerns within these discussions—as reflected in many apocryphal texts—is the nature of Jesus. Was he human? Was he divine? How do those two concerns relate to each other, if at all? The early **ecumenical councils** of the church were explicitly concerned with such christological controversies, so it is no surprise to see these discussions taking place in some of these early Christian writings.

Excerpt: The Gospel of Peter

In 1886, a parchment manuscript dating from the late eighth to early ninth century was discovered in the grave of a monk in the upper Egyptian region of Akhmim. The manuscript contained several Greek fragments, including 1 Enoch, the Apocalypse of Peter, and a text that has come to be known as the Gospel of Peter. Containing material obviously drawn from the canonical Gospels, the Gospel of Peter recounts a fantastic story of Jesus' descent into hell, accompanied by his cross. The cross eventually emerges from the grave and begins to speak about what it has seen. While most scholars are convinced that this is a much later tradition, at least one scholar has argued that the cross material in the Gospel of Peter reflects some of the earliest preaching of the church.[7] Others have suggested that this story, while fanciful in what it recounts, may have been close to the way some early Christians told the story of Jesus' resurrection and defeat of death. Provided below is an excerpt from the Gospel of Peter:

7. John Dominic Crossan has argued that there was originally a Cross Gospel, presenting a passion narrative now reflected in three closely connected units in the Gospel of Peter. For more on this subject, see his book *The Cross That Spoke: The Origins of the Passion Narrative* (San Francisco: Harper & Row, 1988).

That stone which had been cast before the entrance rolled away by itself and moved to one side; the tomb was open and both young men entered. When the soldiers saw these things, they woke up the centurion and the elders—for they were also there on guard. As they were explaining what they had seen, they saw three men emerge from the tomb, two of them supporting the other, with a cross following behind them. The heads of the two reached up to the sky, but the head of the one they were leading went up above the skies. And they heard a voice from the skies, "Have you preached to those who are asleep?" And a reply came from the cross, "Yes." They then decided among themselves to go off to disclose what had happened to Pilate. While they were still making their plans, the skies were again seen to open, and a person descended and entered the crypt. Those who were with the centurion saw these things and hurried to Pilate at night, abandoning the tomb they had been guarding, and explained everything they had seen. Greatly agitated, they said, "He actually was the Son of God." (lines 37–45)[8]

The Apostolic Fathers

The corpus of writings known to us as the Apostolic Fathers represents the earliest Christian writings that have been preserved outside the NT. These documents were written in Greek during what is sometimes called the **postapostolic era** (ca. 70–150 CE), a period within which some of our later NT documents were also being composed. This was a critical period in the life of the earliest church since it was no longer possible to learn directly from one of the apostles. There was a serious concern about which voices and texts were authoritative and which practices were normative for the Christian life. Thus, as postapostolic Christianity began to move in the direction of orthodoxy, there was a call for clarity about Christian practice and authority; these concerns are reflected in the writings of the Apostolic Fathers. In recent years, it has become common for scholars to group these texts with other writings that emerged slightly later under the heading "Early Christian Fathers."

The phrase "Apostolic Fathers" was probably first used in the sixth century by a monophysite Christian named Severus, though the modern collection of texts that goes by that name did not emerge until the late seventeenth century.[9] As with other collections discussed in this chapter, there is no official list of works that make up the Apostolic Fathers. Texts generally found in volumes on the Apostolic Fathers include 1–2 Clement, the Letter of Polycarp to the

---

8. From Bart D. Ehrman and Zlatko Pleše, *The Other Gospels: Accounts of Jesus from Outside the New Testament* (Oxford: Oxford University Press, 2014), 199.

9. The monophysites understood the divine and human natures of Christ to be commingled, or confused, which was deemed a **heresy** by the Fourth **Ecumenical Council** at Chalcedon in 451.

Philippians, the Martyrdom of Polycarp, the Didache, the Shepherd of Hermas, the Epistle to Diognetus, and the **Epistle of Barnabas**. Also included are seven letters attributed to Ignatius of Antioch, though some scholars doubt the authenticity of several of those letters. Most texts in the Apostolic Fathers are epistles, though we also have examples of **apologetic** texts, lists of instructions, and martyrdom stories. As in the case of the NT Apocrypha, it appears that one purpose of these texts was to supplement the NT, though in some cases certain writings appear to have rivaled their NT counterparts.

It is often said that the authors of the texts we include among the Apostolic Fathers knew or had worked directly with the apostles, though in fact most of the writings are anonymous, and there is little evidence to establish a direct connection with the apostles. Some have attempted to argue that Clement of Rome, to whom two epistles are attributed, was associated with either Peter or Paul, but this is little more than speculation.[10] Though we cannot establish a link between Clement and Paul, the letter known as 1 Clement contains important parallels in tone and subject matter to Paul's writings that should not be ignored. The letter was written to the Corinthian church around 95 CE and makes an appeal to the Corinthian Christians to handle their disagreements in a peaceful manner, referencing Paul's correspondence with the Corinthians in several places (see 1 Clem. 13.1; 34.8; 37.3).

Other themes of importance to the early Christian experience that are found in the Apostolic Fathers include the development of the *regula fidei* (or **rule of faith**, a summary of basic Christian teaching) and an emphasis on moving toward a single-bishop system of church polity (monepiscopacy). In addition, a trend that runs throughout the Apostolic Fathers is the move toward institutionalizing certain elements of early Christian practice.

The Apostolic Fathers contribute to our study of the Bible in numerous ways. First, they contain traditions about Jesus that both parallel NT traditions and add to what we already know. Second, they provide some of the earliest interpretations of specific passages or entire books of the NT. Third, they contain traditions about the authorship of various NT writings as well as other traditions relating to the development of practices in the earliest Christian churches.

Excerpt: The Didache

The Didache (also known as the Teaching of the Twelve Apostles) was discovered in the late nineteenth century in a monastery in Turkey. Although

---

10. 1 Clement was commissioned by presbyters in Rome to address problems in the Corinthian church. Clement, a well-known member of this group, may have been its leader, and thus his name is associated with this letter.

the work was known by its title from various references in early Christian writers, this discovery yielded the first full version of the document. Generally dated as early as 100 CE but no later than 150 CE, its material is thought to have circulated for decades before it was formally written down. Functioning as a manual for early Christian behavior and worship, the Didache is divided into two major sections. The first (1.1–6.2) summarizes basic instructions about the Christian life for catechumens (those being instructed in the faith prior to formal entrance into the church), and the second (6.3–16.8) contains instructions about baptism, fasting, prayer, and the **Eucharist** (Communion). Numerous NT texts attest to this foundational early Christian practice (e.g., Mark 14:22–24; 1 Cor. 11:23–26). Specific guidelines for the observation of the Eucharist are also found in the Didache:

> Now concerning the Eucharist, give thanks as follows. First, concerning the cup: "We give you thanks, our Father, for the holy vine of David your servant, which you have made known to us through Jesus, your servant; to you be the glory forever." And concerning the broken bread: "We give you thanks, our Father, for the life and knowledge that you have made known to us through Jesus, your servant; to you be the glory forever. Just as this broken bread was scattered upon the mountains and then was gathered together and became one, so may your church be gathered together from the ends of the earth into your kingdom; for yours is the glory and the power through Jesus Christ forever." (9.1–4)[11]

Conclusion

It is not enough for serious students of the Bible to know only the content of the canonical writings. We must also be aware of the vast amount of literature related to, and contemporaneous with, the Old and New Testaments. This chapter has surveyed some of the major categories of nonbiblical Jewish and Christian writings with which students of Scripture should gain familiarity, but the material covered here is by no means exhaustive. Those who wish to go further would do well to investigate the religious and mythological texts of ancient Mesopotamia; the various Jewish writings such as the **Mishnah** and the **Talmud** (along with other rabbinic writings), the **Targums**, the Samaritan Pentateuch, the **Septuagint** (which is, in many ways, not merely a translation but an alternate version of the OT),[12] and the works of Philo and Josephus; the Corpus Hermeticum; and **Greco-Roman** authors such as Tacitus, Suetonius,

---

11. English translation from Holmes, *Apostolic Fathers in English*, 167–68.
12. Every translation of a text is an interpretation; this is especially true with respect to the Septuagint.

and Plutarch.[13] There is no shortage of material to help us understand the wider world from which the Bible emerged, and the literature of various regions in which the Old and New Testaments were written is a helpful starting point. Against that backdrop, students who wish to immerse themselves in the social, historical, and religious contexts of the Bible should also familiarize themselves with the particulars of each culture in which the biblical writings materialized, including those of the Babylonian, Persian, Greek, and Roman Empires. These avenues of investigation will help students situate their Bible reading in a wide historical context and provide broad exposure to key developments within Judaism and Christianity.

QUESTIONS FOR REFLECTION AND DISCUSSION

1. Although many of the writings discussed in this chapter were in circulation at the same time as writings that became part of the canon and had an obvious impact upon developments within Judaism and Christianity, they were not included in either canon for one reason or another. How does this recognition help you in thinking about the processes that led to the eventual canonization of the Bible?

2. Part of a contemporary Judeo-Christian religious experience is the privileging of a set of formalized sacred writings. However, it is also true that within various expressions of both Judaism and Christianity (especially Roman Catholicism and Orthodoxy), ongoing traditions are also considered authoritative for faith and practice. How might this comparison assist us in thinking about the value of these nonbiblical writings for ancient Jews and Christians?

3. Some scholars have estimated that in order to situate the Old and New Testaments in their original historical and religious contexts, one would need to be familiar with around five hundred ancient texts. How might this claim inform and/or change your approach to studying the Bible?

FOR FURTHER READING AND STUDY

Bauckham, Richard, James Davila, and Alex Panayotov, eds. *Old Testament Pseudepigrapha: More Noncanonical Scriptures.* 2 vols. Grand Rapids: Eerdmans, 2013. Up-to-date translation of and commentary on the OT Pseudepigrapha, containing many texts previously unpublished.

13. The Mishnah, Talmud, and Targums are discussed briefly in ch. 9.

Bockmuehl, Markus. *Ancient Apocryphal Gospels*. Interpretation: Resources for the Use of Scripture in the Church. Louisville: Westminster John Knox, 2017. A nontechnical introduction to the apocryphal gospels, their relationship to the canonical Gospels, and their significance.

Burke, Tony. *Secret Scriptures Revealed: A New Introduction to the Christian Apocrypha*. Grand Rapids: Eerdmans, 2013. Extremely useful, student-friendly overview of the major works and genres that compose the Christian Apocrypha.

Burke, Tony, and Brent Landau, eds. *New Testament Apocrypha: More Noncanonical Scriptures*. Vol. 1. Grand Rapids: Eerdmans, 2017. Collection of thirty little-known and, for the most part, previously untranslated texts.

Charlesworth, James H., ed. *The Old Testament Pseudepigrapha*. 2 vols. Peabody, MA: Hendrickson, 2010. Definitive translation of sixty-five writings with brief commentary by each contributor.

Collins, John J. *The Apocalyptic Imagination: An Introduction to Jewish Apocalyptic Literature*. 3rd ed. Grand Rapids: Eerdmans, 2016. Best available introduction to the Jewish apocalyptic writings of the Second Temple period.

Docherty, Susan. *The Jewish Pseudepigrapha: An Introduction to the Literature of the Second Temple Period*. Minneapolis: Fortress, 2015. Up-to-date, student-friendly introduction to the most important writings of the Second Temple period.

Ehrman, Bart D. *Lost Scriptures: Books That Did Not Make It into the New Testament*. Oxford: Oxford University Press, 2005. Lay-friendly introduction to many important works that influenced developments within early Christianity but did not become canonical.

Evans, Craig A. *Ancient Texts for New Testament Studies: A Guide to the Background Literature*. Grand Rapids: Baker Academic, 2012. Scholarly introduction to and summary of the kinds of writings discussed in this chapter, and others.

Goodacre, Mark. *Thomas and the Gospels: The Case for Thomas's Familiarity with the Synoptics*. Grand Rapids: Eerdmans, 2012. A critical scholarly engagement with the question of Thomas's awareness of synoptic traditions.

Holmes, Michael. *The Apostolic Fathers in English*. 3rd ed. Grand Rapids: Baker Academic, 2006. Best available translation of the Apostolic Fathers in English.

Jefford, Clayton N. *Reading the Apostolic Fathers: A Student's Introduction*. 2nd ed. Grand Rapids: Baker Academic, 2012. Introduces nonspecialists to the issues involved in studying the Apostolic Fathers.

Kasser, Rodolphe, Marvin Meyer, and Gregor Wurst, eds. *The Gospel of Judas*. 2nd ed. Washington, DC: National Geographic, 2008. Complete text of the Gospel of Judas reconstructed and translated into English, with commentary.

Lewis, Nicola Denzey. *Introduction to "Gnosticism": Ancient Voices, Christian Worlds*. Oxford: Oxford University Press, 2012. Useful, student-friendly introduction to the major issues and documents associated with the label "gnosticism."

Magness, Jodi. *The Archaeology of Qumran and the Dead Sea Scrolls.* Studies in the Dead Sea Scrolls and Related Literature. Grand Rapids: Eerdmans, 2003. Introduction to the world behind the Dead Sea Scrolls by a leading archaeologist.

Meyer, Marvin, ed. *The Nag Hammadi Scriptures: The Revised and Updated Translation of Sacred Gnostic Texts Complete in One Volume.* San Francisco: HarperOne, 2009. The most up-to-date, definitive translation of the Nag Hammadi texts available in English.

Skinner, Christopher W. *What Are They Saying about the Gospel of Thomas?* Mahwah, NJ: Paulist Press, 2012. Overview of recent scholarly opinion on three important questions: Thomas's date, relationship to the NT, and theological outlook.

VanderKam, James. *The Dead Sea Scrolls Today.* Rev. ed. Grand Rapids: Eerdmans, 2010. A leading authority considers the story of the discovery, the community that produced the documents, the various genres and texts found, and the path to getting the scrolls published.

6

From Books to Library: The Formation of the Biblical Canons

MICHAEL W. HOLMES

This chapter is devoted to the complex topic of the **canon** of the Bible. More accurately, it is about the *canons* (plural) of the Bible, for as we have already seen in various chapters, there always has been, and still is, more than one scriptural canon. The chapter begins with the question of defining the word, looks briefly at the Jewish canons, and then examines in more depth (because of more data) the various Christian canons for both Testaments.[1]

Introductory Issues

An initial challenge when discussing canon is defining the term. Of its many meanings, two are particularly relevant for this chapter. One is canon as a rule, norm, or guide, as in Galatians 6:16, "Peace and mercy to all who follow this rule" (Greek *kanōn*). The other is a list, register, or catalog (*katalogos*).

---

1. This chapter is based in part on my essay "The Biblical Canon," in *The Oxford Handbook of Early Christian Studies*, ed. Susan Ashbrook Harvey and David G. Hunter (New York: Oxford University Press, 2008). Used by permission of Oxford University Press. For modern canons of Scripture, see figs. 1.2–5 in ch. 1 of the present book.

In **Second Temple Judaism** and early Christianity, Scripture unquestionably functioned as a "norm" or "guide"—we may label this "canon 1"—for life, worship, and morality. But the fact that Scripture functions as a rule or guide (canon 1) does not necessarily mean that it is also "canonical" in the sense of being part of a list or catalog—"canon 2," if you will. There can be "Scripture" (in the sense of "religiously authoritative writings") without a "canon"—that is, a list or catalog—but no canon without Scripture, because there would be nothing to put on the list.

In developing this idea of canon as a list or catalog (canon 2), we may ask, what kind of a list is it? An "open" list, whose contents can be changed? Or a "closed" list, whose contents are unalterable? Many scholars contend that only this latter idea properly catches the idea of canon: a closed, official list, incapable of alteration, one that consciously both includes and excludes. Indeed, some argue that it is precisely closure that differentiates a canon from an ordinary list or catalog.

Other scholars have challenged this narrow formal definition for several reasons. First, closure can be the result of habit, custom, or tradition, and not just formal official action. Second, informal actions can be as influential or consequential as formal ones. Third, a focus on "formal" decisions can turn stages in the process leading up to the formal decision into "preliminary" or "incomplete" stages, whereas the people actually living in those stages may not have viewed their canon or circumstances that way at all. (To put it a bit differently, telling the story in terms of its outcome can obscure the experiences and perspectives of those living the story.) Fourth, a narrow formal definition is inadequate for the complexity of the history of the topic.

Finally, discussion of the idea of a canon should keep in mind the nature of its physical representation. For books written on scrolls, "the Scriptures" comprised multiple scrolls, kept in a basket, container, or storage cupboard. However "closed" the collection may have been, there was still a physical openness to it, as scrolls could easily be added or removed. But by the mid-fourth century CE, when we encounter the earliest surviving examples of all the books considered to be Scripture bound into a single **codex** volume, the physical finiteness of a single bound volume contributed a very different sense of "closure" than did a basket of scrolls.

The Jewish "Canon" in the Late Second Temple Period

The idea of authoritative written documents (Scripture) is at least as old as the Ten Commandments. The early story of the formation of collections of

Scripture, however, is difficult to discern, due largely to an absence of evidence (especially with regard to how and why) and to the ambiguity of what little evidence there is. The authoritative collection of the Five Books of Moses (the **Torah**, or **Pentateuch**) was the first to assume a fixed shape (and relatively stable text), and eventually two other collections coalesced alongside or around it: the **Prophets** and other **Writings**. The earliest reference to this emerging three-part collection is probably the Prologue to Sirach (Ecclesiasticus), sometime after 132 BCE, where there is a triple mention of "the Law and the Prophets and the other books of our ancestors."

The relatively frequent references to "the Law and the Prophets" in late **Second Temple** (mid-second century BCE–70 CE) Jewish writings, including early Christian writings, indicate that the second division—comprising both historical books and prophetic writings—had also achieved a recognizable, though not necessarily fixed, shape during that time. The same cannot be said about the third division. Unlike the first two, it does not have a consistent label or contents in this period. The Prologue to Sirach terms it "the others," "the other books," and "the rest of the books"; other possible references to this third part of the tripartite structure (including Luke 24:44) display a similar fluidity of terminology.[2] The variability of contents is particularly evident in the **Septuagint** (**LXX**), the Greek translation of the Hebrew Scriptures read by Jews whose primary language was Greek. As noted in previous chapters, its collection of "writings" is considerably larger than that of the Hebrew Scriptures, they are organized differently, and some books (most notably Jeremiah) have a different textual form.

During the late Second Temple era, were there any discussions about, or attempts to specify, which books were Scripture and which were not? If so, no evidence survives; there is no indication of any formal canonization of the Jewish Scriptures (canon 2) in this period. Yet Jews everywhere acknowledged the **authority** of the Scriptures and followed them as a guide for life (canon 1). Moreover, when a rabbi declared that "Scripture teaches," he seemed to take for granted that his audience had some general idea of what he was referring to. Indeed, a shared commitment to Scripture was one of the defining marks of Second Temple Judaism, a commitment that differentiated Jews from gentiles.

At the same time, the existence of varied opinions about the boundaries of "Scripture"—and also its interpretation—was a differentiating mark within Judaism. The Pharisees, for example, gave nearly the same weight to **oral**

2. Other possible references include 4QMMT 95–96, from the **Dead Sea Scrolls** (ca. 150 BCE); 2 Macc. 2:13–15 (after ca. 100 BCE); and Philo, *On the Contemplative Life* 3.25 (ca. 20–40 CE).

tradition as they did to Scripture, viewing both Torah and their traditions as given by God through Moses. The Sadducees, however, rejected the Pharisaic emphasis on tradition, insisting on the authority of the written text alone. Then there are the sectarians at **Qumran** (where most of the Dead Sea Scrolls were found), who seem to have viewed additional books as being as authoritative as Scripture; their "canon" was larger than that of either the Pharisees or the Sadducees. One could also mention the Samaritans, who were not Jews but acknowledged some shared history with them: they had their own Torah (known as the Samaritan Pentateuch, which has its own distinctive wording at a few key points) and accepted it alone as Scripture. And even when different groups accepted the same book as Scripture, they sometimes differed about how to live out or practice its teachings.

To summarize: even though there is no evidence of a "formal" canon of Scripture in late Second Temple Judaism, Scripture nonetheless functioned "canonically" (in both senses of the term), and there is evidence of competing "informal" canons throughout the period.

Near the end of the first century CE, after the fall of Jerusalem, we first encounter claims that could be taken as evidence of a definitively "bounded" set of Scriptures. These come from Josephus (*Against Apion* 1.37–43) and 4 Ezra 14.44–45, which refer, respectively, to the "twenty-two" and "twenty-four" books of the Jewish Scriptures (using two different ways of counting the letters of the Hebrew alphabet). Nothing, however, is said about the names or precise arrangement of the specified number of books.[3] The first lists that name specific books come from a century or more later. The earliest is a Christian list, given by Melito of Sardis (d. ca. 190 CE), of the contents of the Septuagint, while the first list enumerating the contents of the Hebrew Bible comes from a tractate of the Babylonian **Talmud**.[4] It lists the basic contents of what became, by the ninth century, the "standard" form of the rabbinic Hebrew text of Scripture, called the **Masoretic Text** (though again we have no evidence that this form was ever "authorized" by any authoritative body or action).[5] This in turn became the "standard" form of the Jewish Hebrew Bible from the late fifteenth century onward, and later the "Old Testament" text of the Protestant reformers in the sixteenth century.

3. Josephus refers to five books of Moses, the prophets after Moses in thirteen books, and the four remaining books of hymns to God and counsel for life. For an illuminating discussion of whether these two numbers ("22" and "24") should be interpreted as quantitative or symbolic numbers, see Eva Mroczek, *The Literary Imagination in Jewish Antiquity*, 159–71.

4. The Babylonian Talmud text (Baba Batra 14b–15a) is possibly from the second century CE, though more probably the third century or later.

5. The **Masoretes** were rabbinic scholars. The term "Masoretic Text" is abbreviated **MT**.

Figure 6.1. A page of Genesis from the Leningrad Codex, the earliest complete copy of the Hebrew Bible (1009 CE), known as the Masoretic Text, showing both the text and critical notes in the margins.

Canons of Scripture in Early Christianity

From Christianity's earliest days, two categories of authoritative traditions gave it shape and direction: the Jewish Scriptures and the gospel (the good news about Jesus, including his teachings and narratives about him), with the latter providing the **hermeneutical** (interpretive) key to the former. Each of these two categories eventually gave rise to a **Testament**; together, the two Testaments constitute the Christian Bible as we know it today.

From "Scripture" to "Old Testament"

The early Christian movement was largely a Greek-speaking and -writing movement, so it is no surprise that for most Christians in the early centuries their Scriptures were the Septuagint. There were exceptions: the **Peshitta** OT read by **Syriac**-speaking Christians (a significant strand of Christianity in the second and subsequent centuries) was largely translated from Hebrew, and a few Christian scholars in the second through fourth centuries (Melito of Sardis, Origen, Jerome) voiced support for the Hebrew version. For most early Christians, however, the Septuagint (or daughter translations into Latin and **Coptic**) served as their Scriptures.

There is no doubt that the early Christians sought to live by Scripture, viewing it as a guide or rule for life (canon 1). Yet there is no evidence that Jesus or his followers discussed its boundaries (canon 2) during the first century or so of the Christian movement. The early Christians used Scripture extensively, but did not, apparently, debate its limits.

Second-Century Developments

In fact, even near the middle of the second century, the matter of how to interpret the LXX seems to have been a more pressing concern than defining its boundaries. Three contemporaries, Ptolemy, **Marcion**, and Justin Martyr, each wrestled with this matter. In its most basic form, it was the problem of what to do with the many commandments in the Jewish Scriptures (such as the Sabbath and dietary laws) that Christians no longer followed.

Ptolemy, a Valentinian (**gnostic**) teacher, resolved the problem by differentiating first between human and divine contributions, and second between obsolete and still relevant elements of the divine parts. For Ptolemy, the Law was to be evaluated by the teachings of Jesus: all of it is "Scripture," but only that which Jesus affirmed is binding on Christians.

Marcion, a Christian from Bithynia in Asia Minor, moved to Rome in the mid-second century. Deeply influenced by the letters of Paul, Marcion made a fundamental differentiation between "law" and "gospel." But what for Paul was a tension between these two concepts became for Marcion a simple contradiction, which he resolved by rejecting the Jewish Scriptures as the work of a lesser god, not to be identified with the true God revealed by Jesus the Messiah.

Justin Martyr solved the same hermeneutical problem by viewing the Jewish Scriptures primarily as "prophecy" rather than "law." This enabled him to affirm a prophecy-and-fulfillment relationship between the Jewish Scriptures and the gospel about Jesus. He also argued for the divine inspiration of the entire LXX by reworking a Jewish legend about its origins (preserved in the Letter of Aristeas). Thus, the LXX became for Justin the "authorized" form of the Jewish Scriptures.

The writings of Ptolemy, Marcion, and Justin Martyr reveal that in the middle of the second century, Christians were deeply concerned about how to interpret the Septuagint. There is, however, no corresponding evidence, apart from Marcion, of any similar concern to determine its boundaries.

Just a decade or two later, however, there is evidence of interest in the boundaries. Melito of Sardis presents two important firsts: the first-known Christian list of the contents of the "Jewish" Scriptures, and the first occurrence of the phrase "Old Testament." In a passage preserved by Eusebius (writing in the early fourth century), Melito mentions traveling "to the east" to determine "the accurate facts" about both the number and the order of "the ancient writings." There he "learned accurately" the "books of the Old Testament": the Pentateuch, Joshua, Judges, Ruth, 1–4 Kingdoms (= 1–2 Samuel, 1–2 Kings), 1–2 Chronicles, Psalms, Proverbs (or Wisdom), Ecclesiastes, Song of Songs, Job, Isaiah, Jeremiah, the Twelve, Daniel, Ezekiel, and Esdras (= Ezra-Nehemiah?).

Numerous questions arise: Where did Melito learn this, and from whom? Is this concern about the limits of Scripture a new or a continuing issue, and in either case, what prompted it? Unfortunately, we do not know. The overall arrangement is clearly Septuagintal, not Masoretic (e.g., 1–2 Chronicles are among the historical books, rather than grouped with the Writings). It also has some quirks (Esther is missing, and the Book of the Twelve is in the middle of the other prophets). This first witness, rather than settling matters, raises additional questions.

Even though Melito does not use the term "canon"—Eusebius labels Melito's list a *katalogos*—it is evident from his interest in the number and order of the books that the concept of a defined list of Scriptures (canon 2) is in mind. Moreover, only a few years later we find, in a comment by an anonymous writer (perhaps Polycrates of Ephesus) as preserved by Eusebius, the earliest known occurrence in Christian literature of what would become a widely repeated phrase: the concern "neither to add nor take away" anything from "Scripture" (an idea earlier voiced by Josephus in *Against Apion* 1.42).[6] By the end of the second century, a growing interest among Christians in defining the contents of the LXX is clearly evident.

6. See also texts such as Deut. 4:2 and Rev. 22:18–19.

The Third and Fourth Centuries: Lists and Boundaries

From this time onward, primary evidence of concern for boundaries comes in the form of lists of, reports about, or manuscripts containing the books of what is now termed, with increasing frequency, the "old testament." Eusebius, for example, reports that Clement of Alexandria (d. ca. 215) used certain books found in the LXX but not in the Hebrew Bible—namely, the Wisdom of Solomon and Sirach. Eusebius does so, however, in a way that tells us more about his own perspective—he labels them "disputed writings"[7]—than it does about Clement's views regarding the contents of the LXX.

Origen (d. 254), well known for his work comparing the Greek text of the LXX with the Hebrew text, presents an ambiguous picture with respect to its contents. Sometimes he seems to have preferred a shorter collection similar in content (but not arrangement) to the Hebrew Bible. Other times, however, he indicates, in explicit contrast to the Jewish Scriptures, a clear preference for "our bible" (i.e., the LXX), including additions such as Susannah. Unfortunately, he never specifies in full what he thinks are the contents of the LXX.

After Origen, surviving evidence comes from the fourth century, primarily in the form of lists, no two of which agree completely. There is also some important testimony from biblical manuscripts (discussed below). In addition, the earliest known instance of the term "canon" used to mean a "list of books" (canon 2) occurs shortly after 350, in the writings of Athanasius of Alexandria. This makes Athanasius's list, in which he speaks of the "canonical books" (*biblia kanonizomena*), of particular interest. (Furthermore, technological improvements in bookmaking that made it possible to bind all the books of Scripture in a single large *biblos*, "bible," gave added urgency to the question of boundaries, i.e., what to include and exclude from such a bound collection.)

This later list appears in Bishop Athanasius's "Easter letter" of 367 CE. He opposes two influential groups because they do not follow the ancient traditions for Easter celebrations. Athanasius and his followers, in contrast, "celebrate the feast according to the traditions of our forefathers, because we have the holy scriptures; they are sufficient to instruct us perfectly." The possibility that opponents might mislead some believers on the basis of other books, "so-called **apocryphal** writings," motivated Athanasius to list "in order the writings that have been put in the canon, that have been handed down and confirmed as divine." He then declared: "In these books alone the teaching of piety is proclaimed. Let no one add to them or take away from them anything."

---

7. A term Eusebius also applied to Hebrews, **Letter of Barnabas**, 1 Clement, and Jude, all of which were used by Clement.

Clearly Athanasius is promoting, in a polemical context, a "closed canon" of the LXX (as well as the NT; see below), which in his estimation represents the inherited tradition of the church. It is also evident that the context of this list implies the existence of competing canons utilized by his opponents. Two centuries after Melito's efforts, there is still controversy surrounding this topic.

Athanasius describes three categories of books: "canonical" books, "non-canonical" books (to be read by new converts), and "apocryphal" writings (whose titles he avoids mentioning and which, according to him, should not be read at all). In the first category are twenty-two books: the Pentateuch, Joshua, Judges, Ruth, 1–2 Kings, 3–4 Kings, 1–2 Chronicles, 1 Esdras (= Ezra–Nehemiah), 2 Esdras, Psalms, Proverbs, Ecclesiastes, Song of Songs, Job, the Twelve, Isaiah, Jeremiah + Baruch + Lamentations + Letter of Jeremiah, Ezekiel, and Daniel. Noncanonical "books to be read" include Wisdom of Solomon, Sirach, Esther, Judith, and Tobit.

In view of the intensity with which Athanasius promotes his canon against its competitors, it is interesting to compare it with the contents of the two earliest (and originally complete) manuscripts of the LXX that we have, Codex Vaticanus and Codex Sinaiticus, which were copied within a few years before or after Athanasius's letter. Vaticanus presents in a single codex exactly the books Athanasius names in his first two categories. The order and arrangement differ, however: the "books to be read" that Athanasius places "outside" his canon appear in Vaticanus interspersed among and undifferentiated from his "canonical" books. Codex Sinaiticus offers an independent order after 1–2 Esdras and adds 1 and 4 Maccabees.[8]

By the late fourth century, it is evident that the LXX is unquestionably the primary form of the Old Testament used by the Christian movement, as it had been from the movement's earliest days. (Jerome's vigorous arguments during this time in favor of adopting the Hebrew canon proved unpersuasive, and not until after the Protestant Reformation did more than a few supporters follow his lead.) It is equally clear, however, that the boundaries of the LXX are still fluid: there is no single definitive canon of the LXX. Rather, the overall situation in the late fourth century is as follows:

- First, there is wide agreement as to a central core of writings, which (with the occasional exception of Esther) corresponds closely to the contents of the Masoretic Hebrew "canon."

8. The fifth-century Codex Alexandrinus, the third of the major codices, presents an independent order after Chronicles and adds five additional books: 1–4 Maccabees and Psalms of Solomon. A comparison of lists promulgated by various church councils held between 363 and 692 CE reveals a situation similar to that found in the manuscripts.

- Second, the order and arrangement of this central core in the LXX (a) differ significantly from the basic Masoretic (Hebrew) arrangement, and (b) differ among the various lists themselves—significantly so in the second half of the core collection.
- Third, there is persistent disagreement as to the status, size, and arrangement of a smaller variable fringe of "Septuagintal extras."

To summarize: Christians nearly everywhere agreed that their Old Testament included the books in the Jewish Hebrew Bible. Most also viewed the Septuagintal "extra books" (in later Roman Catholic terms, the deutero-canonical books) as Scripture, though there was continuing uncertainty about just which of these books were included. The Western Roman Catholic branch had its list (though it was not officially ratified until 1546 at the **Council of Trent**), while the list acknowledged by the Eastern **Orthodox** branch included four additional items (1 Esdras, Prayer of Manasseh, 3 Maccabees, Psalm 151), and the Ethiopic church included even more writings.

The Formation of a New Testament

From Christianity's earliest days "the gospel"—the good news about Jesus, including his teachings and narratives about him—gave the new religious movement both shape and direction. At first transmitted orally, some of these teachings and narratives were committed to writing sometime during the second half of the first century CE, and for some decades both oral and written forms of transmission continued side by side. By the middle of the second century, however, the traditions survived largely in written form, primarily (though not exclusively) in documents known as "gospels."

Even before there were written gospels, however, there were other authoritative writings in circulation, mostly letters to fellow believers composed by followers of Jesus in the course of carrying on his mission. Thus, by the early second century, the emerging Christian movement possessed two kinds of "normative" (canon 1) documents: Jewish Scriptures, and Christian writings composed by (or attributed to) early followers of Jesus—primarily gospels and letters, but also a book of "Acts" and an **apocalypse**.

In other Christian writings composed during the last decade of the first century or in the first half of the second—roughly, from Clement of Rome (late first century) to Justin Martyr (d. 165)—we find these earlier Christian documents utilized in basically the same manner as the Jewish Scriptures. Both categories of documents were treated as authoritative guides for Christian faith, identity, and morality. Furthermore, writings from both categories were read and expounded when congregations gathered for worship. In short, these new Christian writings came to function in the same way as the Jewish Scriptures. It is no surprise, therefore, that the label "Scripture" began to be applied as well to these Christian writings, certainly by the middle of the second century (and probably earlier), or that common usage increasingly linked the Jewish "Law and Prophets" with the Christian "Gospels and Apostles" as similarly authoritative documents.

Collections

The first hints of collections of early Christian writings are also evident during this time. Clement of Rome certainly knew 1 Corinthians and probably also Romans and Hebrews. Polycarp's *Letter to the Philippians* (ca. 120–135) reveals knowledge of at least four (and possibly seven) Pauline letters, as well as 1 Peter and 1 John. But whether these groupings represent deliberate collections (like Polycarp's collection of seven letters from Ignatius of Antioch) or merely circumstantial accumulations is unclear.

The same question hangs over early collections of Gospels. The use by Christians of the codex format (a late first-century innovation) meant that the technology to gather multiple Gospels into one volume was available, but it is not clear when such collections first appeared (the earliest surviving copies date from the late second or early third century). Irenaeus (late second century) offers probably the earliest testimony to an intentionally defined set of four Gospels.

In short, by the mid-second century or so Christians were treating an increasing but still indeterminate number of Christian writings as "Scripture." A widely used core group, consisting of about twenty documents—four Gospels (Matthew, Mark, Luke, John), Acts, thirteen Pauline Letters, plus 1 John and 1 Peter—is beginning to emerge, but these are only the core of a larger unbounded group. Furthermore, believers continued to write new documents in increasing numbers (letters, gospels, acts, instruction manuals, sermons, treatises, an apocalypse or two), evidence of the flourishing diversity within the church. There are ambiguous glimpses of efforts to collect or consolidate smaller subgroups, but (as with the Septuagint at this time) no hint of any focused effort to define the precise contents or boundaries of a collection— that is, to create a canon (canon 2).

The Traditional View

At this point, a brief sketch of the traditional view of the rise of the NT canon may be useful. Typically it involves four stages:

- First (mid-first through mid-second centuries): the creation and rise of Christian writings to the status of "Scripture" (described above).
- Second (ca. 150): Marcion (mentioned earlier for his rejection of the Jewish Scriptures) claims that only ten letters of Paul and a shorter version of the Gospel of Luke (Paul's colleague)—edited to remove later contamination, such as references to Jewish Scriptures—really count as Christian Scripture. Marcion's collection is often viewed as the first "canon" of Christian writings.
- Third (late second to mid-fourth centuries): informal acknowledgment, in response to Marcion's "canon," of a group of about twenty documents (see previous paragraph), around which floated a penumbra of an indeterminate number of books whose status as "Scripture" was subject to debate or uncertainty.
- Fourth (last half of the fourth century): the formal canonization of a twenty-seven-book NT, as authoritative decisions are made regarding which books to include and which to exclude.

This way of telling the story has two notable weaknesses. First, it tells the story in light of its outcome—that is, it knows how the story ends, and works from there back to its beginning. Second, it pays too much attention to formal canonicity and consequently overlooks the existence and significance of informal canons of Scripture that existed prior to formalization.

That first weakness leads to the tracing out of a single line of development as though it were somehow natural and inevitable. As a result, it gives no attention to other possible directions the whole matter might have gone, or of how the people involved may have viewed matters in their own time. This ties in with the second weakness; to describe some books as "disputed" is not inaccurate, but it obscures what was really going on: people were arguing about whether certain books were or were not "Scripture." Some said yes, some said no. This in turn implies that both sides of the argument had some sense of a "list"—a *katalogos*, to use Melito's term—of which books were or were not Scripture. This is the basic idea of "canon" (i.e., canon 2), even if the term itself is not yet being used. From Eusebius's perspective in the early fourth century, his predecessors are "waypoints" or "stages" along the way to a final outcome—but that is almost certainly not how those predecessors viewed themselves.

Canon and Interpretation

With this in mind, let us return to the narrative, resuming with Marcion and bringing in an observation from the preceding discussion of the Septuagint canon. There a key issue in the mid-second century was not merely boundaries but also interpretation—in short, hermeneutics. Marcion's dismissal of the Jewish Scriptures, for example, was the logical outworking of his basic interpretive perspective. The same holds for his handling of early Christian writings. His law-versus-gospel hermeneutic led him to accept as authoritative only a limited number of Christian documents (and those only in a revised form).

To put the matter a bit differently, Marcion was arguing for a particular definition of what it means to be a follower of Jesus, one shaped by claims about both a hermeneutical perspective and a body of authoritative writings. If we look at the canon question in this light, it becomes possible to see it as part of a larger issue that confronted early Christianity during the second, third, and fourth centuries CE—namely, self-definition. At the heart of this matter, in both **rabbinic Judaism** (like Second Temple Judaism before it) and early Christianity, was the question of which traditions to accept as normative and how to interpret them.

During (approximately) the third quarter of the second century, Marcion is only one of a number of individuals or groups proposing answers to this question. Tatian's hermeneutic had a definite Encratite (ascetic) leaning, and he created a single continuous Gospel (the Diatessaron) to serve as his authoritative form of Gospel tradition, in place of the separate Gospels he used as sources. Similarly, Irenaeus reports that other Christians used only a single Gospel. Marcion was not alone in proposing a set of authoritative writings smaller than the emerging "core."

Other groups proposed an expanded set of authoritative revelations or traditions. The Montanist movement, for example, had a Spirit-oriented hermeneutic and argued that new revelations should be given as much (or more) authority as existing traditions. The individuals or group(s) associated with the Gospel of Thomas or the Apocryphon of James each had their own dualistic or "gnostic" hermeneutic, respectively, and also additional documents claiming to embody secret traditions that went beyond the emergent "core" group, not in the sense of replacing it, but rather as building upon it.

In contrast, **Valentinus**, a famous "gnostic" teacher, apparently was content to work with the basic core group of authoritative documents; his particular self-identity was not based on a varying or additional group of written documents, but on his distinctive hermeneutical perspective. It is hermeneutics, not the shape of the canon, that is the key point of disagreement between Valentinus and Irenaeus, his best-known critic.

For his part, Irenaeus—a representative of the **proto-orthodox** strand of early Christianity (the forerunners of the group that formulated the orthodox **Nicene Creed** in the fourth century)—supplies evidence that the boundaries of the core group (for which he is a key witness) are still undefined. His arguments in favor of a closed four-Gospel collection reveal how unsettled opinions still were on this major point; further, his own core group included, in addition to the twenty documents named above, Revelation and the Shepherd of Hermas.

In addition to Scripture, Irenaeus too had a distinctive hermeneutic: the **rule of faith** (*kanōn tēs pisteōs*). Essentially an oral summary of the common

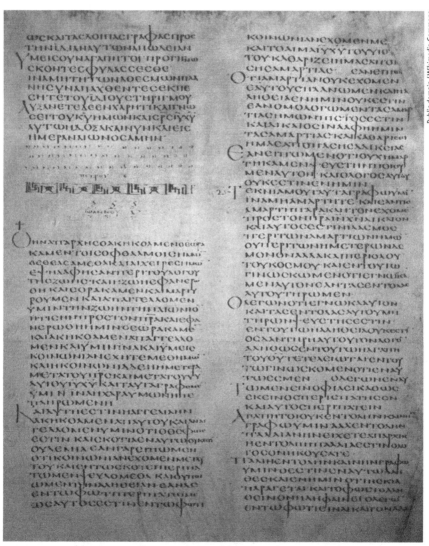

Figure 6.2. A page from the fifth-century codex Alexandrinus, showing the end of 2 Peter and the beginning of 1 John in the left column.

inherited foundational beliefs received from the apostles and transmitted from generation to generation ever since (cf. *Against Heresies* 1.10.1–2), it provided an apostolic norm (canon 1) by which to interpret the written form of apostolic tradition—that is, Scripture.

If by the late second century there was as yet no formal canon in the sense of a closed collection of Scriptures, there were, without question, emerging proto-canons, different groupings of authoritative writings by which different strands of the Christian movement defined themselves—virtually always, it would seem, in conjunction with a hermeneutical perspective that decisively and distinctly shaped their interpretation. Each strand offered its own take on what it meant to be a Christian, its own perspective on what the essence of Christianity was, and this was often accompanied by a different view of which writings counted as Scripture.

From Stable Core to Closed Canon

With Irenaeus and the others, however, the story is, chronologically, only about half over. By the end of the second century (as noted in discussing the LXX) the idea of a collection of writings concerning which nothing could be added nor taken away was gaining traction, even if such a collection did not yet exist. In fact, during the two centuries between Irenaeus and Athanasius, at least nineteen books formed a part of the variable fringe around the relatively stable core group: not just 2–3 John, 2 Peter, Jude, James, Hebrews, and Revelation but also the Gospel of the Hebrews, the Gospel of the Egyptians, Acts of Paul, Acts of Peter, 3 Corinthians, Letter to the Laodiceans, Apocalypse of Peter, Didache, 1–2 Clement, Letter of Barnabas, and Shepherd of Hermas—each of which was considered to be Scripture by someone at some time.[9]

How or why this number was eventually reduced to seven and agreement reached about the twenty-seven books that came to compose the NT canon is, due to an absence of evidence, uncertain. Criteria that may have influenced the process include age, apostolic connections, agreement with the rule of faith, and widespread usage. Most of the available information consists of lists that, as in the case of the LXX, reveal more of the what than the why or how.

Possibly the earliest (and certainly most controversial) extant list of early Christian writings is the Muratorian Canon. It lists four Gospels, Acts, thirteen Pauline Letters, Jude, Revelation, Wisdom of Solomon, and Apocalypse of Peter, but mentions just two Johannine letters, and none by James or Peter, nor Hebrews. Current opinion is deeply divided over whether it dates from

9. Discussion of some of these texts may be found in ch. 5.

the late second or the fourth century. Various features of the document make it something of an odd duck in either period, and its value has probably been overrated.

From the mid-third century, Origen offers another snapshot. His categories of "acknowledged" books (four Gospels, fourteen Pauline Letters, Acts, 1 Peter, 1 John, Jude, Revelation) and "disputed" books (James, 2 Peter, 2–3 John) embody the concept of a canon (canon 2), even as they reveal that the question of boundaries was still fluid—especially in light of Origen's apparent treatment of 1 Clement, Barnabas, and Shepherd of Hermas as Scripture.

In the early fourth century (ca. 325–330) Eusebius's observations on the state of the question, framed in categories similar to Origen's, reveal a continuing uncertainty with regard to certain books. The shape of the core group of twenty from the time of Irenaeus remains stable, while debate continues about seven others (Hebrews, James, 2 Peter, 2–3 John, Jude, and Revelation). What stands out about Eusebius's report is the absence of debate about additional books (such as 1 Clement or Shepherd of Hermas). The "variable fringe" has, apparently, been shrinking, even as opinions continue to differ about whether these should be included or not.

Yet this does not mean that people were holding these books in suspense. Some treated them as Scripture, and some did not, and each side of the argument probably felt that it was right in its opinion. In effect, most folks probably had some sense of a "canon" of Scripture (canon 2); they just differed regarding its content.

As with the Septuagint, Athanasius (whose emphasis on the importance and centrality of tradition echoes the arguments of Irenaeus) marks the beginning of the end of the process. His Easter letter of 367 (whose social context was discussed above) contains the first-known list to characterize as "canonical" exactly the twenty-seven books that today constitute the NT. The same list was later ratified by the Council of Carthage (397) and subsequent councils.

Even after the creation of a formal, authoritative, closed canon of the NT, however, not all variation disappeared. Scholars such as Didymus of Alexandria (Athanasius's home city) continued to work with a larger group of Scriptures. Some books, such as Hebrews (in the West) and Revelation (in the East), remained under a cloud of suspicion. Major early manuscripts include additional books as part of the NT, including Codex Sinaiticus (fourth century: Letter of Barnabas and Shepherd of Hermas) and Codex Alexandrinus (fifth century: 1–2 Clement). Many Latin manuscripts include a Letter to the Laodiceans, and the Armenian canon includes 3 Corinthians. The Syriac Peshitta NT (late fourth–early fifth centuries) lacks the minor Catholic Letters and Revelation; these did not make their way into the Syriac NT until the seventh century. Closure, it seems—even after formal official council action—was still a relative matter. Indeed, for many Christians in the eastern fringes of the old Mediterranean empires, who spoke languages such as Armenian or Georgian, closure did not occur until the arrival centuries later of printed versions of the NT brought by Western missionaries.

QUESTIONS FOR REFLECTION AND DISCUSSION

1. Is the canon of Scripture a list of authoritative books, an authoritative list of books, or perhaps an authoritative list of authoritative books?
2. Is the canon of Scripture intrinsically authoritative, or does its authority derive from something outside of itself?
3. How important is it to the church (or a church) to have a formal closed canon of Scripture?
4. Suppose a genuine but previously unknown letter written by Paul were to be discovered. Should it be added to the NT canon? On what basis should the decision be made? And by whom?

FOR FURTHER READING AND STUDY

Beckwith, R. T. *The Old Testament Canon of the New Testament Church*. Grand Rapids: Eerdmans, 1986. Classic statement of the view that the Hebrew Bible was canonized no later than the Maccabean period, ca. 160 BCE.

Carr, David M. *The Formation of the Hebrew Bible: A New Reconstruction*. New York: Oxford University Press, 2011. Utilizes an "oral-written" model of Israelite literature and the canon in the context of Israel's history.

Halbertal, Moshe. *People of the Book: Canon, Meaning, and Authority*. Cambridge, MA: Harvard University Press, 1997. A Jewish perspective on the role of the canon in Judaism.

Hengel, M. *The Septuagint as Christian Scripture: Its Prehistory and the Problem of Its Canon*. Grand Rapids: Baker Academic, 2002. Reliable, accessible treatment.

Hovhanessian, Vahan, ed. *The Canon of the Bible and the Apocrypha in the Churches of the East*. New York: Peter Lang, 2012. Important Orthodox perspective.

Kruger, Michael J. *The Question of Canon: Challenging the Status Quo in the New Testament Debate*. Downers Grove, IL: InterVarsity, 2013. Argues for a Reformed view that the canon *is* Scripture and therefore was closed the moment the last book of Scripture was penned. Redefining "canon" this way shifts the focus from "formation" (the orientation of this chapter) to "discernment," but the central historical question remains the same: Why did it take God's people so long to either form or discern the boundaries of the canon?

Law, Timothy Michael. *When God Spoke Greek: The Septuagint and the Making of the Christian Bible*. New York: Oxford University Press, 2013. A passionate plea for reclaiming a role for the Septuagint.

Lim, Timothy H. *The Formation of the Jewish Canon*. New Haven: Yale University Press, 2013. Argues that until ca. 100 CE there was a plurality of collections that were authoritative for different communities.

McDonald, Lee M. *Formation of the Bible: The Story of the Church's Canon*. Peabody, MA: Hendrickson, 2012. Accessible and comprehensive popular-level treatment.

———. *The Formation of the Biblical Canon*. 2 vols. London/New York: Bloomsbury T&T Clark, 2017. An exhaustive, scholarly treatment of all the issues related to the formation of the Old and New Testaments as Scripture and as canon.

McDonald, Lee M., and James A. Sanders, eds. *The Canon Debate*. Peabody, MA: Hendrickson, 2002. Major collection of quality essays on a very broad range of canon-related topics.

Metzger, Bruce M. *The Canon of the New Testament: Its Origin, Development, and Significance*. Oxford: Clarendon, 1987. Essential, comprehensive, and authoritative discussion.

Mroczek, Eva. *The Literary Imagination in Jewish Antiquity*. New York: Oxford University Press, 2016. Argues that the literary world of early Judaism was a story rather than a library and that the number of its authoritative scrolls endlessly varied.

Ulrich, Eugene. "Qumran and the Canon of the Old Testament." In *The Biblical Canons*, edited by J.-M. Auwers and H. J. De Jonge, 57–80. Leuven: Leuven University Press, 2003. Highlights the importance of the Qumran discoveries for the history of the canon.

Wilson, Jonathan. "Canon and Theology: What Is at Stake?" In *Exploring the Origins of the Bible: Canon Formation in Historical, Literary, and Theological Perspective*, edited by Craig Evans and Emanuel Tov, 241–53. Grand Rapids: Baker Academic, 2008. Observes that a desire for certainty and control led Protestantism to rely on the canon, Catholicism to emphasize the church, and modernism to focus on human reason (while postmodernism relativizes all three).

7

From There to Here: The Transmission and Translation of the Bible

Michael L. Barré

Most modern readers of the Bible recognize that they are not reading the exact words of Jeremiah or Jesus, of Isaiah or Paul, for none of them spoke or wrote in English, French, Swahili, or even modern Hebrew and Greek. Rather, there was a long process of transmitting the texts of the Bible and of translating them into foreign languages, a process that continues to this day. How did (and does) this process take place? That is the subject of this chapter.

The Bible: Origins in Speech and Writing

The Oral Character of Biblical Traditions

When we think of the Bible, we naturally visualize a book. In fact, as explained in chapter 1, the word "Bible" comes from the ancient Greek word for "book" (*biblion*). It is a collection of historical and religious traditions that has come down to us in written form. It is important to remember, however,

John Kselman and Michael Gorman contributed to the final form of this chapter, for which the author is grateful.

that a good percentage of these traditions were originally handed down by word of mouth. Only later were they written down, eventually assuming the form of a book.

In the nineteenth century there was a great deal of interest in the oral origins of the Bible. Biblical researchers began to notice and then to investigate the similarity between the shape of many biblical passages and folklore traditions in modern societies. This led to the realization that many of the biblical stories once existed in oral form. Of course, not all biblical books had an oral background—for example, the Letters of Paul in the NT, though even Paul received and then cited early Christian **oral tradition** (e.g., 1 Cor. 11:23–26; 15:3–7). These investigations resulted in the conclusion that the Bible was not—at least not entirely—the product of writers who sat down and penned the texts that we now call the Bible.

In many instances, even after oral traditions came to be written down, they continued to be recited (for example, in rituals or storytelling). Because it was not fixed like the written version, the oral version continued to develop. Over time various additions or changes would occur in the oral form of the tradition. Eventually this process could affect the written word.

Two brief examples may be given to exemplify the oral background of the OT:

- Many of the stories about the patriarchs (or ancestors) were classified as "sagas." A **saga** was a short, easily memorized, simple folk story that had little in the way of plot or character development and was handed down from generation to generation by word of mouth. This category includes the various stories about Abraham, Isaac, and Jacob in Genesis.
- The oral aspect of biblical traditions can also be seen in the Psalter. The psalms were originally sung prayers in poetic form that were later written down. They continued to be sung—from memory—in temple services. Psalm 18 and 2 Samuel 22 are two versions of the same psalm, though there are many divergences in the wording of these two versions. Many experts in the Psalms today believe that the divergences stem partly from the fact that this prayer continued to have an oral existence even after being cast in written form.

To take an example from the NT, most biblical scholars today agree that Matthew's version of the Lord's Prayer originally did not contain the words "For thine is the kingdom, and the power, and the glory. Amen" (Matt. 6:13 KJV). But at least by the early second century CE this brief "doxology" had come to be added to the original prayer as it was prayed privately and publicly by Christians (as can be seen in the Didache, one of the writings from the Apostolic Fathers discussed in ch. 5). As a result, some scribes added it to the written biblical text, probably in the margin at first. Later copyists took this marginal addition to be part of the biblical tradition and so added it to the text. This is why it appears in older, traditional Bible translations such as the King James Version. But since it is no longer believed to be part of the original tradition, this doxology does not appear in most modern translations of the Bible except in a marginal note.

The oral background of the Gospels is also evident from the way in which the traditions about Jesus were handed down by the early church. Before the age of critical study of the Bible, it was assumed that the Gospels were essentially like modern biographies of Jesus, with eyewitnesses as their sources. In the last century or so, this view was thoroughly called into question.[1] The position of the majority of scholars today is that while the Gospels give us certain reliable traditions about the words and deeds of Jesus, there is not enough from which to construct his biography (at least in the modern sense of that word). This realization marked the end of the lives-of-Jesus movement in the nineteenth century, which attempted to reconstruct the life of Jesus from NT sources. The predominant view among NT scholars today is that our four Gospels are products of a chain of memory and tradition:

- the first disciples and apostles recalled the words and actions of Jesus in their preaching;
- these traditions were kept alive in the early Christian churches by being recounted and meditated on; and
- the **evangelists**, or Gospel writers (perhaps preceded by other early Christian writers), selected from these traditions (and perhaps some early written sources) and used them in putting together their Gospels.

The first two of these stages involved oral tradition exclusively, or nearly so. Current research on **social memory,** the shared knowledge and memories of a social group (see ch. 10), may alter our understanding of the processes of transmission, but it will not discount the importance of orality.

Social memory and oral transmission are important for understanding the NT writers, writings, and recipients since they lived in a largely oral culture, without a high rate of literacy. Oral processes continued to flourish even after

---

1. An important, though not widely accepted, exception to this trend is the work of the noted NT scholar Richard Bauckham, *Jesus and the Eyewitnesses: The Gospels as Eyewitness Testimony* (Grand Rapids: Eerdmans, 2006).

the first letters and Gospels were written. The NT writings themselves were likely not merely read but in some cases "performed" when they were received and used in the various communities.

The Work of Biblical Scribes

Once biblical traditions began to be written down, scribes made copies of these written texts for future generations. In general these transmitters of the tradition did a commendable job of accurately passing down the Scriptures. However, error-free copies of long texts were virtually impossible in ancient times. In the OT and NT, therefore, it was inevitable that over the centuries errors would find their way into the text. These errors are apparent from occasionally unintelligible passages, which have suffered some kind of corruption in the transmission process, and also (in the case of the OT) from a comparison of the standard Hebrew text with the ancient **versions** (translations).

Not all scribal changes to the text were the result of accidental error. Some were deliberate, with the purpose of updating the text (e.g., by replacing an obsolete word or grammatical form with a current one), expanding the text in some cases (as in the Lord's Prayer), perhaps "fixing" wording that could be interpreted for unorthodox purposes, and generally making the text relevant to those who would read what the scribe was writing. Thus, in transmitting the biblical text, scribes were not human copying machines but to some extent interpreters and shapers of the tradition. In a real sense they were part of the canonical process.

On rare occasions, scribes would change the text in order to avoid something that sounded blasphemous to them. For example, in Job 2:9, after a host of tragedies befalls Job, his wife says to him, "Curse God, and die!" (exclamation added). But the Hebrew text that has come down to us actually says, "Bless God, and die!" (see NRSV note). The textual evidence (including that of the LXX) for this and similar OT texts suggests that some pious, pre-Masoretic scribe found the original wording in Job too blasphemous to be included in the sacred text and so replaced "Curse" with "Bless." The NRSV, recognizing this scribal change, rightly translates the intention of Job's wife according to the biblical writer.

The Textual Traditions of the Bible

Earlier generations viewed the text of the Hebrew OT and the Greek NT quite simplistically. They naively tended to assume that any copy of the Hebrew Scriptures was virtually the original Hebrew text as written by the biblical authors and editors, and that a copy of the Greek NT was identical to what the NT authors had written.

Later generations assumed that the **Masoretic Text (MT)**, the standard edition of the Hebrew Scriptures since the end of the first millennium CE, was identical with the original biblical text. Early Jewish and Christian tradition held that it was dictated directly by God to the inspired biblical authors, letter by letter. Today only the most conservative believers hold such a view. The evidence of the **Dead Sea Scrolls** has demonstrated that the matter is not so simple. Parts of all the books of the OT, except Esther, have been found among the scrolls. Study of these scrolls has shown that between the years 300 and 100 BCE there grew up a variety of Hebrew texts of the OT. Scholars divide them into three "families": the Palestinian, the Egyptian, and the Babylonian. While all of these contained *basically* the same text, they differ in many details. Some contained a shortened text of a particular book or passage, while others expanded the text by adding material. This discovery makes it difficult to maintain, as many scholars had in the past, that the MT is a text superior to all others. Increasingly, translators of the OT today are making more use of the ancient Hebrew and Greek versions, together with the MT, in their work.

Eventually there came a time when many Jews were no longer able to read or understand the Hebrew text. Already in the time of Nehemiah (fifth century BCE), when the Hebrew Scriptures were read publicly, it was necessary to provide a running translation so that the people could understand what was being read (Neh. 8:7–8). This situation eventually led to the first translation of the Hebrew Scriptures into another language. As earlier chapters have already discussed, in the third century BCE the **Pentateuch (Torah)** was translated into the universal language of the day, Greek. This probably took place in Alexandria, Egypt, a major Jewish intellectual center outside of Palestine, at the end of the OT period. Later the **Prophets** (i.e., the **Former Prophets** and **Latter Prophets**) were also translated. This Greek translation, as we have also noted in earlier chapters, came to be known as the **Septuagint (LXX)**, Latin for "seventy," since in popular legend it was translated by seventy (or seventy-two) Jewish elders. The LXX is thus the oldest and most important of the biblical versions.

As time went on, translations were made into other languages. Aside from the Septuagint, the most important version was St. Jerome's translation into Latin in the late fourth to early fifth centuries CE. Earlier Latin translations already existed, but many of these were judged to be of poor quality. In 382 Pope Damasus commissioned Jerome to prepare a new translation. The result, primarily the work of Jerome, was the **Vulgate**, from the Latin meaning "vernacular, popular." The translation of the OT was made partly from the Hebrew text and partly from the Septuagint. The translation of the NT, of course, was made from the Greek. The Vulgate came to be the official Bible of the Roman Catholic Church and was officially recognized as such at the **Council of Trent** in 1546. Until 1943, Catholics were not permitted to translate the Bible from the original languages; they could translate only from the Vulgate.

In the history of the NT textual tradition there was no single form of the text that commanded the same esteem as the MT did for Jews. The earliest manuscripts were written on **papyrus** or **parchment**. Fragments of the NT on papyri as early as the second century CE are known. At first these were written as **scrolls**. But scrolls that held more than one average-size biblical book were cumbersome to use. Already in the second century CE, as well, the **codex** appeared, in which individual pages were bound together similarly to modern books. With the codex, one could find a particular passage rather quickly, without unrolling a large scroll. Two of the major codices containing all or part of the NT are Codex Sinaiticus (signified by ℵ [aleph, the first letter of the Hebrew alphabet]) and Codex Vaticanus (signified by B). Sinaiticus, a fourth-century codex containing most of the OT and the entire NT, was kept at the Monastery of St. Catherine on Mount Sinai, where it was discovered between 1844 and 1859 by Konstantin von Tischendorf, a professor of New Testament at Leipzig. Codex Vaticanus is a mid-fourth-century codex that has been housed in the Vatican Library since the fifteenth century. Today about five thousand manuscripts containing all or part of the NT text are known.[2]

Ancient Biblical Texts and Textual Criticism

Since we do not possess the original texts written by the biblical authors, virtually all translators of the Bible today use the science of **textual criticism** to try to establish something approximating the earliest form of the text, a text that is as free of scribal additions and errors as possible. The result is known as a **critical text** of the Hebrew OT and the Greek NT.

Since the Masoretic Text is still the normative Bible of Judaism and continues to be the standard edition of the biblical Hebrew text, the text printed in **critical editions** (technical scholarly editions) of the OT uses a manuscript from this scribal tradition, the Leningrad Codex, from 1009 CE; it is the earliest dated complete copy of the Hebrew Bible. Even though critical editions of the

2. In addition, there are more than 2,000 **lectionaries** (collections of biblical texts for use in worship) that preserve NT passages. There are altogether more than 7,000 manuscripts or manuscript-like witnesses to the NT text, plus early translations (into Syriac, Coptic, Latin, and so forth) and citations in the post-NT Christian writings of the early church.

489   ΠΡΟΣ ΡΩΜΑΙΟΥΣ   4,15–5,2

κληρονόμοι, κεκένωται ἡ πίστις καὶ κατήργηται ἡ ἐπαγ-
γελία· **15** ὁ γὰρ νόμος ὀργὴν κατεργάζεται· οὗ ⸂δὲ οὐκ   1,18! · 3,20; 5,13.20; 7,8.
ἔστιν νόμος οὐδὲ παράβασις.   **16** Διὰ τοῦτο ἐκ πίστεως,   10s.13 G3,19
ἵνα ᵀ κατὰ χάριν, εἰς τὸ εἶναι βεβαίαν τὴν ἐπαγγελίαν   15,8 2P1,19!
παντὶ τῷ σπέρματι, οὐ τῷ ἐκ τοῦ νόμου μόνον ἀλλὰ καὶ   G3,29
τῷ ἐκ πίστεως Ἀβραάμ, ὅς ἐστιν πατὴρ πάντων ἡμῶν,
17 καθὼς γέγραπται ὅτι *πατέρα πολλῶν ἐθνῶν τέθεικά*   Gn 17,5 ⅏ Sir 44,19
σε, κατέναντι οὗ ἐπίστευσεν θεοῦ τοῦ ζῳοποιοῦντος τοὺς   H11,19 2K1,9
νεκροὺς καὶ καλοῦντος τὰ μὴ ὄντα ὡς ὄντα.   **18** Ὃς   Is 48,13 2Mcc 7,28
παρ' ἐλπίδα ἐπ' ἐλπίδι ἐπίστευσεν εἰς τὸ γενέσθαι αὐτὸν   2Bar 21,4 etc 1K1,28 |
πατέρα πολλῶν ἐθνῶν κατὰ τὸ εἰρημένον· *οὕτως ἔσται τὸ*   Gn 15,5 ⅏
*σπέρμα σου*ᵀ, **19** καὶ μὴ ἀσθενήσας ᵀ τῇ πίστει ᶠ κατ-
ενόησεν τὸ ἑαυτοῦ σῶμα °[ἤδη] νενεκρωμένον, ἑκατον-   Gn 17,17 H11,11
ταετής που ὑπάρχων, καὶ τὴν νέκρωσιν τῆς μήτρας Σάρ-
ρας· **20** εἰς δὲ τὴν ἐπαγγελίαν τοῦ θεοῦ οὐ διεκρίθη τῇ   Mt 21,21
ἀπιστίᾳ ἀλλ' ἐνεδυναμώθη τῇ πίστει, δοὺς δόξαν τῷ θεῷ   H11,34 · L17,18
21 °καὶ πληροφορηθεὶς ὅτι ὃ ἐπήγγελται δυνατός ἐστιν   14,5 Kol 4,12
καὶ ποιῆσαι. **22** διὸ °[καὶ] ἐλογίσθη αὐτῷ εἰς δικαιο-   3!
σύνην.   **23** Οὐκ ἐγράφη δὲ δι' αὐτὸν μόνον ὅτι *ἐλογίσθη*   15,4 1K9,10!
αὐτῷ ᵀ **24** ἀλλὰ καὶ δι' ἡμᾶς, οἷς μέλλει λογίζεσθαι, τοῖς   1K9,10!
πιστεύουσιν ἐπὶ τὸν ἐγείραντα Ἰησοῦν τὸν κύριον ἡμῶν   5! · 8,11! 10,9 G1,1
ἐκ νεκρῶν, **25** ὃς παρεδόθη διὰ τὰ παραπτώματα ἡμῶν   E1,20 1P1,21 1K6,14!
καὶ ἠγέρθη διὰ τὴν δικαίωσιν ἡμῶν.   8,32 Is 53,12 ⅏

                                                               5,18 1K15,17

5 **5** Δικαιωθέντες οὖν ἐκ πίστεως εἰρήνην ⸀ἔχομεν πρὸς   G2,16! · Is 32,17 · Kol
    τὸν θεὸν διὰ τοῦ κυρίου ἡμῶν Ἰησοῦ Χριστοῦ **2** δι' οὗ   1,20! · 1J3,21
καὶ τὴν προσαγωγὴν ἐσχήκαμεν ⸄[τῇ πίστει]⸅ εἰς τὴν χάριν   E3,12! · 1P5,12

15 ⸂γαρ ℵ² D F G K L P Ψ 365. 630. 1175. 1241. 1505. 1739. 1881. 2464 𝔐 sy ¦ *txt* ℵ* A
B C 81. 104. 945. 1506 syʰᵐᵍ • **16** ᵀ ᾗ A 1505 • **18** ᵀ ως οι αστερες του ουρανου και
το αμμον της θαλασσης F G ar • **19** ᵀ εν D* F G ¦ ᵀ ου D F G K L P Ψ 33. 104. 630.
1175. 1241. 1505. 1881. 2464 𝔐 it vgᶜˡ syʰ; Meth Ambst ¦ *txt* ℵ A B C 6. 81. 365. 1506.
1739 m vgˢᵗ syᵖ co ¦ ° B F G 630. 1739. 1881 lat syᵖ sa; Meth Ambst ¦ *txt* ℵ A C D K L P
Ψ 33. 81. 104. 365. 1175. 1241. 1505. 1506. 2464 𝔐 m syʰ** bo • **21** ° F G latt
• **22** ° B D* F G b m syᵖ co ¦ *txt* ℵ A C Dʲ K L P Ψ 33. 81. 104. 365. 630. 1175. 1241.
1505. 1506. 1739. 1881. 2464 𝔐 lat syʰ • **23** ᵀ εις δικαιοσυνην Dᶜ 1241 vgᶜˡ syᵖ
¶ **5,1** ⸀εχωμεν ℵ* A B* C D K L 33. 81. 630. 1175. 1739* *pm* lat bo; Mcionᵀ ¦ *txt* ℵ¹ B² F
G P Ψ 0220ᵛⁱᵈ. 104. 365. 1241. 1505. 1506. 1739ᶜ. 1881. 2464. *l*846 *pm* vgᵐˢˢ
• **2** ⸄εν τη πιστει ℵ¹ A vgᵐˢˢ ¦ − B D F G 0220 sa; Ambst ¦ *txt* ℵ*·ᶜ C K L P Ψ 33. 81.
104. 630. 1175. 1241. 1505. 1506. 1739. 1881. 2464 𝔐 lat

Figure 7.1. A modern critical edition of the Greek New Testament, showing the critical apparatus containing textual variants for Rom. 4:14–5:2.

MT rely on the Leningrad Codex, they can accurately be called critical texts because with the Hebrew text on each page is a **critical apparatus** containing evidence of other ancient versions (DSS, LXX, Vulgate, and so forth), citations from ancient authorities, and suggestions for alternative readings of words or passages in the MT. The standard critical text of the OT is the fourth edition of *Biblia Hebraica Stuttgartensia* (*BHS*), edited by K. Elliger and W. Rudolph. The fifth edition, *BHQ* [*Quinta*], is currently in preparation. Furthermore, the Society of Biblical Literature has begun The Hebrew Bible: A Critical Edition (HBCE), with the first volume (on Proverbs) having appeared in 2015. Its goal is not simply to reproduce the MT, like *BHS* and *BHQ*, but to create a truly eclectic critical edition by using various manuscripts.

Critical editions of the Greek NT (see fig. 7.1, p. 139) are eclectic reconstructions of the text based on textual-critical evidence; they do not match any single manuscript. Newer editions continue to improve the text to arrive at what experts in NT textual criticism regard as the most accurate reading of a word or passage. There are three main critical editions of the text of the Greek NT: the twenty-eighth edition of the Nestle-Aland *Novum Testamentum* (known as NA[28]); the fifth edition of the American Bible Society's *Greek New Testament* (known as UBS[5]), with the same text as NA[28] (but a different critical apparatus); and an alternative critical text of the NT published by the Society of Biblical Literature in 2010, the *SBL Greek New Testament* (SBLGNT), edited by Michael Holmes, a contributor to this book (see ch. 6). The SBLGNT differs from the NA/UBS text in about five hundred places. The NA[28] and the SBLGNT are available in electronic form.

One striking achievement of this modern textual-critical approach to the Bible is found in the New Revised Standard Version (NRSV): the unprecedented addition of a paragraph to the biblical text that has never appeared in any translation of the Bible for over two thousand years. At the end of 1 Samuel 10:27 is a brief narrative about Nahash, king of the Ammonites, found (though fragmentary in character) in one of the DSS manuscripts of 1 Samuel. It is supported also by the writings of Josephus, a well-known Jewish historian (first century CE).

Translating the Bible in Modern Times

Significant Translations in the Middle Ages and Early Renaissance

The Middle Ages saw sporadic translations of parts of the Bible into vernacular languages. St. Bede the Venerable (ca. 673–735) is said to have translated the Gospel of John into Anglo-Saxon shortly before his death, though nothing of this translation has come down to us. His translation was made from the Vulgate and was not disseminated.

Only the most highly educated of the laity could read Latin in the Middle Ages. Since the only Bible permitted by the Catholic Church was the Vulgate, the Bible was unavailable for reading by the great majority of people. In fourteenth-century England, John Wycliffe (ca. 1330–1384) was part of a movement (the Lollards) that believed the Scriptures should be accessible to the general public in their own language. Wycliffe and his Lollard colleagues produced the first complete translation of the Bible into English (1380–1392). It was translated from the Vulgate. (At this time in Europe the biblical languages [Hebrew, Aramaic, and Greek] were virtually unknown to European Christians.) Because the church did not permit any translation of the Scriptures except the Vulgate, Wycliffe's Bible was later condemned, and copies of it were burned.

The Renaissance and Its Effects: Erasmus

The **Renaissance** (French for "rebirth") marked a period of intense intellectual renewal and activity throughout Europe. To a large extent it was a revival of interest in the Latin and Greek classics as well as the beginning of humanism. Up to this point the intellectual life of Europe had been largely dominated by clerics. The Renaissance ushered in the intellectual rise of the laity, as evidenced in such early Renaissance figures as Dante (1265–1321) and Petrarch (1304–1374). Certain contemporary events on the fringes of Europe and beyond also contributed to this movement, notably the fall of Constantinople to the Turks in 1453. After this event, many Christian scholars from the East sought refuge in Italy and brought with them the tradition of Greek scholarship, as well as numerous important manuscripts from that tradition. The Renaissance, in about 1450, saw the invention of the printing press by Johannes Gutenberg, which made possible the wide dissemination of Bible translations—at first only the Vulgate, but later, after the Protestant Reformation, translations into various languages.

The effects of the Renaissance on intellectual Europe and on Bible research may be seen in the work of Desiderius Erasmus (ca. 1469–1536), which marked a turning point in NT studies in Europe. A philosopher and humanist, Erasmus learned Greek and studied the Greek classics. The influence of Renaissance humanism on him was evident first of all in his insistence on turning to early sources. Erasmus was one of the first practitioners of textual criticism, insisting that any translation of the Scriptures had to be preceded by establishing the most accurate text of the book(s) in question. In this task

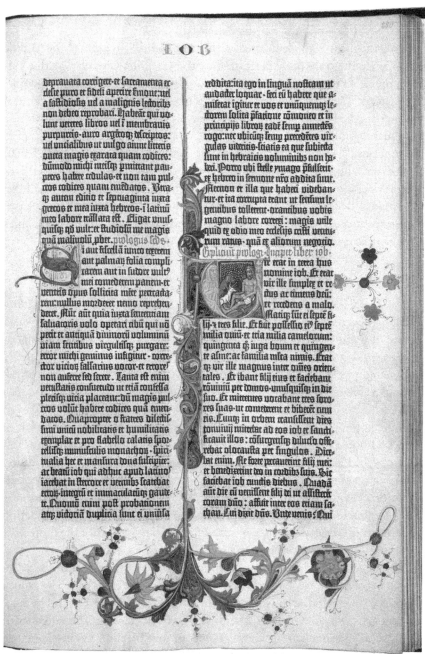

Figure 7.2. The prologue to the Latin text of the book of Job from the fifteenth-century Gutenberg Bible, printed ca. 1455–56 with movable letters and adorned with hand-painted initials, a small depiction of Job, and marginalia.

he employed the techniques of Italian humanists of the fifteenth century in his linguistic research on the Bible and the **church fathers**. In 1516, Erasmus prepared the first critical text of the Greek NT, which served as the basis for later critical editions.

English Translations after the Renaissance[3]

The first translation of the Bible made from the original biblical languages into English was that of William Tyndale (1494?–1536). Since translations of the Bible other than the Latin version were still not permitted by the Catholic Church during his lifetime, the local bishop refused to support his translation project, which forced Tyndale to do his work in Germany and the Netherlands rather than in England. The project took him ten years, from 1525 to 1535. Copies of his translation were smuggled into England, where church authorities confiscated and destroyed them whenever possible. A year later Tyndale was declared a heretic and killed near Brussels. His translation survived, however, and had a great influence on the King James Version (KJV), or **Authorized Version** (AV), almost a century later (see below).

Slightly later than Tyndale's Bible was the Roman Catholic Douay-Rheims translation into English, which began to be printed in 1582. Given the polemical atmosphere of the time, its notes were **apologetic** (defensive) in nature, but this was partly a response to the anti-Catholic tone of those in the earlier English-language Geneva Bible (1557–1560), published by Protestant refugees from England in Geneva. The non-Catholic translators of the AV at times followed the Catholic Douay-Rheims Bible.

At the Hampton Court conference in 1604, the president of Corpus Christi College at Oxford proposed a new translation of the Scriptures. The project was begun in 1607 and published in 1611 during the reign of James I. The result was the Authorized Version, commonly known in America as the King James Version (KJV) or King James Bible. The work was done by over fifty of the best scholars in England, including professors of Hebrew and Greek at Oxford and Cambridge. It was based on the translation of the Bishops' Bible (1568), and in style it was much indebted to Tyndale's translation. Even today it is one of the best-selling Bible translations in English, despite its archaic language and its reliance on manuscripts that are not the most ancient or accurate.

---

3. Although translations into many languages would occur in the wake of the Renaissance and in connection with the Protestant Reformation, we concentrate here and in the next section of the chapter on translations into English.

The translation of the Bible into German by Martin Luther (1483–1546) is ranked as a monumental achievement of German literature. Luther began translating the NT in 1521 and published it the following year. He was aided by Philipp Melanchthon (1497–1560), who was more proficient in the biblical languages than Luther. After the completion of the NT, Luther began translating the OT, and the entire project was completed in 1534. For the next decade he kept revising his translation, the last edition appearing in 1545, a year before he died.

Twentieth-Century Translations of the Bible into English

Modern Bible translations are often classified as "**formal-equivalence**" or "**dynamic-equivalence**" translations. (The latter type is also referred to as "**functional-equivalence**" translation.)[4] In ancient times, translators basically attempted to render the biblical text word for word, or literally, although some paraphrasing could occur. The reasoning was that only such a translation would be accurate. In many cases the result was hardly idiomatic in the target language, and it was sometimes incomprehensible to anyone who was not familiar with the original language. Modern formal-equivalence translations of the Scriptures (such as the Revised Standard Version or the New Revised Standard Version) are not as wooden, though they emphasize close agreement with the exact form and wording of the original text.

In contrast, the primary aim of a dynamic-equivalence translation (such as the Good News Bible or the Contemporary English Version) is to reproduce as accurately as possible the sense (or function, hence "functional equivalence") of the biblical passage in the target language, thus allowing readers to receive fundamentally the same communicative message the original audience received. The result is a translation that changes the *form* of the original text, when necessary, for the sake of *meaning*, or communicative intent.[5] (This is sometimes, though inaccurately, called paraphrasing.)

The following are brief descriptions of some of the better-known recent translations of the Bible into English, most of which have appeared in various editions, including study Bibles.

---

4. Popularly, these are sometimes called "word-for-word" and "thought-for-thought" translations, respectively.

5. A simple example would be translating the Greek phrase *agapē theou* (= "love of God") not as "love of God" but as either "God's love" or "love for God," depending on the context. (This little example demonstrates that every translation is in fact an interpretation!)

The Revised Standard Version (RSV) was a revision of the American Standard Version (1901), itself a revision of the AV, and was intended for use in private and public worship. The NT was published in 1946, followed by the OT in 1952. In 1977 an edition appeared with the Apocrypha. This translation was intended to preserve as much as possible the elevated style of the AV, while eliminating archaic English. Nevertheless, the RSV was based on the latest text-critical research of its time. It is basically a formal-equivalence translation and is still highly regarded by biblical scholars even today.

The New International Version (NIV) was sponsored by a consortium of conservative **evangelical** bodies in the United States. The NT appeared in 1973 and the OT in 1978; it was revised in 1984. While it gave precedence to accuracy of translation, it strove to be more than a word-for-word translation, contemporary but not dated, in clear and natural English. The project was sparked by the negative reaction of many conservative Protestants to the RSV. The NIV often translates OT passages so that their fulfillment in the NT is more readily apparent (e.g., "virgin" in Isa. 7:14 [cf. Matt. 1:23], although strictly speaking, the Hebrew word does not mean this).

An inclusive-language version of the NIV, the NIVI, was published in England in 1996. It was never published in the US and was later discontinued. The NIV itself was revised (NT, 2002; OT, 2005), with more gender-neutral language in regard to humans, as well as other changes, as Today's New International Version (TNIV). In 2011 the publisher (Zondervan) replaced the TNIV with the updated NIV. The family of NIV translations does not include the Apocrypha.

A revision of the RSV, the New Revised Standard Version (NRSV), was published in 1989 under the direction of Bruce Metzger of Princeton Theological Seminary. In some respects it was an ecumenical and even interfaith translation, as its translation committee included men and women of Protestant, Roman Catholic, Greek Orthodox, and Jewish faith traditions, and it includes the Apocrypha. The translators tried to retain the style of the RSV while updating it and taking advantage of recent scholarship. One new feature was the use of gender-inclusive language for humans.

The New American Bible (NAB), by members of the Catholic Biblical Association of America, was the first Roman Catholic translation of the Bible into English from the original languages, inspired by Pius XII's **encyclical** (circular letter) *Divino Afflante Spiritu* (1943; see discussion in ch. 13). It was begun in 1944 and completed in 1970. A revised edition of the NT appeared in 1986 and of the Psalms in 1991, both of which featured the use of inclusive language for people. (The author of this chapter was one of the OT revising translators.) In 2011 the New American Bible, Revised Edition (NABRE) appeared, with the 1986 NT and a fully revised OT that was less gender-inclusive, especially in the Psalms. Plans for another revised NT are underway.

A significant Jewish translation, by the Jewish Publication Society (JPS), is *Tanakh, The Holy Scriptures: The New JPS Translation according to the Traditional Hebrew Text* (NJPS). The project was done in three stages, representing the three parts of the Hebrew Bible: the Torah (Pentateuch) in 1962, the Prophets in 1978, the Writings in 1982, and a complete text in 1985. Since the MT (Masoretic Text) is the Bible of Judaism, the translation was made from this authoritative text. The aim was to make the best possible sense of the MT. In places where the meaning of the text is difficult, footnotes indicate readings of the versions and conjectural solutions. A revised edition appeared in 1999.

In 1966 the American Bible Society published Good News for Modern Man, also known as The New Testament in Today's English Version (TEV). This was followed in 1976 by a translation of the OT, and then by an edition containing the Apocrypha in 1979. Known as the Good News Bible (GNB), it is perhaps the most popular example of a dynamic-equivalence translation. This translation puts great emphasis on clarity and simplicity of language that is comprehensible to all readers of English, often using paraphrasing to do so. In 1995 the American Bible Society issued a new translation, the Contemporary English Version (CEV). It reflects translation principles similar to those of the TEV/GNB and attempts to be more sensitive to certain aspects of the biblical text, especially NT references to Jews.

The NET (New English Translation) Bible, produced by the Biblical Studies Foundation, was published in 2005. The work of twenty-five anonymous scholars, it advertises high-quality biblical research available to anyone without charge. The NET features almost 61,000 textual notes, which it claims make the original languages far more accessible to the reader, allowing one to "look over the shoulder" of the translators in the process of translation. In addition, it provides an alternate "literal" translation of each verse of the biblical text. Both online and in print, the NET is regularly updated after input from scholars and others.

The CEB (Common English Bible), the work of 120 scholars from twenty-four faith traditions, was completed in 2011. One of its principal aims was to make the Bible accessible to a broad range of people and ages. Another was to ensure that those who use it have a smooth and natural reading experience. Most editions of the CEB include the apocryphal/**deuterocanonical** books. A large study Bible appeared in 2013, under the leadership of Joel Green, a contributor to this book (ch. 10), who was also the NT editor for the CEB.

Bible Translation Globally

Despite legitimate concerns about the way Bible translation as a missionary endeavor has sometimes reinforced colonial powers, there can be little doubt that it is valuable for people to have access to the Bible in their own language. Several entities have such translation work, as well as Bible distribution, as a major dimension, or even the primary focus, of their corporate Christian mission. These organizations include Wycliffe Bible Translators and its affiliate organization, SIL (founded as the Summer Institute of Linguistics), as well as the United Bible Societies (UBS) and its two hundred national and territorial member societies around the world. The UBS has also sponsored translations into Braille and various sign languages, and some local Bible societies have produced audio and digital versions of various translations.

There are nearly 7,000 languages spoken among the world's 7.2 billion people.[6] According to both Wycliffe and the UBS (as of 2016), about 550 languages have a complete translated Bible; more than 1,300 have the NT; about 1,000 have portions of the Bible; nearly 2,300 languages have Bible translation projects under way; and as many as 1,800 languages have no Bible or current translation project.[7] The last two statistics, including more than 4,000 languages, represent nearly half a billion people.

Recent developments in linguistic and translation theory, as well as **postcolonial criticism** and theology, place increasing emphasis on the culture of the language into which translations are made. Issues of formal versus functional equivalence may be less important than effectiveness in a given culture. Translations of the Bible in various languages may be found at www.biblegateway.com.

Conclusion

In this chapter we have briefly explored the processes, operative within both Judaism and Christianity, of transmitting sacred traditions and of translating sacred texts so that people of later generations and of different languages (including our own) could hear and read them. Many readers or hearers of Scripture may not fully appreciate the complexity of this process, even though they benefit from it on a regular basis. Perhaps the best way to begin to learn firsthand the task that transmitters and translators face is to study Hebrew

---

6. "Translation," United Bible Societies, April 15, 2016, https://www.unitedbiblesocieties.org/translation.

7. "Why Bible Translation?" Wycliffe Bible Translators, April 15, 2016, https://www.wycliffe.org/about/why; and "Global Scripture Access," United Bible Societies, April 15, 2016, https://www.unitedbiblesocieties.org/translation/global-scripture-access.

and Greek and then to read the Bible in its original languages. Those who do so gain not only a greater appreciation of the transmission of the Bible, but also of its meaning.

QUESTIONS FOR REFLECTION AND DISCUSSION

1. What is the significance of the oral character of ancient cultures for our understanding of how the Bible came to be?
2. How do you account for the large number of translations available in English? From what you see in this chapter, and from good educated guessing, what do you think are the elements of a good Bible translation?
3. Why are the ongoing tasks of textual criticism and Bible translation important?
4. What additional new insights and what new questions have emerged for you while reading this chapter?

FOR FURTHER READING AND STUDY

Cheung, Andy. "A History of Twentieth Century Translation Theory and Its Application for Bible Translation." *Journal of Translation* 9, no. 1 (2013): 1–15. https:// www.sil.org/resources/publications/entry/53005. A helpful survey of theories and trends.

Dewey, David. *A User's Guide to Bible Translations: Making the Most of Different Versions.* Downers Grove, IL: InterVarsity, 2004. A basic presentation of the task of translation and a description of numerous translations into English across the centuries.

Fee, Gordon D., and Mark L. Strauss. *How to Choose a Translation for All Its Worth: A Guide to Understanding and Using Bible Versions.* Grand Rapids: Zondervan, 2007. A readable presentation of the issues involved in Bible translation, with a brief overview of English versions.

Metzger, Bruce M. *The Bible in Translation: Ancient and English Versions.* Grand Rapids: Baker Academic, 2001. A valuable study of ancient and modern (English) Bible translations by a world-renowned expert in NT manuscripts and in translation.

———. *The Making of the New Revised Standard Version of the Bible.* Grand Rapids: Eerdmans, 1991. An overview by the chair of the translation committee.

Metzger, Bruce M., and Bart D. Ehrman. *The Text of the New Testament: Its Transmission, Corruption, and Restoration.* 4th ed. New York: Oxford University Press, 2006. A classic work on NT manuscripts, early versions (translations), the work of scribes, and the practice of NT textual criticism.

Nicolson, Adam. *God's Secretaries: The Making of the King James Bible*. New York: HarperCollins, 2003. An interesting account of the story behind the King James Bible as a landmark of biblical scholarship and a masterpiece of English literature.

Porter, Stanley E., and Andrew W. Pitts. *Fundamentals of New Testament Textual Criticism*. Grand Rapids: Eerdmans, 2015. A readable, up-to-date introduction to ancient writing, NT manuscripts, and textual criticism.

Rogerson, John, ed. *The Oxford Illustrated History of the Bible*. Oxford: Oxford University Press, 2001. An easy-to-read but informative history of the Bible, abundantly illustrated.

Tov, Emanuel. *Textual Criticism of the Hebrew Bible*. 3rd ed. Minneapolis: Fortress, 2012. A standard treatment of the topic.

Ulrich, Eugene. *The Dead Sea Scrolls and the Developmental Composition of the Bible*. Vetus Testamentum Supplements 169. Leiden: Brill, 2015. A comprehensive study of the Scrolls' impact on the history of the OT text.

The Interpretation *of the* Bible *in* Various Traditions *and* Cultures

The Letter to the Hebrews begins, "Long ago God spoke to our ancestors in many and various ways by the prophets, but in these last days he has spoken to us by a Son" (Heb. 1:1–2a). Although Christians affirm that Jesus Christ, the Son of God, is the incarnate Word of God, the Scriptures that Christians also call the Word of God, the witnesses to that in-person revelation, have surely been interpreted in "many and various ways" over the centuries and across the globe.[1]

In part 2 of this book we introduce you to the reception and interpretation of the Bible, including the phenomenon of its reception over time and in diverse ways (reception history), premodern interpretation, modern and postmodern methods of interpretation, and theological interpretation. We

1. The editor owes this analogy to Craig Koester.

also consider scriptural interpretation among the four major branches of Christianity (Protestants, Roman Catholics, Orthodox, and Pentecostals) and within four broad sets of cultural contexts (African, African American, Latino/Latina, and Asian and Asian American).

As noted in the introduction to this book, it is impossible in a book of this size, and perhaps any size, to be truly comprehensive with respect to the various ways Scripture has been interpreted throughout time and across the globe. Nonetheless, we believe that the following chapters are a good and helpful representation of the global and ecumenical character of biblical interpretation, past and present. For three reasons this part of the book gives some extra attention to aspects of biblical interpretation in the North American context: (1) this book had its origin in that context; (2) that context has had a major impact on biblical interpretation globally, perhaps for both good and ill; and (3) North American biblical interpretation is increasingly a "hybrid" enterprise that includes African American, Asian American, and other perspectives, and it is therefore expanding to include more global points of view.

Each chapter in part 2 concludes with a list of recommended reading for further study specific to that chapter. A few general resources on "**hermeneutics**" (interpretation) and "**exegesis**" (literary, historical, and theological analysis of, and engagement with, the text of Scripture, from the Greek for "lead out") are included here.

General Works on Hermeneutics and Exegesis

Briggs, Richard. *Reading the Bible Wisely: An Introduction to Taking Scripture Seriously.* Rev. ed. Eugene, OR: Wipf & Stock, 2011. A concise, insightful overview of the Bible and its interpretation.

Davis, Ellen F., and Richard B. Hays, eds. *The Art of Reading Scripture.* Grand Rapids: Eerdmans, 2003. Important essays by leading theological interpreters, both biblical scholars and theologians.

Gorman, Michael J. *Elements of Biblical Exegesis: A Guide for Students and Ministers.* Rev. and exp. ed. Grand Rapids: Baker Academic, 2009. A companion volume to the present book, this guide introduces exegesis: careful literary, historical, and theological analysis of, and engagement with, the text of Scripture.

Jasper, David. *A Short Introduction to Hermeneutics.* Louisville: Westminster John Knox, 2004. A useful survey of the history of biblical interpretation, focusing on major figures.

McKim, Donald K., ed. *Dictionary of Major Biblical Interpreters.* Downers Grove, IL: InterVarsity, 2007. More than two hundred articles on key figures and their interpretive strategies.

Zimmermann, Jens. *Hermeneutics: A Very Short Introduction*. Oxford: Oxford University Press, 2015. A general introduction to hermeneutics as a philosophical school of thought applicable to reading generally, to law, and to theology.

More Advanced Works on Hermeneutics

Barr, James. *The Semantics of Biblical Language*. Reprint, Eugene, OR: Wipf & Stock, 2004. A classic treatment of the abuse and proper use of words, grammar, and other linguistic phenomena in biblical exegesis and theology more generally.

Bultmann, Rudolf. "Is Exegesis without Presuppositions Possible?" In *Existence and Faith: Shorter Writings of Rudolf Bultmann*, edited by Schubert M. Ogden, 289–96. New York: Meridian, 1960. A classic essay by a giant of twentieth-century biblical scholarship, answering no to the question posed.

Gadamer, Hans-Georg. *Truth and Method*. Revised and translated by Joel Weinsheimer and Donald G. Marshall. 2nd ed. 1989. Reprint, London and New York: Bloomsbury Academic, 2013. A highly influential philosophical treatise on interpretation, first published in 1960 and translated into English in 1975, that argued for the fusion of two horizons: the past horizon of the work being interpreted and the present horizon of the interpreter.

Levering, Matthew D. *Participatory Biblical Exegesis: A Theology of Biblical Interpretation*. Notre Dame, IN: University of Notre Dame Press, 2008. A significant account of biblical interpretation as transformative participation in the divine life that also takes careful historical study seriously.

Ricoeur, Paul. *Hermeneutics and the Human Sciences*. Translated by John B. Thompson. New York: Cambridge University Press, 1981. Essays on the history and practice of hermeneutics.

———. *Interpretation Theory: Discourse and the Surplus of Meaning*. Fort Worth: Texas Christian University Press, 1976. In this short book of four essays, philosopher Ricoeur argues for the existence of a "surplus of meaning" in texts.

Starling, David I. *Hermeneutics as Apprenticeship: How the Bible Shapes Our Interpretive Habits and Practices*. Grand Rapids: Baker Academic, 2016. A consideration of the ways various biblical authors interpret Scripture, offered as models for our interpretive work.

Thiselton, Anthony C. *Hermeneutics: An Introduction*. Grand Rapids: Eerdmans, 2009. A historical overview and critique of hermeneutical approaches from antiquity to today.

———. *New Horizons in Hermeneutics: The Theory and Practice of Transforming Biblical Reading*. Grand Rapids: Zondervan, 1992. A challenging, comprehensive review of hermeneutical approaches together with Thiselton's own thesis, drawing upon speech-act theory, about the ways Bible reading can and should transform readers.

————. *The Two Horizons: New Testament Hermeneutics and Philosophical Description*. Grand Rapids: Eerdmans, 1980. A groundbreaking work about NT interpretation in light of Gadamer, Ricoeur, Bultmann, and others.

Vanhoozer, Kevin J. *Is There a Meaning in This Text? The Bible, the Reader, and the Morality of Literary Knowledge*. Grand Rapids: Zondervan, 1998. A significant proposal about the possibility of textual meaning in the postmodern context.

Zimmermann, Jens. *Recovering Theological Hermeneutics: An Incarnational-Trinitarian Theory of Interpretation*. Grand Rapids: Baker Academic, 2004. A trinitarian approach to hermeneutics in light of the Protestant Reformation and the philosophical concerns of the twentieth century.

8

The Reception of the Bible and Its Significance

CHRISTINE E. JOYNES

What is the significance of the Bible's **reception history** (a term used to refer to how biblical texts have been interpreted across the centuries in diverse contexts and media)? Can we indeed speak of reception history of "the Bible" at all, given that there are so many different biblical versions? It might be argued that the story of the Bible's emergence in its variant forms and translations should be regarded as part of the story of its reception. Furthermore, within the Bible itself one finds evidence of its texts being received, as in the case of the Synoptic Gospels, where Matthew and Luke function as early interpreters of Mark. Hence **redaction criticism** (the study of how authors use their sources) could also be regarded as "reception of the Bible."

The dominant method for interpreting the Bible since the eighteenth century, the **historical-critical method**, has focused on identifying an "original meaning" of a given biblical text.[1] Since the latter part of the twentieth century, however, the primacy given to original meaning has been questioned, with more emphasis placed upon discovering how a text has been received and

---

1. The historical-critical method emerged during the **Enlightenment** and has dominated academic study of the Bible to the present day, using historical criteria to assess the intelligibility and meaning of biblical texts. See discussion in ch. 10.

has made an impact throughout history, tracing its journeys, trajectories, and transformations. From coins to canvas, stained-glass windows to sacred-book illuminations, the reception history of the Bible encompasses a vast array of diverse interpretations extending far beyond the classic commentators of Jewish and Christian tradition. Indeed, a hallmark of reception history has been its enlarging of the definition of "biblical interpreter" to include artists, writers, and musicians. Sermons, commentaries, hymns, art, poetry, music, drama, film—all can provide rich resources for identifying the reception history of a biblical text.

Reception History as a Field of Study

Is It a Method?

Defining reception history is by no means straightforward. The label "reception history" has come to be widely used as synonymous with the concept *Wirkungsgeschichte*, the German word best translated as "effective history" or "history of influence" and derived from the philosophy of Hans-Georg Gadamer (1900–2002); yet the different origins of the two terms (*Wirkungsgeschichte* and "reception history") are noteworthy and may perhaps account for some of the current debate about terminology.

The term *Wirkungsgeschichte* first appears in Gadamer's book *Truth and Method*.[2] Underpinning Gadamer's philosophical approach is the recognition that *all* interpretation is historically and linguistically situated. Therefore, a text's meaning does not depend on "the contingencies of the author and his [*sic*] original audience. . . . It is always co-determined also by the historical situation of the interpreter and hence by the totality of the objective course of history" (*Truth and Method*, 307). Gadamer highlights here that the reader is not simply a passive recipient of the text but actively plays a part in constructing its meaning. For Gadamer, understanding takes place through the fusion of two horizons: the horizon of the *work* (located in a distant past) and the horizon of the *interpreter* (in their own subjective historical location).

Building on his teacher Gadamer's philosophical **hermeneutics** (philosophy of interpretation), Hans Robert Jauss (1921–1997) sought to further define the dynamic relationship between text and reader in the field of literary studies through his aesthetic of reception (*Rezeptionsaesthetik* or *Rezeptionsgeschichte*). Jauss proposes that texts operate within a literary series that includes

---

2. The German original was titled *Wahrheit und Methode: Grundzüge einer philosophischen Hermeneutik* (Tübingen: Mohr, 1960).

prior and subsequent works, with "epoch-making moments" marking the contours of this tradition. Perhaps most significantly, in his seven theses for literary studies, Jauss implies that reception history is a method of literary analysis that can be adopted by interpreters precisely because a literary work does not exist by itself, but always in relation to other works. At this point, we should notice Gadamer's *critique* of methodologies, since his focus was not on a work per se, but rather on the process of understanding, exploring the nature of an individual's relationship to history.

"History of Interpretation" and "Reception History": What's the Difference?

The ideas of Gadamer and Jauss were firmly placed on the map of biblical studies with the groundbreaking work of the Swiss New Testament scholar Ulrich Luz. His Matthew commentary in the Evangelisch-Katholischer Kommentar (EKK) series demonstrates in practice how the use and influence of the Matthean text can be compiled and analyzed, offering new interpretive possibilities. Alongside a historical-critical analysis of Matthew, Luz devotes a significant amount of space to exploring the Gospel's reception history, asserting that the history of interpretation and influence of the text is not an optional extra but an integral part of interpretation.

Luz's work raises a further issue of note, the relationship between "history of interpretation" and "reception history." Again the labels are frequently used interchangeably, and what constitutes the distinction is by no means self-evident. Luz employs "history of interpretation" to refer to exposition in theological commentaries, contrasting this with a more broadly defined *Wirkungsgeschichte*, which includes different media such as hymnody and art. However, he clearly states that "history of interpretation" is for him a subcategory within *Wirkungsgeschichte*.

Although Luz sometimes uses the term "reception history," he attempts to distinguish this from *Wirkungsgeschichte* by emphasizing that the former "connotes . . . primarily the *people who receive the text*, while *Wirkungsgeschichte* suggests . . . the *effective power of the texts themselves*" (Luz, *Matthew 1–7*, 61, emphasis added). But despite defining this theoretical distinction, Luz suggests that in practice the two terms can nevertheless be treated synonymously (7).

Changing the Nomenclature?

I have spent some time outlining the terminological background because this lies at the root of various scholarly challenges to reception history. So, for example, Timothy Beal argues that a Gadamerian reception-history approach cannot be regarded as a method to be applied to the Bible at all ("Reception History and Beyond," 369). For this and other reasons he advocates instead the term "cultural history of the Bible." Similarly, Choon-Leong Seow expresses dissatisfaction with the terminology currently in use, preferring to come up with his own label, "history of consequences," to encompass all the variety of engagements and encounters with the Bible. Alternative scholarly labels that have been suggested include "reception criticism" (Susan Gillingham) and "reception **exegesis**" (Paul Joyce and Diana Lipton), on the basis that these terms better highlight an analytical rather than a merely descriptive approach.

The reception-history approach to the Bible also presents difficulties associated with the vast quantity of material to be assessed, leaving the interpreter open to the accusation of being a dilettante, jack-of-all-trades and master of none, blundering across disciplines where one is ill equipped to judge. Similarly, the principles of selection used by scholars engaging in reception history have also come under fire for giving priority to **ecclesial** traditions of interpretation, classic readings, and authoritative interpreters. Is there a place for marginal or even maverick interpretations in the discussion?

Reception History and the Historical-Critical Method

Biblical reception history has made a significant impact since the start of the twenty-first century. Indeed, Timothy Beal goes so far as to describe the rise of reception history as "revolutionary," exercising an influence comparable to that of **source criticism** and **form criticism** in the late nineteenth and early twentieth centuries. For some, however, reception history is not revolutionary enough, precisely *because it remains beholden to the historical-critical method.* Unsurprisingly, the entrenched dichotomies between historical-critical and literary approaches to biblical texts here become apparent. Does reception history *assist* historical-critical inquiry, bringing interpreters closer to the original meaning? Or does reception history *undermine* the very notion of original meaning? Again the great variety of stances among practitioners of reception history prevents a straightforward response to our question.

Complementary or Contradictory Approaches?

A complementary perspective is evident in Susan Gillingham's work. She argues that reception history of the Hebrew Bible in essence starts where historical criticism ends, with the so-called final form of the Hebrew text. Similarly, Luz's commentary on Matthew succeeds in holding both historical criticism and reception history together in one volume, as mutually enriching approaches. For both Gillingham and Luz, then, reception history is perfectly compatible with historical-critical approaches.

Other scholars, such as Joyce and Lipton, have felt more uncomfortable with the idea that historical criticism is "a kind of foundation on which reception history might be built as a second-stage superstructure." To avoid this implication, they argue that historical-critical study of the Bible should be viewed itself as "a relatively recent phase in the long story of its reception" (*Lamentations through the Centuries*, 11).

More recently, the challenges to reception history for being simplistically added onto traditional modes of exegesis have intensified. For example, Brennan Breed, in response to what he perceives to be historical-critical assumptions underlying some ventures in reception history, has argued for a new theoretical basis. In view of our earlier discussion about definitions, it is worth noting that Breed does not suggest jettisoning the term "reception history" but rather defines his own particular reception-history methodology.

Breed's 2014 monograph, *Nomadic Text: A Theory of Biblical Reception History*, is particularly concerned to question the primacy given to original form and original meaning as naturally preferable to later forms and later meanings. The essential issue he grapples with is "Where do receptions begin and where does the original end?" After highlighting the complexities of the Bible's emergence as a single entity, Breed writes as follows:

> Reception history is nothing if reception history is understood as studying that which comes after the original. There is no such thing, since there was nothing original in the first place. In the first place, there was the secondary. But everything is reception history if reception history is understood as studying how unoriginal audiences take unoriginal texts and give them unoriginal meanings, which is simply to say if it is understood as "people taking a text and doing something with it." (*Nomadic Text*, 115)

Breed is also at pains to emphasize the role of the reader in the interpretive process. Thus he observes,

> At times biblical scholarship focuses so much on the moment of the inscription of a text that it overlooks the moment of reading, which generally occurs well outside the context of inscription. *The very function of a text is to be readable outside of its context of production.* (94, emphasis added)

Breed is, however, alert to the relativizing charge against reception history and the accusation that it promotes *all* interpretations as valid interpretations. He acknowledges that biblical texts *do* have exegetical limits. Nevertheless, within these exegetical limits we find a multiplicity of potential meanings that cannot be contained by whatever context one decides is original.

At this point one further detail to highlight is that much of the above discussion about the meaning of reception history has been framed in terms of texts and readers. However, as noted earlier, an important contribution of biblical reception history is to expand the definition of a biblical **exegete** to include artists and musicians. This further complicates terminological discussion, since the dimensions of seeing and hearing need to be included alongside reading.

In sum: recent discussions of biblical reception history clearly illustrate that its exponents have widely differing views of what it involves. Some suggest that it cannot be reconciled with historical-critical approaches, whereas others seek to hold the two approaches together. Some rejoice in the evident plurality of approaches, in contrast to others who are concerned to define terms more precisely to avoid ongoing confusion.

Reception History in Practice: The Gospel of Mark

To illustrate some of the benefits in using a reception-historical approach to the Bible, I offer a brief case study from Mark's Gospel. Given the tendency to interpret reception in terms of texts, I have selected my example to highlight the insights that emerge from engaging with biblical art.

My example brings the Markan account of John the Baptist's beheading (Mark 6:14–29) into dialogue with Hinrik Funhof's 1483 altar painting *The Feast of Herod*, produced for the St. Johanniskirche in Lüneburg, Germany, where it can still be found today. The devotional context of this artwork should be noted and can be contrasted with the differing functions of other representations of the Baptist's death, which often foreground the dancing girl's role in the events.

Funhof presents us with a synthesis of narrative moments from the biblical text. He focuses on two different elements of the beheading episode: the presentation of the Baptist's head to the girl by the executioner (on the left-hand side of the altarpiece), and her delivery of the head to her mother (depicted on the right-hand side). The artist also contrasts the beheading episode with other Gospel passages, including the birth of the Baptist and his baptism of Jesus (in the background).

St. Johanniskirche, Lüneburg

Figure 8.1. Hinrik Funhof, *The Feast of Herod*, detail from the Altarbild in St. Johanniskirche, Lüneburg, Germany.

Funhof's juxtaposition of different features from the beheading story with other Gospel passages highlights a significant contribution of art to biblical exegesis: its production of a synchronic dialogue between narratives, drawing our attention to **intertextual** resonances.[3] Thus, the association of the

---

3. "Synchronic" (meaning "at or within the same time") here refers to bringing historically disparate events alongside each other to be analyzed at the same time.

beheading incident with the baptism of Jesus prompts the viewer to reflect upon the relationship between these accounts. However, despite Funhof's synthesis of different narrative moments, the dance of the girl is not represented. This leaves the onlooker to consider how the head ended up on the plate. It also reminds us that noticing *what is omitted* in a picture is just as significant as analyzing what an artist includes.

As in the Markan Gospel, Funhof's altarpiece leaves the nature of the dance entirely to the viewer's imagination. The artist focuses rather upon the banquet setting of the narrative, drawing our attention to the food imagery in the story. While biblical commentators have often dismissed the request for the Baptist's head on a platter as a gruesome detail, Funhof highlights the significance of this feature by drawing a striking parallel between the meat joint on the table and the severed head, which is presented as one of the courses at this royal banquet. Herod holds a knife ready to eat, and Herodias's gaze is directed toward the food on the table as her daughter comes to present her prize.

The feasting imagery in the beheading episode is particularly significant given that Matthew and Mark—both of whom include the narrative of the infamous banquet—place this story immediately before the feeding of the five thousand account. This suggests a contrast between the feeding of the multitude—prefiguring both the messianic banquet and Jesus' self-sacrifice—and Herod's banquet, where the Baptist's sacrifice is portrayed.

The interpretation of the Baptist's death as foreshadowing Jesus' own was well known in the medieval church, with the head on the platter regarded as a symbol of the **Eucharist**. Accordingly, an early seventh-century commentator on Mark's Gospel, Pseudo-Jerome, suggests that the plate on which John's head lies is a reminder of the plate used at Mass to hold the eucharistic bread: "The body of John is buried, his head is laid on a dish: the letter is covered with earth, the spirit is honoured and received at the altar."[4] Similarly, the late fifteenth-century York breviary reads, "St John's head on the dish signifies the body of Christ which feeds us on the holy altar."

The widespread eucharistic interpretation of the Baptist's death is evidenced by sculptures, seals, paintings, and domestic ornaments of John's head that were produced. This veneration continued throughout the fifteenth and sixteenth centuries, when alabaster tablets depicting the head of John the Baptist on a dish, known as "Saint John's heads," were particularly popular. In the light of this cultural situation, we can infer that Funhof's use of the

---

4. Pseudo-Jerome produced the first full-length commentary on Mark's Gospel. Because of its attribution to Jerome, the commentary was widely copied and influential until its authenticity was questioned by Renaissance scholars.

beheading incident as the focus for his altar painting was not coincidence, but rather reflects the eucharistic overtones commonly associated with the story.

Pausing to engage with a particular reception of John the Baptist's beheading, as in Hinrik Funhof's altarpiece, can open up new vistas on the Gospel text, highlighting a multiplicity of meanings overlooked by contemporary historical-critical commentaries. It illustrates the prevalence of a (now-neglected) eucharistic interpretation of the episode, which was widespread in diverse periods and contexts. Furthermore, by analyzing the biblical text in art, we are reminded that understanding the text occurs not simply through elucidation of its statements, but by engaging all the senses and involving the whole human being.

The Theological Significance of Reception History

Besides being an interesting exercise in intellectual history and a fruitful means of enlarging our interpretive vision, what might be the theological significance of reception history?

Ecumenical Dialogue

A key contribution offered by reception history is its juxtaposition of different interpretive traditions from across the centuries, bringing them into dialogue. It therefore has significant **ecumenical** potential, enabling religious communities to better understand their differences and current situations. In contrast to the suggestion that reception history has moved beyond retrieving long-lost readings and the correction of exegetical amnesia, I argue that there is much more still to be gained from reception history in this area.

Furthermore, by analyzing the reception of the Bible, one is challenged to surrender any claims to control the biblical text. As A. K. M. Adam recently argued:

No *one* signifying practice controls a uniquely privileged methodological or ethical key to interpretive legitimacy; within each interpretive practice, indigenous conventions will raise up some interpretations as sounder and more compelling, and will discountenance others as uninteresting, poorly-executed, unsound. In order to have made sense of everything we have experienced in all our lives, we must have had viable conventions and criteria by which we venture and assess interpretations. The same capacities will serve us well as we undertake interpretations of the Bible; though we may falter at first, and err more often than we would like, we will in short order be able to acclimatise ourselves to interpretations authorised on the strength of characteristics that do not depend primarily on their deference to an unreachable "correct" meaning.[5]

Perhaps surrendering the quest for a single correct meaning will lead to ecumenical bridges being built between different theological traditions.

Reconnecting with the Past

A further theological benefit offered by reception history is the renewed attention it has given to precritical interpretations and their contributions, as illustrated by the attention these interpretations have received from practitioners of **theological interpretation** (see ch. 11). Reception history has promoted growing interest in **patristic** exegesis (interpretations in the early church; see ch. 9), previously dismissed by biblical scholars as irrelevant allegorization. In addition to highlighting the multivalency of the Bible and its rich exegetical traditions, engagement with **typological** and **christological** readings of the Bible often prompts the interpreter to wrestle with difficult issues, particularly in the area of Jewish-Christian relations.

Voices from the Margins

By enlarging the parameters of biblical studies, reception history has also opened up opportunities for hearing voices from the margins. While some practitioners of reception history still focus on "major interpreters" (see, for example, John Riches's Blackwell Bible Commentary on Galatians), reception history can also bring to the fore readings from the margins (as demonstrated by Judith Kovacs and Christopher Rowland's Revelation commentary in the same series).

Attention to these voices from the margins—advocates of minority positions—can often challenge the exegesis of the majority, thereby pointing to the ambiguity of the text to which the reader is invited to return. While some have expressed reservations about **feminist** and **postcolonial criticism** being subsumed under the reception-history umbrella, its potential to support marginal voices in the history of biblical interpretation is significant.[6]

Acknowledging Ideological Commitments

Finally, by mapping the trajectories of biblical interpretations, their relationships to their own times and places, and the proliferation of their ongoing

---

5. A. K. M. Adam, "Short Bit from Sensuous Hermeneutics," *Akma*, April 2, 2016, http://akma.disseminary.org/.

6. For brief discussions of feminist and postcolonial criticism, see chs. 10 and 11.

effects, reception history clearly shows that all interpretation of the Bible, including our own, is socially, politically, and ideologically committed. Theological commitment is therefore also something to be identified and acknowledged alongside these other commitments.

Concluding Reflections

This chapter has aimed to give an overview of the significant contribution that reception history makes when interpreting the Bible. It has highlighted the vexed question of defining reception history and pointed to the variety of opinion concerning the relationship between reception history and historical criticism. I have suggested that while these two approaches are not necessarily mutually exclusive, nevertheless any idea of a single, definitive "original meaning" is incompatible with reception history.

The chapter has pointed to the way in which reception history highlights **ideological** commitments and the significance of interpretive context, as well as the challenge reception history provides to the widespread scholarly assumption that early means better. By engaging with interpretations from across the centuries and beyond the confines of academic scholarship, reception history can enlarge our own horizons, offering fresh perspectives on biblical texts and alerting us to the limitations of our own readings.

QUESTIONS FOR REFLECTION AND DISCUSSION

1. What are some of the different terms used to refer to reception history? What is the significance of these various terms, and why is there debate about terminology?
2. Does reception history assist historical-critical inquiry, bringing interpreters closer to the original meaning? Or does reception history undermine the very notion of original meaning?
3. What do you see as the contributions of reception history to biblical interpretation?

FOR FURTHER READING AND STUDY

Beal, Timothy K. "Reception History and Beyond: Toward the Cultural History of Scriptures." *Biblical Interpretation* 19 (2011): 357–72. Helpful analysis of the benefits and pitfalls of reception history.

————, ed. *The Oxford Encyclopedia of the Bible and the Arts*. 2 vols. Oxford: Oxford University Press, 2015. A wonderful distillation of numerous reception-history examples in a variety of media.

Breed, Brennan W. *Nomadic Text: A Theory of Biblical Reception History*. Bloomington: Indiana University Press, 2014. A good outline of the challenges that reception history poses to biblical studies.

England, Emma, and William John Lyons, eds. *Reception History and Biblical Studies: Theory and Practice*. London: Bloomsbury, 2015. Wide-ranging collection of essays offering examples of reception history in practice.

Evans, Robert. *Reception History, Tradition and Biblical Interpretation: Gadamer and Jauss in Current Practice*. London: Bloomsbury, 2014. Helpful analysis of the potential that Gadamer offers to biblical studies.

Exum, J. Cheryl, and Ela Nutu, eds. *Between the Text and the Canvas: The Bible and Art in Dialogue*. Sheffield: Sheffield Phoenix, 2007. Insightful essays exploring the reception of the Bible in Western art.

Gadamer, Hans-Georg. *Truth and Method*. 2nd ed. Revised and translated by Joel Weinsheimer and Donald G. Marshall. 1989. Reprint, London and New York: Bloomsbury Academic, 2013. A highly influential philosophical treatise on interpretation, including the introduction of his term *Wirkungsgeschichte*, first published in 1960 and translated into English in 1975.

Gillingham, Susan. "An Introduction to Reception History with Particular Reference to Psalm 1." *Revue des sciences religieuses* 85 (2011): 571–99. Further helpful insights on the contribution that reception history makes to biblical studies.

Gowler, David B. *The Parables after Jesus: Their Imaginative Receptions across Two Millennia*. Grand Rapids: Baker Academic, 2017. Accessible and groundbreaking exploration of the NT parables and their reception history.

Joyce, Paul M., and Diana Lipton. *Lamentations through the Centuries*. Wiley-Blackwell Bible Commentary Series. Oxford and Malden, MA: Wiley-Blackwell, 2013. Engaging example from the innovative reception-history commentary series published by Wiley-Blackwell.

Klauck, Hans-Josef, et al., eds. *Encyclopedia of the Bible and Its Reception*. Berlin: de Gruyter, 2009–. Thirty-volume ongoing project to chronicle the expanses of biblical reception history in encyclopedic form.

Kovacs, Judith, and Christopher Rowland. *Revelation: The Apocalypse of Jesus Christ*. Blackwell Bible Commentary Series. Oxford and Malden, MA: Blackwell, 2004. Pioneering contribution to this reception-history commentary series.

Luz, Ulrich. *Matthew [1–7; 8–20; 21–28]: A Commentary*. 3 vols. Minneapolis: Fortress, 2001–2007. Pivotal commentary on Matthew that placed reception history on the map of biblical studies.

————. *Matthew in History: Interpretation, Influence, and Effects*. Minneapolis: Fortress, 1994. Offering further engagement with the significance of reception history (or "history of influence," the term Luz prefers).

Parris, David Paul. *Reception Theory and Biblical Hermeneutics*. Eugene, OR: Wipf & Stock, 2009. Focuses particularly on the contributions made by Hans-Georg Gadamer and Hans Robert Jauss to biblical studies.

Roberts, Jonathan, and Christopher Rowland, eds. *Journal for the Study of the New Testament* 33, no. 2 (2010). Special edition of the journal dedicated to discussion of reception history's significance, including (importantly) the contribution of visual exegesis.

Seow, Choon-Leong. "Reflections on the History of Consequences: The Case of Job." In *Method Matters: Essays on the Interpretation of the Hebrew Bible in Honor of David L. Petersen*, edited by Joel M. LeMon and Kent Harold Richards, 581–86. Atlanta: Society of Biblical Literature, 2009. Defense of an alternative label, "history of consequences."

———, ed. Illuminations. Grand Rapids: Eerdmans, 2013–. New series of critical commentaries that pays attention to the importance of reception history.

Sherwood, Yvonne. *A Biblical Text and Its Afterlives: The Survival of Jonah in Western Culture*. Cambridge: Cambridge University Press, 2000. Excellent example of the reception history of Jonah in a wide range of contexts across the centuries.

Wiley-Blackwell Bible Commentaries (formerly Blackwell Bible Commentaries). Oxford and Malden, MA: Wiley-Blackwell, 2004–. Innovative and accessible series of reception-history commentaries on each biblical book.

9

Premodern Interpretation of the Bible

CAROLE MONICA C. BURNETT

Jewish and Christian approaches to biblical **exegesis**—the careful analysis and interpretation of texts—share a common ancestry: the self-interpretation evident within the Hebrew Bible / Old Testament itself. Exegesis is performed there when psalmists and prophets ruminate on Israel's **oral traditions** and recorded experiences. Among many possible examples, Psalm 78 can be cited as an interpretation of previously written Scripture, in that it is a retelling of the exodus story from the perspective of David's kingship. The **postexilic** books of Ezra and Nehemiah reflect a focused effort to interpret preexilic writings as moral specifications for the reconstructed nation of Israel. It is from such OT roots that the impulse for subsequent exegesis sprang.[1]

In this chapter we survey many of the issues and approaches that have marked the development of the ongoing relationship between the Bible and faith communities of diverse times and places, ranging from the beginning of the **Common Era** to the sixteenth century. (A time line is provided at the end of the chapter.) Some of these issues still stimulate discussion among people of faith today.

1. See the beginning of ch. 8, where it was suggested that this interpretation of earlier texts within the Bible itself is the earliest manifestation of the reception history of the Bible.

Jewish Exegesis around the Beginning of the Common Era

In ancient Israel, as in any **theocracy** (religiously based government), political and social leaders interpreted and applied Sacred Scripture in their daily decisions. In the centuries immediately preceding the Common Era, however, formal biblical exegesis emanated from two sources, the synagogue and teams of scholars who collaborated on resolving exegetical questions. Line-by-line exposition of Scripture, a method known as **pesher**, was practiced very early, especially at **Qumran**, home to the **Dead Sea Scrolls**. The Hebrew term **midrash** (from the Hebrew verb "search") refers to the interpretation of texts, which can be divided into two primary areas. One is **halakah** (related to the Hebrew verb "walk"), the derivation from Scripture of concrete regulations governing individual behavior and social practices. The other is **haggadah** ("tale," "telling"; related to the Hebrew verb "tell"), the detailed interpretation of biblical narratives, employing historical, philosophical, and philological approaches, as well as humor, and usually drawing a moral from the story. Passages from one portion of Scripture were elucidated by references to other portions of Scripture.

The **rabbinic** scholars active before about 200 CE, called **Tannaim**, transmitted and contributed to both oral and written exegetical traditions. Many of these materials provided specific rules and wise sayings to assist Jewish communities in regulating their everyday transactions and maintaining their Jewish identity. Near the end of the Tannaitic era (ca. 200 CE) the halakic teachings, with haggadic traditions, were compiled in written form to produce the **Mishnah**. Subsequently there developed commentaries on the Mishnah known as the **Gemara**. The Mishnah and the Gemara together are called the **Talmud**, of which there are two editions, or recensions: the Palestinian (ca. 450 CE) and the Babylonian (ca. 550 CE). The painstaking scholarship they represent took place in Tiberias (of Galilee) and in Babylon, respectively; Jerusalem could no longer serve as a locus of scholarship after its devastation by the Romans in 70 CE. Yet another exegetical tradition resides in the **Targums**, **Aramaic** translations of Scripture dating from around 250 BCE to around 300 CE. These qualify as exegesis because, in addition to the intrinsically interpretive nature of any translation, the Targums also contain explicitly interpretive material.

It is within the realm of haggadah that two first-century Jewish writers widely known today, Josephus and Philo, flourished. Josephus's *Jewish Antiquities* and *Against Apion* render patriotic accounts of Israel's history aimed at **Greco-Roman** sensibilities. Philo, a luminary of the Hellenistic Jewish academy of Alexandria in Egypt, was heir to the tradition of synthesizing scriptural revelation with Greek philosophy, which is conspicuous in the apocryphal/ deuterocanonical books of Sirach (Ecclesiasticus) and 4 Maccabees. Greek philosophers had long been utilizing **allegory** to interpret Greek myths and legends. In the **allegorical** method of interpretation, characters and events are assigned a symbolic significance as representing spiritual realities; for example, an enemy army may symbolize moral vices attacking the human spirit. Whatever Philo's goal may have been, the allegorical approach appears in his scriptural commentaries and essays, most strikingly in his *Life of Moses*, where he identifies the two cherubim on the mercy seat of the ark as symbols of the creative and the kingly powers of God (Exod. 25), and the uplifted arms of Moses at the battle against the Amalekites as a symbol of the celestial realm (Exod. 17).

Ancient Christian Exegesis

Early Apologetic and Polemical Uses of Scripture

Just as Philo and Josephus used exegetical approaches intelligible to educated gentiles, second-century Christian writers likewise strove to offer an account or defense (Greek *apologia*, as in 1 Pet. 3:15; hence the English word "**apology**," meaning "defense") of their faith that would make sense to Jews. In dialogues with the Jewish community, these writers agreed with the rabbinical view of canonical Scripture as a single, undivided divine revelation, but included Christian literature as expressing the culmination of that revelation. (The formation of the Jewish and Christian canons is described in ch. 6.) The task of defending the Christian proclamation and explaining its relationship to Israel's salvation history lent itself to the **typological** method of exegesis, which was adopted by, among others, Justin Martyr and the anonymous author of the Epistle of Barnabas in the second century CE. These authors interpreted OT narratives as **types**, or symbolic precursors, of NT events. They depicted as precursors of Christ's crucifixion both (1) the scapegoat of Leviticus 16, who bore the sins of Israel; and (2) Moses supervising with outstretched arms the battle against the Amalekites in Exodus 17 (a different symbolism from that of Philo; see above).[2]

Another occasion for invoking symbolism was the conflict between **orthodox** Christian authorities and the world-denying **gnostics**, who took Plato's dualistic philosophy to extremes and thus rejected the physical creation and

---

2. This approach does not differ substantially from that of the NT itself. Recall the portrayal of Jesus as successor to Moses in the Gospel of Matthew, Paul's linkage of Israel's rock in the desert to Christ (1 Cor. 10:4), and the metaphor of Christ as the ultimate high priest in Heb. 9.

its creator, along with the OT that described them. In order to refute the gnostics and their kin (including the infamous presbyter **Marcion**), ecclesiastical writers were compelled to defend the canonical status of the OT. One response, formulated by the second-century bishop Irenaeus, stressed the original goodness of the creation prior to Adam and Eve's sin and promised a future restoration of this fallen world to its former blessedness. Another approach, emanating from the third-century Christian catechetical school of Alexandria, was the use of allegorical interpretation, also employed by the Hellenistic Jewish philosopher Philo (a native of the same city). When the OT was viewed as allegory, the apparently vengeful acts of its God could be explained as allegorical rather than as evidence of moral inferiority, of which the gnostics accused Israel's God. Clement of Alexandria, the director of the catechetical school, postulated that the highest level of spiritual development was to become a "Christian gnostic" attuned to the allegorical sense of Scripture.

Origen's Allegorical Exegesis

Allegorical exegesis was more systematically expounded and its parameters defined by Clement's successor, the brilliant Origen (d. 254). Influenced by Platonism, Origen found it eminently reasonable to regard the physical, earthly phenomena described by Scripture as signposts pointing to intangible, spiritual realities. Nevertheless, Origen cautioned that all such theological speculations must be kept within the boundaries of the church's traditions—boundaries often referred to in early Christian literature as "the rule of faith" (Latin *regula fidei*). Thus Origen precluded individualistic departures from the orthodoxy of his day. Moreover, he supported his allegorical approach on the basis of Scripture itself, citing Galatians 4 with Paul's interpretation of Sarah and Hagar as an "allegory" (*allēgoroumena*, 4:24) of the two covenants.

The burning issue for Origen's exegesis was how to handle scriptural statements that simply do not make sense or that attribute to God qualities uncharacteristic of divinity. Because he regarded it as axiomatic that the same Holy Spirit was responsible for the entirety of sacred Scripture, and because he stipulated that the majority of scriptural passages could be taken literally, he utilized easily understood passages in interpreting more challenging ones. Some intractable exegetical problems, however, were not conducive to this intrabiblical approach; these, Origen thought, had been intentionally designed by the Holy Spirit as incentives to push the reader into a quest for a nonliteral meaning.

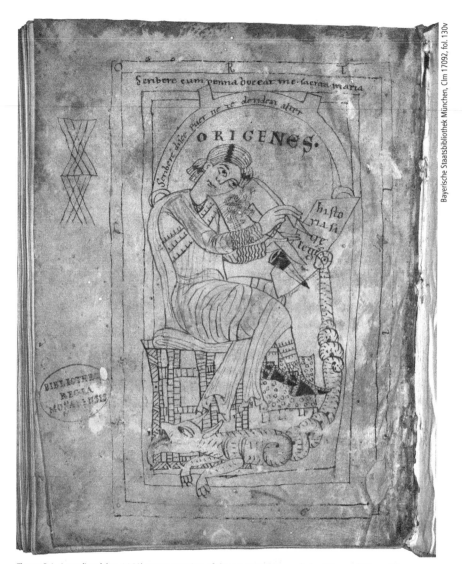

Figure 9.1. A medieval (ca. 1160) representation of the great Scripture scholar Origen of Alexandria (ca. 185–254); originally from the Schäftlarn monastery in Germany, it is now housed in the Bayerische Staatsbibliothek in Munich.

According to Origen, then, Scripture has three possible meanings or **senses**: the **literal**, the **moral**, and the **spiritual** senses. A passage may possess all three, because a historical event, reliably recounted by the biblical author, may itself symbolize moral and spiritual truths. No literal meaning, however, can reside in passages that are patently illogical, such as the account in Genesis 1 of three evenings and mornings having occurred before the creation of the sun and moon. And Paul's declaration of his own unworthiness in 1 Corinthians 15:9 is not to be taken at face value, but is to be regarded as a moral lesson— namely, that all souls are capable of both good and evil; here the second, or moral, sense of Scripture is operative.

The concept of extracting multiple meanings, including allegorical ones, from biblical texts survived in Christian theology for centuries to come. Originating from the Alexandrian Jew Philo, then adapted by Clement and Origen, this approach was disseminated first in the Mediterranean world and then in medieval Europe. Christian allegory was imported to the Latin-speaking church by Ambrose (d. 397), the bishop of Milan whose allegorical sermons enabled the young Augustine to perceive that the OT offers timeless truths. Augustine's biblical interpretation, to be examined below, exerted a far-reaching influence.

Scriptural and Theological Controversy in Late Antiquity

Allegorical exegesis provoked fierce controversy in the eastern Mediterranean world of the fourth and fifth centuries, generating two basic hermeneutical approaches, sometimes labeled the **Alexandrian** and the **Antiochene** schools of thought after their cities of origin (Alexandria in Egypt and Antioch in Syria, respectively). Diodore of Tarsus and his younger contemporary Theodore of Mopsuestia, both leaders of the Antiochene school, rejected allegory as too subjective and individualistic. They preferred to approach scriptural texts as literal accounts of human experiences, to be examined within their respective historical contexts and, if appearing similar to later events in biblical history, to be seen as foreshadowings, or types. Utterly rejecting Origen's view of the Song of Songs as an allegorical metaphor for the intimate union between God and the soul, or between God and the church, Theodore regarded the book merely as erotic poetry. Likewise, with only minor exceptions, he understood royal language in the Psalms not to allude typologically to Christ, but rather to refer to its contemporary setting in King David's court.[3]

Yet another Antiochene **exegete** and pupil of Diodore, John Chrysostom, who was acclaimed more for his powerful preaching than for theological speculation, drew homiletic exhortations from the literal interpretation of Scripture, taking care, for example, to interpret the Pauline Epistles in light of the pastoral problems that Paul encountered. John (dubbed "Chrysostom," or "Golden-mouthed") began his ecclesiastical career in his native Antioch

3. The few exceptions were psalms that ancient Jewish exegesis had already identified as messianic references.

and subsequently became bishop of Constantinople. He disliked allegorical exegesis but, in an ironic turn of events, met his downfall by providing safe haven to four controversial Egyptian monks loyal to Origenism and its use of allegory.

An example of the use of allegory to interpret an OT narrative appears in Gregory of Nyssa's fourth-century treatise *The Life of Moses*, which was influenced by Origen's exegetical writings of the previous century. Origen's view was that any narrative element obviously unworthy of God—such as the anthropomorphic (humanlike) depiction of God as walking in the garden of Eden and as searching for Adam there (Gen. 3:8–9)—must be interpreted figuratively, not as literal fact. Gregory of Nyssa (d. ca. 394) raises this issue in regard to the deaths of the Egyptian firstborn (Exod. 11:1–12:32). Is it worthy of the divine nature for God to punish Pharaoh by killing babies? "How can the history so contradict reason?" asks Gregory.[4]

Gregory resolves the quandary by expounding a "spiritual meaning," which actually involves two of Origen's approaches: first a moral lesson and then an allegory. Morally, the annihilation of the Egyptians' infants indicates that Christians must eradicate evil at its very inception in the soul: lust must be extinguished before it matures into adultery; anger, before it gives rise to murder. Allegorically, the smearing of blood on the Israelites' doorposts and lintels highlights the truth that the highest of the three parts of the human soul, the rational, is necessarily supported by the two lower parts (represented by the doorposts and lintels), the appetitive and the spirited (emotional). The tripartite model of the soul, drawn from Plato's philosophy, is the preconception driving Gregory's allegorical exegesis.

It was Origen who had laid the foundation for Gregory to extract both (1) moral instruction and (2) figurative representation of invisible realities from this OT narrative of death. In a homily on this text, Origen had drawn the same moral lesson from the story, that evil must be quashed immediately so as to prevent its growth, but his allegorical interpretation was brief. He proposed that the slain offspring represent either the evil spiritual powers whom Christ has vanquished or the originators of pagan religions that have been eclipsed by Christian faith.

The disagreements on the value of allegory were paralleled by the christological controversies (arguments about the doctrine of Christ's humanity and/or divinity) spanning the fourth and fifth centuries. Diodore and Theodore

4. Quoted words in this and the following paragraph are from Gregory of Nyssa, *The Life of Moses*, trans. Abraham J. Malherbe and Everett Ferguson, Classics of Western Spirituality (New York: Paulist Press, 1978), 75–77.

both believed that scriptural passages describing Jesus as suffering could be applied only to Jesus' humanity, not to the divine Word, or Logos, for the reason that God Almighty cannot change or suffer. A younger contemporary of Theodore, Nestorius, who became bishop of Constantinople in 428, took this two-natures **Christology** further by insisting that Jesus as an infant had not yet received his divine nature, and that therefore scriptural passages referring to Jesus' growth and development (Luke 2:40, 52) must be applied only to his human nature. According to Nestorius, NT texts must be categorized according to which of Christ's two natures, divine or human, is being described.

This division of scriptural texts was abhorrent to the passionate Cyril of Alexandria (d. 444), the archenemy of Nestorius. Trumpeting his view of Christ as a single entity resulting from a true union—a **"hypostatic" union**—of God with humanity, Cyril condemned Nestorius's exegetical approach on the grounds that texts describing Jesus as changing or suffering pertain to the self-limitation that God imposed on himself in making himself incarnate. Cyril's views eventually gained only a partial victory: an **ecumenical council** at Chalcedon in 451 repudiated Nestorius's perspective on the infant Jesus, but affirmed the two natures of Christ and the validity of categorizing scriptural texts as Nestorius had done.

Farther to the East, in the region that now includes eastern Syria, southeastern Turkey, Iraq, and Iran, the language of Christian discourse was not Greek (as it was for most of the theologians in the East), but **Syriac**, which is intimately related to Aramaic. The most famous of the Syriac-speaking theologians is Ephrem the Syrian (d. 373), who served churches in upper Mesopotamia. While his hymns and verse homilies are studded with symbolism, including typology, his lesser-known commentaries on Genesis and Exodus (as found in the **Peshitta**, the Syriac version of the Bible) adhere to the literal narrative, but with Ephrem's own explanations of the characters' motivations. After Ephrem, the Syriac exegetical tradition, rich and varied, continued through the thirteenth century.

Augustine as Exegete

Meanwhile, in the western, Latin-speaking area of the Roman Empire, Augustine (d. 430), bishop of Hippo in North Africa, was composing a prodigious number of theological works, including his *On Christian Teaching*. In this work he set forth exegetical guidelines that included, as Origen had done, the concept of multiple meanings in Scripture, the **authority** of the church's rule of faith, and the use of lucid scriptural passages in wresting the meaning from obscure ones. Like Origen, Augustine believed that God had intentionally sprinkled difficult passages here and there in the Bible; his explanation was that these strenuous exegetical challenges are meant to spur the reader to overcome pride and to cherish the interpretations obtained by such effort. In addition to these observations, Augustine explained the *Rules* for exegesis written by Tyconius, a fellow North African who belonged to a schismatic sect. Tyconius's rules dealt with figures of speech and literary devices found in Scripture. Above all, said Augustine, the ultimate criterion for accepting an interpretation must be whether it promotes the growth of charity: "Whoever, then, thinks that he understands the Holy Scriptures, or any part of them, but puts such an interpretation upon them as does not tend to build up this twofold love of God and our neighbor, does not yet understand them" (*On Christian Teaching* [*Doctrine*] 1.36.40).

Medieval Exegesis

In the fifth century, the **Roman Empire** crumbled in the West, while Eastern imperial power remained intact, to thrive as the Byzantine Empire. There ensued the era that Westerners call "the Middle Ages," which hummed with exegetical activity in three arenas: Latin-speaking **Christendom** in the West, the Greek-speaking Byzantine Empire, and Jewish academic circles, especially in Spain.

The Christian West

In Western Europe, the Latin biblical translation prepared primarily by Jerome (d. 420), called the **Vulgate**, gained authoritative status, and with it a new **genre** of biblical commentary became widespread. Previous exegetical formats had been those of the homily, the line-by-line commentary, the essay (or tractate), the epistle, and the dialogue. Now that monastic scribes were producing copies of the Bible itself, interpretive comments crept into the copies, written between the lines or in the margins of the biblical text. These comments, which sometimes consisted merely of a single word, were called **glosses**; in the early medieval period they were extracted and compiled into books.

During this period, the content of Western scriptural commentary and other theological thought was dominated by Augustine's weighty legacy. His influence is embedded in the works of Caesarius of Arles, a sixth-century bishop in France, and of Bede, the erudite and prolific eighth-century English monk who nourished the growth of scholarship in a time when continental Europe was teeming with tribal warfare. Bede embraced the exegetical guidelines provided by Augustine in *On Christian Teaching*, including the rules of Tyconius reproduced there. He advocated an expansion of the threefold exegetical methodology expounded by Origen and approved by Augustine; this expansion added a fourth possible meaning to be found in Scripture: the **anagogical sense**, which describes the afterlife. This **fourfold exegesis**, which seeks to uncover (1) the historical (or literal), (2) the **tropological** (or moral), (3) the allegorical, and (4) the anagogical meanings in Scripture, had originated in late antiquity with the fifth-century monk John Cassian. Thanks to its dissemination by Bede and others, it persisted throughout the Middle Ages as the standard methodology of biblical interpretation.[5]

In the so-called High Middle Ages (roughly 1000–1300), the mode of theological instruction was transformed as the centers of scholarship moved from the monasteries to urban cathedral schools, which spawned the medieval universities. In its early stages, classroom teaching consisted of the *lectio* (similar to a lecture), in which the professor read and commented upon each individual line of Scripture or other ancient writing—a classroom procedure that today's students likely would refuse to tolerate. In preparing his *lectio*, the professor found compilations of glosses extremely useful. Pedagogical methodology shifted, however, as the *disputatio* gained popularity. In the *disputatio*, theological questions were identified, to which opposing responses were proposed, supported by evidence gleaned from the Bible, ancient Christian scholarship, and classical philosophy. A concluding resolution was offered for each question, and a professor's conclusions were expected to be comprehensive and logically consistent with one another.

Into this movement, called "Scholasticism," a milieu of lively debate and meticulous logic, the theological giant Thomas Aquinas stepped. Not since Augustine had such deep footprints been imprinted in Christian academia. Aquinas (d. 1274) and his colleagues at the University of Paris eagerly pored over the newly discovered writings of the pre-Christian philosopher Aristotle. Long lost in the Christian world, these works had been carefully preserved by Muslim scholars. This introduction of Aristotle's logic and science injected an urgency into the issue of the authority of faith versus that of reason (for which Aquinas is celebrated as having discovered a satisfying synthesis).

Combining the new focus on Aristotle, whom Aquinas referred to respectfully as "the Philosopher," with the format of the academic *disputatio*, Aquinas articulated his formidably comprehensive theological system in his

---

5. Some contemporary theological interpreters have proposed the recovery of the fourfold sense by relating it to the literal sense and then to the theological virtues of faith (allegorical), hope (anagogical), and love (tropological).

Figure 9.2. A page from a fourteenth-century illuminated manuscript of a missal, preserved in the Abbey at Altenburg, Austria, showing two monks reading the Bible.

tome entitled *Summa Theologiae*. Although he wrote commentaries on some NT books, the starting point of his theology was not Scripture. Rather, by the methodology of the *disputatio*, he set out to demonstrate how human beings can come to know and to participate in God's holiness; in so doing, he presented insights from Scripture as one source among many. Like other medieval theologians, he upheld the fourfold interpretation of Scripture presented earlier by Bede; in doctrinal formulations, however, Aquinas admitted only the literal sense, which for him consisted of the meaning intended by the biblical author within his own particular historical context. The other three senses of Scripture could serve as edification and inspiration, but no doctrine could be based upon them. In this way Aquinas tried to attain objectivity, or at least to steer clear of individualistic interpretations not demonstrable by academic reasoning.

In the twilight of the Middle Ages, Nicholas of Lyra (d. 1340), utilizing the insights of the Jewish scholar Rashi (see below), expanded on the theories of Aquinas. Nicholas posited the existence of two literal senses, both implanted by God: one was the meaning of a text within its original historical context, and the other was the message intended for subsequent generations. Like Aquinas, Nicholas was not appreciated in his own lifetime.

The Christian East

In the Byzantine Empire, the theological work of monastic scholars continued in a smooth progression from the days of the ancient Christian writers. There is no real distinction between "ancient" and "medieval" theology in the Byzantine church. Controversies and councils continued to arise. One of these upheavals, the Iconoclastic Controversy, elicited the support of John of Damascus (d. 749) for the veneration of **icons**, which are distinctive painted images of Christ and of saints. In response to the critics of icons (iconoclasts) who argued on the basis of the divine prohibition of images in Exodus 20 and Deuteronomy 5, John highlighted the historical context of this commandment, which had been issued to the Israelites in the wilderness at the time when the golden-calf episode had clearly exhibited their inclination to worship statuary. Distinguishing between "worship" and "veneration" of images, he pointed out that God had commanded that figures of cherubim be put on the mercy seat, and that Solomon's Temple, approved by God, had contained many images of animals. God had not forbidden the use of images, concluded John; rather, for a particular people in a particular situation (the Israelites in the wilderness), God had prescribed a particular remedy. Thus, John pursued verbal and historical analysis to determine whether a given scriptural passage was applicable in his own day.

Besides John, a host of Byzantine scholars produced a wealth of theological insights. Two of these, Photios (d. 891) and Symeon the New Theologian (d. 1022), were noted exegetes—Photios in addressing a variety of issues, including the procession of the Holy Spirit from the Father only, and Symeon in his advocacy of immediate spiritual experience and of the unbroken continuity of his own day with the NT age of miracles and charisms (spiritual gifts).

Medieval Jewish Exegesis

During the same era, Jewish scholarship was thriving in a golden age of biblical and philosophical study in both East and West. By the time the two Talmuds were completed at the end of the fifth century or so, Hebrew was no longer a spoken language, having been replaced by Aramaic. This shift endangered the accessibility of the sacred text to laypeople, who might be stymied by the uncertainty surrounding its pronunciation. Between the sixth and the ninth centuries CE, therefore, the **Masoretes**, erudite rabbinic scholars headquartered in Tiberias and in Babylon, inserted vowels, punctuation marks, and section divisions into the biblical text, in addition to identifying the authoritative textual version. The resulting text, still in use today, is known as the **Masoretic Text**.

In the tenth, eleventh, and twelfth centuries, Jewish learning flowered in France and especially in Moorish (Muslim) Spain. Two major fields of investigation for the Spanish Jewish scholars were biblical philology (the exploration of the exact meanings of words in Scripture) and the relationship between philosophy and biblical faith. The most illustrious representatives of this school were the rabbis Abraham Ibn Ezra (d. 1167) and Moses Maimonides (d. 1204). The latter's famous philosophical and exegetical work, *Guide for the Perplexed*, allows the use of Aristotelianism for interpreting some texts, and allegory for others, but carefully limits both. Meanwhile, the French Jewish exegete Rashi (d. 1105) and his grandson, Samuel ben Meïr, emphasized the indispensability of literal interpretation and philological analysis.

In summary, while Byzantine Christian scholars were exploring a broad array of theological questions, both Jewish and Christian scholars in the medieval West focused on Aristotelian philosophy, with its concomitant problem of the relationship between faith and reason, and adopted a multifaceted exegetical approach that permitted allegory. Soon the European Renaissance would bring new factors into play.

Renaissance and Reformation

The **Renaissance**, which began in fourteenth-century Italy and spread to northwestern Europe in the next century, was driven by a humanistic revival of interest in classical (ancient Greek and Roman) art and literature. A consequence of this *ad fontes* (to the sources) movement for Christian biblical studies was an increased focus on the primary source of faith—that is, the Bible in its original languages. Among other scholars, the fifteenth-century philologist Lorenzo Valla examined the NT books of the Vulgate, the official Latin biblical text, in light of the original Greek text, and the sixteenth-century German Johannes Reuchlin studied both the Hebrew and the Greek Scriptures, publishing a Hebrew grammar textbook and dictionary.

During Reuchlin's lifetime, the Protestant Reformation—with its slogan *sola Scriptura* (Scripture alone)—ushered in a widespread rejection of Aristotelian philosophy, of imaginative allegory, and of church tradition as a criterion for biblical exegesis. Biblical passages were to be understood through the application of other biblical passages, not of any external standard such as ancient or medieval theological statements; thus, the Bible was to be regarded as self-interpreting. As we have seen, the exegesis of Scripture by means of Scripture had been done throughout the centuries, though not to the exclusion of other methods.

In particular, Martin Luther's interest in the self-evident meaning of Scripture can be partially attributed to the influence of Nicholas of Lyra, and through Nicholas to Rashi. Luther's doctrine of "the priesthood of all believers" extended a role to the individual interpreter within the parameters set by the church, and justification by faith alone (*sola fide*) became a guiding principle.[6] Moreover, Luther identified a **canon within the canon**, meaning that biblical books that preach Christ and support the concept of *sola fide*, such as Romans and Galatians, were to be esteemed more highly than those that do not; in fact, Luther all but relegated the Epistle of James, with its exhortation to good works, to the junk pile, calling it an "epistle of straw." For Luther the OT was a prefiguration of, and preparation for, the advent of Christ, who is the reason for the Bible's very existence, although he also stressed the difference between the (OT) law and the (NT) gospel.

John Calvin endorsed the *sola fide* and *sola Scriptura* theology of Luther, but he added an emphasis on the revelatory role of Scripture and on the ongoing usefulness of the law for Christians (the so-called third use of the law). Because the human eye is obscured by sin, said this second-generation reformer, God has graciously provided scriptural revelation to function as a pair of eyeglasses in enabling nearly blind humanity to perceive God. Not everyone, however, will accept Scripture as authoritative or understand it accurately; therefore, God bestows the internal guidance of the Holy Spirit to enable believers to interpret the Scriptures correctly. To the Christian exegete is

6. Interestingly, although Luther preached the doctrines of *sola fide* and *sola Scriptura*, his theology consistently supported the ancient creeds and councils.

imparted a sense of assurance that the gift of the Spirit has been given. Calvin remarked that "the testimony of the Spirit is superior to reason" (*Institutes of the Christian Religion* 1.7.4) and that

> the Lord has so knit together the certainty of his word and his Spirit, that our minds are duly imbued with reverence for the word when the Spirit shining upon it enables us there to behold the face of God; and, on the other hand, we embrace the Spirit with no danger of delusion when we recognize him in his image, that is, in his word. (*Institutes of the Christian Religion* 1.9.3)[7]

The newer approaches to scriptural interpretation, independent of papal authority and less reliant on medieval methods of exegesis, played a part in the transition to a different and innovative phase of Christian history. The widening chasm between Catholics and Protestants and the resulting decades of bloody warfare exhausted Europeans and produced receptivity to seventeenth- and eighteenth-century **Enlightenment** perspectives, which laid the groundwork for the modern era, including its distinctive approaches to biblical interpretation. These are explored in the next chapter.

Figure 9.3. Time Line of Premodern Interpretation of the Bible

Before the Common Era (BCE)	
400–350	• Plato (d. 348/347) envisions the material world as consisting of imperfect copies pointing to perfect, eternal forms, thus laying the foundation for the concept of allegory.
350–300	• Aristotle (d. 322) expounds ethics, cosmology, and causation in the visible world. • Alexander the Great (d. 323) disseminates Hellenistic culture.
300–250	• The Septuagint is begun: the Hebrew Scriptures are translated into Greek.
250–200	• Beginning of Targums: the Hebrew Scriptures begin to be translated into Aramaic with an interpretive approach, a task that will continue for the next five centuries.

The Common Era (CE)	
1–50	• Philo (d. ca. 45), an Alexandrian Jew, adopts a Platonist approach to Scripture, using allegory.
50–100	• Paul (d. before 68) employs allegory in Galatians and 1 Corinthians. • Josephus (d. ca. 100) presents Israelite history to Greco-Roman readers.
100–150	• The pseudonymous Epistle of Barnabas (ca. 130) interprets the Hebrew Scriptures by means of typology, or prefigurations of Christ. • Justin Martyr (d. ca. 165) employs typology in the *Dialogue with Trypho* (ca. 150), an example of Christian apologetics.

---

7. Quotations are from John Calvin, *Institutes of the Christian Religion*, trans. Henry Beveridge (Edinburgh: Calvin Translation Society, 1845), http://www.ccel.org/ccel/calvin/institutes.html.

150–200	• Irenaeus of Lyons (d. late second century) defends the value of the Hebrew Scriptures against gnostic opposition to them.
200–250	• Clement of Alexandria (d. ca. 215) opposes gnostics, upholds the spiritual meaning of the Hebrew Scriptures, and promotes allegorical interpretation for advanced believers. • Origen of Alexandria (d. 254) employs allegorical exegesis and identifies three levels of meaning in Scripture: literal, moral, and spiritual.
300?	• The Peshitta, the Bible in the Syriac language, is now accepted in Syriac-speaking churches of the East.*
350–400	• Gregory of Nyssa (d. ca. 394) draws upon Philo and Origen for his use of allegory in his *Life of Moses*. • Ephrem the Syrian (d. 373) sees symbolism in literal narratives. • Diodore of Tarsus (d. ca. 392), regarded as an originator of the Antiochene school of thought, rejects allegory. • John Chrysostom (d. 407), a product of Antioch, emphasizes the moral meaning of Scripture. • Tyconius of North Africa (d. ca. 390) formulates his *Rules* for exegesis. • Ambrose of Milan (d. 397) imports allegorical exegesis into the Latin-speaking West.
400–450	• Jerome (d. 420) translates directly from Hebrew into Latin in creating the Vulgate. • Augustine (d. 430) expounds exegetical methodology in *On Christian Teaching*, upholds the three levels of meaning described by Origen, and utilizes the *Rules* of Tyconius. • Theodore of Mopsuestia (d. 428), of the Antiochene school, rejects allegory and seeks literal-historical meanings. • The Palestinian Talmud is completed, ca. 450. • Nestorius (d. probably in the 430s) and Theodoret of Cyrrhus (d. ca. 457), proponents of a two-natures Christology, maintain that Scripture passages can be selectively applied to the human nature or to the divine nature of Christ.
450–500	• The Council of Chalcedon (451) validates the selective application of Scripture in Christology (see immediately above). • The reign of the last Roman emperor in the West ends in 476.
500–550	• The Babylonian Talmud is completed, ca. 550.† • Caesarius of Arles (d. 543) promotes Augustinian theology and exegesis.
600–650	• Muhammad (d. 632) gathers followers and transmits the Qur'an.
700–750	• Bede (d. 735), an English monk and scholar, expands upon Origen and Augustine in proposing a fourfold exegetical approach. • John of Damascus (d. 749) emphasizes the historical context of Scripture passages in defending the veneration of icons.
800–850?	• Finalization of forms of the Masoretic Hebrew text by rabbinic scholars, after work that took place over several centuries.
850–900	• Photios (d. 891), a Byzantine patriarch, interprets Scripture to uphold Eastern pneumatology.
1000–1050	• Symeon the New Theologian (d. 1022), a Byzantine monk, reads Scripture through the lens of spiritual experience.

1050–1100	• The French-Jewish rabbinical scholar Rashi (d. 1105) applies philological analysis to the Hebrew Scriptures.
1150–1200	• Jewish and Muslim scholarship has been thriving for approximately two centuries in Moorish Spain. • The Spanish-Jewish exegete Abraham Ibn Ezra (d. 1167) explores biblical philology and employs philosophical concepts. • The Jewish scholar Moses Maimonides (d. 1204) incorporates both Aristotelian and allegorical exegesis in his *Guide for the Perplexed*.
1250–1300	• Scholasticism and universities are in full swing. • Thomas Aquinas (d. 1274) incorporates Aristotelian thought in his comprehensive theological system, integrating faith and reason.
1300–1350	• Nicholas of Lyra (d. 1340) draws on Aquinas and Rashi to propose two literal senses.
1450–1500	• The Renaissance scholar Lorenzo Valla (d. 1457), a leader in the *ad fontes* (to the sources) movement, returns to the original Greek text of the Christian Scriptures, bypassing the Latin Vulgate.
1500–1550	• Johannes Reuchlin (d. 1522) studies the Scriptures in their original languages, Hebrew and Greek. • Martin Luther (d. 1546) interprets Scripture in the original languages, rejects Aristotelianism, and advocates the principles of *sola fide* and *sola Scriptura*.
1550–1600	• John Calvin (d. 1564) emphasizes Scripture as revelation as well as the role of the Holy Spirit in interpreting it, writes *The Institutes of the Christian Religion*, and perceives a positive value to biblical law in the Christian life.

* The date is debated, with scholarly estimates ranging from the second to the fourth or fifth century.
† This date is debated, with scholarly estimates ranging from the second or third century to the sixth.

QUESTIONS FOR REFLECTION AND DISCUSSION

1. Allegorical exegesis depicts events, objects, animals, or human characters as symbols pointing to spiritual realities. Although ancient Christian allegory was based on Greek philosophy, which is no longer prevalent in most churches, have you ever heard an allegorical interpretation in a homily or sermon? Can it be legitimate and useful to employ allegory in biblical preaching today? If not, why not? If so, what criteria would you apply in assessing each particular use of allegory?

2. Recall that typology involves an event, object, animal, or human character in one part of the Bible as a prefiguration of an event, object, animal, or human character in a later part. Protestant and Catholic lectionaries tend to pair an OT reading and an apparently related NT reading. Have you witnessed the typological approach at work in such pairings? (For Orthodox Christians: What instances of typology seem to you to be most striking in your hymns?)

3. We have seen that at various times throughout history, scriptural interpretation has been shaped by philosophical frameworks or by the exigencies of contemporary controversies. What presuppositions or debates might be at work in twenty-first-century exegesis, whether in academic study, preaching, or informal Bible study?

4. What might be the value of a multilevel approach to biblical interpretation today? Attempt a three- or four-level analysis of a text such as Joshua 6, the conquest of Jericho.

FOR FURTHER READING AND STUDY

George, Timothy, series ed. Reformation Commentary on Scripture. 28 vols. projected. Downers Grove, IL: InterVarsity, 2011–. Commentary on biblical texts from both famous and less-known leaders of the various Protestant and Catholic reformation movements of the sixteenth century.

Hall, Christopher A. *Reading Scripture with the Church Fathers*. Downers Grove, IL: InterVarsity, 1998. Lively introduction to the ancient schools of biblical interpretation and a persuasive argument for the relevance of the church fathers to contemporary Christian thought.

Hauser, Alan J., and Duane F. Watson, eds. *A History of Biblical Interpretation*. Vol. 1, *The Ancient Period*. Grand Rapids: Eerdmans, 2003. Essays on topics pertaining to ancient exegesis of sacred Scripture, both Jewish and Christian.

————. *A History of Biblical Interpretation*. Vol. 2, *The Medieval through the Reformation Periods*. Grand Rapids: Eerdmans, 2009. Wide-ranging exploration of exegetical developments in Jewish and Christian thought over a thousand-year period.

Kanarfogel, Ephraim, and Moshe Sokolow, eds. *Between Rashi and Maimonides: Themes in Medieval Jewish Thought, Literature, and Exegesis*. New York: Michael Scharf Publication Trust of the Yeshiva University Press, 2010. Comparative exploration of the lasting contributions of two giants of medieval Jewish scholarship.

Kannengiesser, Charles, ed. *Handbook of Patristic Exegesis: The Bible in Ancient Christianity*. Leiden: Brill, 2006. Exhaustive compendium, presenting research of renowned patristic scholars, with extensive bibliographies.

Lubac, Henri de. *Medieval Exegesis: The Four Senses of Scripture*. Vol. 1 translated by Mark Sebanc. Vols. 2–3 translated by E. M. Macierowski. 3 vols. Ressourcement: Retrieval and Renewal in Catholic Thought. Grand Rapids: Eerdmans, 2009. Monumental exploration of Western European biblical exegesis in the Middle Ages, with special attention to allegorical interpretation.

Montague, George T. *Understanding the Bible: A Basic Introduction to Biblical Interpretation*. New York and Mahwah, NJ: Paulist Press, 1997, chapters 1–4. Survey of the interpretive methods used by the most renowned scholars of early and medieval Christianity, as well as by the biblical authors themselves.

Oden, Thomas C., series ed. Ancient Christian Commentary on Scripture. 29 vols. Downers Grove, IL: InterVarsity, 2000–2010. A compilation of samples of patristic commentary on selected texts from every book of the OT and NT.

O'Keefe, John J., and R. R. Reno. *Sanctified Vision: An Introduction to Early Christian Interpretation of the Bible*. Baltimore: Johns Hopkins University Press, 2005. Examines major topics, including Christology, typology, allegory, the rule of faith, and the holy life in biblical interpretation.

Reventlow, Henning Graf. *History of Biblical Interpretation*. Vol. 1, *From the Old Testament to Origen*. Translated by Leo G. Perdue. Resources for Biblical Study. Atlanta: Society of Biblical Literature, 2009. A study of the interpretive methods of the biblical writers interpreting their own scriptural sources, the Septuagint translators, the early rabbis, Philo, and Christian thinkers of the first three centuries CE.

———. *History of Biblical Interpretation*. Vol. 2, *From Late Antiquity to the End of the Middle Ages*. Translated by James O. Duke. Resources for Biblical Study. Atlanta: Society of Biblical Literature, 2009. Survey of influential biblical scholars from Ambrose of Milan through John Wycliffe.

———. *History of Biblical Interpretation*. Vol. 3, *Renaissance, Reformation, Humanism*. Translated by James O. Duke. Resources for Biblical Study. Atlanta: Society of Biblical Literature, 2010. A discussion of European biblical interpretation during the fifteenth through seventeenth centuries.

Simonetti, Manlio. *Biblical Interpretation in the Early Church: An Historical Introduction to Patristic Exegesis*. Edited by Anders Bergquist and Markus Bockmuehl. Translated by John A. Hughes. London: T&T Clark, 1994; paperback reprint, 2001. Thorough but succinct exposition of the varieties of patristic exegetical thought and the influences on each.

Wilken, Robert Louis, series ed. The Church's Bible. Grand Rapids: Eerdmans, 2003–. Ancient and medieval exegesis compiled and organized into volumes, with each volume dealing with a particular book of the Bible.

Yarchin, William. *History of Biblical Interpretation: A Reader*. 2004. Reprint, Grand Rapids: Baker Academic, 2011. Survey of Jewish and Christian exegetical approaches from 150 CE to the present.

Young, Frances. *Biblical Exegesis and the Formation of Christian Culture*. 1997. Reprint, Peabody, MA: Hendrickson, 2002. Bold research into the interplay between ancient biblical interpretation and the literary, religious, and philosophical milieu that shaped it and in turn was shaped by it.

10

Modern and Postmodern Methods of Biblical Interpretation

JOEL B. GREEN

Although central to modern and postmodern biblical interpretation, concern with method predates the rise of the modern period in the late eighteenth century, as noted in the previous chapter. In *On Christian Teaching*, St. Augustine (354–430), for example, expressed his aim to identify and explain rules for interpreting the Scriptures. He and other patristic and medieval interpreters developed strategies for discerning the various **senses** of a scriptural text. And the Reformation saw the rise of handbooks for interpretation focused on criteria for achieving legitimate readings. Interaction with Augustine's rules, medieval **fourfold exegesis**, or these later handbooks sets in sharp relief the significance of method in the modern era, however.

Augustine concerns himself with a number of problems arising from ambiguities in biblical texts, but his most memorable claim is his insistence that readings of Scripture must be judged on the basis of whether they cultivate love of God and love of neighbor (*On Christian Teaching* 1.36.40). In the Middle Ages, the fourfold sense of Scripture meant that literal and spiritual meanings were not in competition with each other. And to cite a single illustration from the post-Reformation era, Augustus Herman Francke (1663–1727) arranged his book *A Guide to Reading and Study of the Holy Scriptures* around "the letter of the Scriptures" (focusing, for example, on grammar, history, and literary structure) *and* Scripture's spiritual meaning (with reference, say, to the church's doctrine and the cultivation of holiness). Interpreters in the pre-modern era might introduce historical questions in order to clarify foreign habits of thought and expression or to ward off uncontrolled mysticism or spiritualizing. In their hands, historical inquiry did not challenge the basic unity of Scripture, however, nor question the capacity of Scripture to disclose God's voice or threaten the central affirmations of Christian faith. This would all change dramatically with the emergence of modern biblical interpretation.

The Modern Turn: Autonomy

Among the labels we might use to characterize modern biblical interpretation, *autonomy* may be the most apt description. Biblical interpreters must operate autonomously, or independently—independent of the interpreter's own faith (or lack of faith), independent of the church's theology, and independent of the church's (or any other) authority and influence. Biblical interpreters should go wherever the text leads them. As for the biblical materials, they must be read without consideration for how they have been read by previous interpreters, without reference to their location within the biblical canon, and indeed, quite apart from their status as Scripture. This approach reflects the values of the eighteenth-century **Enlightenment** and its aftermath.

Johann Philipp Gabler (1753–1826) articulated this autonomy early on when he distinguished methodologically between **dogmatic theology** and **biblical theology** in his 1787 inaugural lecture at the University of Altdorf. "Biblical theology," he taught, originates in the past, when the biblical texts were first penned, whereas "dogmatic theology" (today we might say "**systematic theology**") refers to the later teachings of theologians in particular times and places. Thinking of biblical theology, Gabler outlined a three-stage process: (1) careful linguistic and historical analysis of the Bible; (2) engagement in a synthetic task, the purpose of which is to identify the ideas common among the biblical writers; and (3) arrival at the timeless and universal principles of the Bible. Then beginning with these timeless principles, it was the task of dogmatic theologians to adapt them to particular contexts. According to this formulation, biblical studies in the modern era would concern itself with what the biblical materials meant when uttered or written by the prophet or priest, the evangelist or the apostle, regardless of their significance for subsequent faith communities. Such a goal required the development of new interpretive methods.

Modern Methods of Biblical Interpretation

In time, modern approaches to biblical interpretation came to be known simply as "biblical criticism," and especially as "historical criticism." Accordingly, those who do not use historical-critical methods have sometimes been regarded as "uncritical" in their reading of the Bible. Similarly, scholars sometimes refer to biblical interpreters before the eighteenth-century rise of modern biblical criticism as "precritical." These assessments are problematic, though, since they assume that readers in the modern era are the first to have the necessary tools and methods for judging between right and wrong, or good and bad, readings of the biblical materials. This way of telling the story of biblical interpretation assumes that the only (or the primary) way to decide between good and bad readings is by studying the history behind the biblical text. Such an approach arrogantly locates modern biblical criticism as the high point of good interpretation; blindly overlooks how literary, theological, missional, and other interests might shape what constitutes a "good" reading of the Bible; and ironically fails to acknowledge the degree to which modern biblical criticism itself arose in a certain time (the post-Enlightenment era) and place (in the West) and, rather than promoting neutral and objective interpretation, is itself contextually shaped.

Historical Criticism

"Historical criticism" refers to a family of methods characterized by commitment to the model of a supposed neutral or objective interpreter and its nonnegotiable emphasis on interpreting biblical texts with reference to their historical contexts alone. Interpreters are thus known as historians and are tasked with the ideal of setting aside their own interests (whether those interests are philosophical or religious or political or social) as they work with these ancient texts. Biblical texts must be read in terms of the literary and social-cultural conventions of their time, against the backdrop of past times and places as they really were, and with safeguards in place to ensure that readers do not interpret the past in light of the present. Modern study of biblical texts requires an array of closely related methods, or **criticisms**, including historical criticism, **source criticism, form criticism, tradition criticism**, and **social-scientific criticism**.

Although "historical criticism" can be used as a catchall description of modern biblical interpretation, it can also refer more specifically to the method by which historians draw on whatever ancient sources are available to them in order to reconstruct past events for the purpose of narrating the story of the past. Among these sources, the biblical text is only one, and it is placed alongside other texts and/or archaeological evidence from approximately the same time. In addition to sifting among ancient sources, historians also work with certain assumptions about what could have happened in the past, or about what counts as an adequate explanation for historical events. Historians, for example, assume that historical events and processes can be explained in terms of natural causes and effects, without reference to divine influence or intervention. "Truth," for historical criticism, is not theologically determined, nor can it be found by reading the biblical text itself. Truth is found behind the text, as a property of historical events that are discovered or constructed by historians. When biblical interpreters attempt to explain what really happened in the formation of Israel as a people, raise questions about the historical existence of David, or try to write an "accurate" biography of Jesus, they are doing the work of historical criticism.

Source Criticism

Source criticism involves the analysis of biblical texts for evidence of the written or oral sources on which they are based. This approach arose in the late nineteenth century in the work of the German scholar Julius Wellhausen (1844–1918). Regarding the composition of the **Pentateuch**, he developed a theory that has come to be called the "**Documentary Hypothesis.**" According to Wellhausen, the first five books of the Old Testament, or Hebrew Bible (Genesis, Exodus, Leviticus, Numbers, and Deuteronomy), were composed by using four independent sources:

- J—the Jahwist (Yahwist) source, which originated in the southern kingdom of Judah in the mid-900s BCE, uses the name YHWH ("Yahweh") for God (in German, "Jahweh" begins with J);
- E—the Elohist source, which derived from the mid-800s BCE in the northern kingdom of Israel, is noted for using the name "Elohim" for God;
- D—the Deuteronomist source, dating from the late 600s BCE, in Jerusalem; and
- P—the Priestly source, which arose in the mid-400s BCE.

In short, the Pentateuch was not written by Moses, as was widely assumed, but was a compilation of these sources by a later editor, or **redactor**. Since the late twentieth century, scholars have championed more complex models for the writing of the Pentateuch, but modern biblical criticism continues to assume that these books have a complex history, with many hands working over several centuries before what we know as the first five books of the Bible reached their present form.

Source criticism quickly spread from study of the Pentateuch to study of the New Testament Gospels. Modern analysis focuses especially on the relationships among the **Synoptic Gospels**: Matthew, Mark, and Luke ("synoptic" since they take a "common view" of Jesus' career). In Pentateuchal source criticism, attention might center on alternation among names for God, on the presence of other identifiable theological tendencies, or on seams in the text that suggest one style of writing has given way to another. With the Gospels, the focus is somewhat different, since in this instance we have multiple versions of the same episode. For example, consider the synoptic accounts of Jesus' prayer on the night of his arrest (fig. 10.1).[1]

Figure 10.1. Synopsis of Jesus' Prayer

Matthew 26:39–45	Mark 14:35–41a	Luke 22:41–46
Then he went a short distance farther and fell on his face and prayed,	Then he went a short distance farther and fell to the ground. He prayed that, if possible, he might be spared the time of suffering. He said,	He withdrew from them about a stone's throw, knelt down, and prayed. He said,
"My Father, if it's possible, take this cup of suffering away from me. However—not what I want but what you want."	"Abba, Father, for you all things are possible. Take this cup of suffering away from me. However, not what I want but what you want."	"Father, if it's your will, take this cup of suffering away from me. However, not my will but your will must be done."
		Then a heavenly angel appeared to him and strengthened him. He was in anguish and prayed even more earnestly. His sweat became like drops of blood falling on the ground. When he got up from praying, he went to the
He came back to the disciples and found them sleeping.	He came and found them sleeping.	disciples. He found them asleep, overcome by grief.
He said to Peter,	He said to Peter, "Simon, are you asleep?	He said to them, "Why are you sleeping?
"Couldn't you stay alert one hour with me?	Couldn't you stay alert for one hour?	

1. The text is from Joel B. Green and W. Gil Shin, eds., *Common English Bible Gospel Parallels* (Nashville: Abingdon, 2012), 218–19 (§308).

Matthew 26:39–45	Mark 14:35–41a	Luke 22:41–46
Stay alert and pray so that you won't give in to temptation. The spirit is eager, but the flesh is weak."	Stay alert and pray so that you won't give in to temptation. The spirit is eager, but the flesh is weak."	Get up and pray so that you won't give in to temptation."
A second time he went away and prayed, "My Father, if it's not possible that this cup be taken away unless I drink it, then let it be what you want."	Again, he left them and prayed, repeating the same words.	
Again he came and found them sleeping. Their eyes were heavy with sleep.	And, again, when he came back, he found them sleeping, for they couldn't keep their eyes open, and they didn't know how to respond to him.	
But he left them and again went and prayed the same words for the third time. Then he came to his disciples and said to them, "Will you sleep and rest all night?"	He came a third time and said to them, "Will you sleep and rest all night?"	

Even when one reads these parallel accounts in a contemporary English translation like the Common English Bible, it is easy to observe that (1) all three accounts tell basically the same story; (2) at a number of points, two or three of these accounts correspond closely in terms of word usage and word order; and (3) at other points, one or two of these accounts go their own way in telling the story. Close examination of a Gospel **synopsis**, which places the narratives of the Gospels in parallel with one another, like this short example, quickly reveals that this kind of overlap is found throughout the Synoptic Gospels, though more rarely when comparing the Gospel of John with the other NT Gospels. In fact, the Gospels of Matthew, Mark, and Luke share a high degree of similarity in content, so that about 95 percent of the Gospel of Mark is also found in the Gospels of Matthew and Luke. They share the same basic structure. And they share a startlingly similar vocabulary and literature style—startling because (1) these similarities are present in spite of the fact that most or all of these stories would have originated in **Aramaic** and are now told in **Greek**; (2) Greek word order is relatively free in comparison to English, but the similarities in the Gospels often extend to word sequence; and (3) there is little likelihood that three evangelists, working at different times and in different parts of the Roman Empire, would have related the same account using exactly the same words.

Observations like these led scholars to assume that these three Gospels share some sort of literary relationship, though scholars differ in how they explain that relationship. A list of prominent theories includes these four:[2]

1. In the **Four Document Hypothesis**, Mark's Gospel was written first ("**Markan priority**"), and the authors of Matthew and Luke used Mark, as well as two of three other documents: **Q** (usually understood as an abbreviation for the German word *Quelle*, "source"), **M** (Matthew's special source), and **L** (Luke's special source).

2. In the **Two Document Hypothesis**, Mark's Gospel was written first, and the authors of Matthew and Luke used the Gospel of Mark and Q, but also knew and used other **oral traditions**.

3. In the **Farrer Hypothesis**, advocated by Austin M. Farrer (1904–1968) and championed in recent times by Mark Goodacre, Mark was the first Gospel, Matthew used Mark (and other sources), then Luke used both Mark and Matthew.

4. In the **Griesbach Hypothesis**, proposed by Johann Jakob Griesbach (1745–1812), the first Gospel was Matthew's, Luke made use of Matthew, and Luke and Matthew were used by Mark.

From a source-critical perspective, then, the four Gospels were not written by the **evangelists** whose names they carry (Matthew or John, for example), but are the products of a careful combination and editing of earlier sources. Since, from the standpoint of historical criticism, earlier materials tend to be prioritized over later materials, source criticism is important for the way it allows access to oral and/or written traditions behind the final texts of the Gospels.

Form and Tradition Criticism

Form criticism classifies units of the biblical text according to literary patterns, or forms, and then seeks to identify the relationship between the forms of those units and their functions in the sociohistorical settings of the communities in which they were orally transmitted. Hermann Gunkel (1862–1932) pioneered the method, seeking to classify the genre of each psalm (e.g., lament, royal psalm) or, in the case of Genesis, of a textual unit, and to inquire into the role of that sort of text within Israel's communal life, such as

2. Scholars use various descriptive phrases for these basic theories; students should attend primarily to the content of the theories rather than to the labels.

in the wake of a national disaster, at the birth or coronation of a king, or in a pilgrimage to Jerusalem. In NT studies, form critics focused on small units of text called **pericopes,** classified according to **genre** or form (e.g., parable, miracle story); they then associated each form with a particular setting-in-life (German *Sitz im Leben*), such as missionary apologetic, community instruction, or worship. Using this reading strategy, students of the Bible tried to open a window into the life of the communities that preserved, fashioned, and transmitted the oral traditions that would eventually find their way into the texts we read today.

"Tradition criticism" refers to the study of the process by which historical events came to be recounted, shaped into oral and written traditions, and included in the Bible's historical narratives. For example, tradition critics work to get behind the biographies of Jesus we have in the Gospels, or the story of the early church in the Acts of the Apostles, in order to ascertain what actually happened. Today these critics tend to work in one of three ways.

The first is the more traditional and is characterized by the use of **criteria of authenticity** to ascertain the kernels of sayings and events thought to give us genuine access to the historical Jesus.[3] The list of such criteria is lengthy, including the following:

- *multiple attestation*: multiple sources bear witness to the same saying or event;
- *dissimilarity*: a saying attributed to Jesus is unlike both what we find in contemporary Judaism apart from Jesus and what we find in early Christian preaching; and
- *embarrassment*: sayings that the early church would not have manufactured because they would have shamed its leaders.

Thus, a saying attributed to Jesus that appears in multiple sources (e.g., Mark and Q), is unlike material found in Jewish or early Christian texts, and is potentially embarrassing (e.g., a criticism of the disciples' lack of faith) is considered more likely to be an authentic word from Jesus. Having determined what they believe to be authentic sayings of Jesus or events in his life, historians then arrange these data into narrative sequences in order to provide—as an alternative to the New Testament Gospels—a purportedly more historically accurate representation of the past.

The second approach adopts a less skeptical posture toward the evidence and begins from a likely, historical big picture of what happened. Data from

3. This method was made known to the public by the Jesus Seminar.

the Gospels and Acts are then arranged into a narrative based on their coherence with that overarching grasp of what is likely to have happened. This is the basic approach, for example, of N. T. Wright.

The third and most recent approach brings lessons from the study of **social memory** into study of the Gospels and Acts. This approach neither seeks historical kernels nor begins with a theory about the overarching story of what probably happened. Instead, the historian analyzes how events and sayings make sense within their existing narrative frameworks in the New Testament. This method serves the critic's interest in conceptualizing and articulating how social groups appropriate the past in the service of the present; it asks which inferred *actual past* best explains the *narrative representations of the past* that we find in the Bible.

Redaction Criticism

Redaction criticism focuses on how the reformulation, or redaction, of early traditions is significant for a later community. Thus, redaction criticism assumes the results of source and form criticism and studies how those oral and written sources have been edited (or redacted) in the preparation of a new text. Although the form critics cleared away very little space for the theological or literary contributions of the authors of biblical books, redaction criticism highlights such contributions—both in terms of what the authors adopt from their sources and with regard to how they adapt those sources for their own purposes.

Consider the differences between Matthew, Mark, and Luke in the account of Jesus' prayer on the night he was arrested (quoted earlier). If the author of Matthew knew and used Mark's Gospel as a source, how do we explain the changes, both minute and large, he has made to Mark's Gospel? What purpose do those editorial amendments serve? What might the author's (or redactor's) theological aim(s) have been?

Social-Scientific Criticism

Social-science criticism, or social-scientific criticism, a recent extension of historical criticism, works to understand the social worlds within which the biblical texts were written. Typically this method serves two broad aims. On the one hand, social-scientific criticism challenges today's readers to take seriously that what we take for granted in the modern world may be, and often is, quite different from the social conventions assumed by the biblical writers and their communities. Social-scientific investigation is thus a deterrent against the ethnocentrism of modern readers (that is, the assumption that all people in all times and all places experience the world the way we do). On the other hand, social-scientific criticism examines how biblical texts embody and reflect, or challenge and undermine, the social worlds within which they were written. Either way, then, this approach provides students of the Bible with the sensibilities and tools needed to understand and traverse the ancient worlds within which the biblical materials were written.

Like historical criticism more generally, there is no single social-scientific method in biblical interpretation, though two broad approaches are generally taken. The first centers on describing ancient contexts on the basis of an examination of different material aspects of the ancient world. This might include population numbers, attitudes toward children, life in the city versus life in the village, perspectives on ancient economics, and so on. The second, indebted to social-scientific theory, emphasizes the construction of typical social models and cultural scripts, often through observations of other, presumably comparable cultures, by which to interpret social behavior described in biblical texts.

Once our eyes have been opened to them, social-scientific questions relevant to biblical texts easily multiply: Who is in a group, who is out, and on what basis? What threatens those definitions? How are boundaries maintained? Who is up (on the "social ladder"), who is down, and how do people of different social statuses relate to one another? How are certain people addressed—with terms that denote kinship, like "loved ones" or "sisters" or "children," or with terms that connote different levels of authority, like "slave" or "lord"? Who wears what kind of clothes, and what do they signify? What kinds of behavior does a particular text seem to reinforce? To what sources of authority does the text or a character within the text appeal?

Postmodern Methods of Biblical Interpretation

The shift from modern to postmodern biblical interpretation traverses ambiguous boundaries that are not easily mapped. **Postmodernism** began as a reaction to **modernism**, and particularly to modernism's assumed objectivity. Accordingly, postmodern approaches to biblical interpretation are held together less by a common commitment to a certain method or even constellation of methods, and more by their critical sensibilities. On the one hand, in contrast to modernist, Enlightenment thinking, postmodern interpreters urge that we have no objectively determined ledge of truth on which to stand in order to make value-free judgments in the work of making meaning. Interpreters cannot hide behind the veil of presumed ideological neutrality. For many postmoderns, on the other hand, "truth" does not exist as an abstract reality apart from human knowing. Thus, for students of the Bible, "meaning" is not simply a property of the text that the reader must discover or excavate but is somehow the product of the interaction of readers with texts.

We can point to additional differences, too. Modern methods tend to seek after the one, correct meaning of a biblical text, whereas postmodern readers are often content to suggest an additional reading alongside other possibilities; as a result, postmodern interpreters tend to argue less over the single right meaning and more over better or more helpful readings, versus worse or less helpful readings. Moreover, postmodern interpretation does not require, but actually seems to work against, the modern notion that the world of the text and the world of the reader are, and must be kept, separate.

Some methods occupy the borderlands between modern and postmodern study of the Bible. One example is social-science criticism (see above), an approach to reading biblical materials that can serve to distinguish the past of the biblical world from the present world of the reader (a modern approach), but also allow present readers to imaginatively find themselves in the biblical story (a postmodern approach). Other examples include **narrative criticism** and **rhetorical criticism.**

Narrative Criticism

Narrative criticism draws together a range of interests and practices for the study of biblical narratives. Narrative study has its roots in a narrow focus on texts, apart from the people who created them or the worlds within which they were given form. Early narrative critics thought that texts could and ought to be studied as self-contained verbal artifacts, with each text understood as its own unique and privileged source of meaning. For them, "meaning" is available to the interpreter primarily by means of careful attention to a text's language and structure, without regard for concerns of a social-historical kind, and with no sensible way to account for how or why different readers at different times might understand the same narrative differently. Today, however, narrative study increasingly blurs the lines among author, text, and reader, so that we understand better how narratives can both embrace and critique ancient and modern worlds and thereby challenge their diverse readers in different ways. From the influx of narrative interests into biblical studies in the early 1980s to narrative study today, then, we can trace a shift in narrative criticism from modern to postmodern sensibilities.

As a modern method, narrative criticism attends to the dynamics or artistry of biblical narratives, including a relatively stable series of narrative elements. These include, but are not limited to, the following:

- *sequence*—that is, how the organization or structure of events discloses how one event is causally related to another;
- *staging*—that is, the location of a scene in space and time, and what characters are present;
- *time*—that is, the connection between time as it might be experienced in the real world and time as recounted in the narrative, so that months or years can be captured in a single sentence or a few hours can be re-counted in minute detail; and
- *characterization*—that is, how a narrative develops and constrains what we know about those who act within it (whether those actants are people, animals, or angels).

From a postmodern perspective, narratives are more than the summation of their essential elements. They have intended effects on their readers. A narrative is "action," not merely a source of information and not simply "a good read." Narrators seek to draw readers into their plots. For example, biblical narratives use a variety of means to urge that their accounts communicate what is true: references to divine intervention and the supernatural, quotations of and allusions to other scriptural texts, imitation, patterns of prediction and fulfillment, and the like. For postmoderns, narratives ought to be read as acts of persuasion, not reduced to their literary artistry.

Rhetorical Criticism

Rhetorical criticism also spans the borders between modern and postmodern methods. This method concerns itself with the nature of the argument and artistry by which biblical writers have tried to persuade their readers of the truth of their beliefs. As a modern method, rhetorical criticism might be deeply rooted in concerns with an author's intention, historical context, and blending of form and content. Alternatively, rhetorical critics might analyze NT writings, for example, according to the standards of rhetoric developed and practiced in the ancient Mediterranean world. The first of these approaches focuses on the aesthetic properties of biblical literature. The second explores how we might hear the words of early Christian authors as they would have been heard by Greek-speaking audiences of the first century, audiences more or less influenced by long-standing and prevalent Greek and Roman interests in persuasive speech.

Postmodern rhetorical approaches are not content only with describing how a text might persuade an audience. Instead, postmodern rhetorical critics are interested in how texts exercise power. How do biblical texts motivate their audiences to act in certain ways? How do they animate certain convictions, provoke certain emotions, and cultivate certain ways of thinking?

Three Approaches to Locating Meaning

In recent years, many students of the Bible have learned to catalog old and new interpretive strategies with regard to where each locates meaning in relation to the biblical text. Some approaches focus *behind* the text, others *in* the text, and still others *in front of* the text.

- **Behind-the-text approaches** address the text as a window through which to access and examine the deposit of "meaning." These approaches, then, locate meaning in the history assumed by the text, the history that gave rise to the text, and/or the history to which a text gives witness.
- **In-the-text approaches** recalibrate their focus on the qualities of the text itself, its architecture and texture.
- **In-front-of-the-text approaches** orient themselves around the perspectives of various readers of the text, on communities of interpretation, and/or on the effects that texts have on their readers. In this case, readers do not simply *identify* but also help to *produce* meaning.

Of course, these are "ideal types" that rarely appear in such pure forms. Using this catalog, though, we can readily see that postmodern methods prioritize readers, and thus in-front-of-the-text approaches, since these approaches emphasize how our attempts to understand texts are shaped by what we bring with us to the text: our formation, our interests, our questions.

It may be easy to accept the commonsense view that reading is more than an act of perceiving what a text says, that reading is more than the discovery of textual meaning. Texts, after all, are inert until revived by their readers. "Meaning" is not actualized by an author or by a text, but only when we take up the text and read. Thus, reading pushes past perception to production, and "meaning" is what happens at the intersection of textual interests and readerly interests. Although most agree that texts place certain constraints on their interpretation, postmodern approaches recognize that readers come in all sizes and shapes, from many cultural backgrounds; they are formed within widely divergent traditions; they represent crisscrossing religious commitments, including deeply held commitments and no particular commitments at all; and they bring to biblical texts their fully embodied social-political-religious selves. Even if they experience the same texts, then, they experience those texts differently. Postmodern methods take for granted that we always read from "a place," with "place" or "social location" capable of being explained in numerous ways—for example, in terms of gender or racial-ethnic identity, ecclesial tradition or socioeconomic status, and so on.

Here again we see the problem with thinking of postmodern "methods" of reading the Bible. "Method" typically refers to the procedures or protocols one uses to help one make sense of a text. What makes a method "postmodern," though, is less procedure and protocol than it is orientation and commitment. Postmodern interpreters might make use of historical analysis, for example, or practice literary methods, but they do so with their own biases. (What is more, postmodern interpreters insist that everyone else works with their own biases, too, even when those biases are not recognized or acknowledged.)

Postmodern Approaches and Aims

Postmodern commitments express themselves, accordingly, in various ways. Feminist criticism, for example, refers to a spectrum of ways to engage biblical texts—not to a method as such, but to acts of interpretation that expose how the biblical materials themselves and/or biblical interpreters have cultivated attitudes and practices that restrict women's roles in households, churches, and societies. Feminist critics might press forward to encourage women's equality and opportunity in those same spheres of life and influence. Some of this work is literary and historical: Where and how are women present in biblical texts? How do we understand their actions, their voices? Some of this work is perspectival and rhetorical: How do peasant women in Nicaragua identify themselves (or not) with Rahab or Mary or the Samaritan woman? How can biblical texts implicated in patriarchal societies be heard as good news from a gracious God? How is God portrayed in relation to the weak and powerless, including widows and many other women besides, as well as children, slaves, and the poor?

African American criticism, together with readings of the Bible outside of the United States among those of African descent, likewise refers to a range of commitments and interests. (For further discussion, see chs. 16 and 17.) Traditionally, and among some today, the Bible has served and continues to serve as an instrument of survival and liberation. This is because Black readers, particularly those relegated to society's margins, have traditionally identified with the recipients of God's beneficence in the Old and New Testaments. African American criticism today might concern itself with highlighting the presence of Africa and Africans in the Bible; pressing against racist interpretations of the Bible; or struggling with certain assumptions of biblical texts themselves, such as the Bible's general lack of explicit denunciation of the practice of human slavery. Additionally, African American approaches to the Bible might draw on African American sources (slave narratives, spirituals, sermons, and hip-hop, for example) in order to bring African American experiences into conversation with the Bible and its interpretation.

Additional examples easily multiply. As a general category, **intercultural** or **contextual criticism** urges that there is no universal, ideal reader, but only flesh-and-blood readers who come to the biblical texts from their particular contexts and with their distinctive questions. **Womanist criticism** is related to both feminist criticism and African American criticism and refers to the use of a wide range of interpretive practices in the service of concerns for the flourishing of African American women, their communities, and other oppressed communities. **Latino/Latina criticism** in the United States foregrounds the Hispanic American experience, recognizing the inherent hybridity of Hispanic identity while remaining ever sensitive to the artificial nature of a term like "Hispanic," which describes not a unified people but many national, ethnic, and language groups from the Caribbean and Latin America. (See further discussion in ch. 18.) **Postcolonial criticism** refers less to a method and more to one's heightened sensitivity to the power structures within which both texts and their interpreters are embedded—and so whether texts might be used (or have been used) to support or critique the powerful and/or the disempowered.

Theological interpretation is defined by its self-consciously ecclesial location, understood with regard especially to the church's confessions, interpretive traditions, and liturgical life throughout history and today (see ch. 11). **Missional hermeneutics** locates the Bible and its interpretation within the arc of God's mission (the *missio Dei*) as this is articulated in Scripture; it also inquires into how the Bible might shape the church's contemporary identity and mission (see ch. 24). **Pentecostal hermeneutics** represents the ongoing negotiation of the triad of Scripture, church, and the Holy Spirit as it works out the implications of its convictions about the Holy Spirit's dynamic presence in and through both Scripture and the Christian community (see ch. 15). And **everyday hermeneutics**, sometimes called **congregational hermeneutics**, concerns itself with how nonspecialists actually work with biblical texts and how they might be faithfully formed by and for their reading of Scripture.

Conclusion

The Bible can be read in many ways, depending on the aims of the reader. We can read it as literature, for example, since we find within its pages poetry and letters, historical narratives and visions, proverbs and oracles, and numerous other literary forms. We might turn to it as history. After all, we find among the biblical writings a keen interest in the beginnings of Abraham and Sarah's people, the gathering of a tribal people as a nation, the rise and fall of leaders and kings, the story of Jesus' life and ministry, and the church's spread across the Roman Empire. Or we might come to the Bible because of its religious significance, convinced that the Old and New Testaments together compose the authoritative witness to God's work in the world. Different readers, and communities of readers, turn to the Bible with different interests, and their interests and aims will lead them to choose different tools from the toolbox of interpretive approaches. From this perspective, what might at first seem an unruly mixture of interpretive methods can actually help us in our diverse efforts to read Scripture well.

QUESTIONS FOR REFLECTION AND DISCUSSION

1. In what ways, if any, are modern and postmodern methods of reading the Bible similar? What are the chief differences between modern and postmodern methods of reading the Bible?
2. Think about the distinctive roles of authors, texts, and readers. What role is given each of these in redaction criticism? narrative criticism? African American criticism?
3. What new insights about biblical interpretation has this chapter provided for you? What kinds of questions has it generated?
4. Given your present understanding of biblical interpretation, do you think we should prioritize behind-the-text, in-the-text, or in-front-of-the-text approaches? Explain your answer.

FOR FURTHER READING AND STUDY

Adam, A. K. M., ed. *Handbook of Postmodern Biblical Interpretation.* St. Louis: Chalice, 2000. With the next entry, a two-volume set documenting the postmodern turn in literary and cultural studies, justifying postmodern approaches in biblical studies, and illustrating exegetical insights deriving from those approaches.

————, ed. *Postmodern Interpretations of the Bible: A Reader*. St. Louis: Chalice, 2001. See previous entry.

Archer, Kenneth. *A Pentecostal Hermeneutic: Spirit, Scripture, and Community*. 2005. Reprint, Cleveland, TN: CPT, 2009. A key attempt both to understand the history of Pentecostal reading of the Bible and to propose a Pentecostal hermeneutic.

Blount, Brian K., ed. *True to Our Native Land: An African American New Testament Commentary*. Minneapolis: Fortress, 2007. One-volume commentary on the New Testament by African American scholars.

Goldingay, John. *Models for Interpretation of Scripture*. Grand Rapids: Eerdmans, 1995. Approaches the task of reading the Bible from the perspective of four models for understanding the Bible: "witnessing tradition," "authoritative canon," "inspired word," and "experienced revelation."

Gorman, Michael J. *Elements of Biblical Exegesis: A Guide for Students and Ministers*. Grand Rapids: Baker Academic, 2009. Accessible guide to careful analysis of, and engagement with, the biblical text.

Green, Joel B., ed. *Dictionary of Jesus and the Gospels*. 2nd ed. Downers Grove, IL: IVP Academic, 2013. Includes up-to-date articles on African American criticism, canonical criticism, feminist and womanist criticisms, form criticism, historicisms and historiography, Latino/Latina criticism, narrative criticism, postcolonial criticism, social-scientific criticisms, synoptic problem, and theological interpretation.

————, ed. *Hearing the New Testament: Strategies for Interpretation*. 2nd ed. Grand Rapids: Eerdmans, 2010. Provides introductions and illustrations of a wide array of approaches to New Testament interpretation, as well as an annotated bibliography for each method.

————. *Seized by Truth: Reading the Bible as Scripture*. Nashville: Abingdon, 2007. Accessible guide to theological interpretation, including its relationship to historical and other concerns.

Greenblatt, Stephen, and Giles Gunn, eds. *Redrawing the Boundaries: The Transformation of English and American Literary Studies*. New York: Modern Language Association of America, 1992. The field of biblical studies often adapts interpretive methods developed in university departments of literature. This anthology introduces a wide range of such approaches, such as feminist criticism, psychoanalytic criticism, cultural criticism, postcolonial criticism, and African American criticism.

Keener, Craig, and M. Daniel Carroll R., eds. *Global Voices: Reading the Bible in the Majority World*. Peabody, MA: Hendrickson, 2012. Essays on various biblical texts and topics by interpreters in varied contexts around the world.

Keith, Chris, and Anthony Le Donne, eds. *Jesus, Criteria, and the Demise of Authenticity*. London: T&T Clark, 2012. A critical reassessment of the tradition-critical criteria that have played a central role in modern study of the historical Jesus.

Kroeger, Catherine Clark, and Mary J. Evans, eds. *The IVP Women's Bible Commentary*. Downers Grove, IL: InterVarsity, 2002. One-volume commentary on the Bible, representing a variety of feminist commitments and approaches.

Newsom, Carol A., Sharon H. Ringe, and Jacqueline K. Lapsley, eds. *Women's Bible Commentary*. 3rd ed. Louisville: Westminster John Knox, 2012. One-volume commentary on the Bible, representing a variety of feminist commitments and approaches.

Powell, Mark Allan. *What Do They Hear? Bridging the Gap between Pulpit and Pew*. Nashville: Abingdon, 2007. Provides intriguing examples of the importance of social location in reading the Bible.

Rogers, Andrew P. *Congregational Hermeneutics: How Do We Read?* Explorations in Practical, Pastoral, and Empirical Theology. Burlington, VT: Ashgate, 2015. Groundbreaking study of what churches actually do with Scripture; this analysis of everyday hermeneutics also proposes an apprenticeship model for cultivating hermeneutical virtues at a congregational level.

Sugirtharajah, R. S., ed. *Voices from the Margin: Interpreting the Bible in the Third World*. 3rd ed. Maryknoll, NY: Orbis, 2006. Essays on various biblical texts and topics by interpreters in varied contexts around the world.

Troeltsch, Ernst. "Historical and Dogmatic Method in Theology." In *Religion in History*, 11–32. Translated by James Luther Adams and Walter F. Bense. Minneapolis: Fortress, 1991. Originally published in 1898, a classic statement of the historical method.

11

Theological Interpretation of the Bible

STEPHEN FOWL

The present chapter follows two chapters on premodern, modern, and postmodern biblical interpretation. It also precedes discrete chapters on the interpretation of the Bible within specific Christian churches and traditions. It seems appropriate to take advantage of this placement in order to consider **theological interpretation**. In the light of the chapters that precede this one, this chapter will lay out several issues concerning the importance of premodern strategies for reading Scripture and the relationship between theological interpretation of Scripture and **historical-critical** study of the Bible. In the light of the chapters that follow, this chapter will address theological concerns and strategies related to interpreting Scripture in the context of church division.

Theological Interpretation, Premodern Interpretation, and the Rise of Historical Criticism

Premodern interpretation of Scripture, discussed in chapter 9, was theological from beginning to end. That is, the various interpretive practices common in the premodern period arose from and were governed by Christian theological convictions. Reading the Bible was a religious activity. Scripture was seen as God's gift to the church. Scripture was the central, but not the only, vehicle by which Christians were able to live and worship faithfully before the Triune God. Moreover, faithful living, thinking, and worshiping shaped the ways in which Christians interpreted Scripture. This was because, ultimately, scriptural interpretation, worship, and Christian faith and life were all ordered and directed toward helping Christians achieve their proper end (or goal; Greek *telos*) in God.

Nevertheless, it is also clear that premodern interpretation was very different from the types of interpretation one encounters in a modern biblical commentary or article. For many students, their encounter with premodern interpretation can strike them as alien. It may be tempting to think that the difference between premodern interpreters and us is that they had a naively literalistic understanding of the Scripture and that they neglected or glossed over textual puzzles. Alternatively, one might be tempted to dismiss premodern interpretation as merely a collection of fanciful and fantastic **allegorical interpretations**. Although there may be some examples of these interpretive flaws, they are not characteristic of premodern interpretation at its best. Premodern interpreters understood that Scripture was extraordinarily diverse and that it contained various textual puzzles and obscurities.

The chief difference between premodern interpreters and the historical critics who came to dominate academic study of the Bible from the late eighteenth century down to the present is that premodern interpreters granted theological concerns, interests, and strategies priority in interpreting Scripture. They did so because they understood that Scripture could only fulfill its role in bringing Christians to their proper end in God if scriptural interpretation shaped and was shaped by theological concerns. Modern biblical study is most clearly distinguished from premodern interpretation because of the priority granted to *historical* concerns over *theological* ones.

The Seismic Shift in Biblical Interpretation

The first step in interpreting Scripture theologically is to grant priority to theological concerns. As a way of leading to that point, it is useful to explore, at least briefly, why textual puzzles, ruptures, and obscurities that were relatively well known began—sometime in the mid- to late eighteenth century—to generate concerns that led to the rise of historical-critical methods of interpretation. During this period there was a fundamental shift in the practices of biblical interpretation. Prior to this shift, in the premodern era, Scripture was believed to be the most important of God's providential gifts for ordering, understanding, and making the world accessible to humans. Scripture (interpreted theologically) presented a unified narrative through which people could develop coherent views of the world. The evident diversity and rich detail of Scripture called forth a variety of reading practices, both literal and nonliteral (**figural**), that nonetheless presented a common narrative. The rich variety of reading strategies characteristic of premodern biblical interpretation was essential if the Bible was to provide Christians with a way of rightly understanding and living within their past, present, and future.

> Since the world truly rendered by combining biblical narratives into one was indeed the one and only real world, it must in principle embrace the experience of any present age and reader. Not only was it possible for him, it was also his duty to fit himself into that world in which he was in any case a member, and he too did so in part by figural interpretation and in part of course by his mode of life. He was to see his disposition, his actions and passions, the shape of his own life as well as that of his era's events, as figures of that storied world.
> (Hans Frei, *The Eclipse of Biblical Narrative*, 3)

To perhaps oversimplify the matter, this sort of interpretation initially moves from *text* to *world*. The presumption was that it is often difficult to figure out how to live and move in the world in ways that will enhance one's prospects of living and worshiping faithfully before God. Scripture, despite its evident obscurities, was believed to provide a relatively clear and God-given set of lenses for viewing the world and faithfully negotiating one's path through it.

But a seismic shift in interpretation occurred when the relationship between text and world was reversed in the eighteenth century with the rise of the historical-critical methods of interpretation during the **Enlightenment**. At that time, scientific, social, and philosophical changes made it seem that the world was, more or less, immediately (directly) intelligible to all rational people, apart from both faith and Scripture. The "real" world became detached from its biblical rendering. In the light of this transformation, interpreters of the Bible began to believe that

> the real events of history constitute an autonomous temporal framework of their own under God's providential design. Instead of rendering them accessible, the narratives, heretofore indispensable as means of access to the events, now simply verify them, thus affirming their autonomy and the fact that they are in principle accessible through any kind of description that can manage to be accurate either predictively or after the event. It simply happens that, again under God's providence, it is the Bible that contains the accurate descriptions.
> (Hans Frei, *The Eclipse of Biblical Narrative*, 4–5)

Consequences of the Shift

The causes of this transformation are numerous and complex. They are related to the scientific, political, economic, and philosophical upheavals that accompanied the rise of what we have come to call modernity. For the purposes of this chapter, it is less important to explain how this transformation took place than to explain some of its consequences for the study of the Bible. For example, as we have just noted, "the real" or "the historical" became its own realm, accessible to all, even if not immediately evident to all. Thus, scriptural, theological, and ecclesial concerns were not only separated from concerns of historical investigation; they also became actively *excluded* from such investigation. As a result, scholars began to devote a great deal of intellectual effort to such projects as inquiring into the historical accuracy of the Bible. Further, if "the real" or "the historical" was now its own autonomous (independent, self-sufficient) realm, then a great deal of effort would also be devoted to developing procedures and methods for supposedly understanding and interpreting reality as such, rather than viewing reality through the lenses of scriptural interpretation.

Once the shift was made from reading Scripture in order to more faithfully understand and live before God within the world, to reading Scripture in order to see if it matched up with an already known and understood reality, a gap opened up between the alleged "real" world and its past, on the one hand, and the world depicted in Scripture, on the other hand. It was within this historical context, and within this set of concerns, that historical criticism developed. Theological concerns were no longer given priority in biblical interpretation.

The Ascendancy of Historical Criticism

Although people often speak of historical criticism as if it were a single organized whole, it really reflects three recurring and interrelated issues.

The first issue concerns the policing of the scholar's confessional stance (worldview and beliefs). Once "the historical" is presumed to be an autonomous realm, it is a small step from presuming that that realm is providentially ordered (whether by the Christian God or the impersonal god of Deism) to presuming that history itself must provide its own standards of meaning and intelligibility independent of one's confessional stance. Once this step is taken, historical critics must seek to root out any seepage from their own or another scholar's confessional commitments into their historical work. This has forced the vast majority of biblical scholars to learn how to separate their public historical research from their private beliefs.

The second issue concerns questions about the historical reliability of the biblical texts. Initially this issue was concerned with the nature and scope of evidence about Jesus. Scholars focused on the character of the evangelists and their honesty. Very soon, however, the focus of this question shifted to the Gospel texts themselves as scholars tried to develop a variety of methods for getting behind the final form of the Gospel texts to find data about what really happened in the life of Jesus and/or the early church. Further, as more extrabiblical sources became available, they too became part of the mix of possible pieces of evidence. Rather than being a set of lenses for interpreting the world theologically, the biblical texts became relatively discrete pieces of evidence for a variety of historical questions ranging from concerns with the authors of these texts and the sources they used to the insight these texts might provide into particular periods in the early church or, in the case of OT texts, the history of Israel.

The third issue concerns the interpretive framework used to organize the evidence. Once history is thought to be an autonomous realm with its own set of methods for establishing intelligibility or meaning, then scholars must not only figure out which pieces of information will count as evidence; they must also develop ways of ordering and interpreting the evidence.

As long as biblical scholars treated the world, past and present, as more or less immediately (directly) accessible to them, then the practices, methods, and results of historical criticism confidently dominated academic biblical study. Theological concerns were largely pushed to the margins. To the extent that theological concerns received a hearing among biblical scholars, it was only as those concerns arose from the assumptions common to historical critics.

Challenges to the Dominance of Historical Criticism

Scientific, cultural, political, and philosophical movements created conditions for the rise of historical criticism. It is not surprising, then, as noted at the end of the previous chapter, that changes in these areas would make an impact on historical criticism. The past century has witnessed great changes in the intellectual, social, and political climate. These changes worked both to undermine the dominance of historical criticism and to open possibilities for theological and political, **ideological interpretation.**

Recall that historical concerns took precedence over theological concerns only when people assumed they could comprehend the world and its past in more or less immediate or direct ways, apart from the lenses provided by Scripture read theologically. Numerous genocidal conflicts, the rise of quantum physics, the ideological critiques of Marx, the psychoanalytical explorations of Freud, and many other factors now make it clear that we never perceive or comprehend the world and its past without our own set of lenses. That is one of the chief claims of **postmodernism** (discussed in the previous chapter).

However, the recognition that we all view the world and its past through a set of lenses, and not immediately, does not mean that all lenses result in 20/20 vision or that all lenses are equal. For the purposes of this chapter, it is sufficient to note that if the dominance of historical criticism depended on the assumption that the world and its past were immediately available to us, then the recognition that the world is not immediately available must affect the claims of historical criticism.

New Developments: Feminist and Marxist (Liberationist) Interpretation

Since the late 1960s, therefore, professional biblical scholarship has seen an explosion of interpretive strategies driven by scholars with particular sets of interests and commitments that go beyond presenting the past as it (supposedly) actually was. These strategies do *not* grant historical concerns priority over all others. Among these ideological interpretations, the most prominent are **feminist criticism** and **Marxist interpretation**, which are both strategies of **liberationist interpretation**, concerned with revealing and correcting ways in which biblical interpretation has ignored or oppressed certain marginalized people (see chs. 10, 16–19, 22).

The field of biblical studies as it exists today, therefore, appears much different and more fragmented than it did even fifty years ago. The concerns and practices characteristic of historical criticism are still around, but they exist in a chastened form. Historical critics can no longer claim to offer an immediate, objective, and definitive view into the past. Rather, they pursue their specific historical investigations as one among many sets of scholarly interpretive interests. Practitioners of newer, liberationist methods still rely on the tools of historical criticism as a foundation for further investigation to explore a new set of **hermeneutical** (interpretive) interests and questions.

It is as problematic to speak of "feminist biblical interpretation," as a single enterprise, as it is to speak of historical criticism as a single enterprise; feminist interpretation is constantly engaging new voices and new interpretive questions. Nevertheless, beginning students can expect to find at least two strategies that are commonly labeled "feminist." The first strategy seeks, through rigorous historical investigations, to uncover and document the lives of women in the biblical period. In this respect the Bible is simply one piece of evidence among many. (Other pieces of evidence would include, for instance, socioeconomic and archaeological data.) The second strategy brings various contemporary feminist concerns to bear on the practice of biblical interpretation. Thus, this strategy can focus on structures within the academy or the churches that work to silence or marginalize women scholars or women in general, with an even broader concern for all marginalized or silenced people. Additionally, it can address and develop ways of reading the Bible that might advance a feminist agenda.

In the same manner, Marxist strategies of interpretation engage in historical work from a Marxist perspective, examining social structures and means of production in the ancient Near East or the Mediterranean world. Again, the Bible is simply one piece of evidence for a scholar inclined in this way. Additionally, as with feminist criticism, contemporary Marxist interpretive strategies and agendas can be brought to bear on the biblical texts with an eye toward the contemporary world.

The demise of the conceptual apparatus that allowed for the dominance of historical-critical interpretation of the Bible has not led to the elimination of historical criticism, nor should it. It has, however, opened the door to critical approaches to the Bible that do not grant historical concerns priority over all others. In theory this means that there is now room for theological concerns to reenter the scholarly realm. However, this has been slow to happen, and it is still a work in process.

Reinvigorating Theological Interpretation

The first thing that must be said is that theological interpretation of Scripture never really stopped. Although it was largely exiled from academic biblical studies, Christians have been consistently interpreting Scripture theologically because their identity as Christians compels them to do so. Reading Scripture theologically does not depend on the support of academics for its survival. Nevertheless, disciplined and scholarly attention to interpreting Scripture theologically can only benefit the practice within the church.

Second, numerous generations of scholars came of age when historical criticism, which is not particularly concerned with theology, was the dominant form of academic biblical studies. Thus, the interpretive practices and strategies that arise when theological concerns and aims are given priority in scriptural interpretation fell into disuse.

Moreover, the academic practice of theology was separated from the practice of academic biblical studies. These two disciplines came to jealously guard their autonomy, making it difficult for scholars to try to work in both fields. It has only been since about the mid-1980s that scholars have started to bridge the gap between theology and biblical studies with the aim of reinvigorating the practice of theological interpretation.

Here is the heart of the matter: *if there is to be a revival of theological interpretation of Scripture among scholars and students, theological concerns must be given priority over other concerns.* At the same time, it will not always be clear how and in what ways the priority of theological concerns will need to take shape in specific times and places. Theological interpretation will always to some degree be constituted by ongoing arguments and debates about how to bring theological concerns to bear on scriptural interpretation, and vice versa. At the very least, however, granting theological concerns priority will involve a return to the practice of using Scripture as a way of ordering and comprehending the world, rather than using the world as a way of comprehending Scripture.

Although, as we have seen, this was the standard practice before the eighteenth century, we today need to relearn this habit for our own time. Exactly how it can be done remains to be seen. Nevertheless, at least two common theological interpretive strategies need to be reinvigorated.

The Rule of Faith

First, Christians will need to read Scripture, as the early church did, in accord with the church's **rule of faith** (the church's basic teachings and traditions, formally represented in **creeds** and functioning as a standard of **orthodoxy**; see also chs. 6, 9, and 12 for discussion). Reading according to the rule of faith is not like following an instruction manual, simply following a set of instructions in order to construct a product. Rather, the rule of faith works more like a moderately flexible framework within which one can order the pieces of a puzzle in order to render an image. While one could argue that the rule of faith operates from the very beginning of Christian scriptural interpretation, it receives an early formulation in St. Irenaeus's dispute with the **gnostic Valentinus** (late second century).

Both Irenaeus and Valentinus recognized that Scripture is an extraordinarily diverse set of writings. Their dispute concerned how to order that diversity. Valentinus and his followers devised a philosophical cosmology (belief system about the universe) that provided a certain order to Scripture. Irenaeus's objection to this strategy was that the cosmology did not originate in the Scriptures themselves, and therefore it was imposing an external order.

Although Valentinus's type of interpretive strategy provides a sort of order to Scripture, it does so at some cost. Above all, it commits one to adopting a set of views that requires so much revision of essential Christian claims about God and the world that the result is not recognizably Christian. Irenaeus argued that such an account is "scriptural" only to the extent that it is stocked with biblical verses. Ordering these verses within a framework provided by a Valentinian cosmology results in a twisted version of the biblical story. Irenaeus likened this procedure to someone who constructs a story from Homeric verse. It is possible to take some texts from the *Odyssey*—in no particular order—and intersperse them with texts from the *Iliad*—again, in no particular order—and thus create a story. This story would contain only Homeric language; it would contain only Homeric characters. Moreover, it could easily convince the uneducated that it was a true Homeric story. Nevertheless, its connections to Homer would be only superficial, and its assertions and narrative would not be Homeric at all (Irenaeus, *Against Heresies* 1.9.4).

Irenaeus's brilliant alternative is to make use of the so-called rule of faith. He develops an account of God's economy (plan) of salvation that has its definitive and climactic moment in the incarnation, death, and resurrection of the Word. By clarifying the economy of salvation in the light of the crucified and risen Lord, Irenaeus can give a coherent account of the various movements of God's economy. This summary account of the whole of God's economy is what he calls the apostolic faith, a faith that is formally represented in the creed. This then provides the framework within which the diversity of Scripture can be rightly ordered so that it can be directed toward advancing the apostolic faith in the life, teaching, and worship of the church—a life, teaching, and worship that is acknowledged throughout the world (*Against Heresies* 1.10.1–3). Of course, what is so striking about Irenaeus's account of the divine economy and the rule of faith is that it is derived from Scripture.

Clearly there is a circular movement here. The diversity of the NT poses a problem that is solved by ordering that diversity in the light of the apostolic faith. Only in the light of the NT, however, does that apostolic faith receive its definitive formulations. As Rowan Greer puts it:

> We could say that the quest which Irenaeus accomplishes is basically the discovery of a principle of interpretation in the apostolic Rule of faith. At the same time . . . it is in another sense Scripture itself that supplies the categories in which the principle is expressed. Text and interpretation are like twin brothers; one can scarcely tell the one from the other. (Kugel and Greer, *Early Biblical Interpretation*, 157)

This circularity is not vicious as long as one recognizes that theological considerations and church tradition are intimately and complexly connected to

Christian interpretation of Scripture. At the same time, the rich and varied history of biblical interpretation following in the wake of Irenaeus indicates that interpreting within the rule of faith does not demand an erasure of Scripture's diversity.

Figural Interpretation

The second consideration that is important if theological concerns are to regain and retain their priority in the theological interpretation of Scripture has to do with the importance of **figural reading**. Figural reading is a practice that is integral to Jewish and Christian study of their respective Scriptures. It is common to contrast figural interpretations with the "**literal sense**" of Scripture. In the Christian theological tradition, however, the "literal sense" does not precisely correspond to our modern notions of "literal." For now, let me propose the following working notion of the "literal sense" of Scripture: the meanings that Christians conventionally ascribe to a passage in their ongoing struggles to live and worship faithfully before the Triune God.[1]

This means that the literal sense of Scripture will be primary; that is, it will be the basis and norm for all subsequent ways of interpreting the text. At the same time, and because God is the ultimate author of Scripture, a passage may have several meanings within its literal sense (as defined above). Think of this famous example from Isaiah 7:14, "Behold, a maiden [LXX, "virgin"] is with child and will bear a son and will name him Immanuel" (author's translation). Read in the context of Isaiah 7–8, the text seems rather clearly to indicate that the child in question here is the son born to Isaiah of Jerusalem in 8:1–4.[2] Some would argue, especially from a "modern" perspective, that this is the only "literal" meaning of the verse. It is equally clear, however, that Matthew's Gospel and the Christian tradition generally take this verse to be a prophetic announcement of the birth of Jesus almost 750 years later. Christians, therefore, can grant that *both* of these are the literal sense of Isaiah 7:14, because God is capable of intending both of these meanings.

---

1. Although in contemporary usage we often understand the word "literal" as referring to the meaning of a text strictly in its original context, my proposal is intended to reflect a broader understanding of "literal" that is characteristic of Christian biblical interpretation through the centuries. Even a dictionary definition of "literal" can allow for this: "taking words in their usual or primary sense and employing the ordinary rules of grammar" (*Concise Oxford Dictionary*, 11th ed. [Oxford: Oxford University Press, 2005]).

2. Readers of Isaiah and Matthew's Gospel will note that neither child takes on the name "Immanuel." Instead, "Immanuel" serves as a designation and a promise.

If we use this working definition of the literal sense, then figural interpretations will rely on a variety of interpretive techniques to extend the literal sense of Scripture in ways that enhance Christians' abilities to live and worship faithfully in the contexts in which they find themselves. The primary importance of figural reading comes from the fact that there will be times when the literal sense of Scripture may not offer us a sufficiently sharp vision to account for the world in which we live.

A Figural Account of Christian Division

Let me offer an example of figural interpretation. The chapters that immediately follow this one will explore the interpretation of Scripture in Protestant, Roman Catholic, Orthodox, and Pentecostal Christian traditions. The fact that these different chapters need to be written at all is tacit recognition that the church of Christ is divided. I do not have the space to explore all of the hows and whys of church division. Instead, as a way of illustrating the nature and importance of figural reading, I want to look at some scriptural passages that might provide Christians with ways of thinking theologically and faithfully about divisions within Christ's one body.

First, we need to notice that the problems of a divided church are not really the same problems as those faced by Catholics and the various reformers of the sixteenth century. Rather, the problems of a divided church as we know it today are really the result of **ecumenism**. The more that Catholics and non-Catholics, for example, recognize one another as true Christians (rather than heretics or members of different religions), the greater the problem of their division, the sharper the pain of this fracture.

If Christians today are to think about this division theologically and scripturally, we need to begin by recognizing that the NT will be of very limited use here. The NT has, for example, some things to say about divisions within the Corinthian church, but those are not at all of the same nature and scope as the divisions we face today. Indeed, if we are to find scriptural lenses for viewing contemporary church divisions, I suggest that we begin by turning to the OT. Interpreted figurally, biblical Israel and its divisions may provide us with ways of thinking and living in our own divided churches.

Passages such as Psalm 106 and Jeremiah 3 lead us to view Israel's division into northern and southern kingdoms as one of the results of Israel's persistent resistance to the Spirit of God. Division is simply one manifestation of this resistance, along with such things as grumbling against God and Moses in the wilderness, lapses into idolatry when Israel occupies the land,

and the request for a human king. Interestingly, each of these manifestations of resistance becomes a form of God's judgment on Israel.

Take the example of Israel's request for a human king in 1 Samuel 8. Although Samuel takes this as a personal affront, God makes it clear that it is simply part of a pattern of Israel's rejection of God's dominion that has carried on from the moment God led the Israelites out of Egypt. This rejection of God results in the granting of a king. The granting of this request becomes the form of God's judgment on Israel as kings become both oppressively acquisitive and idolatrous (cf. 1 Sam. 8:10–18; 12:16–25).

Here we see that one of the forms of God's judgment is giving us what we want. If we treat division in this light, it becomes clear that division is a sign that we are willing to live, and even *desire* to live, separate from our brothers and sisters in Christ. And it is also God's judgment upon that desire. Our failure to love, especially to love our brothers and sisters with whom we are at odds, lies at the root of our willingness and desire for separation. This separation, in the form of church division, is God's judgment on our failure to love as Christ commands.

One of the by-products of Israel's resistance to God's Spirit is that the people's senses become dulled so that they are increasingly unable to perceive the workings of God's Spirit. The prophet Isaiah makes this particularly clear in Isaiah 6:10; 28:9; and 29:9–13. Readers who know the prophets well will recognize that this sort of stupefaction and blindness is a precursor to judgment. At those times when Israel is most in need of hearing God's word and repenting, the people's sin has rendered them least able to hear that word. Because God's covenant is everlasting, however, the judgment that follows leads to restoration. Importantly, it is restoration of a *unified* Israel, as declared in passages such as Jeremiah 3 and Ezekiel 39. Such a vision of restoration may be both a sign of coming judgment on the churches and the basis for hope in a future restoration.

If we look at the divided church in the light of a figural reading of biblical Israel and its division, then we face several conclusions. First, division is one particularly dramatic way of resisting the Spirit of God. Such resistance further dulls our senses so that we are less able to discern the movements and promptings of God's Spirit. Thus we become further crippled in reading God's Word. Throughout their messages, the prophets call for a definite response to this phenomenon: repentance. Whether our senses are so dulled that we cannot discern the proper form of repentance, whether God's judgment is so close at hand that we cannot avoid it, we cannot say. Instead, we are called to repent and to hope in God's unfailing plan of restoration and redemption in Christ.

Conclusion

There is much more to say here if one were to develop this account further. I have merely tried to indicate how figural reading might look today as it extends the literal sense of passages about divided Israel in order to help Christians today view their own divided state.

As a way of concluding, let me state that reading according to the rule of faith, developing habits of figural reading, and more generally maintaining the priority of theological convictions in scriptural interpretation are central practices of theological interpretation. Yet we need to recognize that historical-critical, feminist, Marxist, or other strategies of interpreting the Bible may well yield insights that will be important for theological interpretation. There is little point in advocating the elimination of these other strategies. Rather, Christians can appropriately make use of their results as long as they are keeping their own ends and purposes for interpreting Scripture primary. This calls for wisdom as Christians move in and among the various strategies for interpreting Scripture with an aim toward ever deepening their love of God and of their neighbors (and enemies).

QUESTIONS FOR REFLECTION AND DISCUSSION

1. Rather than being a precise method of interpretation, theological interpretation is more like the exercise of a type of wisdom. How is that wisdom formed in interpreters?
2. Theological interpretation recognizes that a text could have a variety of legitimate interpretations. How might that variety be both a strength and a weakness?
3. How might one make judgments among competing theological interpretations of a passage?

FOR FURTHER READING AND STUDY

Billings, Todd. *The Word of God for the People of God: An Entryway to the Theological Interpretation of Scripture.* Grand Rapids: Eerdmans, 2010. This volume is indeed a very good entryway, particularly from the perspective of the Reformed tradition.

Blowers, Paul. "The *Regula Fidei* and the Narrative Character of Early Christian Faith." *Pro Ecclesia* 6 (1996): 199–228. Useful article relating the importance and function of the rule of faith.

Davis, Ellen F., and Richard B. Hays, eds. *The Art of Reading Scripture*. Grand Rapids: Eerdmans, 2003. Essays by leading theological interpreters, both biblical scholars and theologians.

Fowl, Stephen. *Cascade Companion to the Theological Interpretation of Scripture*. Eugene, OR: Cascade, 2009. Accessible introduction to many of the issues that come up in this chapter.

———. *Engaging Scripture: A Model for Theological Interpretation*. 1998. Reprint, Eugene, OR: Wipf & Stock, 2008. More scholarly than *Reading in Communion* (see below), this book offers a more detailed account of the importance of theological interpretation and outlines some of the central practices and assumptions of such interpretation.

———, ed. *The Theological Interpretation of Scripture*. Oxford: Blackwell, 1997. Essays about theological interpretation and examples of theological interpretations of Exodus 3, Isaiah 53, Matthew 5–7, and Romans 9–11 from patristic, medieval, Reformation, and modern interpreters.

Fowl, Stephen, and L. Gregory Jones. *Reading in Communion*. 1991. Reprint, Eugene, OR: Wipf & Stock, 1998. Accessible volume on the importance of reading Scripture in the context of Christian communities.

Frei, Hans. *The Eclipse of Biblical Narrative*. New Haven: Yale University Press, 1974. Difficult but groundbreaking work that lays out some of the most crucial interpretive shifts that occurred in modernity, why they happened, and what was lost as a result.

Gottwald, Norman. *The Hebrew Bible: A Socio-Literary Introduction*. Philadelphia: Fortress, 1985. A continuation and development of the work started in *The Tribes of Yahweh*.

———. *The Tribes of Yahweh*. New York: Orbis, 1979. One of the first Marxist materialist interpretations of Israel's history.

Green, Joel B. *Seized by Truth: Reading the Bible as Scripture*. Nashville: Abingdon, 2007. Another accessible guide to theological interpretation, including its relationship to historical and other concerns.

Hays, Richard B. "Reading the Bible with Eyes of Faith." *Journal of Theological Interpretation* 1 (2007): 5–22. Proposes twelve "marks," or characteristics, of theological exegesis.

Johnson, Luke. "Imagining the World Scripture Imagines." *Modern Theology* 14 (1998): 165–80. Part of an entire issue of *Modern Theology* devoted to theological interpretation of Scripture, Johnson's work is among the most thoughtful from those who interpret Scripture theologically and can provide a Catholic perspective to balance Watson (below).

Kugel, James L., and Rowan A. Greer. *Early Biblical Interpretation*. Vol. 3. Library of Early Christianity. Philadelphia: Westminster, 1986. Clear and incisive introduction to the history of biblical interpretation in early Judaism and Christianity.

Legaspi, Michael. *The Death of Scripture and the Rise of Biblical Studies*. Oxford: Oxford University Press, 2010. Lucid and closely argued account of the rise of academic study of the Bible in Germany in the eighteenth and nineteenth centuries.

Radner, Ephraim. *Time and the Word: Figural Reading of the Christian Scriptures*. Grand Rapids: Eerdmans, 2016. A study of the theological and philosophical foundations of figural reading, its methods, and its contemporary significance.

Schüssler Fiorenza, Elisabeth. *In Memory of Her*. New York: Crossroad, 1983. Feminist reconstruction of Christian origins that was very important in articulating issues in feminist interpretation of Scripture.

———, ed. *Searching the Scriptures*. 2 vols. New York: Crossroad, 1994. An introduction to Scripture and one-volume commentary on the Bible written by a wide variety of feminist scholars; a good place to begin a study of feminist interpretation.

Seitz, Christopher, and Kathryn Greene-McCreight. *Theological Exegesis*. Grand Rapids: Eerdmans, 1999. Essays celebrating the work of Brevard S. Childs, whose scholarly treatment of the OT as canon has been very influential in opening up questions about how to interpret Scripture theologically.

Treier, Daniel. *Introducing the Theological Interpretation of Scripture: Recovering a Christian Practice*. Grand Rapids: Baker, 2008. A very clear, cogent, accessible account of theological interpretation.

Watson, Francis. *Text, Church, and World*. Edinburgh: T&T Clark, 1994. A vigorous, detailed argument for the importance of the theological interpretation of Scripture that is heavily influenced by Karl Barth and repays careful study.

12

Protestant Biblical Interpretation

Michael J. Gorman

Protestant Christians—those whose churches have their roots in the protests and reformations of the sixteenth century—have often thought of themselves, like the Jewish people, as "people of the book," as Christians who derive their beliefs and practices from the Bible. This is entirely natural and appropriate for people whose churches were born with the words *sola Scriptura*, "Scripture alone," on their lips. Under the influence of Martin Luther, Protestants also stressed the "priesthood of all believers." The corollary of that principle for biblical interpretation was the right, even the duty, of all Christians to read and interpret the Bible themselves. This practice has traveled with Protestant communities and missionaries throughout the world.[1]

Although it is true that the Bible has always been the foundation of Protestant beliefs and practices, it is self-evident from the large variety of Protestant churches, doctrines, and moralities—all claiming to be "biblical"—that this commitment to the centrality of Scripture has not yielded uniformity in its interpretation. Furthermore, despite the great heritage of Protestant commitment

1. This chapter does not deal explicitly with Anglicanism, though many Anglicans around the world would identify closely with Protestantism and with the approaches to the Bible and the surrounding issues discussed here. Anglicans self-identify in various ways; they may share perspectives on Scripture (and more) with Protestants as well as with Pentecostal, Roman Catholic, and Orthodox Christians.

to Scripture, there is concern among many Protestants that the people (and even the pastors) in their churches have become (1) biblically illiterate; and/or (2) disrespectful of the biblical text, especially when it seems to challenge their own presuppositions; and/or (3) skilled at manipulating the text for their own ends. Such concerns are shared fairly equally across the theological spectrum.

In this chapter we briefly examine some of the persistent issues and current trends in the interpretation of Scripture among Protestants, especially as they are manifest in the North American context from which I write.

The Protestant World(s)

This relatively brief chapter cannot possibly speak for or about all Protestants in North America, much less globally (hence the importance of other chapters in this book), but it will consider aspects of biblical interpretation in three Protestant streams that exist in various forms around the world: so-called **mainline churches** and traditions as well as **evangelical** and (to a lesser degree) **fundamentalist** churches and traditions. Much of this chapter is relevant as well to various so-called megachurches, missional churches, postevangelical churches, and intentional Christian communities that are largely indebted to Protestant traditions, especially evangelical ones, even if they do not explicitly self-identify as Protestant.[2]

2. Some representative entities of mainline Protestantism in the United States include the Presbyterian Church (USA) and the United Methodist Church (which is actually a global church); *The Christian Century* magazine; Princeton Theological Seminary (more moderate) and Harvard Divinity School (more liberal); and the National Council of Churches. Globally, mainline Protestantism is symbolized by the World Council of Churches.

Some representative entities of evangelical Protestantism include the Presbyterian Church in America and the Church of the Nazarene; significant "wings" within mainline churches; numerous smaller denominations, including some that have separated from mainline denominations; the magazine *Christianity Today*; Wheaton College (IL); Fuller Theological Seminary (more moderate), which has had an unusual global impact, and Gordon-Conwell Theological Seminary (more conservative); InterVarsity Christian Fellowship; and the Billy Graham Evangelistic Association. (As of this writing in late 2016, the definition of "evangelical" in the United States is in flux and its future uncertain.) Globally, evangelical Protestantism is represented by the World Evangelical Alliance, the International Fellowship of Evangelical Students, and similar entities, as well as many churches and theological schools. (Worldwide, Pentecostalism, discussed in ch. 15, has much in common with broader evangelicalism.) "Progressive" or "liberal" evangelicalism is symbolized in the United States by *Sojourners* magazine. In general, evangelicals around the world have become more socially concerned in the last half-century; globally, many self-defined evangelicals are politically "left of center." (Note: in some parts of the world, "evangelical" means "Protestant" or "Lutheran.")

Fundamentalist Protestantism has been represented in the United States and globally by certain independent Baptist, Pentecostal, and nondenominational churches that are often loosely affiliated with one another (and frequently with US-based churches or mission bodies), as well

One way to organize the streams of contemporary Protestantism is to consider three dimensions of **ecclesial** existence in the world: (1) the church's response to the modern and postmodern intellectual ethos and also to biblical criticism; (2) its theological, social, and political agendas; and (3) its approach to **ecumenical** relations (relations with other professing Christians). Figure 12.1 is a highly simplified way of depicting the wide ecclesial spectrum within Protestantism.

Figure 12.1. An Overview of the Protestant Spectrum

Protestant Tradition	Response to Modern and Postmodern Intellectual Ethos and to Biblical Criticism	Theological, Social, and Political Agendas	Ecumenical Relations
Mainline	General acceptance	Moderate to liberal/ progressive	Dialogue and cooperation with ideologically similar Protestants as well as with Roman Catholicism and Orthodoxy
Evangelical	Gradual and cautious acceptance	Varied: historically conservative to moderate; at times more liberal/ progressive	Interdenominational cooperation primarily with ideologically similar Protestants, but also with more traditionalist Roman Catholics and with Orthodox Christians
Fundamentalist	General rejection	Very conservative	Separatist approach to interchurch cooperation requiring agreement on certain theological convictions (derived from the five "fundamentals")* and, often, social and political views

* The five fundamentals formulated during the fundamentalist-modernist controversy of the early twentieth century were articulated with some differences but generally included the inspiration and inerrancy of Scripture, Christ's deity and virgin birth, his substitutionary atonement, his bodily resurrection and imminent bodily return, and the historicity of miracles. Theologically and sociologically, however, there is much more to fundamentalism.

Because Protestant Christianity constitutes a broad theological spectrum, it is difficult to characterize it fairly into three (or more) categories. Furthermore, there is significant overlap among the branches of Protestantism and their contemporary descendants. For instance, evangelicals focus on biblical **authority**, theological **orthodoxy**, and personal conversion to Christ, but

as by related Bible colleges. In the United States, it is symbolized as well by institutions like Bob Jones University, Liberty University, and Grace Theological Seminary; and by organizations like the (creationist) Institute for Creation Research.

such believers are found in most mainline churches. On the other hand, social justice concerns have generally been associated with mainline or liberal
Christians, but in the last two generations, justice has emerged as central to
many evangelicals, both in the West and especially in the **Majority World**.
And a growing number of mainline Christians as well as evangelicals express
significant theological concerns about modern biblical criticism.

This chapter, then, represents a perspective that has sometimes been called
"generous orthodoxy," an approach to Christian faith and life that affirms
the historic creeds and practices of Christianity with a spirit of openness to
others and to differences of interpretation within the large Christian family.
It might be considered a hybrid of mainline and evangelical Protestantism.[3]

Protestants as People of the Book

Despite their wide diversity, Protestants have historically been unified in naming
the Scriptures as their primary authority for faith and life. Protestants, one
could say, seek to be a "Scripture-shaped community"—so Richard Hays in
his article by that name. (This in no way implies that other Christian traditions do not seek to be Scripture-shaped.) From the Reformation onward, this
devotion to Scripture has been intimately connected to the life of the Triune
God, seeing Scripture as a word from God that bears witness to Christ by the
inspiration and ongoing testimony of the Spirit. The centrality of Scripture
in Protestantism reveals itself in several ways.

First, Protestant worship aims to be biblically shaped and centered. The
sermon is frequently the central and longest element of the worship service,
averaging fifteen to twenty minutes in many mainline churches and thirty to
forty-five minutes in many evangelical and fundamentalist churches. For many
Protestant churches, communion is only a monthly or quarterly event, and
the sermon is the primary aspect of worship by which members are spiritually nourished. Protestant ministers are generally expected to be informed,
well-prepared, relevant, and inspiring preachers.

Protestants have a long tradition of reading Scripture at worship and of
using biblical language in their corporate prayer (whether spontaneous or
prepared) and song. Many Protestant churches have regularly read or sung a
psalm at every service, and some have regularly recited the Ten Commandments

---

3. The term "generous orthodoxy" was coined by Yale theologian Hans Frei and popular-
ized by, e.g., pastor-author Brian McLaren and preacher-author Fleming Rutledge. My use
of the term as shorthand for this chapter's approach, however, is not an endorsement of any
particular interpretation of the term.

(the **Decalogue**). In recent decades, some churches have instituted the use of a **lectionary**, or compilation of Scripture readings for each Sunday, which in some denominations is obligatory while in others optional. Some churches, however, read only a single biblical passage that is the text for the sermon. Protestant hymnody is generally rich in biblical language and imagery, from the great traditional hymns of Martin Luther, Charles Wesley, and Isaac Watts to the praise songs of contemporary worship.

Second, the Bible is central to Protestant Christian education (increasingly called "formation") and life together ("fellowship"). Protestant churches have historically stressed having children learn Bible stories and memorize key Bible verses. For youth and adults, the focus is often on understanding biblical "principles" and applying them to daily life. Protestant publishers, representing the entire theological spectrum, have issued books claiming to expound biblical principles for living—everything from raising children to making love to accumulating wealth (or giving it away). Newer approaches to biblical interpretation have also affected Protestant Christian formation, such as the notion of inhabiting the world and narrative of Scripture, or finding our stories in the biblical story and its stories.

Protestant publishers have also produced untold numbers of Bible study guides for personal or group use inside or outside the church. These tend to be based on what is often called the "inductive" method of Bible study, a kind of commonsense approach in which participants ask questions of the text, sometimes with little reference to its historical context. In addition, many church-related publishing houses have produced more sophisticated education materials, including video series that feature biblical scholars. Moreover, Bible study leaders are generally encouraged to consult commentaries, of which there are many (of varying quality) accessible to laypeople.

Third, Protestants have generally promoted biblical scholarship. Protestant biblical scholars are plentiful in the Society of Biblical Literature, the largest organization of professional biblical specialists in the world; in most national or regional professional societies around the world; and even in the Catholic Biblical Association. In addition, evangelical societies such as the Institute for Biblical Research and Tyndale Fellowship for Biblical and Theological Research contribute to biblical scholarship internationally. Protestant pastors are generally expected to benefit from the best biblical research, first as seminary students and then, through continuing study of commentaries and other works of scholarship, as lifelong learners in their pastorates.

Fourth, the Bible is at the heart of Protestant personal spirituality and, when it is present in a church, social action. One of the norms of Protestant piety is a daily time of "devotions," sometimes called a "quiet time," in which believers read Scripture and/or a scripturally based meditation and engage in (primarily intercessory) prayer. This time can vary from a few minutes to an hour, but it is entered into with the presupposition that God speaks to individuals through Scripture (and perhaps an inspirational writer or devotional booklet). More recently some Protestants, both mainline and evangelical, have turned to regular communal prayer, often using a form of Anglican or Catholic **liturgical** prayer.[4]

From their commitment to the authority of Scripture, Protestant Christians also often find their mandates for social and political action in addition to personal conduct. While they may agree on certain basics (e.g., the importance of feeding the hungry and clothing the naked), Protestants are less likely to agree about matters that the Bible does not explicitly address (e.g., abortion), only cursorily addresses (e.g., homosexual relations), or addresses ambiguously (e.g., male-female relations). Nevertheless, statements from Protestant churches on social, political, and ethical matters are generally filled with biblical references and biblical interpretation; a proposed statement will not be passed, or an existing statement long endure, unless it is thought by the decision makers in the church or denomination to address and rightly interpret Scripture. This is the stuff of which church wars are made, and it suggests that biblical interpretation is as much a *problem* as it is a distinguishing trait for Protestant churches.

The Problem of Biblical Interpretation

It has often been said that common sense is not so common. So too, perhaps, with Scripture: the plain sense may not always be so plain, so clear.

An Example

An example will illustrate the problem: it was self-evident to many white, Protestant slave owners in the United States that the plain sense of the Bible was that whites were superior to blacks (believed to be descendants of Ham, cursed by Noah in Gen. 9:25) and entitled to own them. Similar arguments for apartheid were mustered by Dutch Protestants in South Africa until late in the twentieth century. The clear biblical texts and principles to which whites

---

4. See especially the popular *Common Prayer: A Liturgy for Ordinary Radicals* (Grand Rapids: Zondervan, 2010) by Shane Claiborne, Jonathan Wilson-Hartgrove (a contributor to this book [ch. 23]), and Enuma Okoro.

zealously clung were not so clear to the blacks they oppressed, nor are they clear to us today. What has changed? Our understanding of the biblical text? Yes and no. To be sure, we have a more informed and sophisticated understanding of texts about Ham and Shem, about ancient and more recent forms of slavery, about oppression and justice. More importantly, however, we have a better comprehension of the process of reading and interpreting texts. We have learned, for example, that our perception of the "plain sense" of Scripture is greatly affected by the traditions and communities, small and large, within which we read the biblical texts. Exegesis without presuppositions is impossible, as the Protestant biblical theologian Rudolf Bultmann proclaimed early in the last century. That is to say, we are shaped by ideologies or "-isms"— together with the practices those "-isms" entail—that surround us. (Later in the chapter we will return to the importance of practices for interpretation.)

The Context(s) of (Mis-)Interpretation

For several decades now, Christians have been becoming increasingly aware of the effects of racism and sexism on their biblical interpretation. More recently the theologian Stanley Hauerwas has convinced many Western Protestants that we are also inappropriately formed by modern liberalism, democratic pluralism, and nationalism. And biblical theologian Walter Brueggemann has argued convincingly that much Western scriptural interpretation is distorted by what he calls "military consumerism" or "commodity militarism."[5] These interpretive tendencies are sometimes more explicit in fundamentalist and conservative evangelical churches, but they are hardly absent from the mainline traditions. And due to Western influence on global Christianity, both during and after colonialism, these sorts of interpretive postures have been exported around the world. Today it is common to hear certain Protestant preachers in the Majority World, for instance, offer a thoroughly North American prosperity gospel.

An example more recent than slavery or apartheid will serve to illustrate these sorts of concerns. On September 14, 2001, three days after 9/11, in the Washington National Cathedral, US President George W. Bush (a United Methodist) concluded his address by quoting an abridged version of Romans 8, which includes the words "nothing can separate us from the love of God in Christ Jesus our Lord." Bush deleted the reference to Christ and implicitly

5. See Walter Brueggemann, *Theology of the Old Testament: Testimony, Dispute, Advocacy* (Minneapolis: Augsburg Fortress, 1997), 486, 718–20, and his other books. Brueggemann argues that Scripture offers a counternarrative to the West's metanarrative (grand story) of militarism and consumerism.

interpreted the word "us" as a reference to the people of the United States. The service concluded with a military color guard marching forward as the congregation sang the "Battle Hymn of the Republic," after the president, the Reverend Billy Graham, and others had assured everyone listening of God's blessing as the war on terror began. Here was a subtle but sophisticated misreading of a key biblical text: a de-Christianizing, universalizing interpretation shaped by pluralism, on the one hand, and by militarism and nationalism, on the other.

In some respects, the various methods of biblical interpretation that thrived in the twentieth century were attempts at curbing supposedly plain-sense readings and making readers acknowledge their presuppositions and the cultural distance between them and the biblical texts. Attempts at more "scientific" or "historical" readings, and then at more "literary" ones, were ways of addressing the problem. Ultimately, however, these approaches revealed more problems than they solved.

The peculiar problem we are describing derives from the close relationship between Christianity and culture since the first Europeans settled in what is now North America. It is certainly not the only issue. Some, in fact, would claim that the more pressing issue is that of biblical authority, in either theology or ethics or both. But we cannot really discuss biblical authority without having first considered the cultural context of interpreting the Bible as our authoritative text.

Questions of Authority

For many years, most Protestants assumed that biblical authority was the Protestant alternative to the authority of the pope or the authority of tradition. Indeed, some non-Protestants (and even some Protestants) have accused certain elements in the Protestant tradition of having a "paper pope" or even of "bibliolatry" (Bible worship).

The acceptance of biblical criticism, the advent of more sophisticated approaches to reading and interpretation, and the modern and postmodern challenges to traditional Christian theology and ethics in the past century generated a widespread crisis in authority within nearly all the Christian churches. The authority of the Bible—both the existence and the nature of that authority—became a matter of dispute. Today the most pressing question for Protestants may well be, what is the role of Scripture in relation to other authorities? Many Protestants implicitly recognize some form of the so-called **Wesleyan quadrilateral** of four authorities, or guides: Scripture, tradition, reason, and experience. Which is the primary locus of authority? How do we interpret and utilize each of them? How do these authorities relate to one another, especially when they seem to be in conflict?

- Is the primary authority *human experience*? If so, then do we risk remaking God in our own image?
- Is it *the theological tradition*? If so, which part(s) of the broad Christian tradition?
- Is it *the Spirit*? If so, how do we know what the Spirit is saying? Can the Spirit speak apart from or even against the Scriptures?
- Is it *the Bible*, the canonical Scriptures, or is it *part of the Bible—a canon within the canon*? If either of these, does the authority reside in the text itself? Which parts of the text? Or is it in the overarching scriptural narrative? And which interpreter or tradition is the authoritative voice concerning the canon, the canon within the canon, or the trajectory of the canon?
- Is it *the eternal Word* to which the Scriptures bear witness? If so, is that Word the living Christ, the Christ of the Gospels, or the historical Jesus? And which aspect of the life and teaching found in the Gospels, or which version of the historical Jesus, is the church's authority?
- Or does the authority reside in *the interpretive community* to which the text speaks and which the text forms? If so, which "community"?

An obvious example of the crisis of authority is in the question of human sexuality. Protestant Christians differ on every imaginable point:

- what the biblical texts that are explicitly about sexuality actually say, and why;
- which other biblical texts and themes (about inclusion, justice, purity, holiness, diversity, and so forth) might or might not be relevant, and why;
- the ignorance of biblical authors concerning modern discoveries and theories about human sexuality, and whether that ignorance matters;
- the reliability and relevance of those modern discoveries and theories;
- the problem of whether the church's tradition and historical practice is known, or knowable, or just, or relevant;
- the issue of whether the Spirit can lead the contemporary church along paths that alter the "plain sense," the literal reading, or the "traditional interpretation" of the biblical text; and

- the question of the cultural and ideological contexts (e.g., political liberalism or conservatism) that shape the church's interpretive practices.

Despite a certain emerging ethos regarding human sexuality among many North American and European Protestants, this ethos has met with firm resistance among most Protestants in the Majority World, often raising a new form of the issue of colonial oppression from Western powers and causing splits within ecclesial bodies.

For Protestant Christians, the challenge of biblical interpretation and authority within these sorts of contexts and concerns has created a constellation of persistent issues as well as emerging trends. To these trends, many of which are echoed globally, we now turn.

Some Trends in Protestant Biblical Interpretation

Like any human endeavor, biblical interpretation is not a static but rather an evolving discipline. Though it would be misleading to suggest that the trends discussed below have developed among all Protestants, or that older ways of interpretation have died out, it is nonetheless fair to say that there have been dramatic shifts in emphasis. The following discussion identifies seven of these shifts, even as we stress that there still exists great diversity in Protestant biblical interpretation, and that the evolution we are describing is still filtering down from academic biblical interpreters to pastors to laypeople.

The Focus of Interpretation: From the Nation to the Kingdom of God

Since their nation's founding, most Protestants in the United States have had some sense that their land and nation have a special place in the divine economy (**American exceptionalism**), that it is the "city on a hill" of Matthew 5 (cf. 5:14–15), ordained to give the light (of freedom, democracy, and so forth) to all the world. This has resulted in the mission of creating some form of implicit or explicit "Christian America" or Christian culture, however that might be understood and despite the alleged separation of church and state. Protestants in European countries often lived within a state that had an established church (e.g., Lutheran or Anglican) and thus a more explicit **Christendom**. Within both forms of Christendom, the focus of biblical interpretation (not to mention other theological endeavors, especially ethics) is not merely or even primarily the Christian individual or church. It is the nation-state and its citizens.

Today most Protestants recognize that such a Christendom no longer exists. Although some US Protestants (especially fundamentalists and the most conservative evangelicals) acknowledge this reality with chagrin and try to re-Christianize the country's people and its government, an increasing number of Protestants realize that the experiment was a failure because it was flawed. The focus of the Christian Bible is not the United States, or any other nation-state, but the kingdom of God, which both transcends and incorporates all the world's peoples. The Christian Bible is addressed to a distinct people (the church) called out from the nations, and it is therefore to be interpreted by and for that distinct people as it seeks to spread the good news of the kingdom throughout *all* nations. Living "after Christendom" (see, for example, Stanley Hauerwas's book with that title) means reading the Bible with this sort of ecclesial (church) focus, not with an eye on what the Bible means "for our country." For many under the influence of John Howard Yoder, who wrote from within the Anabaptist tradition (the "peace churches"), and for Hauerwas (who is himself influenced by Yoder), this shift also means understanding the church as an alternative culture, or political entity, and reading Scripture to form the church in its concrete social existence.

This is not to say, of course, that Protestants now think that nation-states have no accountability to biblical standards. Quite the contrary is the case, in fact, for if *no* nation is the special focus of God's activity, then *no* nation has a claim to special status, but *all* nations are equally answerable, for instance, to the prophetic demands for social justice. This does not mean, however, that all Protestants always agree on what justice is.

The Locus of Interpretation: From the Individual to the Christian Community

This shift in *focus* has also entailed a shift in the *locus* (location, context) of interpretation. Protestant Christians increasingly interpret the Bible in and as the church, rather than merely as individuals. But this shift poses a challenge to the supposed ideal of the Reformation as many came to understand it, in which the individual believer is so central. Recently many Protestants have come to see that this interpretation of the Reformation was a classic case of the pendulum swinging too far in one direction. Neither the earliest Christians nor the Reformers understood biblical interpretation as a private affair, even if it is the responsibility of each person within the church.

Since NT times, Christian communities have been called to mutual instruction and admonishment, which is to say, interpreting Scripture and the ongoing work of the Spirit together, *in communion* (see Fowl and Jones, *Reading in Communion*), not merely in private. For many Protestants, this recent recovery of community has also meant a renewed appreciation for previous generations of interpreters, both great (like Augustine, Luther, and Calvin) and small, and thus also a new respect for tradition. For a growing number of Protestant theologians, this recovery of tradition means also a commitment to biblical interpretation within the framework of the church's core convictions, or *regula fidei* (rule of faith; see chs. 6, 9, and 11). This is one aspect of the movement known as **theological interpretation** (see ch. 11). Christian theological interpretation affirms, therefore, that scriptural interpretation should be explicitly Christocentric (which does not mean **Marcionite**—dismissive of the OT) and done within a trinitarian framework.

To be sure, this development does not mean the end of the Protestant Christian's private reading of Scripture. Rather, it seeks to situate that experience within a larger, communal context that provides a rationale for personal biblical interpretation, as well as a means of correction for the individual when it is needed. It does mean, however, that it is primarily the church, rather than the individual, that discerns the contours of faithful and appropriate biblical interpretation, spurred on from time to time (paradoxically but necessarily) by a prophetic voice that runs counter to both the community as community and to its many individual voices.

The Perspective of Interpretation: From the Powerful to the Powerless

The need for that kind of prophetic voice, in fact, leads to the next recent shift in Protestant biblical interpretation: a shift in perspective from the powerful to the powerless. When Western Protestant Christianity as a whole believed that its perspective on the world and on the faith was the right one (by virtue of its specially "blessed" location), it was looking out from the perspective of power and privilege. But for several decades now, prophetic voices have been calling Protestants (and others) to see things from the margins, from the perspectives of the oppressed: the poor, women and minorities, the socially outcast. There has been a call, and in many circles an affirmative response, to read the Bible with Christians in the Majority World and with the persecuted church—to interpret the Bible as the revelation of the God of the oppressed (see the classic books by Robert McAfee Brown and James Cone).

This shift began in more liberal Protestant circles but has been embraced by many evangelicals as well. An increasing number of younger evangelicals have deliberately moved into places "abandoned by empire," often in small intentional communities, in order to follow Jesus—and interpret Scripture—among the poor (see ch. 23).

The Presupposition of Interpretation: From Inerrancy or Suspicion to Polyvalence and Trust

John Calvin talked of Scripture as divine accommodation to human weakness, while Luther compared Scripture to the hay-filled manger that housed the divine Word at its incarnation. But after the eighteenth-century **Enlightenment**, and especially in the late nineteenth and twentieth centuries, many Protestants increasingly felt the need to defend the Bible's inspiration against the attacks of detractors. Strict defenders of the Bible's inspiration argued that it was free of error even with respect to history and science. The fundamentalist-modernist controversy, exemplified in the famous Scopes trial about evolution, was perhaps the most well-known manifestation of this phenomenon, which split some American Protestant denominations and institutions.

The debate about the Bible's **inerrancy** continued, especially among fundamentalists and evangelicals, through the middle and even into the latter part of the twentieth century, often very stridently. These Protestants asked: Is the Bible without error in scientific and historical matters as well as matters of faith (theology and ethics)? Is it better to describe the Bible less strictly as "infallible" (unable to fail in its divine intention) or simply as "inspired"? Many mainline Protestants, eventually joined by more progressive evangelicals, adopted the neo-orthodox approach of theologian Karl Barth, who saw the Bible not as revelation but as *witness* to revelation. They soon began wondering if there were limitations inherent in the Bible, due to its fully human character as a product of ancient (especially patriarchal) times, and even if there were "errors" in its theology and ethics. The "Bible's attitude" toward women, slaves, LGBTQI (lesbian, gay, bisexual, transgender, queer or questioning, and intersex) persons, and so on—or that of the Bible's interpreters—was seen by some as oppressive.

Carried to an extreme, this line of reasoning led (and leads) certain interpreters to embrace a radical **hermeneutic of suspicion** toward the Bible, a kind of guilty-until-proven-innocent approach to the text. Having concluded that some or even much of Scripture is inherently patriarchal, oppressive, exclusive, or otherwise problematic, these interpreters often adopted a **hermeneutic of liberation**: the Bible's inspiration and authority lie in its power to liberate, and texts perceived to be nonliberating ought to be subordinated to Scripture's liberating and inclusive trajectory. Such concerns are expressed not only about parts of the OT but also, and often, about the writings of Paul, which are frequently (but misguidedly) contrasted with the Gospel accounts of Jesus' life and teachings.[6]

---

6. For a corrective, see J. R. Daniel Kirk, *Jesus Have I Loved, but Paul? A Narrative Approach to the Problem of Pauline Christianity* (Grand Rapids: Baker Academic, 2011).

The wide Protestant spectrum of opinion about the Bible's inspiration—from theories of complete inerrancy (some even assuming divine dictation) to the hermeneutics of suspicion—will probably never be compressed into one mediating position. Nevertheless, in recent years there has been a more balanced tendency to acknowledge the complex character of the Bible as both human and divine word, on analogy to the incarnation of the eternal Word as fully human and fully divine (see Goldingay, *Models of Scripture*). This perspective allows for a certain "weakness" in the Bible, by virtue of its humanity, without denying its power as inspired divine word (see Richard Hays, "A Hermeneutic of Trust").

Many Protestants today are more comfortable with the idea that all texts, even biblical texts, have (or generate) a **surplus of meaning**, sometimes described as the **polyvalence** of the text. This approach also attempts to avoid the extremes of the hermeneutic of suspicion, which is sometimes too quick to dismiss texts that appear (at the moment) to be oppressive or obsolete. A **hermeneutic of trust**, which expects our encounter with Scripture to effect a **conversion of the imagination** (the terms of Richard Hays), invites the text to speak afresh in new situations, in spite of its real or perceived limitations. At the same time, a postmodern *Christian* commitment to polyvalence is an invitation, not to "anything goes," but to what some have called "creative fidelity" or "responsible plurality" (see the volume edited by Porter and Malcolm).

The Prerequisite of Interpretation: From Knowledge to Character

The notion of a hermeneutic of trust suggests yet another recent shift: the idea that proper interpretation of the Bible is dependent on interpreters' having a certain character that predisposes them toward the biblical message. This is quite a subtle yet radical shift.

For a long time, Protestants have operated on the assumption that the most important thing needed for biblical interpretation is knowledge. Fundamentalists and some evangelical Christians have thought that the more intimately one knew Scripture (through memorization and study of the text's "plain sense"), the better one could interpret it, especially by comparing Scripture with Scripture. Other evangelical Christians, as well as many mainline Protestants, have put their stock in the sort of knowledge one gains from academic study of ancient history and biblical languages.

Both types of knowledge are, of course, valuable. But the recent emphasis in Protestant biblical interpretation has been on the requisite *character* of the interpreter, not on his or her *knowledge*. In other words, interpretation is a function of certain practices that make interpretation both possible and meaningful. This means, for example, that a person or community cannot rightly interpret the teachings of Jesus about forgiveness and nonviolence without practicing forgiveness and nonviolence. This principle finds an analogy in music and the arts generally. For example, the best interpreter of Bach's music is not simply one who knows a lot about the composer's life and times, or even about the theory of contrapuntal music. Certainly these are valuable and perhaps even necessary fields of study for the interpreter of Bach—the conductor or organist, for instance. But to really conduct or play Bach, one must *love* Bach, one must *imbibe* Bach. Similarly, many Protestants now say, one must embrace and live the biblical message before one can truly interpret it. And this leads naturally to the very meaning of the word "interpretation."

The Goal of Interpretation: From Information to Formation/ Transformation and Mission

For many Protestants, the interpretation of the Bible has been understood as an intellectual endeavor, whether done in a church Bible class or in a meeting of a professional academic guild. Although few would have denied the need for the "application" of biblical principles to personal or church life, they would have seen—and some still see—the goal of interpretation as the accumulation of more accurate "information," or the acquisition of a more biblically rooted theology.

Good information and sound theology are certainly not bad per se, but neither do they constitute the true goal of interpretation, according to the most recent interpreters of interpretation. The proper goal of interpretation, they say, is not *information* but *formation* and *transformation*. Character, in other words, is not only the *prerequisite* of interpretation but also the very *purpose* of interpretation. In fact, many say (and as the analogy to music from the previous section suggests), the best way to define interpretation is as *performance*: the essence, the goal, of interpretation is a faithful but creative performance of the text in a new setting (see Laytham, "Interpretation on the Way to Emmaus"). This understanding of interpretation makes it inherently a spiritual and ethical task, not merely an intellectual one. It also reinforces the importance of community. If the goal of interpretation is performance, then an orchestra of musicians, or a cast of characters, is needed to bring the text to life and achieve the goal of interpretation.

One way of describing this goal is to say that the purpose of biblical interpretation is for the community of faith to become a ***living exegesis*** of the text—an embodiment of, say, the justice of God or the love of Christ to which the Scriptures bear witness. Such an approach to Scripture has been recently labeled a **missional hermeneutic** (see ch. 24). For instance, to understand that in Christ, God was reconciling the world means to practice Christlike peacemaking and reconciliation in the home, church, and world. This shift in the goal of interpretation also coalesces with the shift from the nation to the kingdom of God as the focus of interpretation. The goal of interpretation is growth in *discipleship* and *witness to the kingdom* rather than *citizenship*.

Scriptural interpretation is thus a process of individual and communal discernment about becoming a faithful witness to and participant in God's project of bringing saving life to the world. At the same time, such an approach needs to be grounded in a deeply spiritual reading of the Bible for personal and communal formation in Christlike holiness (see ch. 20).

The Means of Interpretation: From Excavation to Engagement

Finally, these new understandings of interpretation raise questions about the means to do biblical interpretation in the twenty-first century. When interpretation is understood primarily as the discovery of knowledge about the Bible, or the Bible in its cultural and linguistic worlds, the Bible is treated like an archaeological site—something to be excavated for all the information about the artifacts and their world that it can provide. Archaeology is a noble academic discipline, and the sort of understanding of the biblical text it provides can be useful; but it is not sufficient for biblical interpretation in the church.

Rather, the trend that has emerged in recent discussion and practice is the focus on fully engaging the text as God's word, as divine address to the church. Interpretation understood as biblical excavation, however fascinating and useful, is an abortive process. This means that even the most sophisticated tools of excavation, such as the various methods of **historical-critical** inquiry and literary analysis discussed in chapter 10, are inherently insufficient for the task because they help us to encounter the text merely in its humanity. Such tools may be helpful and even necessary, though some interpreters—and not just fundamentalists—argue that they not only fail to engage the holiness and inspired character of the biblical text, but also that they are in some cases inherently alien to the text and thus to its proper engagement.

Thus, these means of biblical analysis must be supplemented (some would even say replaced) by means that allow the church to engage the Bible as sacred text. This has given rise to the movement of ecclesially located and focused scriptural interpretation known as theological interpretation. Some have suggested, for example, that **premodern, precritical** approaches to the text be recovered for use today. There has therefore been a steadily growing interest in **patristic** interpretation of Scripture and in **reception history** of the

Bible more generally (see chs. 8–9). Whether or not the future of Protestant biblical interpretation belongs to the past, one thing is clear: if Protestant churches are going to offer a life-giving word to people, and if they are to face the internal and external challenges of the twenty-first century, they have no choice but to engage the Bible, in their preaching and teaching, with spiritual, prophetic, theological, and missional vigor and imagination.

One Ongoing Challenge

One persistent phenomenon, possibly suggesting that the shifts we have been considering have not fully occurred, is Protestants' fondness for **eschatology** (the doctrine of the last things), and specifically speculation about Christ's second coming (the **parousia**). This phenomenon is as old as Christianity itself, but it has been a major focus of American **fundamentalism** and evangelicalism, and it has been exported globally. In the early twentieth century, the **dispensationalist** theories of John N. Darby, a nineteenth-century British leader of the Plymouth Brethren, became the basis of the notes in the popular Scofield Reference Bible (published in 1909). Darby believed that history was divided into distinct eras called "dispensations," and that the current age was the last dispensation before the return of Christ, to be accompanied by signs and upheavals.[7] By the 1970s these sorts of speculations about the "end times" had made their way into the writings of Hal Lindsey (e.g., *The Late Great Planet Earth*), and a generation later into the best-selling Left Behind series of **apocalyptic** novels by Tim LaHaye and Jerry Jenkins, not to mention innumerable sermons and websites.

Pastors and Bible teachers around the world influenced by this school of thought have constructed elaborate end-time scenarios and timetables. Critics contend that such interpreters use the Bible as a box of puzzle pieces, without examining the original context and purpose of individual biblical texts, to create a coherent story that would, ironically, be incoherent to any of the biblical writers. They find predictions about contemporary world events (particularly concerning the Middle East) in the ancient biblical texts. Again, critics of these interpreters argue that their perspectives reveal more about the interpreters' own politics and fantasies than about the biblical text. A

7. One aspect of this form of biblical interpretation was, and is, belief in the "**rapture**" of faithful Christians (based on particular interpretations of Rev. 4:1; 1 Thess. 4, and certain Gospel texts). While the second coming of Christ is a basic Christian belief, most biblical scholars and theologians do not accept the "rapture"—which essentially says Christ will return twice, once *for* the saints and once *with* the saints (as some have put it)—as a biblical teaching.

more Christocentric, prophetic, and missional reading of Revelation and other apocalyptic biblical texts is needed, and indeed possible (see Gorman, *Reading Revelation Responsibly*).

Conclusion

In many ways the story of Christianity, and especially of Protestantism, is the story of its interpretation of the Bible. In this chapter we have looked briefly at the complexity of that story as it has been recently told in at least some Protestant circles. The trends that we have examined ought not to obscure the fact that Protestantism remains a richly variegated, a complicated, and in many ways a divided house. Whether the trends identified in this chapter continue, and whether they contribute to further rupture or further healing, we cannot yet know. But the future story of Protestant Christianity will no doubt remain the story of its biblical interpretation. Therefore the current divisions will be healed, or not, and the contemporary crises resolved, or not, through processes of biblical interpretation.

QUESTIONS FOR REFLECTION AND DISCUSSION

1. How and why do Protestant Christians, despite their historic deep commitment to the Bible, differ about so many topics and concerns related to Christian faith and life? Is this a good situation, a bad one, or a mixture of both? If you see it as at least somewhat problematic, what are some ways to address the problem?

2. Which aspects of the various shifts in Protestant biblical interpretation described in this chapter have you seen or experienced, whether in the preshift or postshift setting? (For example, either nationalistic approaches to Scripture or more kingdom-oriented approaches? individualistic and/or communal approaches?)

3. What do you think you can gain from the Protestant approach(es) to interpreting Scripture described in this chapter (whatever your own tradition)?

FOR FURTHER READING AND STUDY

Bartholomew, Craig G. *Introducing Biblical Hermeneutics: A Comprehensive Framework for Hearing God in Scripture*. Grand Rapids: Baker Academic, 2015. A sophisticated theological and philosophical exploration of scriptural interpretation.

Brown, Jeannine K. *Scripture as Communication: Introducing Biblical Hermeneu-tics.* Grand Rapids: Baker Academic, 2007. A careful, evangelical approach, both theoretical and practical, to Scripture as "communicative act."

Brown, Robert McAfee. *Unexpected News: Reading the Bible with Third World Eyes.* Philadelphia: Westminster, 1984. An influential demonstration of liberation themes in the Bible and their importance for the church.

Cone, James H. *God of the Oppressed.* New York: Seabury, 1975. A landmark lib-erationist reading of Scripture from a distinguished African American theologian.

Fowl, Stephen E., and L. Gregory Jones. *Reading in Communion: Scripture and Eth-ics in Christian Life.* 1991. Reprint, Eugene, OR: Wipf & Stock, 1998. A modern classic on the role of character and community in understanding interpretation as embodiment.

Goldingay, John. *Models of Scripture.* 1994. Reprint, Eugene, OR: Wipf & Stock, 2002. A theology of Scripture as witnessing tradition, authoritative canon, inspired word, and experienced revelation.

Gorman, Michael J. *Reading Revelation Responsibly: Uncivil Worship and Witness—Following the Lamb into the New Creation.* Eugene, OR: Cascade, 2011. A critique of the Left Behind approach to Revelation and of nationalistic civil religion, offering a Christocentric and missional reading of Revelation.

Green, Joel B. *Seized by Truth: Reading the Bible as Scripture.* Nashville: Abingdon, 2007. An accessible guide to theological interpretation, including its relationship to historical and other concerns.

Hauerwas, Stanley. *After Christendom? How the Church Is to Behave If Freedom, Justice, and a Christian Nation Are Bad Ideas.* Nashville: Abingdon, 1991. An accessible manifesto on the role of the church as an alternative community.

Hays, Richard B. "A Hermeneutic of Trust." In *The Conversion of the Imagination: Paul as Interpreter of Israel's Scripture,* 190–201. Grand Rapids: Eerdmans, 2005. A significant call for the use of a hermeneutic of trust in reading the Bible.

———. "Scripture-Shaped Community: The Problem of Method in New Testament Ethics." *Interpretation* 44 (1990): 42–55. Methodological considerations about how the NT should be used to form the life of the Christian church.

Jenkins, Philip. *The New Faces of Christianity: Believing the Bible in the Global South.* New York: Oxford University Press, 2006. An appreciative study of the role of Scripture among Christians in Africa, Asia, and Latin America.

Laytham, D. Brent. "Interpretation on the Way to Emmaus: Jesus Performs His Story." *Journal of Theological Interpretation* 1, no. 1 (Spring 2007): 101–15. Example of, and argument for, scriptural interpretation as performance.

Porter, Stanley E., and Matthew R. Malcolm. *The Future of Biblical Interpretation: Responsible Plurality in Biblical Hermeneutics.* Downers Grove, IL: InterVarsity, 2013. Essays on theological, historical, and ecclesial responsibility by leading biblical scholars such as Anthony Thiselton, James Dunn, and Walter Moberly.

Wright, N. T. *Scripture and the Authority of God: How to Read the Bible Today.* New York: HarperCollins, 2011. A guide to reading the Bible as Scripture, building on Wright's proposal that the biblical story should be seen as a five-act drama.

Yoder, John Howard. *To Hear the Word.* 2nd ed. Eugene, OR: Cascade, 2010. Essays by a highly influential Anabaptist scholar who advocated Jesus as the norm of the church's social and political witness.

13

Roman Catholic Biblical Interpretation

RONALD D. WITHERUP

The Roman Catholic Church is the only Christian denomination with a substantial body of authoritative teachings about the Bible and its use in the life of the Church. Whereas Protestant traditions have historically emphasized the principle of *sola Scriptura* (see ch. 12), the Catholic Church emphasizes Scripture *and* Tradition as two expressions of one divine revelation. Thus, any discussion of biblical interpretation within Roman Catholicism must take into account the official documents that have expressed and governed this complex relationship between Scripture and Church teaching (see Béchard, *Scripture Documents*). These began as early as the fourth century CE, the time of St. Cyril of Jerusalem, and have continued to the present.

Key Documents

For hundreds of years, until the time of the **Enlightenment,** Catholics—like almost everyone else—accepted the Bible without questioning the historicity of the text. However, Catholics had also developed a great sensitivity to deeper, more spiritual meanings of biblical texts, primarily under the influence of **patristic** commentators (see ch. 9). With the onset of significant scientific studies[1] of the Bible in the eighteenth and nineteenth centuries, most of which were conducted by Protestant scholars, the Catholic Church became fearful of such research. Thus, the tendency was to avoid promoting biblical study and to rely solely on the Church's interpretation of biblical texts. It is no exaggeration to say that Catholics viewed the Bible as the domain of Protestants, while Catholics emphasized the sacraments.

Only near the end of the nineteenth century, under Pope Leo XIII, did a glimmer of light shine on the Church's official stance. Leo's **encyclical** (a papal circular letter to address a specific issue) *Providentissimus Deus* cautiously urged Catholic scholars to participate in biblical research, but in a way that would not raise questions about the historicity of the Bible or cause skepticism on the part of the faithful. In 1902 he also established the Pontifical Biblical Commission (PBC), an official body (originally consisting of cardinals but now composed of Catholic biblical scholars from around the world) whose job was to help guide Catholics in their appreciation of the Bible, albeit in a cautious and vigilant manner. Thus began a tiny ripple that was felt primarily in monastic settings, where a small number of Catholic scholars were already quietly doing biblical research.

From then on, however, the Church's official stance grew in stages. While it is not possible to rehearse all the official documents, certain key texts are worth noting, summarized in figure 13.1 (p. 242).[2] Even though all of these documents constitute official Church teachings, there is a hierarchy of authoritative teachings within Roman Catholicism, indicated in the table by the letters A, B, and C. Texts created by **ecumenical councils**, called "constitutions," have the highest **authority** (A), followed by papal encyclicals (B) and other papally approved writings (C).

These eight documents are the most important in terms of their promotion of historical-critical and other scientific methods of studying the Bible. In essence, in the short span of little more than a century, Roman Catholics came from an underdeveloped and fearful approach to scholarly study of the Bible to a full-fledged participation in it, even to the point of becoming equal dialogue partners with Protestant counterparts.

1. Roman Catholics understand the term "scientific studies" generically to describe all scholarly approaches to the Bible, including both post-Enlightenment **historical-critical** methods, which were dominant until the late twentieth century, and newer ones. The term is meant to be as broad and encompassing as possible and to contrast with simplistic "literal" readings.
2. Customarily, many of these documents have Latin titles that become the convenient title for reference. The English titles of the documents are provided here, though they are not always translations of the Latin.

Figure 13.1. Key Catholic Documents

Document Title	Date	Author	Description	Authority Level
Providentissimus Deus "Encyclical Letter on the Study of Sacred Scripture"	1893	Pope Leo XIII	Papal encyclical that promoted some scientific study of Scripture but within certain limits, to protect the historicity of the biblical data	B
Divino Afflante Spiritu "Encyclical Letter Promoting Biblical Studies"	1943	Pope Pius XII	Papal encyclical sometimes called the Magna Carta of Catholic biblical studies; strongly promoted use of linguistic and scientific means for professional biblical study among Catholic scholars	B
Sancta Mater Ecclesia "Instruction on the Historical Truth of the Gospels"	1964	Pontifical Biblical Commission	Instruction that recognizes three embedded levels of history and tradition even in the Gospels: (1) historical life of Jesus; (2) apostolic preaching; (3) time of each evangelist and his community	C
Dei Verbum "Dogmatic Constitution on Divine Revelation"	1965	Vatican Council II	As a conciliar document, the highest authoritative text that recognizes Scripture and Tradition as the combined source of revelation and promotes the value of the Bible for Catholics and all Christians	A
"The Interpretation of the Bible in the Church"	1993	Pontifical Biblical Commission	Instruction that recognizes strengths and weaknesses in virtually all methods of scientific biblical studies and rejects a fundamentalist approach	C
"The Jewish People and Their Sacred Scriptures in the Christian Bible"	2001	Pontifical Biblical Commission	Significant statement that affirms the ongoing validity of the covenant between God and the Jewish people and recognizes the value of the Christian OT on its own terms	C
Verbum Domini "The Word of the Lord"	2010	Pope Benedict XVI	Detailed apostolic exhortation that emerged from the 2008 synod of bishops on the Word of God; quotes the century-long tradition from Leo XIII through *Dei Verbum*	B
The Inspiration and Truth of Sacred Scripture	2014	Pontifical Biblical Commission	Study requested by Pope Benedict XVI as a means to clarify how inspiration and the truth of Scripture are understood in the Catholic tradition, a topic not fully addressed at Vatican II	C

R. Witherup

Figure 13.2. St. Peter's Basilica at the Vatican in Rome, viewed from St. Peter's Square; constructed from 1506 to 1626 by Michelangelo and others, it was the site of the Second Vatican Council (1962–1965).

The process was not entirely smooth. As in the case of some Protestant churches (see ch. 12), Catholics have periodically fought over the results of modern biblical scholarship. At one point (1905–1914), the PBC issued a series of instructions condemning the results of certain OT studies that called into question such positions as the Mosaic authorship of the Pentateuch. This occurred in the midst of the **Modernist crisis**, a time when the Church felt threatened by "modern influences" it perceived to be out to destroy its authority. These statements no longer inhibit Catholic scholars from pursuing their research freely. Later Church teaching has made it clear that Catholics are free to accept the results of biblical scholarship on such matters (see R. Collins, "Rome"; Brown and T. A. Collins, "Church Pronouncements").

The Role of the Bible in Catholic Life

One cannot exaggerate the impact of the Second Vatican Council (1962–1965, also known as Vatican II) on Catholic appreciation of the Bible. Its fiftieth anniversary (2012–2015) provoked countless publications, addressing how dramatically Catholic life changed after the Council. Many theological experts at the Council were themselves biblical and patristic scholars or theologians familiar with the results of historical-critical study of the Bible. Vatican II brought a breath of fresh air to Catholics who were enthusiastic to learn more about the Bible. The Council promoted more active Catholic appreciation of the Bible in several ways.

Prayer and Liturgy

The first area concerns prayer and liturgy. Catholic monks, religious (brothers and sisters/nuns), bishops, and priests always used the Bible in their obligatory prayer rituals, such as the **Liturgy of the Hours** (monastic recitation of psalms and biblical readings for each part of the day) and *lectio divina* (prayerful meditation on Scripture passages). After the Council, however, the Bible began to play a more prominent role in lay Catholic life. More recently, Pope Benedict XVI promoted the rediscovery of *lectio divina* among all Catholics to encourage deeper reflection and meditation upon the Word of God (*Verbum Domini*, §§86–87). The goal is to increase Catholic awareness that the Scriptures themselves provide a way to encounter the risen Christ on a daily basis. This view sees Scripture not simply as a text from the past but as a living Word that speaks anew to every generation of believers (*Verbum Domini*, §§37–38).

Concerning liturgy, the Council also mandated that excerpts from Scripture be read whenever the sacraments are celebrated. It also reinstituted the ancient practice of following the **lectionary**, a tool that became commonplace among many Protestant Churches as well.[3] The lectionary, a large collection of excerpts from the Bible formulated to coincide with the liturgical year and its seasons (Advent, Lent, and so forth), exposed Catholics to most segments of Scripture that had largely been ignored prior to Vatican II. It encompasses a three-year cycle, with each year devoted to one of the Synoptic Gospels, read in sequence during much of the liturgical year, beginning in Advent. (John appears *every* year through much of Lent and Easter.) In addition, Sunday Mass includes three readings from Scripture (usually excerpts from one OT book; one NT letter, Acts, or Revelation; and always a Gospel) plus a Psalm response. The Council also asked priests to give a **homily** (a short, liturgically centered sermon) expounding the biblical readings of the day and applying them to daily life. Catholic preaching thus became more biblically oriented (see *Verbum Domini*, §59).

3. After the Roman Catholic Church revived the lectionary during the Council, several Protestant churches created a "Common Lectionary" modeled on the Catholic version. In 1992 this publication appeared in a new edition as the "Revised Common Lectionary."

Professional Biblical Studies

A second development was the entrance of Catholic biblical scholars into the broader conversation of professional biblical studies. Many Catholics now obtain doctorates from prestigious Catholic and secular universities, as well as Protestant divinity schools, and they participate fully in the life of the academy. Also, the founding of the Catholic Biblical Association in 1937 (see Fogarty, *American Catholic Biblical Scholarship*) increased the visibility of Catholic Scripture scholarship, as Catholic scholars began to publish both technical and popular biblical studies. Internationally, Catholics participate in all the major associations of biblical scholars in the world, such as the Society of Biblical Literature. Also, the Catholic Biblical Federation, an independent nonprofit organization founded in 1969 and headquartered in Germany, promotes Catholic and **ecumenical** appreciation of the Bible worldwide. It sponsors international symposiums, collaborates with various United Bible Societies, and maintains contact with agencies in the Vatican over issues in biblical studies.

Another international dimension of Catholic biblical studies is the composition of the Pontifical Biblical Commission. Now a consulting body to the Congregation for the Doctrine of the Faith in Rome,[4] the PBC consists of twenty international biblical scholars who research specific topics with a view to publishing teachings issued with papal approval. It meets once a year in Rome and thus far has published thirty-seven major documents in multiple languages.[5] Additionally, in the last half century the Catholic Church has cooperated with the United Bible Societies to produce more than 130 biblical translations in foreign languages around the world (see ch. 7). Although the active presence of professional **exegetes** from Africa, Asia, South America, and Oceania in the professional associations of biblical scholars remains underrepresented, their influence continues to grow (see Okoye, *Scripture in the Church*, 22–37). Two examples illustrate the point. An international team of scholars has produced a one-volume commentary on the Bible from both Catholic and ecumenical perspectives (Farmer, *International Bible Commentary*). Another book, focusing on the NT, represents perspectives from Latino/Latina and feminist experts (Reid, *Taking Up the Cross*). This entire area is likely to expand in the future for Catholic exegetes.

4. This Congregation is the office in charge of all doctrinal matters in the Roman Catholic Church.
5. They are listed at "Pontifical Biblical Commission," The Holy See, http://www.vatican .va/roman_curia/congregations/cfaith/pcb_doc_index.htm.

Bible Study Programs

A third development has been the proliferation of Bible study programs. One of the first and most successful was the Little Rock Scripture Study (1974), which went on to publish a Catholic study Bible as well as many individual programs in English and Spanish. Moreover, the burgeoning publications of Catholic scholars, on both a popular and a scholarly level (e.g., *The Bible Today* and *The Catholic Biblical Quarterly*, respectively), led to further excitement about biblical studies. A landmark publication was *The Jerome Biblical Commentary* (1968), the first one-volume, fully historical-critical commentary produced entirely by Catholic biblical scholars, and its successor, *The New Jerome Biblical Commentary* (1990).[6] The three editors (Raymond E. Brown, Joseph A. Fitzmyer, and Roland E. Murphy) became virtual household names identified with the maturation of Catholic biblical scholarship.

The Bible in Official Catholic Teaching

A fourth development was that the Bible began to exercise considerable influence on the level of formal Catholic teaching. Official documents issued from the Vatican or from local episcopal conferences (regions of bishops, such as the bishops of the United States) now always contain sections that expound the teaching of the Bible on one topic or another. Thus, for example, documents addressing topics like poverty, war and peace, the arms race, immigration, abortion, medical ethics, family life, religious freedom, and so forth begin their reflections with a summary of biblical perspectives on the topic. (Two prominent examples of this development are the US bishops' pastoral letters "The Challenge of Peace" [1983] and "Economic Justice for All" [1985].)[7]

In short, the Bible has become a regular feature in Catholic life and has helped rejuvenate the Catholic Church in multiple ways.

The Distinctiveness of Roman Catholic Biblical Scholarship

Given this rebirth of Roman Catholic interest in the Bible, a vital question has emerged: What is distinctive about a Catholic approach to the Bible? From one perspective, we could say that Catholic biblical scholars are no

---

6. An updated revision of this book is in process.
7. "The Challenge of Peace," http://www.usccb.org/issues-and-action/human-life-and-dignity /war-and-peace/nuclear-weapons/upload/statement-the-challenge-of-peace-1983-05-03.pdf; "Economic Justice for All," http://www.usccb.org/upload/economic_justice_for_all.pdf.

different from their Protestant, Orthodox, or Jewish counterparts. Scholars evaluate research results on the basis of generally accepted, objective scientific criteria. Catholic scholarship is no exception. As is clear from the PBC's 1993 instruction on biblical studies, Catholic scholars are free to use whatever methods are being developed for Scripture research that might help elucidate the text. Thus, Catholic scholars employ textual criticism, linguistics, all sorts of historical-critical methods, and more recent methods, such as rhetorical, canonical, narrative, **reader-response**, and social-scientific criticism, among others (see ch. 10).

The *Catechism of the Catholic Church* (§§112–14), the current official compendium of Catholic teachings, points to three major characteristics of Catholic biblical interpretation, as digested from the teachings of Vatican II:

- First, *Catholics must pay attention "to the content and unity of the whole of Scripture."* This means that there is a unity between the OT and the NT, which is part of God's mysterious plan of salvation.
- Second, *Catholics should interpret the Bible within "the living Tradition of the whole Church."* This is an acknowledgment that the Holy Spirit always guides the process of interpretation, and that no one period of Church history or any single Church teaching encompasses all that the Scriptures can teach. Our understanding of the Bible as God's inspired Word grows and develops over time.
- Finally, *Catholics must pay attention to the "analogy of faith"—that is, "the coherence of truths" contained in God's revelation.* The Catholic approach, then, is not identified with any particular method of interpretation but with the interaction of the Word of God and the ongoing, living Tradition of the Church.

Specific implications flow from these three distinctive principles, summarized in the following seven statements (see also Witherup, *Scripture at Vatican II*).

1. *Catholic biblical interpretation always recognizes the complex relationship between the Bible and Tradition.* These are not *two* sources of divine revelation but *one* source through which the Holy Spirit guides the life of the Church. The Spirit helps interpret the Scriptures and their meaning for each generation of the faithful. This principle is exemplary of the Catholic tendency to prefer a "both/and" approach rather than an "either/or" approach (e.g., Word and Sacrament; human and divine; proclamation and response).

2. *Catholic biblical interpretation always recognizes deeper senses of Scripture beyond but not contradictory to the literal sense.* These additional senses include, but are not restricted to, the traditional categories of the spiritual, moral, allegorical, and anagogical senses of Scripture (see ch. 9). Some Catholic scholars have used the term *sensus plenior* (fuller sense) to describe what the 1993 PBC document calls "a deeper meaning of the text, intended by God but not clearly expressed by the human author" (§II.B.3), but the literal sense must always be considered first (see Brown and T. A. Collins, "Church Pronouncements").

3. *Catholic biblical interpretation does not hold to a specific theory of inspiration or doctrine of verbal* **inerrancy.** Catholics do, however, recognize and honor the Bible as God's inspired Word, which teaches "solidly, faithfully, and without error that truth which God wanted put into sacred writings for the sake of salvation" (*Dei Verbum,* §11; see also *Inspiration and Truth of Sacred Scripture,* §§52–57, 63–64).

4. *Catholic biblical interpretation accepts fully the human dimension of the Bible.* For Catholics, the Bible is God's Word in human words. Interpreters should explore texts in context and read them by using all available methods, recognizing the human conventions employed to express the divine message.

5. *Catholic biblical interpretation views the* **canon** *of Sacred Scripture as the result of a long process directed by the apostolic Tradition and defined by the Church.* Catholics believe that although God is the ultimate author of the Bible, the Church conducted the process of the selection and ordering of the canon under the guidance of the same Holy Spirit who guided the formation of the canonical Scriptures (see ch. 6).

6. *Catholic biblical interpretation gives special but not exclusive precedence to patristic interpretations.* The history of interpretation is important for Catholics, and although the patristic period (the era of the early **church fathers**) is especially revered, medieval, scholastic, and modern commentators are also important.

7. *Catholic biblical interpretation always honors the* **magisterium** *(official teaching authority) of the Church as the official interpreter of biblical texts.* This is true mostly in cases where disputed meanings arise that have doctrinal implications. The Roman Catholic Church does not have an "official" interpretation of every biblical text. In fact, the Church rarely pronounces a definitive meaning of a text but at times points out interpretations that are unacceptable, usually for doctrinal reasons. One example would be the classic explanation of the texts that speak

of Jesus' brothers and sisters (Matt. 12:47; Mark 3:31–32; 6:3; Luke 8:19; John 7:3, 5; Gal. 1:19). Roman Catholics, relying on the explanation of some patristic interpreters, prefer to understand these passages as referring to a wider network of Jesus' relatives rather than to blood siblings. The reason is the Church's doctrine of the perpetual virginity of Mary, a doctrine intimately tied to the doctrine of the Incarnation. In this instance, the Church officially pronounces what the text does not mean, even though there is no definitive explanation of how to understand the Greek or underlying Semitic terms involved.

These seven propositions are crucial to a Catholic approach to the Bible. Other Christian Churches would share some of them, while some might demur on one or another point. Essentially, the Catholic Church has come to incorporate the Bible much more into the mainstream of Catholic life; in doing so it has fostered ecumenical relations with other Christians. For example, Catholic Scripture scholarship has greatly contributed to historic ecumenical agreements, such as the Joint Declaration on the Doctrine of Justification (Oct. 31, 1999) shared by Roman Catholics, the Lutheran World Federation, and the World Methodist Conference.

Catholic Biblical Interpretation in Practice

To illustrate the distinctiveness of Catholic biblical interpretation, we may take the example of sacramental imagery often present in Roman Catholic interpretation of Scripture. The Catholic Church teaches that all seven sacraments have roots in various scriptural passages. Thus, the Church sees in Christ's teaching to Nicodemus to be "born of water and the Spirit" (John 3:5) a direct call for the sacrament of baptism, confirmed in the fact of Jesus' own baptism by water and the Holy Spirit (Mark 1:9–11 and parallels) and the call by the first apostles to baptism (e.g., Acts 2:38). Also, Catholics read the words of institution at the Last Supper, as recounted by the Synoptic Gospels and Paul (1 Cor. 11:23–26), as more than a narrative from Christ's life. It is the moment of the institution of the sacrament of the **Eucharist** whereby the risen Lord is actually present, under the elements of bread and wine, which are transformed mysteriously into the body and blood of Christ. For Catholics, this is not merely symbolic language; it concerns "the real presence" of Christ. When Jesus says, "This *is* my body . . ." and "This cup *is* the new covenant in my blood . . . ," these words are accepted at face value as the identification of Jesus Christ with the bread and wine "transubstantiated" (to use a theological term meaning "transformed") into his body and blood. Catholics also see the "blood and water" that flowed from Christ's pierced side (John 19:34) as symbolically representing baptism and Eucharist, two necessary sacraments for the life of the Church, symbolized in the same passage by Christ's entrusting of his mother and the Beloved Disciple to each other, now representing the new community of faith.

These examples do not mean that Catholics see sacramental imagery everywhere in Scripture, or that Protestant interpreters cannot appreciate similar insights. But Catholic **exegesis** is more sensitive to such sacramental interpretation because of its profound appreciation for the interplay between Scripture and Tradition, mentioned above. Not all forms of Protestantism think positively about this connection, but a more serious concern for Catholics is biblical **fundamentalism**.

Catholics and Fundamentalism

Since the nineteenth century, biblical fundamentalism has continued to be a feature of American life that has had its impact on church and society. Biblical fundamentalism is essentially a loose Protestant movement opposed to modernity and committed to preserving the "literal" truth of the Bible and of certain "fundamental" doctrines. Catholics have not been immune to fundamentalist tendencies. Historically speaking, prior to the twentieth century the Catholic Church took positions on the Bible that were essentially fundamentalist in perspective. Even one section of Pope Leo XIII's otherwise admirable encyclical *Providentissimus Deus* is basically a defense of verbal inerrancy, a position that later changed in Roman Catholic teaching, but one that nonetheless remains current in certain conservative Protestant circles. In the past, moreover, official Catholic teachings tended to use the Bible as a source for **prooftexts** in order to substantiate doctrinal claims, a tendency found also in fundamentalist circles.[8]

Some Catholics are attracted to contemporary biblical fundamentalism because it seems to preserve basic values reflected in the Bible but under attack in contemporary society, particularly in the West, especially with regard to family life and morality. Moreover, fundamentalism is often allied with certain conservative political movements that lure some Catholics. As attractive as biblical fundamentalism is to some people, it is contrary to a Catholic approach to the Bible. In fact, it is the only approach to biblical interpretation

8. A prooftext is a scriptural text used to attempt to justify a belief, usually without consideration of the text's context and in isolation from other texts.

singled out officially as incompatible with a Catholic approach. A quotation
from the 1993 PBC document summarizes why biblical fundamentalism is
unacceptable to Roman Catholics:

> The fundamentalist approach is dangerous, for it is attractive to people who
> look to the Bible for ready answers to the problems of life. It can deceive these
> people, offering them interpretations that are pious but illusory, instead of
> telling them that the Bible does not contain an immediate answer to each and
> every problem. Without saying as much in so many words, fundamentalism
> actually invites people to a kind of intellectual suicide. It injects into life a false
> certitude, for it unwittingly confuses the divine substance of the biblical mes-
> sage with what are in fact its human limitations. ("The Interpretation of the
> Bible in the Church," §I.F; see also *Verbum Domini*, §44; and *The Inspiration
> and Truth of Sacred Scripture*, §4)

Essentially, fundamentalism is incompatible with Roman Catholic biblical
interpretation because of its opposition to historical-critical methodologies
and its concomitant overemphasizing of the divine and underplaying of
the human dimensions of Scripture. Fundamentalists are concerned that
any perceived error in the Bible, even historical or scientific, necessarily
erodes the belief in the Bible as God's Word. Such is not the case with
Catholics. A Catholic approach to the Bible has much more in common
with mainline Protestant and more progressive **evangelical** approaches than
with fundamentalism.

On the other hand, rejecting a fundamentalist approach to the Bible does not
mean rejecting everything fundamentalists hold. Catholics recognize certain
aspects of the faith of fundamentalists that are admirable. Examples include
the fervor for their faith and willingness to testify publicly to it, their promotion of the value of human life, their respect for the integrity of the family as
a sacred institution, and their love and respect for the Bible as God's Word
(see Witherup, *Biblical Fundamentalism*).

Current Issues and Trends

The progress that has been made in Catholic appreciation for the Bible, especially since the end of the nineteenth century, is remarkable. Catholics in
general have become more enlightened about the Bible. Catholic scholars
participate fully in the exegetical and hermeneutical challenges of biblical
scholarship. They are active in the formal academic societies and international
symposiums, and they publish in the most prestigious journals. From this

perspective, they share the challenges facing all biblical scholars. Yet Catholic biblical scholarship also has its own concerns. Five areas seem crucial.

- *Which modern methods of biblical studies will prove to be the most enduring?* Newer methods in biblical studies have been appearing at an astonishing rate. As noted above, in addition to the traditional historical-critical methods (e.g., form, literary, source, and redaction criticism, among others), Catholic scholars have used narrative, rhetorical, canonical, reader-response, social-scientific, and other newer methods (see ch. 10). Some have also used broader approaches that are not exactly methods but are oriented toward specific hermeneutical interests, such as feminist, liberationist, African, and Asian approaches (see chs. 10, 16–19). At issue is also whether some methods, such as semiotics, structuralism, and various postmodern approaches, will have any lasting value or are merely passing fads.

- *What is distinctively Catholic about Catholic biblical studies?* This will remain a burning question among Catholic exegetes. Some scholars wish to promote more use of the imagination in interpretation, others want to import more postmodern interpretive techniques, and still others want to emphasize dogmatic teachings to guide interpretation (see Johnson and Kurz, *Future*). These lead to the obvious question of how one avoids both fundamentalist readings and overly imaginative readings imposed on the text—the results not of exegesis, but of **eisegesis** (reading things *into* the text). Catholics seek a balance in biblical studies, one that accepts the necessary scholarly tools for biblical study but also feeds and nourishes people's faith.

- *How do interpreters relate Catholic teachings to the Scriptures in ways that do not violate the integrity of the Bible?* In Catholicism the close relationship between Scripture and Tradition is fundamental to Catholic interpretation. Relating the two concretely with regard to specific teachings is delicate, however, for it is important to avoid eisegesis. Achieving absolute objectivity is impossible, since everyone brings to biblical texts certain biases. One major flaw in historical criticism is its presumed independent objectivity, something that has been shown to be false. A challenge to Catholic scholars in the future will be how to achieve as much objectivity as possible while interrelating the Scriptures with the Church's teachings.

- *How can Catholics make the Bible more readily present in their daily lives, seeing in it a way to encounter Christ?* Since Vatican II, the Catholic tradition has underscored liturgy as the privileged place to encounter Christ in Word and Sacrament. Recent official documents have emphasized this as well as the fact that for Catholics, the Word of God is first and foremost an encounter with a person, the Word-made-flesh, Christ the Lord (*Verbum Domini*, §7). When it comes to pastoral practice, however, surveys have shown that Catholics remain largely uninformed about the Bible. Scripture hardly impacts the daily life of average Catholics in a way that nourishes them spiritually and makes them aware of God's outreach through the sacred Word as envisioned by the Council and later church teaching (*Dei Verbum*, §23; *Verbum Domini*, §19). Although Catholics have progressed significantly in Bible study, much more needs to be done to make the Word more effectively known.

- *What role will biblical studies play in Catholic relations with other Christians and people of other faiths?* Catholic entrance into biblical studies has clearly impacted ecumenical and interfaith relations. The PBC's recent documents on the Jewish Scriptures and on the inspiration and truth of Scripture (§148), as well as *Verbum Domini* (§§117–20), are examples of the Catholic Church's abiding interest in continuing discussions with other faiths about issues of mutual concern, acknowledging the value of their own sacred literary traditions. Biblical studies will likely be one area where ecumenical and interfaith relations continue to grow.

Conclusion

These five questions are merely highlights of the questions that Catholic scholars are likely to pursue in the years ahead. They clearly overlap with the concerns of other Christians concerning the Bible. While there is a distinctive Roman Catholic approach to Scripture, expressed in official Church documents, much that Roman Catholics believe about the Bible they also share with other Christians. Roman Catholics will join with other Bible-believing Christians in trying to apply the Bible judiciously to the challenges that await as the third millennium advances.

QUESTIONS FOR REFLECTION AND DISCUSSION

1. In what way(s) has the Roman Catholic approach to Scripture evolved over the centuries?

2. Why is a fundamentalist approach to the Bible incompatible with a Roman Catholic approach?

3. How do Scripture and Tradition relate in Roman Catholic thought? What is the magisterium, and what role does it play in Roman Catholic biblical interpretation? How are these aspects of biblical interpretation distinct from the teachings of other Christian denominations?

4. What might non-Catholics learn from Catholic approaches to the interpretation of Scripture?

FOR FURTHER READING AND STUDY

Béchard, Dean P. *The Scripture Documents: An Anthology of Official Catholic Teachings.* Collegeville, MN: Liturgical Press, 2001. Compendium of the most important Catholic documents on the Bible promulgated throughout history up to 2001.

Benedict XVI, Pope. *Verbum Domini.* Vatican City: Libreria Editrice Vaticana, 2010. Online at http://w2.vatican.va/content/benedict-xvi/en/apost_exhortations/docu ments/hf_ben-xvi_exh_20100930_verbum-domini.html. A document that grew out of a worldwide synod of bishops, this is the most important papal teaching on Scripture since Vatican II.

Brown, Raymond E., and Thomas Aquinas Collins. "Church Pronouncements." In *The New Jerome Biblical Commentary*, edited by Raymond E. Brown et al., 1166–74. Englewood Cliffs, NJ: Prentice-Hall, 1990. Good digest of Catholic teaching on the Bible through official documents up to the late twentieth century.

Catechism of the Catholic Church. 2nd ed. Vatican City: Libreria Editrice Vaticana, 1997, §§101–41. Online at http://ccc.usccb.org/flipbooks/catechism/files/assets /basic-html/page-1.html#. The most current authoritative, succinct summary of Catholic teaching on the Bible.

Collins, Raymond F. "Rome and the Critical Study of the New Testament." In *Introduction to the New Testament*, 356–86. Garden City, NY: Doubleday, 1983. Historical survey of how the official Church has dealt with scientific study of the Bible.

Farmer, William R., ed. *The International Bible Commentary: A Catholic and Ecumenical Commentary for the Twenty-First Century.* Collegeville, MN: Liturgical Press, 1998. One-volume commentary targeted toward pastoral application of the biblical text, created by a large team of international scholars from diverse cultural and ethnic backgrounds.

Fogarty, Gerald P. *American Catholic Biblical Scholarship: A History from the Early Republic to Vatican II.* San Francisco: Harper & Row, 1989. The most thorough history of the Catholic Biblical Association of America and its antecedents.

Harrington, Daniel J. *How Do Catholics Read the Bible?* Lanham, MD: Rowman & Littlefield, 2005. Excellent nontechnical introduction to a Catholic approach to Scripture.

Johnson, Luke Timothy, and William S. Kurz. *The Future of Catholic Biblical Scholarship: A Constructive Conversation.* Grand Rapids: Eerdmans, 2002. Scholarly essays arguing for the existence of serious flaws in the historical-critical method and the need to rediscover patristic and theologically oriented exegesis.

"Joint Declaration on the Doctrine of Justification" (Oct. 31, 1999). Online at http://www.vatican.va/roman_curia/pontifical_councils/chrstuni/documents/rc_pc_chrst uni_doc_31101999_cath-luth-joint-declaration_en.html. A revolutionary statement by the Roman Catholic Church and the Lutheran World Federation on their common view of justification and endorsed by the World Methodist Conference in 2006.

Okoye, James Chukwuma. *Scripture in the Church: The Synod on the Word of God and the Post-Synodal Exhortation "Verbum Domini."* Collegeville, MN: Liturgical Press, 2011. A good summary of the 2008 worldwide synod of Catholic bishops and Pope Benedict XVI's subsequent apostolic exhortation, with special attention to international responses to the preparatory documents.

Pontifical Biblical Commission. *The Inspiration and Truth of Sacred Scripture.* Collegeville, MN: Liturgical Press, 2014. Detailed analysis of inspiration, based not on dogmatic theories but on a careful exegesis of many biblical passages.

Reid, Barbara E. *Taking Up the Cross: New Testament Interpretations through Latina and Feminist Eyes.* Minneapolis: Fortress, 2007. Reflections on biblical passages about the passion of Jesus interpreted through the experiences of Latinas from Mexico, Bolivia, and Peru.

Williamson, Peter S. *Catholic Principles for Interpreting Scripture: A Study of the Pontifical Biblical Commission's "The Interpretation of the Bible in the Church."* Subsidia biblica 22. Rome: Pontifical Biblical Institute, 2001. A dissertation on the 1993 document that surveys methods used by Catholic scholars, proposes twenty principles for Catholic exegesis, and discusses an agenda for the future.

Witherup, Ronald D. *Biblical Fundamentalism: What Every Catholic Should Know.* Collegeville, MN: Liturgical Press, 2001. Brief but thorough overview of biblical fundamentalism, its origins, and how a Catholic approach differs from it.

———. *Scripture at Vatican II: Exploring "Dei Verbum."* Collegeville, MN: Liturgical Press, 2014. Popular commentary on the Dogmatic Constitution on Divine Revelation and its importance.

14

Orthodox Interpretation of Scripture

EDITH M. HUMPHREY

Reading the Holy Scriptures is like a treasure. . . . You can get from a small phrase a great wealth of thought and immense riches. The Word of God is . . . like a spring gushing with overflowing waters in a mighty flood. . . . Great is the yield of this treasure and the flow of this spiritual fountain. . . . Our forebears drank from these waters to the limit of their capacity, and those who come after us will try to do likewise, without risk of exhausting them; instead the flood will increase and the streams will be multiplied.

—St. John Chrysostom, *Homily 3 on Genesis*

In this text, the "golden-mouthed"[1] father of the Eastern Church pictures the riches of the Scriptures and how they refresh the faithful: as in reading Scripture, summarizing **Orthodox** biblical interpretation is like drinking from a fire hose. Generally, Orthodox **hermeneutics** (principles of interpretation) emerges in common life and liturgy, rather than in dogmatic statements. After early skirmishes with the heresies of **Marcionism, gnosticism,** and **Manichaeism,** the Orthodox Church had no need to lay down interpretive principles with

1. "Chrysostom" is Greek for "golden-mouthed."

Figure 14.1. Ecumenical Patriarch Bartholomew I at his residence in Constantinople/Istanbul.

precision. Because of this, and also because of the nature of Orthodoxy, which resists systematization, appreciation of Orthodox interpretation comes by reading Orthodox writers and by engaging in the life of the Church. In recent years Orthodox scholars, in contact with Protestant and Roman Catholic colleagues, have described (but not prescribed) their interpretive perspectives. Orthodox interpretation is still, however, not as easily traced as in Protestant traditions, or in the Roman Catholic response to the Reformation.

The Orthodox Church appears as a family of "jurisdictions" with various ethnic and cultural backgrounds. Each jurisdiction, governing its own affairs, is united with the others in sacramental worship, respect for the seven **ecumenical councils**,[2] and recognition of the Ecumenical Patriarch of Constantinople as *primus inter pares*, "first among equals."[3] "Cradle" Orthodox find their roots in Jerusalem, Egypt, Syria (specifically Antioch), Greece, Turkey, Russia, and other countries of Eastern Europe, but Orthodoxy is growing

2. The general councils attended by representatives of the entire undivided Church: Nicaea, 325; Constantinople, 381; Ephesus, 431; Chalcedon, 451; Constantinople II, 553; Constantinople III, 680–681; Nicaea II, 787.
3. This chapter concerns the Eastern Orthodox Church, in distinction from the Oriental Orthodox. The latter do not accept all seven councils, but include communities in Syria, Egypt, Ethiopia, Armenia, and India that rejected the Fourth Ecumenical Council due to differences in their understanding of the person of Christ. In some quarters there is hope that this division may have been partly due to misunderstanding of language, and that the Oriental community may rejoin the Orthodox Church in the near future.

in Western countries such as Great Britain, Canada, and the United States, where many have become Orthodox as adults. Due to cross-fertilization among jurisdictions, there is increasingly a discernible common approach to biblical interpretation, based upon the **Fathers** and responsive to the contemporary world.[4]

It is tempting for Western students to picture Orthodox interpretation as a variant of Catholicism, because of a common stress on liturgy, **Holy Tradition**, and the sacraments. However, Orthodox teaching largely has *not* been shaped through reaction (as with the Reformers and the **Council of Trent**), so questions and answers emerge differently. We will consider historical moments that have informed Orthodox understandings of Scripture, discern approaches and methods patterned by formative ancient theologians, survey the contemporary landscape, and close with a discussion of challenges currently facing Orthodox scholarship.

Historical Overview

The Eastern Church (with the West) faced its first challenge concerning the Scriptures in the second century, as it discerned the value of books such as the Epistle of Barnabas and adjudicated the teachings of Marcion (ca. 100–160). Marcion taught that the first covenant represented by the OT was abolished, not fulfilled, in Christ, and urged that the selection of Gospels and Epistles reflect this. The Epistle of Barnabas exhibited similar doubts concerning the OT narratives but removed the scandal through radical allegorization: God had never objected to the actual eating of rabbit, for example, but symbolically warned against copying the rabbit's licentious sexuality! Marcion and Barnabas, however, did not triumph: in harmony with the NT writers, the second-century Church retained the OT as essential to God's revelation, pointing forward to Christ, while witnessing to God's actions in history.

In St. Irenaeus's *Against Heresies* 1.9 (ca. AD 180), we discern another challenge launched by the many-headed **gnostic** movement. **Valentinian** gnostics, he charged, rearranged Scripture like a mosaic—wrenching details out of context, disregarding the divine authorial intent, reframing the expressions and names—and so deformed the picture of the King (Jesus) into that of a fox. In gnostic writings uncovered at **Nag Hammadi** in Egypt, the fanciful interpretations of the OT bear out his charges: even the goodness and omnipotence of the Creator are questioned. Against these, St. Irenaeus called

---

4. The Fathers are the significant early Christian writers from throughout most of the first Christian millennium, beginning in the late first or early second century CE.

upon even illiterate believers to understand the OT read in the light of Christ, by clinging to the apostolic "**rule** [*kanōn*] **of truth/faith.**" He presupposed that holy books were the domain of the entire Church, understandable by way of the apostolic faith and its custodians.

The Orthodox Church did not formally fix the extent of the OT canon, which they received by means of the **Septuagint** (**LXX**) version, while recognizing that this was a Greek translation from the Hebrew. The "extra" books not found in the Hebrew collection were debated, but typically designated as *Anaginōskomena* (**Readable Books**) for instruction in piety. Since the **creed** was established not by **prooftexts** but by the entire sweep of salvation history in Christ, the precise extent of the OT was not a pressing matter, as it later became in the Reformation. It would be some time (the fourth century) after the NT books were written before the NT canon would be established, a process that included discerning which books were truly "canonical"—that is, written according to the "rule [*kanōn*] of faith" or "truth."[5] In the NT the Church received implicit instruction regarding how the Old and New were related, as "two sisters and two maidens [who] serve one Master" (Chrysostom, *Homily on Luke 2*). This included patterns for **allegory** and **typology** that did not negate the historical nature of Israel's story, and a decisive centering upon God's deepest revelation in Jesus Christ. Wild **apocalypses**, dismissive allegorizations of Torah, strange diversions about Jesus' childhood, and esoteric teaching supposedly written by apostles were eventually rejected.

Working with principles drawn from the NT, **Church Fathers** from the third to the fifth centuries demonstrate a breathtaking yet harmonious variety, proclaiming scriptural themes such as creation, law, prophecy, election, covenant, sacrifice, Incarnation, redemption, atonement, justification, communion, resurrection, and the new creation. They also made use of the cultural riches of their various times—philosophical, philological, historical, and rhetorical—in order to clarify debated matters or to commend the Scriptures to those in doubt. St. John Chrysostom, in particular, exemplifies a style of reading and teaching at once practical and illumined, building a bridge to his congregation, while holding out the hope of spiritual vision (*theōria*) and transformation into the divine image (*theōsis*). In this period, key theologians responded to various **heresies** concerning the nature of the Son and the Holy Spirit, appealing to the Scriptures as they bracketed off various theological dead ends.[6] This they did without reducing the Scriptures to a quarry for

---

5. See ch. 6 on the formation of the canon(s).

6. These included Arianism, Apollinarianism, Monophysitism, Nestorianism, and Pneumatomachianism. A good theological dictionary will explain these movements.

dogma, and while deepening the Church's appreciation of Scripture and its understanding of the Trinitarian mystery. During this time, the **Antiochian** (or **Antiochene**) and **Alexandrian schools** of interpretation emerged, with overlapping methods but different emphases, the latter more dependent on allegory. A comparison of Origen (ca. 185–254), St. Athanasius (ca. 296–373), St. Basil (ca. 330–379), St. John Chrysostom (ca. 349–407), St. Gregory of Nyssa (ca. 330–395), St. Theodore of Mopsuestia (ca. 350–428), and St. Cyril of Alexandria (ca. 376–444) demonstrates great variety. The fruits of this period were not simply the declarations of the first four ecumenical councils and the **Niceno-Constantinopolitan Creed**, but also an enduring interpretive and liturgical tradition.

In the following period, St. Maximos (580–662) explored the Torah, Psalter, Gospels, and Pauline Epistles, correcting earlier theologians (such as Origen) and framing mysteries expounded by Pseudo-Dionysius (late fifth / early sixth century) in a more biblical fashion. St. Maximos also insisted upon the divine and human wills of Jesus (as did the Sixth Ecumenical Council, 680–681), commended the Scriptures' practicality for the common Christian, and firmly established the Orthodox hope of *theōsis*. He was followed by Oikoumenios (sixth–seventh century), St. John Damascene (676–ca. 749), St. Photios the Great (ninth century), St. Symeon the New Theologian (eleventh century), and St. Theophylact (eleventh century). Such theologians looked steadfastly to the earlier Fathers (especially St. John Chrysostom), as they were encouraged to do by canon 19 of the Quinisext Council (691), but also addressed their own day. For example, St. John Damascene was key in defending **icons** as a visual Bible for the faithful, St. Photios engaged in matters that would later worry the historical-critical scholars, and St. Symeon passionately modeled a personal direction by the Holy Spirit, so that the Christian might join the ranks of the pure who shall "see God" (see Matt. 5:8):

> How shall I describe, Master, the vision of Your countenance?
> How shall I speak of the unspeakable contemplation of Your
>   beauty? . . .
> O awesome wonder which I see doubly,
> With my two sets of eyes, of the body and of the soul! . . .
> He took upon Himself my flesh and He gave me His Spirit
> And I become also god by divine grace, a son of God by adoption.
> O what dignity, what glory![7]

7. "Hymn 25," in *Hymns of Divine Love by Symeon the New Theologian*, trans. G. A. Maloney (Denville, NJ: Dimension, 1976).

Symeon's full hymn demonstrates a seamless incorporation of the Transfiguration account (Matt. 17:1–13//Mark 9:2–13//Luke 9:28–36), John 3, Psalm 27:4, John 1, the parable of the publican, Mark 2:17, Acts 9, the exodus narrative (especially Exod. 24), Romans 8, and 2 Peter 1:4, 16–19. His insight into Scripture and the Christian life is later championed by St. Gregory Palamas (1296–1359), whose defense of the **hesychasts** (monks who meditated in quiet, claiming to see God with their physical eyes) included intriguing expositions of the Gospels' Transfiguration episodes and 2 Corinthians 12. While these theologians were writing, the Scriptures made an indelible mark upon Orthodox Tradition, liturgies, iconography, and saints' feast days, which joined past and present.

Though Orthodoxy was not heavily embroiled in the Reformation, we may notice some reactionary responses to the upheaval. One unhappy incident was the prohibition of lay reading of the Scriptures by Patriarch Jeremiah III of Constantinople in 1723—a limitation never imagined by St. John Chrysostom, who encouraged the faithful to read their Bibles in the weekly rhythm of life. During this time and continuing into the modern period, the Orthodox world experienced a partial hardening into tradition*alism*, coupled with what Fr. Georges Florovsky (1893–1979) termed pseudomorphosis—a deformation into Western habits, including ways of looking at the Scriptures, a dismissal of the Readable Books (by Metropolitan Philaret of Moscow in 1823), and the construal of Scripture and Tradition as two separate sources of **authority**. Such reactions, however, did not wholly obscure Orthodoxy's devotion to the Scriptures, enshrined in its liturgy, iconography, and common life. In the next section we will expound some of Orthodoxy's distinctive principles of interpretation.

Patristic Approach and Method

Authentic Orthodox hermeneutical principles from the Fathers have been gleaned by Fr. John Breck (*Scripture in Tradition*, 45–46) and may be briefly rephrased as follows:

1. The "Word of God" refers in the first place to the Son, the personal Logos.
2. True reading of Scripture requires a Trinitarian perspective.
3. Scripture is **theandric**, both human and divine.
4. Interpretation of Scripture is to help the Church and for salvation.
5. NT writings are the norm for the whole Tradition.

6. The OT and NT are related as promise and fulfillment.

7. Scriptural passages should be interpreted by reference one to the other.

8. Scripture must be interpreted within a life of prayer in the Church.

Figure 14.2. A twelfth-century icon of Christ the merciful, holding the Gospel book (Museum für Byzantinische Kunst, Bode-Museum, Berlin, Germany).

The first four principles concern Scripture in the light of the Gospel narrative. The first establishes that Christianity is not a "religion of the Book"—at least not as understood by Judaism and Islam. Christianity's center is the God-Man Jesus, and thus the reading of Scriptures serves to glorify the incarnate Word—that is, to explain and make Him present. The Scriptures therefore assume the power of a verbal icon, not pointing to themselves, but becoming windows to the One who is the Light. The second principle places Scriptures in direct relation to the Tradition that interprets them: without a creedal understanding of the Holy Trinity, the Scriptures remain obscure; yet the creeds were discerned by means of the Scriptures, in the context of the Church (cf. St. Cyril of Jerusalem, *Catechetical Lecture* 4.17, 33). The relationship between creed and Scripture, then, is symbiotic, although the Bible is primary or central: this yields a perspective that is *prima* (not *sola*) *Scriptura*.

In the third principle, the written Word is congruent with the Incarnate Word, both human and divine in nature. As Fr. Georges Florovsky put it, "In Scripture we see God coming to reveal himself to man, and we see man meeting God, and not only listening to his voice, but answering him, too" (*Bible, Church, Tradition*, 21). In the fourth principle, human and divine voices in the Bible indicate its purpose—not to speculate upon mystery, but to bring about reconciliation and health for humanity. Often these voices speak in harmony, although sometimes the human voice must be corrected or modified at subsequent parts of the revelatory text. For example, cultic regulations in Leviticus are not simply dismissed by the NT, but understood as fulfilled in the life, death, and resurrection of Jesus, who makes all things clean (cf. Acts 10:15). Scripture was given over to the whole Church by prophets and apostles for the Church's benefit, not as esoterica to privileged persons; those who transmit the teaching serve the Church, not themselves.

Principles 5–7 illumine interrelationships between the "parts" of God's revelation. The NT, the climax of God's revelation, culminates the story of Adam and Israel. By its light, ancient theologians resolved debates concerning the mysteries of **Christology**, the Holy Trinity, and the nature of the Church. Scripture is thus the core of Holy Tradition, bequeathed by Tradition and interpreted in its light (2 Pet. 1:20–21). Where there is a flat contradiction of a church tradition by the whole Scriptures, something is wrong: it is not *holy* Tradition. In order to understand the whole Scriptures, moreover, the relationship between Old and New must be probed: they are linked together as promise and fulfillment (principle 6), as enshrined in

Jesus' words on the road to Emmaus (Luke 24:13–27), in the Gospel writers,[8] and in the Fathers. Principle 7 goes further, describing the principle of **exegetical reciprocity** shared by rabbis and Fathers (Scripture interpreting Scripture, regardless of chronological order). This is counterintuitive for the twenty-first-century mind, especially when we suspect historical anachronism. However, many of the Fathers were not naive concerning history, but engaged in thematic or figurative analysis that illustrates or clarifies mystery. For example, St. Paul shows how the obedience of Abraham points forward to the Christian obedience of faith; similarly, in ancient hymnody, the burning bush that is not consumed is a sign pointing to the **Theotokos** ("God-bearer"; i.e., Mary), who safely bore within her human body God the Son.

The final principle encapsulates what is arguably the characteristic feature of Orthodox interpretation: reading the Scriptures involves transformation within the Church. Adding to the historical, literary, and theological dimensions of interpretation advocated by N. T. Wright, Fr. Theodore Stylianopoulos insists that authentic Orthodox interpretation also leads to *theōria* (seeing God) and transformation (*The New Testament*, 215–16). Though historical and literary (and some theological) implications of Scripture comfortably emerge in public academic discourse, the transformative element is disclosed among the faithful. Here we understand why the ancient theologians detected four **senses of Scripture**—literal, **tropological** (moral), **allegorical,** and **anagogical,** in various combinations and orders—and reflected on **type** and **antitype** (e.g., Jacob's ladder prefiguring Jesus, who joined heaven and earth).[9] When read so as to disclose not simply history, or a plain sense, but to inform Christian practice, the Bible hints at deeper theology that "leads up" (Greek *ana* / *agōgē*; hence "anagogical") to God. Contemporary scholarship has struggled with these so-called **precritical** methods, sometimes championing typology over allegorization, sometimes accepting allegorization of events but not arbitrary ornamentation (Louth, *Discerning the Mystery*, 115–22).

A reading of the Fathers (and the NT) shows both allegorical and **typological** approaches, sometimes overlapping. Careful analysis shows that these methods were not merely artificial means of rendering the texts relevant, nor intended mainly to tame difficult (OT) texts, though sometimes they are used in this manner. Instead, they were a response to the mysterious iconic

8. See the refrain "that the Scriptures [or prophets] . . . might be fulfilled," in Matt. 2:17, 23; 4:14; 13:14; 26:54; 27:9.

9. See the discussion of typology in ch. 9.

nature of the Scriptures (Louth, *Discerning the Mystery*, 121). Different approaches may complement one another. For example, the historian sees in Jesus' baptism an indication that the early Church understood Jesus as Messiah, "God's Son" (cf. Ps. 2); Orthodox Fathers celebrate the baptism as the event when "worship of the Trinity was revealed"; Orthodox worship, using OT Scriptures that feature water, implies that Jesus' baptism fulfilled and foreshadowed the destiny of humanity's passage from death to life. At best, the allegorical and typological do not deprive the Bible of its historical/natural meaning (for the Incarnation, touching space and time, is its center!) but enrich that meaning. The Scriptures are time*ful* rather than merely time*less:* "Revelation is not a system of divine oracles only. . . . Revelation was the path of God in history. And the climax was reached when God entered history himself, and forever" (Florovsky, *Bible, Church, Tradition*, 21).

Representative Approaches Today

As an actual academic discipline, biblical scholarship is not strongly represented by Orthodox Christians. Moreover, Orthodox biblical scholars typically combine their own specialism with **patristics**, Christian spirituality, practical theology, or ethics. In doing this, they join others who refuse to be confined by the boundaries of disciplines and who write not only for their colleagues but also for a more general readership. Helpful popular approaches to the Bible are offered by biblical scholars Frs. George Barrois, Patrick Reardon, and John Breck, as well as by philosopher George Cronk.

Among those who reflect specifically upon biblical interpretation, there are three tendencies: (1) embracing the historical-critical methods within an Orthodox perspective; (2) expressing serious concern about such atomistic methods; and (3) adopting the more recent integrative approaches, with an Orthodox flavor. In the first category we may place Veselin Kesich as well as Eugen Pentiuc, who enrich the critical methods with patristic approaches. In the second are found Michael Legaspi and Mary Ford. In the third are many, including Fr. John Breck, who stress the literary aspect in his less popular work; Fr. Theodore Stylianopoulos (discussed above); George Parsenios, writing within the Paideia commentary series, which itself stresses the final form of the text; and the present writer (Edith Humphrey), who uses a **rhetorical-literary** method to address theology. There are also theologians who engage in biblical interpretation as integral to a larger project, such as Fr. Georges Florovsky, Fr. Boris Bobrinskoy, and Fr. Andrew Louth.

Contemporary and Future Challenges

By means of these voices we receive complementary explanations of Orthodoxy's approach: the necessity of the **ecclesial** context, the vivification of the Bible in worship, Scripture's iconic nature, the Church as a living Bible in the world, and the call to a **neo-patristic synthesis** for our day: an appropriation of the Fathers' insights that is both faithful and responsive to today. What remains constant is the conviction that the Bible speaks as the vital core of Holy Tradition, not across a divide of two thousand or more years, but through and in the company of the faithful. Rephrasing the philosopher Hans-Georg Gadamer, Fr. Louth offers a quintessential Orthodox challenge:

> In interpreting a piece of writing it is not a matter of my attempting to reconstruct the original historical context in which it was written and thus to divine what was originally meant in an act of imagination, but rather a matter of my listening to what was once written, listening across a historical gulf which is not empty, however, but filled with the tradition that brings this piece of writing to me, and brings me not only that piece of writing but [also] preconceptions and prejudices that enable me to pick up the resonances of the images and arguments used in whatever it is I am seeking to understand. (Louth, *Discerning the Mystery*, 106–7)

In the midst of such riches, Orthodox Christians may be overwhelmed. Protestant believers, with the vestiges of *sola Scriptura* still in place, are frequently satisfied with Bible studies and typically have demonstrated a thorough knowledge of the content of Scriptures, though this is now changing. Orthodox, on the other hand, have a larger canon to master, including the Fathers, and sometimes are not well acquainted with the details—especially in the OT, which has not been read in Sunday Divine Liturgy since the early patristic period. Moreover, practically minded clergy frequently present the faithful with directive homilies sometimes only loosely connected with the readings. Such a procedure is not particularly Orthodox (by way of contrast, consider the detailed sermons of St. John Chrysostom!) but has become the norm. Interventions, however, are making their impact, as seen in recent publications on biblical themes, the popularity of the *Orthodox Study Bible*, and the proliferation of blogs and podcasts associated with *Ancient Faith Radio*.

Similarly, Orthodox academics trained in biblical studies may naturally react to the atomization of their field by engaging in research that more easily expresses their Orthodox instinct for integration: many shift to the subapostolic era (the second century), or the interpretation of Scripture in the patristic age, rather than entering into close discussion with nonorthodox specialists in biblical studies. This drive for integration is salutary in a time when disciplines have been artificially separated, but Orthodox voices will be more clearly heard if biblical scholars actually write within their own discipline and show where biblical studies can be enriched by the Fathers. Indeed, Fr. Anthony McGuckin positions the challenge for Orthodox scholars within the context of the fragmented discipline of biblical studies, inviting biblical specialists to disclose Scripture as the "collective 'song of the community'" ("Recent Biblical Hermeneutics in Patristic Perspective," 308). Eugen Pentiuc likewise closes his bracing survey of the OT with "an invitation to future Orthodox biblical scholars . . . to identify further distinct characteristics" of the Orthodox tradition, so that they "might enter the dialogue with post-Enlightenment approaches to Scripture, overcoming the 'hermeneutics of suspicion' that still overshadows the current conversation in biblical studies" (*The Old Testament in Eastern Orthodox Tradition*, 330). Orthodox biblical scholars are well positioned to adopt a hermeneutic of welcome (i.e., a hermeneutic of trust) as they engage in biblical interpretation, fully aware of their Tradition, not naive regarding historical-critical methods, and responsive to today's engaged approaches.

QUESTIONS FOR REFLECTION AND DISCUSSION

1. What are the limitations and strengths of reading the Scriptures according to the historical-critical method, and how do these compare with the methods of the ancient Fathers?

2. Is a typological approach more congenial to contemporary understandings of Scripture than allegorical interpretation?

3. Is the call to *theōria*, or recognition of an iconic transformative element in Scripture, an element that complicates or enriches public discourse on the Bible?

4. What is the difference between *sola Scriptura* and *prima Scriptura*, and how might this be played out in the work of biblical interpreters?

FOR FURTHER READING AND STUDY

Allen, Joseph, et al., eds. *The Orthodox Study Bible: New Testament and Psalms.* Nashville: Thomas Nelson, 2008. Based on the NKJV and the St. Athanasius Academy Septuagint, with patristic and liturgical insights.

Barrois, George A. *Jesus Christ and the Temple*. Crestwood, NY: St. Vladimir's Seminary Press, 1980. Stresses historical questions and Christology.

Bobrinskoy, Boris. *The Mystery of the Trinity: Trinitarian Experience and Vision in the Biblical and Patristic Tradition*. Translated by Anthony P. Gythiel. Crestwood, NY: St. Vladimir's Seminary Press, 1999. A luminous piece that joins confession with personal insight.

Breck, John. *Longing for God: Orthodox Reflections on Bible, Ethics, and Liturgy*. Crestwood, NY: St. Vladimir's Seminary Press, 2006. Practical exploration of problematic issues for today.

———. *Scripture in Tradition*. Crestwood, NY: St. Vladimir's Seminary Press, 2001. Helpfully distills what is common in early patristic interpretation of Scripture.

Cronk, George. *The Message of the Bible: An Orthodox Christian Perspective*. Crestwood, NY: St. Vladimir's Seminary Press, 1982. Popular treatment by an Orthodox philosopher.

Florovsky, Georges. *Bible, Church, Tradition: An Eastern Orthodox View*. Vol. 1 of the Collected Works of Georges Florovsky. Belmont, MA: Nordland, 1972. Places biblical interpretation in a larger ecclesial context with great insight.

Ford, Mary S. *The Soul's Longing: An Orthodox Christian Perspective on Biblical Interpretation*. Waymart, PA: St. Tikhon's Monastery Press, 2015. Commends the patristic insight that hermeneutical difficulties provide opportunities for spiritual growth.

Humphrey, Edith M. *Scripture and Tradition: What the Bible Really Says*. Grand Rapids: Baker Academic, 2013. Shows the Scripture's indebtedness to and approval of Tradition.

Kesich, Veselin. *The Gospel Image of Christ*. Crestwood, NY: St. Vladimir's Seminary Press, 1992. Commends a renaissance of critical biblical study within Orthodox circles.

Legaspi, Michael C. *The Death of Scripture and the Rise of Biblical Studies*. New York: Oxford University Press, 2010. A provocative contrast between the "academic" and "scriptural" Bibles.

Louth, Andrew. *Discerning the Mystery: An Essay on the Nature of Theology*. Oxford: Clarendon, 1983. A trenchant challenge to the exclusive quest for "original meaning" in biblical interpretation.

McGuckin, John Anthony. "Recent Biblical Hermeneutics in Patristic Perspective: The Tradition of Orthodoxy." *Greek Orthodox Theological Review* 47 (2002): 295–326. Survey by a patristic scholar.

Parsenios, George L. *First, Second, and Third John*. Paideia Commentaries on the New Testament. Grand Rapids: Baker Academic, 2014. Commentary by an Orthodox scholar.

Pentiuc, Eugen J. *The Old Testament in Eastern Orthodox Tradition*. New York: Oxford University Press, 2014. A remarkable survey and analysis of the use of the OT in Orthodoxy.

Reardon, Patrick Henry. *Christ in the Psalms.* Ben Lomond, CA: Conciliar, 2000. A book for the nonspecialist, merging Western and Eastern interpretation of the Psalms.

Stylianopoulos, Theodore G. *The New Testament: An Orthodox Perspective.* Vol. 1, *Scripture, Tradition, Hermeneutics.* Brookline, MA: Holy Cross Orthodox Press, 1997. An Orthodox approach that interacts with Western methods.

————. "Orthodox Biblical Interpretation." In *Dictionary of Biblical Interpretation, K–Z,* 227–30. Edited by John H. Hayes. Nashville: Abingdon, 1999. Succinct overview.

15

Pentecostal Biblical Interpretation / Spirit Hermeneutics

CRAIG S. KEENER

In many respects, Pentecostal biblical interpretation, or **hermeneutics**, is as diverse as the backgrounds and training of Pentecostal interpreters. Some Pentecostal scholars have, for example, embraced qualified postmodern approaches (e.g., Archer), whereas others contend for more traditional **exegesis** (e.g., Fee, Keener, Wyckoff). Lukan scholars such as Roger Stronstad, Robert Menzies, and Martin Mittelstadt use redaction and narrative criticism to support Pentecostal readings. So what makes an interpretation "Pentecostal"?[1]

Who Is "Pentecostal"?

At the outset, it is helpful to define what we mean by "Pentecostal." If we limit **Pentecostalism** to distinctly Pentecostal denominations and churches, the movement stems from some prominent early twentieth-century revivals (most famously, Azusa Street in Los Angeles starting in 1906, with related experiences earlier in the US Midwest and in India, and soon afterward in

---

1. Much of this chapter adapts and condenses material from my book *Spirit Hermeneutics*.

Figure 15.1. The Apostolic Faith Mission, or Azusa Street Mission, in Los Angeles, California, source of the Pentecostal movement beginning in 1906; led by Pastor William J. Seymour, the mission received guests from around the world.

Scandinavia, Chile, Brazil, and elsewhere). Traditional Pentecostalism's adherents worldwide today might number as high as 200 million.

Pentecostals welcomed mainstream **evangelical** Protestant beliefs as well as the emphases of more radical evangelicals of the era who emphasized holiness, divine healing, eschatological anticipation, and apostolic power for mission. They added to these agendas the renewal of more neglected "gifts of the Spirit" (such as prophecy) and especially the association of prayer in tongues (**glossolalia**) with a typically postconversion experience of empowerment by the Spirit.

Although "tongues" was the emphasis that most set the movement apart from other evangelicals of the era, Pentecostalism's primary focus (and ultimately its larger contribution to the wider church) has been the present activity of the Spirit, which equips God's people in relation to him and their mission in the world. Most published contributions to distinctly **"Pentecostal" hermeneutics** currently derive from academicians in this tradition.

Pentecostalism's influence has been greater than its denominational figures indicate, however. In the West, the influence of the renewal began to spread in other denominations, especially in the 1960s and 1970s in the **charismatic renewal,** and Pentecostalism's lively worship and openness to gifts of the Spirit have connected especially strongly with Christians beyond the West.[2] (For the purposes of this chapter, we will define "**charismatic**" Christians as those who embrace in practice the reality of all spiritual gifts but do not belong to denominationally Pentecostal churches.)

The phrase "**global pentecostalism**" (with a lowercase *p*) includes such Christians, whose numbers are sometimes estimated beyond 600 million, making it the second largest movement within Christianity. The highest estimates of global pentecostals are often more sociological than theological, including even some movements with fringe Christologies that nevertheless exhibit lively worship and prophetic practices. The majority of global pentecostals, however, fall within traditional theological **orthodoxy**, ranging from Catholics affected by the charismatic renewal (perhaps some 150 million) to independent churches with high Christologies.

Globally, such pentecostals have multiplied by more than six times in three decades. Patrick Johnstone estimates that "independent" churches will have grown from 1 percent of global Christianity in 1900 to possibly one-quarter by 2050.[3] He also suggests that by 2050 global pentecostalism, to which many independent churches belong, will constitute one-third of Christians and 11 percent of the world's population.[4] Robert Bruce Mullin observes that already by the end of the twentieth century, there were "more Pentecostals worldwide" than mainline Protestants.[5] Stephen Tomkins calls it "the fastest-growing form of Christianity ever."[6]

What unites interpreters classified in this way is more experiential than methodological; for examples of the diversity in the West alone, theologians who self-identify as charismatic include Teresa Berger and Miroslav Volf at Yale, William Abraham at Perkins School of Theology, Andrew Sung Park at United Theological Seminary, and J. P. Moreland at Talbot School of Theology. Among biblical scholars, charismatic Catholics include Luke Timothy Johnson at Emory and the editors of the Catholic Commentary on Sacred Scripture series (Baker Academic), Mary Healy and Peter Williamson. Charismatic Anglicans include N. T. Wright; charismatic Lutherans include Mark Allan Powell; charismatic Methodists include Richard Hays and Ben Witherington. I am a white charismatic ordained in an African American Baptist church

2. The word "charismatic" comes from the Greek word *charisma* (pl. *charismata*), meaning "gift, favor" or "spiritual gift," and is related to *charis*, meaning "grace, benefaction."

3. Patrick Johnstone, *The Future of the Global Church: History, Trends, and Possibilities* (Downers Grove, IL: InterVarsity, 2011), 113.

4. Ibid., 125.

5. Robert Bruce Mullin, *A Short World History of Christianity* (Louisville: Westminster John Knox, 2008), 211.

6. Stephen Tomkins, *A Short History of Christianity* (Grand Rapids: Eerdmans, 2005), 220.

and married to a Congolese Protestant. We exemplify a range of approaches and perspectives.[7]

Some Features of Pentecostal Interpretation

Whether on the narrower or broader definition of pentecostalism (that is, Pentecostal or pentecostal/charismatic), however, certain features usually characterize pentecostal interpretation. None of these is unique to pentecostal hermeneutics, nor is a pentecostal hermeneutic limited to them. But an interpretive approach could not conceivably be called pentecostal without them.

Not Uniquely Pentecostal or Comprehensively Pentecostal

As we will see in more detail below, pentecostal interpreters stress the contemporary significance of the Bible and the illumination of the Spirit in interpretation. Embracing Scripture's message for the present is not uniquely pentecostal, characterizing Christians from patristic preachers to Pietists. *Lectio divina*, for example (see ch. 20), is a meditative approach developed among Benedictines in the fifth century. Historically, Christians also have regularly affirmed the need for the Spirit's illumination in understanding Scripture, in addition to readers' own diligence in study (e.g., Origen, John Chrysostom, Augustine, and Calvin). Luther emphasized the need for faith and the Spirit's illumination, in addition to grammatical and historical exegesis. "Experience is necessary for the understanding of the Word," Luther insisted; it must "be believed and felt."[8] Most interpreters from all Christian traditions seek both to explore the ancient meaning of the texts and to explore their significance for today.

Although the principles described below emphasize the subjective aspect in reception of Scripture, the strong majority of pentecostal interpreters would agree that they must be anchored in the texts themselves. Although there is nothing distinctively pentecostal in this approach, pentecostal **exegetes** value the ancient horizon and not simply the horizon of the interpreter. Most pentecostals, like most other Christian believers, affirm embracing both Word and Spirit and are simply keen to make sure that the dynamic of the Spirit is not neglected. Scripture remains the canon, the most authoritatively inspired arbiter for evaluating all other claims to hear the Spirit; endeavoring to hear God's voice in Scripture therefore inevitably involves a hermeneutical circle.

7. For this paragraph, see my *Spirit Hermeneutics*, 297–302.
8. As cited in Craig G. Bartholomew, *Introducing Biblical Hermeneutics: A Comprehensive Framework for Hearing God in Scripture* (Grand Rapids: Baker Academic, 2015), 198–99.

Because of the movement's rapid growth, many Pentecostals globally lack access to the ancient context, but most Pentecostal scholars, like most other scholars, use it when it is available to them.

Typical Features of Pentecostal Interpretation

Various features characterize specifically pentecostal readings. We will list them briefly and then consider them in more detail.

First of all, global pentecostal reading is a **continuationist reading**: pentecostals ideally shape their expectations of God's activity in their world based on how they see God acting in the world of the Bible. They thus read also with eschatological anticipation, as people of the new era of the Spirit inaugurated on Pentecost. Ideally they read with faith, expecting to meet God in the biblical text.

Second, pentecostals have also always embraced the theological value of narrative. They are thus as interested in God's empowerment of his people in Luke-Acts as in the more detailed argumentation of Paul's Letters. Most therefore also read missionally; indeed, the late nineteenth-century radical evangelical quest for missional empowerment and "missionary tongues" helped birth the movement.

Third, pentecostals today read from a wide range of global locations (cf. Anderson; Miller and Yamamori). Both in the Pentecost narrative in Acts 2 and today, reading Scripture with an emphasis on the Spirit also invites global readings sensitive to the range of cultures in which the message is contextualized.

Fourth, pentecostal revival began and has flourished especially among the marginalized. Although the movement today has expanded into all classes, the majority read from the vantage point of the broken; Scripture nourishes hope and courage for them.

A Continuationist Approach: The Bible for Today

Bultmann, Gadamer, and other interpreters have tried in various ways to bridge the gap between ancient and modern horizons. This has also been a concern of most pentecostal readers.

Continuationism means that we are interested in biblical texts not simply for what they teach us about ancient history or ideas (intriguing as those are), but because we expect to share the kind of relationship with God and spiritual experience that we discover in Scripture.

A continuationist approach—that is, belief that spiritual gifts and the life depicted in the biblical text remain part of the present age—may not seem unusual to Catholic or Orthodox interpreters. This emphasis, however, nourished among late nineteenth-century radical evangelicals, stood in dramatic contrast to the hard **cessationism** that pervaded much of earlier Protestant thought, despite periodic "special providences" (as cessationists described events that looked like miracles) that kept the question of miracles fresh.[9] That most of Protestantism is no longer cessationist is a tribute to the effectiveness of the pentecostal movement's biblical challenge to cessationism as well as to global evangelicalism's not privileging Western theological categories derived from **Enlightenment** skepticism.

Embracing the World of the Text

For continuationists, the supernatural God of the Bible is the God of the present, real world. We see ourselves and our world in the Bible. The line between salvation history in the biblical narrative and continuing salvation history today is thus thin, so that readers approach the text as a model for life and ideally expect God to continue to act in the surprising sorts of ways, at various times and places, that he acted in Scripture. The message of the text shapes the meaning the reader finds in external reality; as Jacqueline Grey contends, Scripture's story offers a metanarrative in which Pentecostal readers "can locate themselves" (*Three's a Crowd*, 160).

Early Pentecostals who believed that they lived in "Bible days" read the text in a sympathetic way that many purely academic approaches and hard cessationist approaches missed. Echoing the Holiness movement and other radical evangelicals, they assumed that the book of Acts models what corporate Christian experience today should look like.

Experiencing the Textual World

In the same way, pentecostals' experience of the Spirit encouraged their sympathetic reading of otherwise alien biblical passages. Because charismatic experience is an important part of New Testament experience, it provides a fuller preunderstanding for engaging the text than does the lack of such experience. **Relevance theory** reminds us that all communicators take for granted, rather than articulate, some information that their audience already shares. As cultural background once shared by biblical authors and their first audiences may help readers to fill gaps in the text, so too shared spiritual experience

---

9. In this context, "cessationism" refers to the belief that the supernatural work of the Spirit, demonstrated in such manifestations as tongues and miraculous healing, ended at the conclusion of the apostolic era or soon thereafter.

may help us relate to many experiences in the text, such as understanding what it feels like (at least in some cases) to experience the Spirit's guidance, visions, or prophecy.

Scripture often invites us to frame our lives in light of the biblical narrative. Biblical narratives offer repeated models of believers willing to be changed by their experiences of divine encounters, as in Acts 10:9–11:18 and 15:6–28, for example, which led to and confirmed the inclusion of the gentiles. Early Pentecostals viewed Acts 28, the book's last chapter, as open-ended, portending the mission's future, a conclusion that narrative critics today have usually re-affirmed. So long as the mission remains to be completed, we continue to need the Spirit's power to fulfill it (Acts 1:8), and that same power is promised to us (Acts 2:39; cf. 1:4). Likewise, we who continue this mission remain part of the continuing, postcanonical narrative of salvation history, to which Acts points.

The book of Revelation similarly speaks of God's people from all nations, and the continuing conflict in this age between the values of Babylon and those of the New Jerusalem. We who follow the Lamb (Christ) remain part of the narrative envisioned in Revelation.

Reading with Faith

Living by faith in God's present activity affects our reception of Scripture. When we read as believers, we read the Bible, as Richard Hays puts it, with a "hermeneutic of trust" rather than with one of suspicion. Reading the biblical narrative with faith means reading its message as *true*. The God of the Bible is our God; the Jesus of the Gospels is our risen Lord; the sorts of angels and demons that inhabit the New Testament exist in our world; and the Bible's verdict on human moral failure is what we see reflected around us continually.

As Allan Anderson observes, "Pentecostal rituals exhibit a worldview that presupposes that worship is about encountering God, including a faith in an all-powerful God" (*To the Ends of the Earth*, 138). Reading with *faith* means reading biblical narratives with *expectation*—expectation that God will speak to us in some way because the God who is active in the narrative world of the text is the real God who is also active in our world. Expecting God to act today as he did in the Bible is closely related to what the Bible calls "faith."

A Subjective, Experiential Aspect of Reading

Personal experience inevitably shapes how texts or communications affect us. The same report of a sports event will affect differently those who were rooting for different teams. A report about the rise in racism may feel more personally threatening to some people (including myself, since my family is interracial) than to others.

Many parts of Scripture overtly invite experiential reading. For example, by their very genre, the Psalms, like other ancient hymns to deities, are meant to be prayed and sung. Psalms evoke feeling, employing a range of rhetorical devices. Likewise, narratives invite us into their world, facilitating reader identification. Indeed, **Greco-Roman** historians and biographers frequently noted explicitly that they intended their narratives to supply models and moral, political, or sometimes theological lessons. Pentecostal hermeneutics affirms and attempts to practice what these genres naturally call forth.

Reading Eschatologically

Although we may rightly question early Pentecostals' allegorization of Joel's "latter rain" (Joel 2:23 KJV) to refer to the contemporary outpouring of the Spirit, their eschatological instincts rang true. In Acts 2:17–21, Peter recognizes that Jesus' followers now live in a special, biblically promised time, the "last days," when God will pour out his Spirit and save those who call on Jesus Christ. This fresh framework for conceptualizing Scripture in light of christological experience is inherently eschatological, involving the "already" as well as the "not yet" of Christ's kingdom. God did not pour out the Spirit on Pentecost, pour the Spirit back for most of history, and then pour the Spirit out again in the early Pentecostals' own day. Nor did God start the last days, revert to some less-than-last days, only to conclude with more-than-last days.

Although early Pentecostal **restorationism** ignored most postbiblical church history, Pentecostals rightly grasped the sense of eschatological existence and anticipation that characterizes the church age in much of NT theology (cf., e.g., Rom. 12:2; 1 Cor. 2:9–10; 10:11; 2 Cor. 1:22; 5:5; Gal. 1:4; Heb. 1:2; 6:5; 1 Pet. 1:20).[10] Contemporary pentecostal hermeneutics attempts to retain the early Pentecostal insight, grounding it more carefully in this common NT perspective.

Embracing the Theological Value of Narrative

From Franciscans to Moravians and Anabaptists, various renewal movements have looked to biblical narratives as models for living. Indeed, NT writers read earlier biblical stories this way (e.g., Rom. 15:4; 1 Cor. 10:11; 2 Tim. 3:16–17).

---

10. "Restorationism" is the term given to movements that seek to restore to the contemporary church forms of church life from the earliest, foundational days in the apostolic period.

Scripture Models Narrative Theology

Biblical narratives teach us about God's actions (such as activities of the Spirit recounted in Acts and Paul's Letters) and provide positive and negative models for our responses to God. Granted, Scripture's narrative frame concerns itself primarily with salvation history and with God lovingly seeking to restore us to himself. God is the character about whose ways we learn consistently, and many of even the most positive human characters are weak. Thus, the controlling thrust of OT historical books in their current form is often to explain the causes of exile, justifying God's anger and promising future restoration.

The same thrust, however, warns against the sins that led to the exile, such as idolatry, sexual immorality, and the shedding of innocent blood. Such sins also include neglecting or refusing to heed and implement the message of the Scriptures and the warnings of God's true prophets, who stood in continuity with the earlier biblical message. These narratives readily lend themselves, then, to continuing applications.

Paul and James plainly use Abram's faith (Gen. 15:6) as a model for believers (Rom. 4:1–25; James 2:21–23). James similarly uses the experiences of the prophets and Job as models for endurance (5:10–11). He not only recognizes Elijah's common humanity with us, but for this very reason also treats his faith for divine action as a model for us (James 5:17–18). In 1 Corinthians 10, Paul does not cite OT examples only to remark, "Such interesting history gets us where we are today." He cites the judgment experienced by ancient Israel as a warning relevant for God's people in his own day. That is, the apostolic church read the Bible as an inspired text that offers patterns for God's continuing dealings with his people.

Reading Missionally

Although a significant stream of popular charismatic interpretation today focuses on personal prosperity, echoing its valuation in the wider culture (and not just in North America or the West), one enduring stream of Pentecostal interpretation from the beginning has emphasized empowerment for mission. Certainly the Spirit also engages us personally (Rom. 8:14–16), but nearly all of Luke's programmatic texts (Luke 4:18–19; 24:45–49; Acts 1:8; 2:16–17; cf. Luke 3:4–6) emphasize God's Spirit empowering believers for our mission. Luke reveals how pivotal this empowerment is by underlining its necessity in both the conclusion of his Gospel and the introduction of his sequel (Acts). The majority of global pentecostals emphasize texts about the Spirit's empowerment for the moral life and ministry, and for the Spirit's witness to Christ (cf. John 16:13–15).

Global Reading

Readers today often have cultural blind spots that can be helpfully addressed by believers in other cultures. **Majority World** hearers, for example, often approach reports of healings or spirits more sympathetically than do Western readers burdened with our legacy of Enlightenment antisupernaturalism.[11] One early twentieth-century Chinese church leader, for example, warned that the theological acumen of some Western Christians would benefit them little in his country if they were not prepared to cast out demons when necessary.

Most Christians function with a de facto **canon within a canon**, prioritizing some texts and teachings above others. Messianic Jewish believers, for example, rightly call gentile Christians' attention to positive texts about the law or the Jewish people that we have historically neglected. Because of traditional Confucian values, Chinese and Korean believers rightly highlight for Westerners the values of honor and respect found in Scripture. On the other hand, some revolutionary contexts in Latin America may invite emphases on justice and liberation that prophetically challenge authority. The Confessing Church in Nazi Germany and antiapartheid Christians in South Africa rightly raised such challenges to churches subservient to demonic political ideologies.

Too often Christian readings domesticate the Bible in ways acceptable to our own contexts, but listening to Christians from different settings helps challenge our hermeneutical blind spots and canons within the canon. This is true whether the corrections come from studying the history of interpretation (**reception history**; see ch. 8) or from global voices of living churches today.

Valuing global readings does not equalize all readings. For example, understanding rebirth in John's Gospel in light of Hindu reincarnation reads the texts in a way starkly divorced from their original setting. But a Western reading should *also* not be privileged over the original setting, and reading texts together with Christians from other cultures and eras can help us all surmount some of our cultural blinders.

Today an increasing number of theologians and religion scholars in the Majority World are Pentecostal or charismatic. Some examples from Africa include Anglican bishop Dapo Asaju (Nigeria), Kwabena Asamoah-Gyadu (Ghana), and the late Kwame Bediako (Presbyterian, Ghana); Asian examples include retired professor and Methodist bishop Hwa Yung of Malaysia, Simon Chan in Singapore, and Korean scholars Wonsuk and Julie Ma.

---

11. "Majority World" is the term preferred by many for the non-Western nations of Africa, Asia, and Latin America.

Given the global dissemination of movements of God's Spirit today, and especially given the biblical model of Pentecost, a true Spirit hermeneutic today must be one that considers a range of concrete **contextualizations**. When executed optimally, contextualizations also help us better identify with how the biblical texts confronted their first audiences. We must listen critically, with believers from all cultures tethered to the same canon that binds us together.

Reading with the Humble

Many early Pentecostals, like most global pentecostals today, were poor and socially marginalized. Sometimes their spiritual experience generated a pride of its own, but in general, they represented much humbler circles than those that dominated the most prestigious theological institutions at the time.

Scripture often indicates that God is near the broken but far from the proud (Ps. 138:6; Prov. 3:34; Matt. 23:12; Luke 14:11; 18:14; James 4:6; 1 Pet. 5:5). We should expect this claim to have hermeneutical implications, as **liberation theology** and biblical theology alike lead us to expect (cf. Matt. 5:3–12; Luke 6:20–26). If God normally reveals himself especially to the broken, why should he reveal himself differently (only to elites) among those who read (or hear) the Bible?

Unfortunately, exegetes are sometimes proud of our knowledge; knowledge does, as Paul noted, tend to lead us to overestimate our status (1 Cor. 8:1). Apparently none of Jesus' earliest disciples were scribes, none belonged to the prestigious sect of the Pharisees, and certainly none belonged to the Sadducean chief-priestly elite in Jerusalem. With few and private exceptions, it was not the intellectual elite of Jesus' day, but the lowly, who followed him. "I praise you, Father," Jesus prayed, "for you hid these matters from the wise and intellectual and revealed them to little children" (Matt. 11:25//Luke 10:21, my translation). Only those who welcome the kingdom like a child will enter it (Mark 10:15).

The humble read Scripture not simply to reinforce their knowledge, but with faith—and often in a situation of desperation—to hear God there. They read with dependence on God, trusting the Holy Spirit to lead them. Today biblical scholarship has vital contributions to make to global pentecostalism; yet we scholars also have much to learn from those who are part of that movement.

Challenges for Pentecostal Hermeneutics

Important challenges loom on the horizon for global pentecostal hermeneutics. First, pentecostal interpreters from given reading locations need to engage in conversation with believers from other locations. Reception history, global readings, and ecumenical discussion can all help challenge individual blind spots.

Second, for our range of contextual readings to be anchored to the same canon, we must hear the biblical texts first in their own cultural setting before translating them into our own fresh contexts. Teaching about the Bible has been hard-pressed to keep pace with pentecostalism's rapid growth, but access to sound information about ancient biblical backgrounds must be provided. Exegesis itself is a cross-cultural activity, requiring us to hear texts originally composed in different languages and addressing different cultures. The very use of an ancient Mediterranean or Middle Eastern text, reflecting ancient genres, composed in Greek or Hebrew, and presupposing particular cultural assumptions—all this invites our attention to the text in the contexts that generated both it and the words that it employs.

Finally, some older pentecostal traditions can become more comfortable in celebrating traditional pentecostal theology than in depending radically on God's Spirit. If the heart of a pentecostal hermeneutic and what it has helped remind other Christians about is its emphasis on the Spirit, pentecostals need to make sure that our biblical interpretation truly reflects humble dependence on God rather than triumphalism about our traditions.

Spirit Hermeneutics

This essay does not address everything one needs for understanding Scripture but focuses on an element regularly emphasized in pentecostal hermeneutics: How do we hear the Spirit's voice in Scripture? Other techniques, common to other sorts of literature, necessarily remain relevant to various genres of Scripture. After all, biblical texts are *texts*, communicated in real language, history, culture, and genres that at least resemble identifiable genres from their historical contexts. The shape of these texts invites interpretive approaches appropriate to their shape.

What is distinctive to Spirit hermeneutics, however, is *believers* reading the texts as *Scripture*. While doing, or once we have done, responsible exegesis, how may we expect the Spirit to apply the text to our lives and communities? Those of us already trained in exegesis are sometimes the ones who most need to be reminded of this latter concern, often neglected in our traditional exegetical methodologies.

Of course, elements that characterize such "pentecostal" hermeneutics should characterize *any* truly Christian and Spirit-led hermeneutic. While careful study of Scripture is essential to counter the unbridled subjectivism of popular charismatic excesses, study that does not lead to living out biblical experience in the era of the Spirit misses the point of the biblical texts. All Christian experience in this era must be properly "pentecostal"—that is, shaped by the experience of Pentecost, the outpouring of the Spirit on the church.

QUESTIONS FOR REFLECTION AND DISCUSSION

1. What similarities and differences do you perceive between pentecostal interpretation of Scripture and the interpretive approaches with which you are familiar, either from personal experience or from study? How might other approaches to Scripture answer the driving question of pentecostal hermeneutics: "How do we hear the Spirit's voice in Scripture?"

2. From a pentecostal perspective, how does the intellectual context of the Western churches sometimes negatively impact Western Christian interpretation of Scripture?

3. What impact on biblical studies, and on the Christian church more generally, do you think global pentecostalism might have in the coming years?

4. What can you appropriate from the pentecostal approaches to the interpretation of Scripture described in this chapter?

FOR FURTHER READING AND STUDY

Anderson, Allan Heaton. *An Introduction to Pentecostalism: Global Charismatic Christianity.* Cambridge: Cambridge University Press, 2004. Global history and analysis of key themes.

———. *To the Ends of the Earth: Pentecostalism and the Transformation of World Christianity.* New York: Oxford University Press, 2013. Main aspects of Pentecostal and charismatic Christianity and its effects, including its part in the shift of the church's center of gravity to the Southern Hemisphere.

Archer, Kenneth J. *A Pentecostal Hermeneutic: Spirit, Scripture, and Community.* 2004. Reprint, Cleveland, TN: CPT Press, 2009. Recognizes some textual polyvalence and welcomes aspects of postmodern interpretation.

Fee, Gordon D. *Listening to the Spirit in the Text.* Grand Rapids: Eerdmans, 2000. Emphasizes understanding the original sense.

Grey, Jacqueline. *Three's a Crowd: Pentecostalism, Hermeneutics, and the Old Testament.* Eugene, OR: Pickwick, 2011. Engages a range of modern approaches.

Jenkins, Philip. *The New Faces of Christianity: Believing the Bible in the Global South*. New York: Oxford University Press, 2006. An appreciative study of the role of Scripture and belief in supernatural activity among Christians in Africa, Asia, and Latin America.

Keener, Craig S. *Spirit Hermeneutics: Reading Scripture in Light of Pentecost*. Grand Rapids: Eerdmans, 2016. Considers biblical epistemology and intrabiblical readings.

Martin, Lee Roy, ed. *Pentecostal Hermeneutics: A Reader*. Leiden: Brill, 2013. Seminal essays from leading Pentecostal interpreters.

Miller, Donald E., and Tetsunao Yamamori. *Global Pentecostalism: The New Face of Christian Social Engagement*. Berkeley: University of California Press, 2007. Studies "progressive Pentecostalism," meaning Pentecostalism that tries to balance evangelism and social ministry.

Oliverio, L. William, Jr. *Theological Hermeneutics in the Classical Pentecostal Tradition: A Typological Account*. Global Pentecostal and Charismatic Studies 12. Leiden: Brill, 2012. Classifies and evaluates various approaches.

Pinnock, Clark H. "The Work of the Spirit in the Interpretation of Holy Scripture from the Perspective of a Charismatic Biblical Theologian." *Journal of Pentecostal Theology* 18 (2009): 157–71. A charismatic theological hermeneutic.

Spawn, Kevin L., and Archie T. Wright, eds. *Spirit and Scripture: Exploring a Pneumatic Hermeneutic*. New York: Bloomsbury, 2012. Includes seminal essays from leading Pentecostal interpreters.

Wyckoff, John W. *Pneuma and Logos: The Role of the Spirit in Biblical Hermeneutics*. Eugene, OR: Wipf & Stock, 2010. Includes historical and epistemological considerations.

Yong, Amos. *Spirit-Word-Community: Theological Hermeneutics in Trinitarian Perspective*. Burlington, VT: Ashgate, 2002. A Pentecostal theologian's approach to interpretation.

16

African Biblical Interpretation

Bungishabaku Katho

Africa is a vast continent consisting of many cultures and countries. Nevertheless, there is something of a shared reality among many Africans due to the common experiences of missionary work and **colonialism** in addition to similar patterns of living that existed prior to, and even after, these historical events. One remarkable fact is that it was with the nineteenth-century missionary movement, which coincided with colonialism, that the Bible was spread throughout Africa south of the Sahara. Since then, the Bible has continuously played a very important role in the lives of many Africans. This chapter examines biblical interpretation among the peoples of Africa.

Historical Overview

Many African scholars trace the origin of biblical interpretation on the continent to the cities of Alexandria in Egypt and Hippo Regius (modern-day Annaba) in Algeria. This enterprise is usually linked with such names as Clement of Alexandria (150–215), Origen of Alexandria (185–254), Augustine of Hippo (354–430), and many others who lived and worked in North Africa during the first four Christian centuries. The works of these early African theologians, especially in Alexandria, were dominated by the **allegorical** method discussed in chapter 9. This method became widely accepted in the Western church until the **Enlightenment**, when it was pejoratively characterized as premodern or uncritical. It was then replaced, in the eighteenth century, by the **historical-critical method**, which reigned until about the middle of the twentieth century, when it was gradually supplemented by **literary** approaches and **social-scientific criticism**.[1] These last approaches became well established and accepted by the great majority of interpreters as the best scientific tools of modern biblical research.

In Africa south of the Sahara, the use of both historical and literary methods began with the appearance of the first universities in the middle of the twentieth century. The first professors who taught in these new African universities were themselves Europeans or Americans, helped by a few Africans who were educated in Europe and the United States, where these methods were dominant. Hence, literary and historical-critical methods dominated all African interpretations of the Bible during that early period. These methods are still widely used today by many scholars on the continent, despite the fact that more than 90 percent of these professors are Africans, mostly trained in Africa. It can therefore be said that biblical interpretation in Africa today is to a certain degree a continuation of these modern methods of Western academic biblical scholarship.

However, a number of scholars are putting forth a great effort to develop a parallel African method in many African universities. The major characteristic of this method is the concern to create an encounter between the biblical text and the African context. What is intended by "African" in biblical interpretation is the integration of the sociopolitical, religious, and economic context of Africa—more precisely, the context of the region where the interpreter is working. Thus, the main characteristic of African biblical interpretation is the focus of the interpreter on the *constant* and *intentional* interaction between the biblical (con)text and the local community of the interpreter that receives the text. There is agreement among biblical scholars that this development of African biblical interpretation can be divided into three periods.

The Early Period (1930s–1970s)

The early period of African biblical interpretation occurred from the 1930s through the 1970s. During this time, the first African scholars mainly focused their work on legitimizing African religions and cultures by showing some similarities between Hebrew and African cultures, primarily through comparative methods. Joseph John Williams was one of this period's earliest scholars.

1. See the discussion of these various approaches and methods in ch. 10.

He published *Hebrewism of West Africa* (1930) to show similarities between the Ashanti language of Ghana and Hebrew, and also between the worship practices of the two peoples who spoke these languages. Many years later, Professor Kwesi Dickson took on the task of researching and writing about the values of African religions (e.g., *Akan Religion and the Christian Faith: A Comparative Study of the Impact of the Two Religions* [1965]; *Biblical Revelation and African Beliefs* [1969]). Generally, these values were studied in the light of similar values in Hebrew life and customs, such as the importance of community life and the omnipresent nature of religion in everyday life. The main idea behind this enterprise was the search for the recognition of African cultures, which were being denied and condemned by many missionaries.

Beyond the need for identity claiming and affirmation, this was also the important period of achieving independence for most African nations (1950s– 1960s). In that context, the few existing universities would consider their mission as contributing to the efforts of national development, politically, economically, and culturally. As a result, many departments of religious studies in public universities also focused their research on African culture, languages, and traditional religions.

The Middle Period (1970s–1990s)

The middle period took place from the 1970s through the 1990s and was dominated by two specific approaches: (1) **inculturation**, also called the **indigenization method**, and (2) **liberation hermeneutics**. The hermeneutics of inculturation is an attempt to understand different meanings of a biblical text while interacting with its original context and with contemporary contexts in which the text is being currently read. With these two approaches, the African context visibly and more intentionally became a resource for biblical interpretation.

Inculturation/Indigenization

Inculturation or indigenization studies focus on the encounter between the Bible and African religion and culture. This is a huge and rich field of research in Africa, including different aspects of theology such as **Christology, ecclesiology**, and social ethics. Research in inculturation is not done just for the sake of finding similarities and dissimilarities, as in the case of comparative studies. The goal is to understand the relationship between the Bible and African culture in order to facilitate understanding and communication of the message of the Bible in Africa, with the hope that, from this new understanding, there would emerge a Christianity that is both African and biblical.

Apart from his own research in inculturation, Bujo Bénézet has also edited three volumes, in French, about major figures of African inculturation theology.[2] It was also during this period that many scholars consciously started conducting research on the presence of Africa and African people in the Bible, sometimes called "the Africa-in-the-Bible approach." There were at least two objectives for this new research. On the one hand, African researchers and those interested in Africa wanted to correct the negative images about Africa and African peoples presented in certain traditional Western scholarly readings of some biblical texts. On the other hand, they also sought to examine the place and the contribution of Africans in biblical texts and history, from which Western scholarship has excluded them. Tuesday Adamo's book *Africa and Africans in the Old Testament* can be considered as the best summary of these efforts.

Liberation Hermeneutics

Inspired by Latin American theologians, many scholars in Africa started developing a means of critical reflection, based on God's Word, to shed light on the African continent as a poor, oppressed, unjust, and exploited society. The goal of this hermeneutic is to restore distorted human dignity by building a much more equitable society. This type of reflection, known as **liberation theology** or liberation hermeneutics, started in the 1950s, but found its champions in the 1970s. Liberation theology has various concerns: economic (the relationship between the poor and the rich), geographical (the economic gap between Western countries and Africa), gender (the brutalization and marginalization of women on the continent), ethnic (specifically, the case of apartheid in South Africa), and cultural (the tendency of Western nations to impose their culture in Africa, especially in the African Catholic Church). Jean Marc Ela is known as one of the best African liberation theologians.[3]

The Modern Period (1990s–)

The modern period of African biblical interpretation started around the 1990s. It emerged from the understanding that both inculturation and liberation have not solved Africa's problems. Many theologians became aware that

---

2. Bujo Bénézet, *Théologie Africaine au XXIe siècle: Quelques figures* [African theology in the 21st century: Some figures], vols. 1–2 ed. Juvénal Ilunga Muya, vol. 3 ed. Bujo Bénézet (Fribourg: Academic Press, 2002–2013).

3. His 2003 book is entitled *Repenser la théologie Africaine: Le Dieu qui libère* [Rethinking African theology: The God who liberates] (Paris: Karthala, 2003).

M. Gorman

Figure 16.1. An ecumenical Scripture conference at Notre-Dame de l'Espérance (Our Lady of Hope) Roman Catholic seminary in Bertoua, Cameroon.

God does not manifest his presence only in the culture but also and more concretely through the faith that works in concrete situations for transformation. From this perspective, inculturation is treated by some African theologians as a distraction from Africa's current real concerns. Thus there emerged two major elements in the interpretation of the Bible in Africa.

The first element is the refinement of a theology of reconstruction and renaissance that seeks (a) to address in concrete ways African realities such as corruption, poverty, and political oppression that are destroying the continent and (b) to find ways to build a better continent. The second element is recognizing the importance of including the community, or ordinary readers, in the process of biblical interpretation for transformation. This element takes into consideration the languages, categories, concepts, needs, questions, interests, and resources of the poor with the goal of helping the vast majority of poor people in Africa transform their spiritual and social conditions through the Bible-reading process. This process has different names: African biblical hermeneutics, African cultural hermeneutics, African biblical transformational hermeneutics, or simply African biblical studies. While talking about the theology of reconstruction and an African biblical hermeneutics of transformation, at least three people come to mind: Jesse N. K. Mugambi, Gerald O. West, and Ka Mana.

Methods and Principles of Contemporary African Biblical Interpretation

Many scholars recognize that African Christian theology is in a methodological crisis. This crisis can be explained by the lack of agreement among African scholars on the standards to adopt for biblical interpretation. But it might also be that the question of method or hermeneutics has not received enough attention from African theologians. There has been more methodological reflection on African philosophical scholarship than in any other research field on the continent. In theology, the concentration has been on the description or the analysis of African realities, but not on *how* to address these realities. The good news is that this methodological reflection is now beginning to emerge. In Francophone Africa, Jean Koulagna's recent work is the best example of an entire volume (though very small) devoted to the question of hermeneutics in African scholarship.[4] In Anglophone Africa, Ukachukwu C. Manus calls for much creativity in doing African biblical interpretation. He proposes a methodology with seven steps. Justin Ukpong suggests four stages. Reflecting on the works of Gerald West, Jonathan Draper ("Old Scores and New Notes") offers a nice summary that reduces African biblical interpretation to three essential elements: **distantiation, contextualization**, and **appropriation**.

Distantiation

The first step, distantiation, comes from an understanding of the following two realities. First, the Bible is a "sacred text," not an ordinary document. As such, it is normative for the believing community. Second, it was written in a different context and for different people, struggling with issues that are similar to, but not exactly the same as, ours. This understanding of the Scripture leads the interpreter or interpreting community to let the text speak for itself, acknowledging that it is important to listen to the sacred text from its own historical, social, cultural, and economic context. This allows interpreters, whether as individuals or as a community, to understand that they

---

4. Jean Koulagna, *Exégèse et herméneutique en contexte: Réflexions méthodologiques* [Exegesis and hermeneutics in context: Methodological reflections] (Yaoundé: Dinimber & Larimber, 2014).

are not the first audience of the Bible, and that there are differences between their situation and that of the first audience.

Contextualization

The second step, contextualization, is the acknowledgment that there is no absolute meaning of a text. While Western interpretation has tended to neglect or elide the contemporary context of the biblical interpreter, African biblical hermeneutics is emphatic about the context from which and for which the biblical text is being interpreted. African biblical interpretation tries to be as meticulous in its analysis of the details of African contexts as it has been about the details of the biblical text in the distantiation phase. Therefore, the interpretation of a text does not stop with what the text meant to its original audience (distantiation), but it must help modern readers to discover themselves as historical persons and communities, rooted in their time and confronted by specific problems in their context.

Appropriation

Appropriation is the highest level of interpretation. It is conceivable only where the Bible is accepted as a normative text for the interpreter or the interpreting community. As said above, in African biblical hermeneutics interpreting the biblical text is never considered an end in itself. The result of biblical interpretation is always about transforming the life or the context of the interpreter(s). Therefore, the kind of dialogue or interaction between the biblical text and the African context is very often determined by the vision of change the interpreting individual or community has in mind. Thus, the responses that interpreters arrive at depend on the questions being asked.

At this point, it is important to recognize that the best appropriation is possible only when there is a profound knowledge of both the biblical context and the interpreters' context. These two contexts must enter an ongoing and deep conversation to produce a new light that can lead to change through appropriation.

Contemporary and Future Challenges

A good interpretation requires a certain expertise. It requires an advanced knowledge of **exegesis**. Yet, in Africa, the vast majority of Bible readers and interpreters are church members with limited education and biblical knowledge who read the Bible on Sunday or during Bible study sessions. They are called "ordinary readers." This means that to become effective, African biblical interpretation needs facilitators to help ordinary readers.

But facilitators or experts must be aware that there are a lot of local resources for a transformative understanding of the Bible. They must avoid the danger of remaining too academic, using only foreign resources. The questions, needs, and experiences of the local community can become enriching ingredients for a better understanding of the Bible, far better than critical and bookish methods. African biblical interpretation insists on the fact that facilitators or theologians must listen to the community where they live. This responsibility requires a conversion of facilitators from the academic, Western "scientific" methods in which they have been trained. It is the conversion from the individual, academic, and Western ways of reading the Bible to a communal, transformative reading of God's word. Understood this way, theology in general and Bible interpretation in particular should avoid being purely speculative discourse for the pleasure of some specialists. It is a reading that must produce a transformation of the readers.

Having said this, we also must recognize that there is a tendency in Africa to use the biblical text as a pretext, reducing it to a simple socially and ideologically unmediated Word of God. This is due to the lack of an adequate and profound analysis of biblical texts, using all possible tools of exegesis. The real test of African biblical interpretation is to remain profoundly biblical and contextually relevant for the continent by going beyond the level of devotional Bible study and making God's Word a tool for the transformation of the continent. In this process, it does not matter whether facilitators start their interpretation with the context (contextualization) or the text (distantiation) itself. What is important is that each stage must be given due weight.

A Sample Interpretation: Hearing Jeremiah 5:1–5 in an African Context

In Jeremiah 5:1–5 God commands Jeremiah to search through the streets and marketplaces of Jerusalem to find out whether there is one righteous person who acts with justice and strives for honesty so that he may forgive the city (v. 1).[5] The prophet carries on the search and finds nobody who is righteous. Then he comes to the first conclusion: the search was done in the wrong place—that is, in the streets and marketplaces—and with the wrong people: the poor (v. 4). Then Jeremiah decides to go to a different location,

5. Part of this text was presented as Bungishabaku Katho, "Hearing Jeremiah in African Context: An Intercultural Interpretation" (paper presented at the annual meeting of the Society of Biblical Literature, San Diego, November 22, 2014).

where the rich live, to find out whether there is one single person who acts with justice. He goes to the rich (v. 5) with a strong hope that he will certainly find a different situation there. Unfortunately, the rich too were unrighteous. The study of this text in my context is guided by four main questions:

1. Why did God send Jeremiah to search for a righteous person in the streets or marketplaces in Jerusalem? Is this choice arbitrary?
2. Why did Jeremiah conclude that the search was done at a wrong place, with wrong people, the poor?
3. Why did Jeremiah assume that the rich must know the way of the LORD, compared to the poor?
4. What can we learn from this text in our context?

Reading the Text in the Streets of Africa's Cities

Jeremiah 5:1 reads, "Run to and fro through the streets of Jerusalem, look around and take note! Search its marketplaces/squares and see if you can find one person who acts justly and seeks truth—so that I may pardon Jerusalem" (NRSV, slightly altered).

Someone from Europe or the United States who visits a city like Nairobi, Kinshasa, Lagos, or Kampala for the first time will be surprised by the number of people in the streets. In those cities, some streets are easily converted into marketplaces, with hundreds of thousands of people, which can make human movement very difficult. YHWH could have sent the prophet to the temple or private homes, but he chose the streets and marketplaces because in the temple people can hide their behavior and pretend that they are spiritual or religious; but in marketplaces they easily forget their masks and reveal their true behavior. Righteousness is not written on the faces, but it is observed through daily lives and interactions in real-life situations. Therefore, the best place to observe it is a public setting like marketplaces and streets.

The result of the search was disappointing for the prophet. Jeremiah found that people in Jerusalem were very religious, for they were swearing all the time by YHWH (v. 2). To swear by God is to call upon his name as the guarantor of any obligation that a person may take upon himself. In the event of a violation of any duty or agreement, YHWH would be expected to visit the covenant-breaker with severe judgment. But in Jerusalem, the oath sworn in YHWH's name had no honesty in it; it was *sheker*: falsehood, deception, lying, pretense, and fraud (v. 2). People used the proper formula for oaths ("as YHWH lives"), but their language was false. Swearing had become a habit, a culture, a mere word, but its meaning and value were forgotten.

Then the prophet draws his first conclusion. The search was probably done in the wrong place, the streets and the marketplaces, and with the wrong people, the poor (v. 4). How should we understand this sentence? Is Jeremiah condemning the poor, or is he justifying their ignorance? Who are these poor, the *dalim*?

In the Hebrew Bible, the *dalim* are sometimes identified as the opposite of the rich (Ruth 3:10), or simply as the powerless and insignificant, as opposed to those who have power and influence (Lev. 19:15). One interpreter thinks that the reference to the word *dalim* in this context means poverty of knowledge and understanding, rather than poverty of an economic kind. But this is to misunderstand what is going on here. My argument is that poverty in this passage is of both knowledge and economy, and that one has an impact upon the other. In other words, the poor in the streets of Jerusalem were economically poor. This forced them to spend the whole day, and part of the night, in the streets, looking for any means of survival. Their understanding of God, who seemed not to respond to their daily needs (while the rich seemed to have everything they needed), might have been profoundly distorted. Their survival and that of their families was more important than keeping covenant, going to the temple, or telling the truth. As a consequence, this economic poverty created a poverty of knowledge and faith in God.

These are the poor who overcrowd most of the streets in African megacities, as Michela Wrong carefully observed in Kinshasa, capital of the Democratic Republic of the Congo (my country):

> In the space of forty-five minutes, as I worked my way through a steaming plate of rice and beans, I was offered the following items without straying from my seat: cigarettes, chewing gum, hard-boiled eggs, cola nuts, spice sachets and carrots (all from a medicinal box aimed at those plagued by bad breath or sore throats), French perfume (two tatty boxes, clearly fake), plastic briefcases and plastic sandals (range of), shoe polish (a small boy knocking his brush against a stool to attract attention), men's trousers, transistor radios (choice of two models), a display of tinny-looking watches and sunglasses, ginger powders, a couple of sports shirts, cheap nylon ties, disposable razors, men's briefs (packet of three), men's shirts, paper tissues, roasted peanuts (in the sachets), grilled prawns (on wooden skewers), socks (variety of colors). . . . It was like watching predators on the savannah as they prowled the long grasses and scoured the horizon, searching relentlessly for a kill.[6]

6. Michela Wrong, *In the Footsteps of Mr. Kurtz: Living on the Brink of Disaster in Mobutu's Congo* (2000; repr., New York: Harper Collins, 2001), 149.

This is how poor people struggle in our cities, in public places where YHWH sent his prophet.

One Woman's Story

This incident also reminds me of the story of Barbara, a young lady who works in an Internet café in Uganda. She opens the office at eight in the morning and closes it at ten at night. She works seven days a week, without twenty minutes for rest, not even on Sunday. I was in the café late one day and noticed that her employer kept calling her every half hour to see whether Barbara had left before ten. When I asked why she accepted such a condition, why she was not able to ask her employer for a day off, especially on Sunday so that she might go to worship God with other believers (Barbara is a Christian), her answer was simple and straightforward:

> The boss will not accept the request, and if I dare to disagree with him, I will be fired and another person will take this job on that same day. What should I do in this country of misery? I spent four years looking for a job. I even made a bad mistake and became pregnant because I needed money. Now that God offered a job for me, why should I leave it for someone else?

This is a *dal* (a poor person) of our day. Barbara has no choice but to serve as a slave and be there in the office despite her unbearable conditions. Should she disobey her boss, go to church on Sunday, and then lose her job? Will this not force her to go back to selling her body and become pregnant again, probably eventually dying with HIV/AIDS? Should she forget about the church and continue with her job? What will be the impact of her decision on her faith if she continues with her job in this way? Does she really have time to pray and meditate on God's Word? These are some of the many questions we should ask about the poor in our streets. Poverty does have a negative impact on our faith.

A Hermeneutic of Compassion

Thus, one interpreter's claim that these people were just shouting in the streets might not be totally true. This might have been a mixed crowd with different concerns, even undergoing a very dire situation. In such a situation, it might not have been a big problem for the poor in the streets of Jerusalem to behave like people who did not know YHWH: telling lies when necessary, making an oath that could not be kept, or stealing if one felt compelled to do so. How many *dalim* do we have in our prisons because they were forced to steal some money for the survival of their families?

It seems to me, and this is an important point to make, that it was with *compassion* that Jeremiah looked at the poor who crowded the streets of Jerusalem, and he noticed that something very important was missing in them: they were too busy for life, and rightly so, but they lacked the proper knowledge of YHWH. In this context, poverty is not to be accepted as a virtue; it is an enemy of faith.

From this discussion, I argue that Jeremiah was trying to *justify* their ignorance. In other words, the poor were faulty but excusable because of the condition in which they found themselves. This is why my translation of verse 4 reads like this: "*But these are just the poor people! This is why they act foolishly, since they do not know the way of YHWH, the manners of their God.*" In this passage, knowledge of YHWH is associated with certain conditions of life. And for the poor, the concern for survival was stronger than the concern for faithfulness to YHWH.

During his ministry, Jesus had a special concern for such poor people of his time. One day, after teaching them for three days, he noticed that the crowd had nothing to eat, and he feared that they might faint on their way back home, probably because most of them had not eaten for some or all those days. There is no doubt that these were very poor people who came to listen to him, expecting a change in their dire condition. He looked at them with a lot of compassion: "Then Jesus called his disciples to him and said, 'I have compassion for the crowd, because they have been with me now for three days and have nothing to eat; and I do not want to send them away hungry, for they might faint on the way'" (Matt. 15:32). What would have happened to them if Jesus had sent them back hungry? They would certainly have forgotten all his good teachings, and Jesus was very much aware of this.

It is clear that the majority in African churches are such poor people, who come to our services, expecting to be fed and healed. What can African churches do to help poor people like Barbara or those crowding our streets? What are other challenges poor people experience in the cities?

Conclusion

The vitality, growth, renewal, and survival of the African church will depend on the right interpretation of the Word of God. It is no longer acceptable for Africans to continue reading the Bible from a Western perspective. African scholars must continue to produce an interpretation that is profoundly biblical and that addresses African issues. The greatest challenge for African scholars is certainly methodological: how to include local resources in our interpretation. This must take into account the oral dimension of the Bible. That most of the texts of the Bible first existed in oral forms can be a real advantage to African interpreters, since most African cultures still favor oral communication.

Another dimension is the understanding that most biblical texts were produced by and for communities. They were not individual works, produced by a few specialists for a limited audience of scholars and their small group of students specializing in the same area, like most of our writings today. They reflect the experience and struggle of a group of people in real-life situations. It is important for African interpreters to keep in mind this community dimension of the Bible.

However, this search for relevance in African scholarship should not be used as a pretext to avoid the rigor of biblical analysis inherited from Western scholarship. Interpreters in Africa should avoid what I call "using the text as a pretext." The search for relevance must be built on the solid foundation of rigorous textual analysis, following all credible classic methods.

QUESTIONS FOR REFLECTION AND DISCUSSION

1. Has the impact of Western scholarship, often originating from colonizing nations, been positive or negative in the African context?
2. Why is it important for African biblical interpreters to develop their own approaches to interpretation?
3. Are the hermeneutical principles of distantiation, contextualization, and appropriation valid outside of the African context? How might they be relevant to your own interpretation of Scripture?
4. How might the concerns of African interpreters to involve the community, including "ordinary readers" (the educationally and economically poor), be relevant in your context?

FOR FURTHER READING AND STUDY

Adamo, David Tuesday. *Africa and Africans in the Old Testament.* 1998. Eugene, OR: Wipf & Stock, 2001. Example of efforts to reclaim a neglected aspect of the Bible.

Draper, Jonathan. "Old Scores and New Notes: Where and What Is Contextual Exegesis in the New South Africa?" In *Towards an Agenda for Contextual Theology: Essays in Honour of Albert Nolan,* edited by T. McGlory Speckman and Larry T. Kaufmann, 148–68. Pietermaritzburg: Cluster, 2001. Three essential elements of African biblical interpretation: distantiation, contextualization, and appropriation.

Manus, Ukachukwu C. *Intercultural Hermeneutics in Africa: Methods and Approaches*. Nairobi: Acton, 2003. A summons to hermeneutical creativity.

Page, Hugh R., Jr., ed. *The Africana Bible: Reading Israel's Scriptures from Africa and the African Diaspora*. Minneapolis: Fortress, 2010. Essays on OT books and topics by scholars from Africa and its diasporas, especially the United States.

Speckman, T. McGlory, and Larry T. Kaufmann, eds. *Towards an Agenda for Contextual Theology: Essays in Honour of Albert Nolan*. Pietermariztburg: Cluster, 2001. Essays for a South African Dominican priest who specialized in contextualization.

West, Gerald O. *The Academy of the Poor: Towards a Dialogical Reading of the Bible*. Sheffield: Sheffield Academic Press, 1999. The importance of the poor, ordinary readers.

———. *Biblical Hermeneutics of Liberation: Modes of Reading the Bible in the South African Context*. Pietermaritzburg: Cluster, 1991. An important work in liberation hermeneutics.

West, Gerald O., and Musa W. Dube, eds. *The Bible in Africa: Transactions, Trajectories, and Trends*. Leiden: Brill, 2001. A massive volume on a wide variety of topics.

17

African American Biblical Interpretation

C. Anthony Hunt

For African American Christians, the Bible has been and continues to be the foundational source for comprehending and appropriating faith in God. To discuss the Bible is to engage in conversation about the church's book. In this respect, the Bible—with its stories, personalities, and places—has taken on life; it is a living document. Its stories are not merely historical episodes but also narratives that have assumed an existential reality for persons over the course of a number of generations.

As Dale Andrews points out, the early African Americans were interested in God's will for them. They focused on God's activity in human history and life in the Spirit. They did not perceive their devotion to the Bible as anti-intellectual. Rather, they accepted it as a book of very real accounts of God, Christ, and God's people (*Practical Theology for Black Churches*, 19).

The Bible has been the primary source of knowledge and experience of God, guidance for the expression of the Christian faith in personal life, and unquestionable strength and wisdom in the development of social values and norms. According to Cain Hope Felder, the Bible has come to occupy a central place in the religions of the black **diaspora** (dispersion from the African homeland). The biblical narrative has inspired and captivated those in the black churches. The Bible has given meaning amid conditions that have often been oppressive, and it has served as a basis of hope for a liberated and enhanced material life (*Troubling Biblical Waters*, 6).

After providing a brief description of the African American churches, this chapter will address African American biblical interpretation from a historical as well as a contemporary perspective, with some considerations about the future.

The African American (Black) Churches

In beginning a discussion of the Bible's role in the African American Christian experience, it is helpful to provide a brief description of the African American (or black) churches. Although the terms "African American" and "black" are not completely synonymous relative to sociocultural context, for the purposes of this chapter, they will be used interchangeably.

To speak of black churches is to speak of a multifaceted set of realities. They are essentially composed of black persons who have arrived in America under various circumstances and who live today amid a variety of conditions. Thus, black churches include people who were born in America; persons who have arrived in America directly from various countries on the African continent; and black persons from the Caribbean, Latin America, and—to a lesser degree—Asia and Europe. Black churches exist in urban, rural, and suburban communities. They are composed of people with various levels of education, from the illiterate to persons with graduate degrees. These churches encompass the economically poor, the middle class, and the prosperous. Socially, politically, and theologically, black Christians are conservatives, liberals, and moderates. Throughout history, it has not been uncommon for persons from many of these divergent categories to worship, exist, and intermingle within the same local congregational setting. Today it is also not unusual to have blacks with ancestry from various different African and non-African countries worshiping in the same American congregation. (It will therefore be wise to keep the previous chapter in mind while reading this one.)

The African American Christian community is also diverse in the sense of being multidenominational. Most black Christians have been (and continue to be) Baptist and Methodist, but many are also Catholic, Episcopalian, and Presbyterian. Today many black churches are **evangelical**, **Pentecostal**, or nondenominational. In fact, over the last two decades, the fastest-growing black churches and denominations are among these latter three groups.

Lisa Hunt

Figure 17.1. *Praise the Lord with Gladness*, a painting by Larry Poncho Brown at Epworth Chapel United Methodist Church in Baltimore, Maryland, depicting a stained-glass image of a community of exuberant worshipers of all ages with Bibles in hand.

The Bible and the Black Church in Historical Perspective

Within the diversity we have just considered, three common features have historically shaped the identity of African American churches.

First, African American churches were formed out of the lived reality of slavery in America and its concomitant dehumanization, racism, subjugation, and oppression. From the time the first blacks encountered Christianity in America in the seventeenth century until today, the songs, prayers, and preaching of the black churches have served as sources of community solidarity, strength, and hope for people who in many other ways have been disintegrated, disenfranchised, segregated, separated, and alienated.

Second, the life and character of African American churches, while linked in some respects to the Christianity of the churches of white Americans, are organically and inherently derived from the experiences of African traditional religions. This is seen today in the rituals, mores, customs, traditions, and values that remain extant in much of the African American religious experience. For example, the importance of preaching in the black church tradition can be directly traced to the role of narrative and narrator (the storyteller, or *jali/fundi/griot*) in African tribal culture. The African storyteller typically held a central role, similar to the role that the black preacher has assumed in African American churches. The preacher, as the central figure in the black religious experience, has been viewed as the person "called by God" who is appointed to "tell the story," thus offering hope found in the gospel of Christ, who can "make a way out of no way" (see Andrews, *Practical Theology for Black Churches*, 16–17).

The third common feature in shaping the African American churches has been the central role of the Bible. Catholic theologian Cyprian Davis states that "American blacks, both Protestant and Catholic, found their roots in the Old Testament and the New, and most particularly in the many references to Ethiopia in the Psalms and the Prophets" (*History of Black Catholics in the United States*, 1).

Davis points out that the suffering of the children of Israel has been likened to the suffering of black people. Many blacks grew up with stories of Abraham, Moses, Jonah, Daniel, Ezekiel, Ruth, and Esther. Identification with suffering, as experienced by the people of Israel, has been considered to be a key to understanding the kingdom of God for black Christians.

Along with the ongoing identification with these biblical stories, themes, and personalities, there has emerged a growing awareness in African American churches that truly understanding the role and the interpretation of the Bible requires careful analysis.

The Development of African American Biblical Scholarship

In the mid-twentieth century, with the groundbreaking research of African American biblical scholars such as Charles Copher, there began a movement to critically analyze the biblical text from the perspective of black persons. Many questions began to surface about the presence of blacks in the Bible. Who were the Cushites, the Nabateans, the Egyptians, and other African peoples in the Bible? Where were Cyrene, Niger, Sheba, and other locations that are mentioned? Who were the Queen of Sheba (1 Kings 10:1–3), Zipporah (Exod. 2:21; Num. 12:1), Ebed-melech (Jer. 38:7–13), Hagar (Gen. 16:1–3), Simon of Cyrene (Mark 15:21), and the Ethiopian eunuch (Acts 8:27–39)?

Today many scholars agree that there is a prominent African presence in Scripture, as evidenced in numerous biblical references to African lands, nations, and people whose ancestral roots were African. It has been proposed that the Eden of the biblical tradition included mainland Africa to the Tigris-Euphrates valley (see the books by Copher and Felder) and that the location of the garden of Eden would have been understood to be totally or partially situated in what has come to be known as Africa. Of the four rivers named in the biblical account of the garden, two of these can be associated with regions in Africa where Hamitic people were significant early developers of civilization.

For African American churches, considering the role of Africans in Scripture has helped to facilitate the ongoing appropriation of the God of Israel as the God of black Christians, and an appreciation of the notion that black persons are indeed created in the image of God (*imago dei*). The contemporary research of OT scholars such as Renita Weems, Randall Bailey, Hugh Page, Valerie Bridgeman, and Temba Mafico, as well as NT scholars like Brian Blount, Brad Braxton, Clarice Martin, and Obery Hendricks Jr., continues to build upon the foundational work of Charles Copher, Cain Hope Felder, Vincent Wimbush, and others by addressing issues relative to how the Bible is read, interpreted, and appropriated given the issues facing black churches and communities. Some of these issues involve the place and role of black women within the framework of the biblical text, along with issues of class, politics, justice, health care, and other matters relative to the plight of African Americans today. In essence, the scholarship of these and other black biblical interpreters has, according to Vincent Wimbush, served as a challenge to the still largely unacknowledged interested, invested, racialized, culture-specific, and ethnic-specific practice of Eurocentric biblical interpretation that is part of an even larger pattern of such interpretation of literatures and of history in the West (*African Americans and the Bible*, 8).

Black biblical interpreters have learned a great deal from developments in black **liberation theology** as put forth in a foundational way by James H. Cone, Jacqueline Grant, J. Deotis Roberts, Dwight Hopkins, and others. Liberation theologians generally agree that the experiences of one's own group are a legitimate context for establishing categories and criteria for theological discourse. Those experiences are also a means of identifying with biblical texts and extracting contemporary meaning from the theological witness of those texts. **Feminist liberation theology** in the African American tradition is known as **womanist theology**.

The Role of the Bible in Shaping African American Identity

As we have been suggesting, over time the African American churches have engaged in the ongoing process of discerning what the Bible, as a foundational document of the church, says and means for them in light of its ancient context. This hermeneutical (interpretive) process has been critical in shaping the identity of blacks, both individually and communally, providing a framework for meaning and relevance in black life.

Many African American biblical scholars and theologians have pointed out that there is clear evidence from the perspective of faith that, through the biblical text, God has continued to speak to the plight of African American Christians. The Bible has been (and continues to be) a source of common story and shared vision, speaking to all the tragedy and triumph of the community. Furthermore, it has been (and continues to be) a means of educating the untutored, inspiring the weak, consecrating the secular, motivating the tired, and transforming the misdirected.

Wimbush points to the significance of the biblical witness as a critical component in shaping black identity:

> In their sermons and testimonies, African Americans interpreted the Bible in light of their experiences. Faith became identification with the heroes and heroines of the Hebrew Bible, and the long-suffering but ultimately successful Jesus. As the people of God in the Hebrew Bible were once delivered from enslavement, so, in the future, the Africans sang and shouted, would they. As Jesus suffered unjustly but was raised from the dead to new life, so, they sang, would they be "raised" from their "social death" to new life. (*The Bible and African Americans*, 24)

The Bible has also served specifically as a point of reference for appropriating and rationalizing the notion of the African American family as critical to black existence. Cain Hope Felder points out that the NT has a distinct concern for quality relationships in the household (Greek *oikos*), which emerges as a theological paradigm for membership in the household of God (the church). Felder sees a particular theological challenge and opportunity to make the biblical story relevant, given the contemporary realities of the black family (*Troubling Biblical Waters*, 150).

This interpretive process of shaping African American identity is connected to several central biblical themes—what Marcus Borg refers to as "**macrostories**" (*Meeting Jesus Again for the First Time*, 121–27). For black Christians, three of these macrostories are the story of the **exodus**; the story of the **exile**; and the priestly story of sin, guilt, sacrifice, and forgiveness.

The Exodus Story

The **macrostory** of the *exodus* is the story of the journey from *bondage* to *freedom*. Humanity's great need here is not for forgiveness or reconciliation, but for freedom. The religious life is a journey to *liberation* as God moves us out of captivity, through the wilderness, and into the land of promise. From this perspective, the problem facing the children of Israel in Egypt was not that they were *sinful*; it was that they were *slaves*.

It is the story of the exodus of Israel from Egyptian bondage (Exod. 14) that continues to serve as the primary liberation motif for black Christians and is thus the foundational biblical paradigm for communal solidarity and hope. God's saving activity in the exodus events resulted in liberation of the Hebrews from enslavement to an oppressive power. This also established a relationship between Israel and God, the Liberator. The exodus motif is reinforced by the famous Lukan text in which Jesus announces his own ministry of liberation (Luke 4:18):

> The Spirit of the Lord is upon me, because he has anointed me to bring good news to the poor. He has sent me to proclaim release to the captives and recovery of sight to the blind, to let the oppressed go free.

The image of God's deliverance continues to empower African American churches and helps to form a theological framework for the struggles of African Americans against systems of oppression that have often stripped persons of their human dignity and left them without hope. Slaves, for instance, would often translate central plots and themes from biblical stories into songs relating to their own struggles (see, e.g., Felder, *Troubling Biblical Waters*, 85–86). The exodus drama of God's intervention against hostile forces to effect deliverance has provided the basis for hope, as seen in the spirituals, such as "Swing Low, Sweet Chariot":

Figure 17.2. "Swing Low, Sweet Chariot"

Refrain: Swing low, sweet chariot, Comin' for to carry me home! Swing low, sweet chariot, Comin' for to carry me home!	*Elijah's chariot ride to heaven (2 Kings 2:1–12) refers to going home to heaven, as well as to escaping to the North or Canada via the Underground Railroad.*
I looked over Jordan, and what did I see, Comin' for to carry me home? A band of angels comin' after me, Comin' for to carry me home!	*The slaves hoped not only for angels to take them to heaven but also for angelic works in the Underground Railroad to take them to safety.*
Refrain	

If you get there before I do, Comin' for to carry me home, Jess tell me friends that I'm acomin' too, Comin' for to carry me home!	*The expectation of a great reunion* *in heaven, or in the North, kept hope* *alive among the slaves.*
Refrain	
I'm sometimes up and sometimes down, Comin' for to carry me home, But still my soul feels heavenly bound, Comin' for to carry me home!	*Sorrows and setbacks did not quench* *hope, either for heaven or for freedom.*
Refrain	
The brightest day that I can say, Comin' for to carry me home, When Jesus washed my sins away, Comin' for to carry me home!	*No matter what the slaves' human* *fate, their salvation, forgiveness, and* *assurance of heaven was their great-* *est joy.*
Refrain	

"Swing Low, Sweet Chariot" is classified as a **coded song** because its biblical allusions and other aspects of the lyrics refer not only to heavenly freedom but also to earthly freedom (probably via the Underground Railroad). This coded language demonstrates the close connection between spiritual and political realities in African American experience and biblical interpretation.

The Story of Exile

The theme of *exile* is epitomized by the Babylonian captivity. Like God's ancient people, humanity is *separated* and *alienated* from the place it truly belongs, rendering people sad, lonely, and desperate. According to the exile story, people are estranged from the center of their being and yearning.

The two interchangeable Hebrew terms for exile are *golah* and *galut*. These terms speak to "captivity" and "deportation," and for black Christians they continue to conjure up images of removal from the African continent and transplantation into the Western Hemisphere. This exile has dimensions that are physical, psychological, social, emotional, spiritual, and relational. Through the **Middle Passage**,[1] slavery, and related experiences over four centuries, blacks have experienced separation not only from their native land but also from family members, language, and culture, as well as religious and spiritual traditions and customs.

1. The Middle Passage refers to the voyage from Africa to the Americas of enslaved persons who were sold into further slavery. Ships were characteristically overcrowded because more slaves meant greater profits. These conditions resulted in much disease and death.

The solution is a journey of *return* to where persons truly belong, and the image is that of a joyful reunion or homecoming. The writer of Ephesians shares a NT vision of belonging:

> So then you are no longer strangers and aliens, but you are citizens with the saints and also members of the household of God, built upon the foundation of the apostles and the prophets, with Christ Jesus himself as the cornerstone. In him the whole structure is joined together and grows into a holy temple in the Lord; in whom you also are built together spiritually into a dwelling place for God. (Eph. 2:19–22)

For persons of the black diaspora, the Bible and its use in the black churches has been a critical source where this return from separation, estrangement, and alienation is seen as a possibility. In the midst of exile, the Bible has offered hope and provided a framework for the actualization of community through worship, service, advocacy, and fellowship.

The Priestly Story

A third theme is that of *sin, guilt, sacrifice, and forgiveness.* Borg calls this the *priestly* story because it is grounded in the institution of temple sacrifice in Israel. Humanity is depicted primarily as sinful, with good reason to be ashamed. Borg sees a problem in that for many people this story has dominated the understanding of Jesus and the Christian life, to the neglect of the other macrostories.

Today the priestly story—and concern with matters such as individual sin, guilt, sacrifice, and forgiveness—tends to be a primary focus of many African American Pentecostal and evangelical churches. But the theme also affects social ethics. For instance, black evangelicals tend to focus on reconciliation, with Christ as reconciling agent. The focus here is on the biblical mandate for the church to work toward overcoming cultural and racial barriers that divide the church and society. Three of the proponents of this perspective are William Pannell, John Perkins, and Tony Evans. Evans claims,

> Racism, whether based on skin color or ethnicity, has always been a terrible sin in the eyes of God, and worthy of His severest judgment. Both white and black people who allow race to determine social and political structure in America need to remember that. (*Let's Get to Know Each Other,* 25–26)

Evans also emphasizes that the Bible is a multiracial book. He further states:

When a person understands the glorious presence of African people in God's drama of redemptive history, Scripture is clearly the primary source for legitimate black pride. Scripture allows us to take pride in who we are and what God has made us, without feeling we have to become something other than what God has created us to be. (*Let's Get to Know Each Other*, 25)

Despite Borg's concerns, for African American Christians the *priestly* story has usually been connected with the stories of the *exodus* and *exile*, and has therefore often played a less dominant role than among some other Christians. But as each of these themes speaks to some dimension of the reality of the African American socioreligious experience, they have all been interwoven to play an integral role in shaping black identity, depicting the ongoing drama and journey of African American Christians.

Future Prospects

For African American Christians, preaching, teaching, singing, praying, and living the hope that is found in Scripture have continued to provide the primary means of survival amid oppressive structures and realities. Jesus' sense of mission, as noted above, is embodied in his striving for the "liberation" of humanity. This notion of liberation beckons the Christian community to deal faithfully with the difficult, perennial problems that segregate persons in the church and society. From both black liberation and black evangelical perspectives, today's churches are called to faithfully interpret what the biblical text says about the treatment of women, persons of color, the poor, and those who are otherwise denigrated, marginalized, and ostracized.

If African American churches persist in taking the Bible seriously, the Scriptures will continue to serve as a source of inspiration, consecration, motivation, and transformation. In the future, African American churches will continue to face the significant challenge of reappropriating ancient biblical stories and themes in ways that are relevant to contemporary realities. This must be accomplished within the context of what philosopher Cornel West refers to as the prevailing condition of the "nihilism of black America"—that is, a certain lovelessness, hopelessness, meaninglessness, and nothingness that pervades and permeates much of African American life today (*Race Matters*, 14).

It is in the midst of such despair that the reality of the Bible, as the living Word of God, must continue to offer the possibility of spiritual and social transformation. This must involve tapping into the deep streams of past African American engagement with the biblical text, while building upon these encounters in ways that facilitate the development of a hermeneutic intentionally promoting the holistic preservation and perpetual progress of African American churches and communities.

It is within the context of the cross—and the concomitant suffering and rejection that Jesus experienced—that African Americans can continue to identify a critical means of comprehending their own suffering. The notion that Jesus is passionately concerned with the condition of all people, and especially the disinherited, is central to black faith. Jesus demonstrated his concern by associating with despised and rejected persons of his own time. For black Christians, there is a clear and indelible connection with the suffering and rejected Christ. Today, Christ continues to take the pain of suffering persons upon himself.

The resurrection of Christ must remain the basis of realized and future hope for African American Christians. The resurrection must continue to speak not merely about immortality and eternity but also about life and hope in places of death and despair. Without ongoing faith in the resurrection, there can be no good news to preach and no faith and hope to sustain humanity.

For African American Christians, resurrection symbolizes the promise of new possibilities for meaning within the existential sense of dread and despair. It means that the oppressed can be set free to struggle against injustice, and humanity can be liberated to move toward an appropriation of hope. For black Christians, the resurrection is God's breaking into history to transform suffering into wholeness—to move persons from being victims to being liberated agents of change.

QUESTIONS FOR REFLECTION AND DISCUSSION

1. In reflecting on the prospect of the Bible being a foundational source for comprehending and appropriating faith in God for African Americans, how do you see this as being the case, historically and contemporarily? How has this changed over time?

2. Given the proposal that Africa and Africans had a central place in the shaping of the Bible, how do you see this as being the case (or not)? How might an appropriation of this proposal shape biblical interpretation, through preaching and teaching, in the black churches today?

3. What do you think of the accuracy and the significance of the proposal that there are three major macrostories—exodus, exile, and priestly—that have shaped and continue to shape African American biblical interpretation?

4. What aspects of African American biblical interpretation should you appreciate, or even consider appropriating, no matter your own interpretive location?

FOR FURTHER READING AND STUDY

Andrews, Dale P. *Practical Theology for Black Churches: Bridging Black Theology and African American Folk Religion.* Louisville: Westminster John Knox, 2002. Includes analysis of the role and use of Scripture and biblical interpretation in shaping black religious life.

Bailey, Randall C., ed. *Yet with a Steady Beat: Contemporary U.S. Afrocentric Biblical Interpretation.* Atlanta: Society of Biblical Literature, 2003. Biblical interpretation in light of African American culture, stressing liberation as a foundational construct.

Blount, Brian K. *Then the Whisper Put On Flesh: New Testament Ethics in an African American Context.* Nashville: Abingdon, 2001. An approach to the NT from the perspective of oppressed African peoples in America, interpreted from the point of view of African American slaves, and revealing the message of liberation.

————, ed. *True to Our Native Land: An African American New Testament Commentary.* Minneapolis: Fortress, 2007. Introductory articles and commentary on each book.

Borg, Marcus. *Meeting Jesus Again for the First Time: The Historical Jesus and the Heart of Contemporary Faith.* San Francisco: HarperOne, 1994. An account of contemporary scholarship on the historical Jesus, with important implications for today's church.

Cone, James H. *A Black Theology of Liberation.* Maryknoll, NY: Orbis, 1970. A groundbreaking analysis of the African American Christian experience from the perspective of liberation theology.

Copher, Charles B. *Black Biblical Studies: An Anthology of Charles Copher.* Chicago: Black Light Fellowship, 1993. Copher's foundational research in biblical, theological, hermeneutical, historical, and cultural perspectives on the Black and African presence in the biblical world.

Davis, Cyprian. *The History of Black Catholics in the United States.* New York: Crossroads, 1990. Analysis of the African American Catholic experience, tracing the African roots of the Bible, OT and NT personalities, and the church, and documenting the contributions of African Americans.

Evans, Tony. *Let's Get to Know Each Other: What White Christians Should Know about Black Christians.* Nashville: Thomas Nelson, 1995. Evangelical perspectives on efforts to foster understanding in order to help break the bonds of racial separation in the church and society.

Felder, Cain Hope. *Troubling Biblical Waters: Race, Class, and Family*. Maryknoll, NY: Orbis, 1989. A groundbreaking, comprehensive look at the significance of the Bible for blacks and the importance of blacks in the Bible.

Hendricks, Obery M. *The Politics of Jesus: Rediscovering the True Revolutionary Nature of Jesus' Teachings and How They Have Been Corrupted*. New York: Doubleday, 2006. Examination of contemporary Christian faith in light of the revolutionary heart of Jesus' teachings.

Page, Hugh R. *The Africana Bible: Reading Israel's Scriptures from Africa and the African Diaspora*. Minneapolis: Fortress, 2010. A critical window into the world of the Bible as lived and read in the multiple diasporas of African peoples.

Powery, Emerson B., and Rodney S. Sadler Jr. *The Genesis of Liberation: Biblical Interpretation in the Antebellum Narratives of the Enslaved*. Louisville: Westminster John Knox, 2016. The role of the King James Bible in the quest for freedom by slaves prior to the Civil War.

Weems, Renita J. *Just a Sister Away: A Womanist Vision of Women's Relationships in the Bible*. San Diego: LuraMedia, 1988. Biblical interpretation from a black Christian, womanist perspective, focusing on the women of the Bible, including relationships, race, and class.

West, Cornel. *Race Matters*. Boston: Beacon, 1993. A classic examination of the most urgent issues confronting African Americans, from discrimination to despair, and how contemporary leadership might address them.

Wimbush, Vincent L., ed. *African Americans and the Bible: Sacred Texts and Social Textures*. New York: Continuum, 2001. A comprehensive anthology addressing issues in African American biblical interpretation.

———. *The Bible and African Americans: A Brief History*. Minneapolis: Fortress, 2003. Five phases of African American biblical reading, showing how the language of the Bible has enabled African Americans to negotiate the realities of church and society.

18

Latino/Latina
Biblical Interpretation

M. DANIEL CARROLL R.

Increased awareness of global diversity is a hallmark of the times. Many of the new voices that are being raised come from marginalized minority groups. Their demographic is growing, which makes it impossible to ignore their presence and increased cultural, sociopolitical, and economic impact. Religious traditions of all kinds, as well as the academy, also are being revitalized by their energy and dedication.

Over the last few decades in the United States, feminist and African American scholars have made important contributions to biblical and theological studies. More recently, **Latino/Latina** approaches, along with other nonmajority views, have begun to secure a more prominent profile.[1]

Reading the Bible *Latinamente*

To begin with, the label Latino/Latina can be controversial. The United States government created the label "Hispanic" for the 1980 census to refer to all

---

1. As this chapter explains, Latino/a biblical interpretation has been influenced by Latin American **liberation theology**. Some important resources are noted in the "For Further Reading and Study" section at the end of the chapter.

peoples of Iberian descent, which includes those from countries south of the US border and most of the Caribbean.[2] This tag, however, put populations of different national histories and of diverse languages and cultures under a single rubric. It ignored the fact that these peoples represent various races and ethnicities, including those of direct Caucasian European descent, the mestizo (or ladino), the mulatto, the Amerindians, zambos, and others who would self-identify as black or Asian.[3] This is not to say that there are no cultural commonalities or shared values across this spectrum. All acknowledge (and celebrate) a broader ethos grounded in a collective *latinidad* (shared Latino/a identity).

Within the larger culture, the term "Hispanic" is now common parlance, but it is resisted by many of these communities. In contradistinction to this externally imposed category, many choose instead "Latino" (Latina is the feminine form; some combine the two as Latin@). There is disagreement as to whether the word "Hispanic" should be used at all, or if it should be limited to those who come from Latin America and the Caribbean, with Latino/a being applied to those born in the United States. Some reverse those referents. Complicating matters further, not a few eschew both labels and favor referring to themselves according to their country of origin. Within academic circles, Latino/a is the preferred term, so that is the one employed in this essay.

Particular Contexts for Reading the Bible

To read the Scripture *latinamente* is to recognize and embrace the distinct realities of Latino/a history that can profoundly mark how the Bible is read.[4] These include the difficulties of longtime social marginalization and discrimination. This experience of inequity goes back over a century and a half to the United States' acquisition of a large swath of Mexican territory through the Treaty of Guadalupe–Hidalgo in 1848 (ending the Mexican-American War) and the Gadsden Purchase of 1853. Other Latin American and Caribbean countries have their own unfortunate experiences with US foreign policy and economic power. In addition, the last four decades have witnessed overwhelming global economic, political, and ecological forces that are triggering the influx of millions of immigrants (both regular and undocumented) to the

---

2. Iberia is the peninsula of Europe that today comprises the countries of Spain, Portugal, and Andorra.

3. "Mestizo" and "ladino" refer to a person of combined European and Amerindian descent; "mulatto" to a person of mixed European and African descent; and "zambo" to a person of mixed African and Amerindian descent. "Mestizo" can also refer generally to people of mixed genealogy.

4. The Spanish suffix "-mente" functions like the suffix "-ly" in English.

United States from Latin America, primarily from Mexico. For various reasons, this phenomenon has generated another layer of prejudice toward Latinos/as. The sense of national disdain is exacerbated by the fact that a large percentage of our people come from the poorer segments of society.

Other factors loom large in Latino/a identity. One has already been mentioned: the complex racial makeup of this population that often is dissimilar to that of the majority culture. The term *mestizaje* (from *mestizo*, "mixed") signifies the hybridity of many Latinos/as, which is in constant flux because of the ongoing ambivalent processes of cultural adaptation and amalgamation, intermarriage, and changing language predilections. Another key dimension is that millions are first-generation arrivals. Additional millions are descendants of immigrants, who continue to cherish their Latin American or Caribbean heritage. This immigrant situation characterizes Latinos/as as a **diaspora** group. This sociocultural, economic, and political condition is connected to a deep feeling of alienation and otherness vis-à-vis the larger context and also to a transnational connection to countries of origin. One finds, as well, a principled solidarity to stand with others who experience a similar plight.

A final element is the importance of unique communal realities of everyday life, *lo cotidiano*. For example, loyalty to the extended family and the significance of the mother and of women to familial, social, and religious relationships are foundational to Latino/a cultural dynamics. In addition, the lively devotion of Latino/a popular religion—whether Roman Catholic or Protestant (especially **Pentecostal**)—reflects the passion, festive spirit, and spiritual instincts of our culture. What is more, immigrant congregations become a place of refuge and encouragement, a substitute for the extended family of the members' homelands as they face the many obstacles of daily life, *la vida cotidiana*.

All of these matters combine in multiple ways to leave an imprint on the way in which Latinos/as engage the Bible. These readers can be, in other words, self-aware contextualized interpreters, whose upbringing and milieu yield fresh understandings of the biblical text. Of course, attitudes toward the Bible vary by religious allegiance. The Scripture plays a more central role within Protestant circles, especially in **evangelical** and Pentecostal churches, than among Roman Catholics, due to the significance of other elements within that tradition. It would be disingenuous, however, to claim that all Latinos/as and their congregations read the Bible in the ways presented here. Many remain settled with customary liturgies, a prosperity gospel, classic systematic theology emphases, or an individualistic ahistorical framework for their faith. Multigenerational Latino/a churches or those Latinos/as attending majority culture churches face their own particular challenges. What follows

AP Photo / Tina Fineberg

Figure 18.1. Latino/a Christians at worship.

is an introduction to an orientation that strives to reflect and respond to the particular needs and aspirations of Latino/a contexts.

Responsibilities in Reading the Bible

An orientation to the Bible determined by these realities should spawn a set of social and **ecclesial** commitments in interpretation, a mind-set that responsible biblical interpretation is a vocation. This reading of the Scripture is undertaken as an active exercise *with*, *from*, and *for* Latino/a families, congregations, and communities. Interaction with the text should not be done in isolation from our people, but rather alongside them and within their world. Awareness of their concrete privations defines the purpose of such study. It ought not to be driven primarily by intellectual curiosity or academic ambition. Biblical preaching, research, and writing have the greater call to affirm the dignity of a people, empower them, and support sociopolitical and economic transformation. An exemplar of this kind of commitment is *mujerista* **theology**, which does theology and biblical work in conversation with **feminist criticism** on behalf of Latinas.

This ethical impulse for biblical scholarship has several corollaries. First, Latino/a scholars are open to working *en conjunto*—that is, together in collaboration—across confessional lines and disciplines. Differences in personal background, faith commitments, training, and institutional affiliation are respected, since everyone can contribute to the larger common good.

Second, from this perspective the evaluation of interpretations of biblical texts has a functional, or praxiological, component. It is not enough to assess the correctness of a reading according to the attention given to the original languages and material and social-scientific backgrounds—all of which must be taken into account. Latino/a biblical approaches are critical of the assumed objectivity and secure positivism of classical critical methodologies that may stand removed from seeking the import of the text on behalf of those who live on the underside of history. They distrust analyses that claim universal results derived from rules established by the Western academic guild. Ultimately, the relevance of the text must be grounded in its interface with today's social challenges. Interpretation should advance *la lucha*, that urgent struggle for constructive change.

Not surprisingly, and third, this biblical interpretation locates some of its roots in Latin American **liberation theologies**.[5] Although the history and context of Latino/a readers are different from those of our neighbors to the south, there are cultural ties, experiences of marginalization, and moral and theological concerns that underpin this connection. Those liberation theologies and current Latino/a biblical studies find their motivation in the desire to resist the status quo and align themselves with greater justice and opportunity. Unmasking the complicity of certain interpretive strategies in the sacralization of exclusionary structures and attitudes also has led some to an interest in **postcolonial** thought. Postcolonial approaches facilitate the exposure of power differentials within a society and its religious constructs; some Latino/a scholars apply that critical attitude to biblical texts, which they perceive as instances of problematic rhetoric and ideologies that cannot be revelatory or salvific. Even so, Latino/a scholarship across the theological spectrum upholds some level of biblical normativity. The occasional **hermeneutics of suspicion** does not negate the Bible's ongoing **authority** and power.

Latino/a Readings of the Bible

What might Latino/a readings look like? What could Latinos/as mine from the Bible to provide hope in *lo cotidiano* (the experience of daily life) and to give diaspora existence significance with God and before others? Textual techniques among Latino/a biblical scholars and theologians might vary, but—whatever

5. Key authors include J. Severino Croatto, Carlos Mesters, and Elsa Tamez.

the method chosen—this orientation offers new insights into the text. There, Latinos/as find meaning for life, analogous experiences of displaced minority peoples, wrestling with hybrid identities, compassionate legislation for the outsider, and the assurance of God's presence in their troubles. At the same time, the Bible can raise the majority culture's awareness of the strangers in their midst. The following discussion is but a small taste of the richness of these contributions. The readings are grouped into two general categories.

The Bible Reveals the Worth of the Stranger

A recurring issue among minority communities is a sense of inferiority. This is not the place to probe the possible reasons for this complex, but the Bible contradicts that powerful lie. All human beings are made in the image of God (Gen. 1:26–28; cf. 2:15). They are the crown of creation and, as God's representatives, they are to subdue, rule, and steward the earth. The foundational truth, then, is that every person has not only worth but also incalculable potential. There should be no doubt in the heart and mind of any Latino/a that they are valuable in the sight of God, irrespective of whatever prejudice they might experience. They should dream and strive and not let themselves be defined by cultural bias or be pulled down by the destructive choices of those Latinos/as who feel disenfranchised. The Bible gives voice to the powerless in its stories (e.g., Gen. 16; 1 Kings 17:7–24) and songs (e.g., the theme of the poor in the Psalter; 1 Sam. 2:1–10; cf. Luke 1:46–55). God walks with the marginalized, because they matter. The creativity of humanity also means that there are aspects of Latino/a culture to enjoy and in which we can rightly take pride; these should be championed as a divine gift to the broader society and not be a source of shame or embarrassment.

The value of the outsider is evident not only in the creation account. It is clear, too, in the sojourner (Hebrew *gēr*) laws of Exodus, Leviticus, and Deuteronomy. No other ancient law code demonstrates a similar level of concern for outsiders. Old Testament law appreciated their vulnerability and mandated a series of directives to safeguard impartiality in legal proceedings, fair wages and rest from labor, and the provision of food (e.g., Exod. 20:10; Deut. 24:14–22). These outsiders were even allowed to participate in Israel's religious rituals, the most precious part of their culture (e.g., Exod. 12:45–49; Lev. 16:29). Israel was reminded of the history of its own sojourning, but most importantly of God's love for the immigrant (Deut. 10:17–22). Lessons for today abound, for those of the Latino/a diaspora as well as for those of the majority culture who claim the Christian faith. The former can trust in divine attentiveness to their condition; the latter should consider ways to tangibly express God's heart for sojourners, whether through charitable projects, social advocacy, or legal initiatives; these newcomers are neighbors whom the people of God are to love (Lev. 19:18, 33–34).

Still another avenue is to explore the concept of *mestizaje* (biological and/ or cultural blending) in the Bible. Virgilio Elizondo's work is relevant at this point. He sought to establish parallels between the borderlands experiences of Mexican Americans and the life and ministry of Jesus, a Jew from the cultural and political backwater of Galilee. This otherness was fundamental to Jesus' identification with the marginalized and his challenge to the religious authorities in Jerusalem. Whatever the shortcomings of Elizondo's proposal, the link between *mestizaje* and Jesus is powerful. Latinos/as can see themselves as connected to Jesus himself in unique fashion. They can begin to appreciate their *mestizaje* as a legitimate *locus theologicus* (formal theological context) This is another foundation on which to stand confidently before what can be unfair and degrading circumstances, and from which to speak truth to power.

The Bible Mirrors Diaspora Experiences

Reading Old Testament Narratives of *Migration* Latinamente

Human history is the history of migration. It is not surprising, therefore, that migration is a major reality in the OT. In the ancient world, like today, migration was either voluntary or forced and was driven by hunger, war, or natural disasters.

A clear example of voluntary migration in the OT is the story of Ruth, a well-known tale that resonates with the experiences of many immigrants. Ruth had married an immigrant from Judah, one of Naomi's sons and, now widowed, becomes herself an immigrant to a foreign land. She takes advantage of her rights as a widow and sojourner to glean in the fields and thereby provide for herself and Naomi. Her hard work gains the respect of the other harvesters, and she catches the eye of the landowner and kinsman Boaz. Later, at the threshing floor she again takes the initiative, at great personal risk, directing Boaz about his next course of action. In the closing chapter Ruth receives accolades from the elders and praise from the townswomen, who had ignored Ruth at her arrival. This resourceful foreigner secures her future by crossing ethnic boundaries and progressively finding her way into the heart of the townspeople. Surely Obed, the *mestizo* son she bears Boaz, would not endure his mother's travails. The genealogy at the book's close reveals that from Obed would come David. The NT extends that link to Jesus (Matt. 1:5, 16). The lesson is profound: God can reward the efforts of immigrants to find a way in their new context and may have a future beyond their imagination for them and their families.

There are several accounts of forced migration in the OT. Not too long after Abram receives the divine promise (Gen. 12), a famine in the land forces him to move to Egypt with his wife (Sarai), nephew, servants, and animals. The Egyptians had built a series of forts along their eastern frontier to monitor the movement of those seeking entry. Because of the Nile River, Egypt was less prone to crop failures, so that people were constantly trying to enter and find sustenance. Abram probably conceived of the scheme to have Sarai present herself as his sister as they approached such an outpost. How to get past the military outpost and cross that *frontera* to survive? This desperate measure of hungry people puts Sarai in a particularly dangerous situation. Parallels abound of modern-day immigrants taking tremendous gambles at the borderlands to seek a better life. That liminal space is the decision point for survival.

Biblical characters embody varying degrees of accommodation that typify the decisions of diaspora peoples. We begin with Joseph (Gen. 37–50). His brothers sell him into slavery, but through a series of divine coincidences in Egypt, he finds himself in Pharaoh's court as second in command. Joseph is given an Egyptian name and an Egyptian wife, but, interestingly, he gives their children Israelite names (Gen. 41:41–52). He never loses his mother tongue and is able to converse with his brothers many years later when he coordinates the admittance of his extended family into Goshen. When Jacob, the aged Bedouin, arrives, Joseph presents him to Pharaoh. Might it have been awkward for Joseph, in his prestigious role, to present his father, someone who practiced a despised profession (Gen. 46:32–34), to one of the most powerful men on the earth? Amazingly, Jacob blesses Pharaoh. This gracious act of a believing immigrant supersedes the cultural strictures of the new host country (Gen. 47:1–12). At the end, Joseph asks to be buried in his homeland (Gen. 50). Although assimilated to Egypt and in a position of privilege, Joseph never forgot his cultural roots.

In the Joseph story we witness the convoluted process of cultural adaptation and his choice not to forsake his ethnic identity or family loyalties. We also can ponder how to follow Jacob's example of blessing those in authority in the host country. Things do not always go as hoped, however. Eventually the descendants of the patriarchs find themselves as slaves to the Egyptians, who feared the growth in Israelite numbers. Cruel measures are put into place to control that foreign population, even as the Egyptians want them to keep working. In the midst of all the suffering, the midwives resist with wisdom and bravery (Exod. 1–2). Those with eyes to see will perceive parallels with contemporary fears of the growing immigrant population coupled with the need for foreign labor.

Centuries later thousands were exiled from Judah after the fall of Jerusalem (587/586 BCE) and relocated in the Babylonian heartland (the **Babylonian exile**). For some, this experience was horrific and humiliating; they loathed their captors (Ps. 137). Some expected a quick return, but Jeremiah counsels these immigrants to invest in their new setting (Jer. 29). There would be a *mañana*, but according to God's timing and means. Archaeological data reveals that a number of Judeans fared well in exile, which explains why at Cyrus's decree many did not join the returnees (2 Chron. 36:22–23; Ezra 1–2) or later accompany Ezra (Ezra 7–8). Through the guidance of her well-to-do kinsman Mordecai, Esther progressively moves from apparent unconcern for her Jewish heritage to maneuvering to save her people. Never, however, is any thought given to leaving Babylon for the province of Yehud (Judah).

Daniel and his friends live in diaspora. They are given new names (a sign of subjection to their Babylonian captors) and are schooled for government positions. How hard it must have been to go through that regimen in order to serve the empire that had destroyed their capital city and temple, taken away their families' possessions, and killed family and friends! Through what must have been painful situations, they maintain their integrity—both religious (the confession of YHWH) and cultural (their diet)—and are exemplary students. As foreigners, they are detested by other officials but willingly stand up for what they know is right (Dan. 1–6). Adaptation to their surroundings there was, but within parameters. Ezekiel, in turn, lived among the diaspora community and worked to convince his people of the sovereign plans of their God. Nehemiah, on the other hand, was cupbearer to the Persian king. His faithful service gained him royal support for rebuilding Jerusalem's walls, after which he returned to work again for the emperor. He too fought religiocultural concessions and bemoaned the loss of the Hebrew language (Neh. 13). Ezra the priest, on the other hand, adamantly opposed anything foreign. He appealed to the empire for help only when necessary, and he acted severely against those who he felt had compromised their way of life (Ezra 9–10).

This range of attitudes and behavior in the diaspora, and the occasional indications of what today we might label transnationalism, are mirrored in the various kinds of integration among Latinos/as. The adaptation process entails the constant negotiation of identity markers. The biblical narratives present different cultural options, even as they portray the characters' faith commitments in those diverse circumstances.

© Wayne Healy and David Botello

Figure 18.2. This mural of "la familia" depicts the family's centrality and variety of roles in Latino/a communities.

Reading New Testament Narratives of Migration Latinamente

To these OT narratives can be added migrant experiences from the NT. Matthew 2 depicts the flight to Egypt by Jesus, Mary, and Joseph (the text is silent about their life there as refugees). The early church was dispersed from Jerusalem by persecution and thereby was birthed as a diaspora people (Acts 8:1–8; 11:19–30). Paul's missionary strategy was marked by diaspora realities. He often began in a city by proclaiming the good news among diaspora Jews; in several locations there also resided displaced gentiles. The leadership of the church at Antioch was from different places and ethnicities (Acts 13:1). Key leaders of the incipient movement were diaspora Christians (e.g., Priscilla and Aquila, Apollos). The apostle's demand for oneness in Christ may have been informed, at least in part, by friction between Jews and gentiles who represented not only different religious views but also dissimilar cultural and ethnic backgrounds (e.g., Acts 6:1–6; Gal. 3:28; Eph. 2:11–22). The Christians addressed in 1 Peter 1:1 as "exiles" (or "aliens") probably had been relocated by the Roman Empire: they were both legal and spiritual outsiders. In sum, migration, diaspora, and hybridity were foundational to the start and growth of the Christian church. The NT helps shift the attention of Latinos/as from perhaps looking only for parallels of their struggles to cognizance of the missional significance of those experiences for their faith.

Migration and the diaspora life are highlighted by their application in the NT to every Christian (1 Pet. 2:11). We have a different citizenship and serve another king (cf. Phil. 3:20; Heb. 13:14). Though Christians live *in* the world, they should not be *of* it; they are to consider themselves strangers in a strange land. A migrant perspective, in other words, can help all Christians better understand their true identity. Said another way, *the churches of the host culture need the presence and voice of the immigrant for their own Christian faith.* Believing Latino/a immigrants should appreciate this divine role! Diaspora faith communities are a God-given blessing.

This brief survey of some Latino/a interpretations demonstrates the new perspectives that these readings bring to academic biblical research and to pastoral work among diaspora and majority cultures alike. They should encourage and empower Latinos/as; at the same time, they might reveal to those of the majority culture areas of systemic injustice and prejudice that must be addressed. They can reorient the convictions of both groups about life, community, and God.

Future Prospects

In some ways Latino/a biblical approaches to the Bible are in their infancy. Much remains to be explored in terms of method and results, and there also is the goal of achieving a broader impact within the academic guild and in institutions of higher learning. A major pioneer has been Justo González, a historical theologian, who has ventured successfully into the arena of biblical studies. He has furthered Latino/a scholarship by being instrumental in the founding of the Association for Hispanic Theological Education (AETH, Asociación para la Educación Teológica Hispana), the Hispanic Theological Initiative (HTI), the Hispanic Summer Program (HSP), and the journal *Apuntes.* Another pioneer and mentor to many is NT scholar Fernando Segovia, who has been key in organizing conferences and editing publications to disseminate the work of Latino/a scholars. Latino/a Roman Catholic biblical scholars are active in the Academy of Catholic Theologians of the United States (ACTHUS), and many of all traditions are involved in national and international professional societies.

As with any such movement, there are at least two possible dangers. One is that conversations get circumscribed to scholarly circles and that actual engagement with the grassroots diminishes, that Latino/a scholars speak for their communities although they are no longer truly connected to *la vida cotidiana* of the marginalized—even as they declare what needs to be said to Latinos/as and to the majority culture. A second danger is that the Latino/a prophetic voice gets co-opted by the guild—that is, domesticated by inclusion. In this case, Latino/a interpretation becomes simply another academic specialty, one more interesting point of view among other minoritized voices.

These are real concerns. Latino/a biblical scholars, however, have been willing to be self-critical, and working *en conjunto* fosters accountability. The set of commitments detailed earlier bodes well for a bright future for Latino/a interpretation. There is much transformative work to be done with the text, in ecclesial bodies, in academic (theological and secular) institutions, and in the larger society. *Estamos construyendo un nuevo futuro* (We are building a new future).

QUESTIONS FOR REFLECTION AND DISCUSSION

1. How does this chapter help your appreciation of Latinos/as as a diaspora people?
2. What aspects of Latino/a biblical interpretation are different from what you have understood to be normative for biblical interpretation?
3. How might your own approach to biblical interpretation be enriched by Latino/a perspectives?

FOR FURTHER READING AND STUDY

Agosto, Efraín. "Latino/a Hermeneutics." In *Hearing the New Testament: Strategies for Interpretation*, edited by Joel B. Green, 350–71. 2nd ed. Grand Rapids: Eerdmans, 2010. Applies Segovia's hermeneutic of engaging the Bible from Latino/a realities to NT texts.

Carroll R., M. Daniel. *Christians at the Border: Immigration, the Church, and the Bible*. 2nd ed. Grand Rapids: Brazos, 2013. Surveys the history of US immigration and immigration law, and presents OT and NT teaching on migration.

———. "Reading the Bible through Other Lenses: New Vistas from a Hispanic Diaspora Perspective." In *Global Voices: Reading the Bible in the Majority World*, edited by Craig S. Keener and M. Daniel Carroll R., 5–26. Peabody, MA: Hendrickson, 2012. Discusses new insights from reading OT narratives through the eyes of diaspora Hispanics.

Carroll R., M. Daniel, and Leopoldo A. Sánchez M., eds. *Immigrant Neighbors among Us: Immigration across Theological Traditions*. Eugene, OR: Wipf & Stock, 2015. Hispanic theologians process immigration through the unique lens of their theological traditions.

Croatto, J. Severino. *Biblical Hermeneutics: Toward a Theory of Reading as the Production of Meaning*. Translated by R. R. Barr. Maryknoll, NY: Orbis, 1987. Argues from a South American context for the potential of new meanings latent in texts generated by *relecturas* (rereadings) on behalf of today's oppressed.

Elizondo, Virgilio. *Galilean Journey: The Mexican-American Promise*. Rev. ed. Mary-knoll, NY: Orbis, 2000. Pioneer text establishing *mestizaje* as a theological category.

González, Justo L. *Santa Biblia: The Bible through Hispanic Eyes*. Nashville: Abingdon, 1996. Groundbreaking classic that presents the central characteristics of reading *latinamente*.

Guardiola-Sáenz, Leticia A. "Latina/o Interpretation." In *The Oxford Encyclopedia of Biblical Interpretation*, edited by Steven L. McKenzie, 1:483–91. Oxford: Oxford University Press, 2013. Surveys the diverse approaches and major figures of Latino/a interpretation.

Lozada, Francisco, Jr., and Fernando F. Segovia, eds. *Latino/a Biblical Hermeneutics: Problematics, Objectives, Strategies*. Semeia Studies 68. Atlanta: SBL Press, 2014. Broad exploration of Latino/a identity and biblical interpretation.

Mesters, Carlos. *Defenseless Flower: A New Reading of the Bible*. Translated by Francis McDonagh. Maryknoll, NY: Orbis, 1989. A Roman Catholic rereading of Scripture grounded in the interpretations of poor people in the small Christian communities of Brazil.

Rivera-Rodríguez, Luis. "Toward a Diaspora Hermeneutics (Hispanic North America)." In *Character Ethics and the Old Testament: Moral Dimensions of Scripture*, edited by M. Daniel Carroll R. and Jacqueline E. Lapsley, 169–89. Louisville: Westminster John Knox, 2007. Detailed presentation of diaspora hermeneutics.

Ruiz, Jean-Pierre. *Readings from the Edges: The Bible and People on the Move*. Maryknoll, NY: Orbis, 2011. Explores responsible interpretive method and highlights texts not commonly used in migration discussions.

Segovia, Fernando F. "Toward a Latino/a American Biblical Criticism: Latin(o/a)ness as Problematic." In *They Were All Together in One Place? Toward Minority Biblical Criticism*, edited by Randall C. Bailey, Tat-siong Benny Liew, and Fernando F. Segovia, 193–223. Semeia Studies 57. Atlanta: Society of Biblical Literature, 2009. Probes the complexities of a Latino/a perspective vis-à-vis the dominant paradigm and other minority approaches.

Tamez, Elsa. *Bible of the Oppressed*. Translated by M. J. O'Connell. Maryknoll, NY: Orbis, 1982. An in-depth analysis of key terms for oppression in the OT from the perspective of the marginalized, by a leading Protestant biblical scholar in Costa Rica.

———. *The Scandalous Message of James: Faith without Works Is Dead*. Rev. ed. New York: Crossroad, 2002. A liberationist, Latin American reading of James that offers a prophetic critique of capitalist economies and reveals God's identification with the poor.

19

Asian and Asian American Biblical Interpretation

K. K. YEO

In Asia, difference surpasses commonality, hybridity takes the place of singularity, and multiplicity overshadows uniformity. With the exception of the interpreters having a shared cultural heritage, there is very little common ground between biblical interpretations of Asians and Asian Americans, or even among Asians themselves. This essay summarizes biblical interpretations in the vast region called Asia and is intended to provide a brief survey for novice readers, allowing them to explore the diversity of Asian and Asian American biblical interpretation in light of their disparate contexts—contexts out of which the Bible is read *and* to which the Bible still speaks. Readers may want to compare and contrast these interpretations—strategies of **contextualization**—with those of the West, Africa, or Latin America and, in doing so, note the fluid and powerful translatability of the Bible across space and time. Because Asian biblical interpretations reflect only a microcosm of the multiple centers of global Christianity, interpreters face the challenge of being **catholic**/global (Rev. 7:9) and **ecumenical**/united (John 17:21) with one another.

Historical Overview

Over time, as the gospel has been proclaimed and the Bible translated, the population center of the church has shifted from the Middle East to Europe and Africa, then to Asia and Latin America. Today the Asian church (along with the African and Latin American churches) constitutes the **Majority World** and is part of the "Next Christendom" (Philip Jenkins).[1] Yet Indian and Chinese Christianities are not new. Even if one considers the apostle Thomas's missionary activity to India in AD 52 and the early **Syriac** missionaries' work in China in the second century (the Han dynasty) as mere legends, there is historical evidence to suggest that the Bible already was part of the Syriac liturgy in India in the sixth century and that the **Nestorians** translated part of the Bible into the Chinese language as early as the seventh century.[2]

Missionaries, together with local collaborators, translated the Bible into the vernacular languages of various people groups, so that individual tribes and nations could understand God and his creative, as well as redemptive, activities in the language of their hearts. Not too far behind the West, where the Tyndale NT was published in 1526 and the King James Bible in 1611, the East saw publication of the Tamil Bible called *Cardila* in 1554, the Malay-Dutch Bible in 1651, and the Jean Basset NT, a Chinese Bible translation, prior to 1707.[3] For several centuries now, local communities of faith have read the Bible in their own languages, out of their own contexts, making sense of God's Word for their specific life situations. While Western missionaries have been responsible for significant contributions to and influences on Asian biblical interpretations, Asian Christians are neither "passive receptors" nor "empty-handed" (Gerald West's term) negotiators in their interpretations, and the following sections will show their *owned* methods of reading the Bible. For the Spirit, blowing as the Spirit pleases (John 3:8), inspires Asian readers to read the Word for salvation and life.

Methods and Principles

We see that within the Bible the original message of God's salvation is re-interpreted as the readers' context changes. The idea of not pouring "new wine

---

1. Philip Jenkins, *The Next Christendom* (New York: Oxford University Press, 2007).
2. The **Nestorians**, also called the Church of the East, were Christians in Persia who used Syriac liturgical rites and believed in the distinctiveness, or independence, of Jesus' humanity and his divinity. Their missionaries went to China via the Silk Road in the seventh century.
3. Tamil is the language of the Tamil people of southern India and Sri Lanka; Malay is the language of Malaysia, Indonesia, and surrounding areas.

. . . into old wineskins" (Matt. 9:17) applies to methods of reading the Bible. Biblical interpretations that emerge from "the womb of Asia" (C. S. Song) need fresh wineskins, which reflect the principle of "four selfs" proposed by Hispanic theologian Justo L. González for the church in the Majority World: self-support, self-propagation, self-administration, and *self-theologizing*.[4] This principle in turn infuses the hybrid identity of Asian biblical interpretations in the following ways.

Indigenous Translations of the Bible Embodied in Asian Worldviews

Bible translation is itself an act of interpretation. In Asia, the Bible has been translated into various indigenous vernaculars and has become embodied in Asian spiritual worldviews. At the same time, however, these translations have been done in dialogue with the original languages and concepts of the Bible. The ancient Chinese cosmology of **"yin-yang"** (which literally means a "shaded area" and a "brightly lit area" that are in constant flux) is often re-appropriated by Asian scholars to speak of the marginality and in-betweenness of theological method (including biblical interpretation). For example, the relational aspects of God's faithfulness (Exod. 3) and of being human (Gen. 1–2) demonstrate this flux respectively between God and his people as well as between male and female. In addition, local metaphors in Asia are used to describe biblical interpretations; for example, Kosuke Koyama, a Japanese missionary in Thailand, sees "water-buffalo" theology as the practical application of biblical readings in and for the nitty-gritty of life; Hwa Yung, a Methodist bishop in Malaysia, uses the image of "mangoes or bananas" of that country as metaphors for authentic Asian-Christian theology; and Thomas Thangaraj in India refers to Jesus as the "crucified guru."[5]

More than simply making the meaning of the Bible accessible to people, Bible translations and interpretations have a saving effect on cultures. Korean scholars use the concept of *han* (the relational consequence of sin) to interpret sin (Andrew Sung Park) and the concept of *jeong* (affection) to interpret **Christology** (Wonhee Anne Joh). In doing so, these scholars nuance and enrich the cultural concepts of both *han* and *jeong* with christological meaning. Similarly, I have shown how the Confucianist word *ren* (moral love) is used to translate *agapē* in the New Testament Chinese Bible; consequently,

---

4. Justo L. González, *Mañana: Christian Theology from a Hispanic Perspective* (Nashville: Abingdon, 1990), 49.

5. We offer numerous examples of biblical scholars and theologians in this chapter whose work, for reasons of space, does not appear in the bibliography. It may nonetheless be found online or in a good theological library.

the moral denotation of *ren* is infused and saturated with the connotation of divine love.

Worldview matters in biblical translation. Asian worldviews are radically different from those of most Westerners, who are "sold out to scientism, materialism, and determinism" (Jenkins, *New Faces of Christianity*, 16). Asian worldviews, similar to biblical worldviews, are dynamically religious. Asian Christians see spirits, witches, and magic at work in numerous dimensions of life: morality, health, natural disaster, and so forth. Biblical texts such as Psalms 31 and 91, Luke 10, and Ephesians 6, with their emphasis on invisible forces and spiritual battle (texts that are not favorites of Western Christians), have become the **canon within the canon** for Asian believers.

In India, where *dalits* (the "oppressed," the "destitute," or the "untouchables": members of the lowest caste in Hindu society) are essentially forbidden to read, Indian churches teach *dalits* to read the Bible first and foremost so that they can participate in the *magical act* of gaining the supernatural power needed to break the curse of being born into a caste worse than slaves. As they read and interpret the Bible for themselves, it nourishes and sustains their freedom and power. To protect themselves and their families from evil spirits, some Chinese Christians in rural China have biblical verses written on red paper and posted on the doorposts of their homes. Intellectual study of the Bible in Asia does not exclude belief in the supernatural world.

A "Glocal," Praxis-Based Engagement of Scripture toward a Catholic Faith

Keeping in mind the fact that the world is local *and* global (thus the term **"glocal"**), Asian biblical interpreters value a practical approach to scriptural engagement that honors the multiple contexts of various cultures but also aims toward building a catholic Christian faith of ecumenical respect and relations.

Natee Tanchangpongs, a Thai scholar, shows the intricate and complex ways in which the following four Asian theologians use their multilayered contexts (religiously, scripturally, linguistically, and racially) to express the doctrine of the Trinity: Raimundo Panikkar and Brahmabandhab Upadhyaya, both Indians; Jung Young Lee, a Korean; and Nozomu Miyahira, a Japanese. Yet, as a faithful Bible reader, Tanchangpongs critically challenges each of these theologians not only to allow Scripture to speak prophetically to their respective contexts but also to begin the global dialogue among non-Asian Christians regarding the Trinity ("Asian Reformulation of the Trinity"). Only an ongoing dialogue that holds to the ethic of humility will allow each biblical reading to move toward an Asian hermeneutic that is both catholic and ecumenical while guarding against blind spots and distorted vision.

In fact, theory and practice are inseparable in Asian biblical interpretation. Living in a pluralistic society, Asian Bible readers cannot afford to have a "private faith" or a narrow vision of faith. Despite the sociopolitical alienation of Christians as a minority in Asia, they are able to read the Bible and claim an identity for themselves as "a royal priesthood [and] a holy nation" (Exod. 19:6; 1 Pet. 2:9), therefore bearing witness to the power of the gospel. James 1:27 speaks to their hearts: "Religion that is pure and undefiled before God, the Father, is this: to care for orphans and widows in their distress, and to keep oneself unstained by the world." Elsewhere I have written, "As our own horizons are pulled away from our immediate communities to tsunamis in India, earthquakes in China, nuclear disaster in Japan, . . . we are wrested away from our centripetal tendencies to linger in the comfort zones of the local and are propelled into the centrifugal tendencies to participate in the global" (Yeo, "Theology and the Future of Global Christianity," 60).

Interpreting the Bible Cross-Culturally in the Context of Real-Life Issues

Because Asian Christians believe the Bible is authoritative in matters of faith and life, Asian biblical interpretations are distinctively cross-cultural enterprises that respond to *real-life issues* of gender (e.g., female prostitution), ethnicity (e.g., rivalry, cleansing), health (e.g., epidemic outbreaks), justice (e.g., human trafficking, child labor), politics (e.g., authoritarian regimes, corruption), and regional concerns (e.g., interreligious and territorial conflicts, environmental devastation). This cross-cultural sensitivity to real-life issues concretely affects interpretation. For example, although the original recipients of the biblical writings were located in the Middle East (which includes Western Asia), contemporary interpreters in the very different cultures of South and East Asia value Genesis for its universal and inclusive creation story, in contrast to the story of Jacob/Israel, which takes on an ethnocentric tone. The social, ecological, and expansive biblical lens guides Asian believers to read Mosaic laws in Exodus as rules of life and basic tenets of human rights and freedom, in contrast to the rather restrictive purpose of the ritual laws in Leviticus. Asian Christians look to Proverbs for practical wisdom. They find in Revelation a message of hope that is illuminating to those living in sociopolitical uncertainty and hardship, while the ecological concern of Revelation jolts their consciences to take care of the world.

Sensitivity to the imbalance of power in the world is one of the understandings or presuppositions that Asian Christians bring to the Bible as they read cross-culturally. The book of Romans is often read in Asian contexts, as it may have been in the original Roman imperial context, as a political "hidden transcript" (James Scott)[6] of resistance to oppression that addresses, for example, the Malaysian occasional Islamic oppression of other racial and religious groups (Hii Kong-hock). In light of the dissymmetry of wealth and oppression of the poor in Korea, 1 and 2 Kings are read in such a way as to critique the prosperity gospel in that country (e.g., Lee Kyung Sook).

Furthermore, many Asian theologies, rooted in Scripture (especially in the Gospels), address real-life issues. Korean interpreters point to Jesus' siding with marginal groups and the *ochlos* (crowd) in the Synoptic Gospels, and construct *minjung* (populace / the common people) **theology** as they give voice to the powerless and poor in Korea. The book of Ruth is read by *dalit* Christian women to overcome their "thrice-oppressions": pollution, powerlessness, and poverty. Like Ruth, these women find dignity, power, and wholeness. Ruth is read christologically so that, through a friendship with Christ, *dalit* Christian women are no longer the "lost sheep" and so that Jesus has become a *dalit* himself among them. In all these cases, the Bible not only speaks comfort, deliverance, and freedom to Asian Christians but also passes judgment on the oppressors and the oppressive system/culture.

Readings in Liminal (In-Between), Marginal, Shifting Spaces

For Asian American Christians living in, and *in-between*, two worlds (i.e., Asia and America), globalization subjects them to rapid change and often threatens their immigrant identity of *double-rootedness*, so they are therefore unable to live fully in either place.[7] This struggle to identify who one really is, unfortunately, is true of Asian Christians as well, but their in-betweenness or liminality exists in the sense of double citizenship in their country and in God's kingdom. A Korean American theologian, Sang Hyun Lee, reads Jesus the Galilean as living in a liminal space of his day in which the presence of God is found. First Peter and James are texts of survival and thriving for Asian Americans, although most of them are not themselves confronted with the problems of exile. Yet the issues of migration, trafficking, and marginality in a shared-space society are real global problems their theologies must engage.

6. See, e.g., James C. Scott, *Domination and the Arts of Resistance: Hidden Transcripts* (New Haven: Yale University Press, 1990).

7. The same could, of course, be said of Asian European Christians, and so forth.

Much of Asian and Asian American biblical interpretation wrestles with the problem of the liminal and marginalized existence in the critical context of empire and colonial hegemony (see, e.g., Kwok Pui-lan, Gale Yee). Children and women are the most vulnerable victims in the system of hegemony and poverty. Many Western Christians misread 1 Timothy 2, 1 Corinthians 11, and Ephesians 5 as reinforcing patriarchal values and the submission of women, yet Asian and Asian American feminist theologians offer a variety of alternative readings that are creative and powerful (see Brock et al., *Off the Menu*).

Like their Asian friends, Asian Americans in general occupy a more privileged social status and achieve higher education at a greater-than-average rate when compared to the rest of society. However, they face the temptations of power, wealth, and money (cf. Matt. 4). Powers and principalities, both inside and outside the church, are thorny issues that Asian Americans seek to unmask as they marshal biblical resources for their public biblical theology.

A Contextualized Biblical Interpretation That Engenders Potent Spirituality

What do these principles mean for the daily lives of Asian Christians?

No one comes to the biblical text with absolute objectivity; each interpreter approaches Scripture with certain lenses and assumptions. The daily challenge to live peacefully in multireligious, racial, and contextual societies means that Asian Christians tend to prefer Isaiah's vision of God's expansive mercy and inclusive love for the world, while they find the narratives in Joshua and Judges to be parochial and unhelpful. They mimic Matthew's **intertextual** hermeneutic between the OT and the teachings of Christ for their own reading of the Bible and cultural classics. They love wisdom literature, such as Proverbs in the OT and James in the NT, for the practical teaching in moral, religious, and communal life found in these writings.

Living in contexts of dislocation, migration, and displacement, Asian Christians find important themes in the following biblical texts: the call of Abraham to leave his hometown for the promised land (Gen. 11:31–12:9); the wilderness wandering of the exodus generation; and the exilic narratives of various captivities in the OT and the NT (see Hebrews, 1 Peter, and James). Asian Christians learn from the Bible that the normative life in God's kingdom is nomadic. Seeing themselves as people of God in sojourn/pilgrimage, they also take seriously the covenantal promise of God for them to be God's "treasured possession," and they pledge their loyalty to obey God's Word faithfully (Exod. 19:5).

Responding to issues of poverty and epidemic, Asian biblical interpretations lay claim to the promise of Jesus as the great "I am." Because they are dealing with the issue of famine, the word of Jesus, "I am the bread of life" (John 6:41–51), speaks volumes to them. In this view, Jesus' heavenly Father still cares for the dispossessed. Bakery businesses and love feasts mark the kingdom ethic of the body of Christ in Asia. Asian interpreters relive the stories of Mary's prayer, the Magnificat, taking solace in God's identifying with the poor and lowly, and passing judgment on the oppressive rich. Asian Christians also rehearse the Elijah and Elisha stories of ministering to the hungry (1 Kings 19:4–8).

Since resources are limited in Asian contexts, especially when natural catastrophe or human mismanagement occurs, many resort to borrowing from friends and banks, loans that come with heavy interest. Thus, the biblical discussion of the unbearable problem of debt as "trespassing" is real to Asian interpreters. As the Lord's Prayer has it, "Forgive us our debts, as we also have forgiven our debtors" (Matt. 6:12); however, this can be a disturbing call for the wealthy bankers to forgive financial debt, not just spiritual wrongs. The Jubilee concept of forgiven debt becomes a sociopolitical message of revolution (Lev. 25:8–13; Luke 4:19) if financial institutions only have ears to hear.

Contemporary and Future Challenges

If Jesus has an "Asian face" (so R. S. Sugirtharajah, Peter C. Phan), I suppose it must look rather colorful, chameleon-like, and spirited. There are many challenges and unanswered questions, however, regarding the kaleidoscopic and animated Asian faces of biblical interpretation in this region.

First, compared with interpretations from other continents, Asian biblical interpretations are more cross-cultural, not only linguistically but also contextually, because of their rich traditions. Yet the question remains: How does extra-Christian or prebiblical revelation relate to biblical theology and revelation? The longer the history and civilization a culture has, the harder it is to provide an easy answer, although we can safely assume that the agency or Spirit of God must be at work in that part of the world since the genesis of time and space (Gen. 1:1–2). Perhaps this is an enduring question regarding the relationship between general/natural revelation and special revelation. While Western Christians seldom question the use of secular philosophy and psychology in their theology and counseling respectively, Asian Christians often are questioned as to whether they can name God as Dao/Tao, Buddha, *Shangdi*, Bhakti, or Allah.

Second, Asians have a spiritual worldview, and many Christians have a superstitious faith; thus the perennial question arises: Is sickness or famine the result of human sin and, therefore, punishment from God—or worse still, a curse from an evil spirit? It is tempting to read Paul's teaching and his handkerchiefs as healing wands (Acts 19:12), raising the question whether Chinese Christians can seek traditional Daoist medicine for healing. It seems that a modern, scientific worldview of demythologizing both the biblical and the Asian worldviews will not solve the problem of superstitious faith. What is needed in the intertextual reading (between text and reader) is not simply reading Scripture *culturally* (i.e., one-way translation), but also ultimately reading the culture *biblically* (i.e., toward the transformation of culture). While Western Christians trust in modern medicine and distrust the power of prayer, should Asian Christian readings affirming that "every facet of life has to do with spiritual forces" be considered not biblical?

Third, in a region where poverty and prosperity are in stark contrast and result in a great division among people, what is the valid biblical preaching that teaches wealth and health as guaranteed for the godly (e.g., 1 Chron. 4:10)? By looking to the Christian West as the model for prosperity, and accepting the belief that biblical principles bless the Western market economy, Asian interpreters may be tempted toward biblical readings that are superficial, partial, or distorted. This raises the question about an ethic of biblical interpretation, which Asian interpreters must face—just as biblical interpreters from other regions must.

Fourth, Asian biblical scholars need to be in constant dialogue with non-Asian scholars rather than simply listening exclusively to their own voices. The challenge in the commitment to ecumenical dialogue is an interpretive *virtue* calling Bible readers to listen to biblical interpretations outside of their own contexts. Monologue or monocultural interpretation has too many blind spots of its own. "Iron sharpens iron" (Prov. 27:17), so one interpretation can sharpen the other. For example, the pain of God and wounded love (*han*) in Japanese and Korean biblical interpretations may sound to Westerners like denying God's impassibility (inability to suffer), recalling the history of judging patripassianism or Sabellianism,[8] and they may see this as **heresy** (cf. 2 Cor. 5:19, 21; 13:14; Matt. 27:46; 28:16–20; 1 John 5:6–8). Is it possible to

8. Patripassianism: the belief, in the ancient Western church, that the Father (*patri-*) suffers (*passio-*) as God is incarnated in Jesus; Sabellianism: the belief, in the ancient Eastern church, that the three members of the Trinity are three modes or aspects of the One God, and therefore not three co-eternal persons within the Godhead.

read Philippians 2 as God's self-emptying of suffering between his love and his wrath, and thereby interpret the pain/wound not simply as God's saving mercy but also as an attribute of *pathos* (as Kazoh Kitamori does)?

Engaging Asian Biblical Interpretations

There are two critical issues that I want to mention briefly as we engage with Asian biblical interpretations.

First, in general, Asian interpretations tend to hold a high view of biblical **authority** in matters pertaining to their moral and religious life. Is it true that "all scripture is inspired by God and is useful for teaching, for reproof, for correction, and for training in righteousness" (2 Tim. 3:16) for the world church? This issue raises the question about our perception of *biblical authority* and the way this authority impacts the way we read the Bible. For example, one of the divisive and painful issues is the use of the Bible (Gen. 19:1–29; Lev. 18:22, 20:13; Rom. 1:18–32; 1 Cor. 6:9–11; 1 Tim. 1:10) with regard to the sexuality of LGBTQI (lesbian, gay, bisexual, transgender, queer or questioning, and intersex) persons.

Second, as mainline denominational lines break down and a charismatic local community emerges as church, nonclergy and congregational preaching and teaching of the Bible in Asia increasingly creates an **ecclesiology** of lay leadership. When there is neither magisterium nor bishop to judge the authentic teaching or to validate a biblical interpretation, then the critical issue is identifying the criteria needed to discern sound biblical teaching. For example, the ways in which Asian Christians experience the Bible in visions, exorcisms, healings, and miracles may be categorized by Western interpreters as unscientific, and thus not "legitimate" interpretations of the Bible. On the other hand, while Western Christians generally trust their government and the stock market, Asian Christians generally distrust the secular order, thus doing a sociopolitical reading of the Bible in critique of government power.

Conclusion

One may ask Christians in Asia the question, "Do you understand what you are reading?" (Acts 8:30). That is a fair question to ask, but only if asked of the world church as well. The ultimate purpose of this essay is to invite all of us to engage with one another in *our* interpretations of the Bible. Then, and only then, will we come to appreciate the inexhaustible meaning of the same biblical text that different regions and peoples have to offer—even though the interpretations may look different or even conflict with one another.

QUESTIONS FOR REFLECTION AND DISCUSSION

1. How would you characterize the similarities and differences between your experience of biblical interpretation in your context(s) and the approaches to biblical interpretation of Asian and Asian American Christians?

2. What great strengths and what potential problems, if any, do you find in the Asian approaches to biblical interpretation and theology discussed in this chapter?

3. What can Western Christians learn about biblical interpretation from Asian and Asian American Christians?

FOR FURTHER READING AND STUDY

Brock, Rita Nakashima, et al., eds. *Off the Menu: Asian and Asian North American Women's Religion and Theology*. Louisville: Westminster John Knox, 2007. Diverse views of Asian and Asian American women scholars on doing theology in a global context of hybridity and change.

Chan, Simon. *Grassroots Asian Theology: Thinking the Faith from the Ground Up*. Downers Grove, IL: IVP Academic, 2014. Reflects on the dynamic faith of Asian Christians in the lived contexts of Asian peoples and cultures.

Cosgrove, Charles, Herold Weiss, and K. K. Yeo. *Cross-Cultural Paul: Journeys to Others, Journeys to Ourselves*. Grand Rapids: Eerdmans, 2005. Six cultural-theological readings of the Pauline Epistles.

Jenkins, Philip, ed. *The New Faces of Christianity: Believing the Bible in the Global South*. New York: Oxford University Press, 2006. Examines biblical interpretation and issues in Asia and Africa.

Lee, Sang Hyun. *From a Liminal Place: An Asian American Theology*. Minneapolis: Fortress, 2010. Relates the Galilean Jesus' living in a liminal space in which the presence of God is found in Asian American experience.

Song, C. S. *Theology from the Womb of Asia*. Maryknoll, NY: Orbis, 1986. Classic work of Asian theology.

Sugirtharajah, R. S., ed. *Frontiers in Asian Christian Theology: Emerging Trends*. Eugene, OR: Wipf & Stock, 2010. Previews emerging themes in Asian theologies.

Tanchangpongs, Natee. "An Asian Reformulation of the Trinity." In *Trinity among the Nations*, edited by Gene L. Green, Stephen T. Pardue, and K. K. Yeo, 100–119.

Grand Rapids: Eerdmans, 2015. Examines and challenges Asian interpretations of the Trinity.

Yeo, K. K. *Musing with Confucius and Paul: Towards a Chinese Christian Theology.* Eugene, OR: Cascade, 2008. Reads Galatians in dialogue with the Analects (a Confucianist text).

———. "Theology and the Future of Global Christianity: Glocal and Public Theologies." In *Theology and the Future: Evangelical Assertions and Explorations,* edited by Trevor Cairney and David Starling, 45–61. Edinburgh: T&T Clark, 2014.

The Bible *and* Contemporary Christian Existence

Part 3 of this book consists of chapters that explore the relationship between Scripture and five aspects of contemporary Christian existence in the world: spirituality, ethics, politics, community, and mission. These five topics do not exhaust the various intimately interrelated dimensions of Christian practice that are affected by biblical interpretation (that would require a much longer book), but each is a significant topic. Moreover, none of these chapters claims to speak the last word on the subject at hand. Each author comes to the chapter with a particular perspective, and other writers would of course address the same topic quite differently. Nonetheless, these contributors are recognized authorities in their subject matter, and each attempts to provide a compelling analysis of the relationship between the Bible and the life of faith.

We do not here provide a general bibliography for part 3, for the topics that are or could be addressed are wide-ranging and not necessarily covered in a single volume. Once again, however, each chapter concludes with a bibliography of relevant books and articles.

St. Augustine said, "Anyone, then, who thinks they have understood the divine Scriptures, or any part of them, but cannot with this understanding increase in the twofold love of God and neighbor has not yet understood them" (Augustine, *On Christian Teaching* 1.36.40, my translation). These words suggest the reason for, and the spirit of, the chapters that follow.

20

The Bible and Spirituality

Patricia Fosarelli and Michael J. Gorman

Throughout the ages, the words of Scripture have encouraged believers to grow in their knowledge and love of God. It is appropriate, therefore, that the ecumenical Christian community in Taizé, France, points those who visit its website to two early Christian theologians who knew that the Bible is "the inexhaustible wellspring by which God gives himself to thirsting human beings" (Origen, third century) and that it is a "letter from God to creatures" that enables them "to discover God's heart in God's words" (Gregory the Great, sixth century).[1] In this chapter we explore the relationship between Scripture and spiritual growth, beginning with a brief definition of the latter before considering how Scripture can promote it.

It may surprise some readers that a chapter about spirituality even appears in this book. This is because there are two common, but misguided, sentiments in some quarters of the Christian church regarding the relationship between spirituality and the academic or intellectual life. One is the belief that intellectual pursuits do not benefit the spiritual life and may even be dangerous to it. The other is the belief that spirituality is somehow "beneath" those who are intellectually serious about Christianity and specifically about the literary, historical, and even theological study of the Bible.

---

1. See "Preparing a Time of Prayer," Taizé, February 1, 2016, http://www.taize.fr/en_article 337.html.

M. Gorman

Figure 20.1. The Church of Reconciliation, the heart of the ecumenical community at Taizé, and some of the thousands of young people gathered to pray and discuss Scripture.

Unfortunately, at times professional theologians and biblical scholars have perpetuated these notions, particularly the second one. However, as practicing Christians and as professors of spirituality and of biblical studies, one Catholic and one Protestant, we have found neither of these sentiments to be true for us or for the majority of our colleagues and mentors—or our students. Moreover, there are many biblical scholars around the world whose academic work is both motivated and nurtured by their deep spirituality, as this book, for example, indicates.

What Is Spiritual Growth?

In his Letter to the Romans, the apostle Paul writes the following:

> I appeal to you, therefore, brothers and sisters, by the mercies of God, to present your bodies as a living sacrifice, holy and acceptable to God, which is your

spiritual worship. Do not be conformed to this world, but be transformed by the
renewing of your minds, so that you may discern what is the will of God—what
is good and acceptable and perfect. (Rom. 12:1–2)

Earlier in the same letter (Rom. 8:2–17, 29), and elsewhere (e.g., 2 Cor.
3:18), Paul reveals that this process of transformation is the work of God's
Spirit and is transformation into the image of Christ. For Christians, to
grow spiritually is to become more like Jesus Christ. Over the centuries,
Christians have had different names for this process of spiritual growth,
including sanctification, or becoming more holy; (ongoing) conversion, in
the sense of continual change; and **deification**, or **theosis**, meaning taking
on, by grace, certain attributes of God such as holiness and, eventually,
immortality.

Since Jesus was a Jew who lived and taught the basic covenantal require-
ments of his Scriptures, to become more like him is to become more loving
and loyal toward God. It is also to become more loving and just toward our
fellow human beings. Putting this in trinitarian terms and echoing Augustine,
Stephen Fowl has defined the meaning of the church's existence—and thus the
goal of engaging Scripture—as the process of entering into ever-deeper communion with the Triune God and with one another (see ch. 11 in this book).
We might say, then, that the heart of spirituality from a Christian perspective
is transformative participation in the life of the Triune God within the community of faith and in mission to the world.

Spiritual growth, therefore, is a deeply *personal* but not a *private* experience. It is the deepening of one's relationship with God, with others, and
indeed with all creation because of this all-encompassing relationship with
God. For this reason the present chapter needs to be seen as integrally related
to the next, which deals with the Bible and ethics.

Because of its outward movement, growth in the spiritual life *must* translate into a deeper fellowship or communion, not only with God but also
with others, whom God also loves. If any practice fails to do this, it does
not foster true spiritual growth. Spiritual growth is not, therefore, primarily
an intellectual exercise, though it involves the mind, as Paul clearly notes
in the Romans text quoted above and as Jesus himself taught (Mark 12:30
and parallels). That is to say, spiritual growth is not so much about gaining
information, as it is about experiencing *transformation*. It means listening
to Scripture, not merely with the head, but primarily with the heart, as great
spiritual writers have said.

Hence, Bible study that *only* results in a greater fund of knowledge
without making an impact on the way a person relates to God and others

is more of a purely academic exercise than a spiritual one. It is tempting to think that because we "know" the Bible, we are growing spiritually, but that is not the case unless greater devotion to God and greater love for others is the result.

Approaching the Scriptures in Trust

The transformation we have been describing can occur when we read and reflect on Scripture, because encountering Scripture can be a discipline, a grace, an icon, and perhaps even a sacrament that permits us to encounter God and God's transforming love. For many centuries, believers have found that they meet God in Scripture.

For several generations now, however, much reading of the Bible, even in churches, has been done with what theologians call a "**hermeneutic of suspicion**" (see discussion in ch. 12). Rather than approaching the Bible as the source of divine revelation and the locus of an encounter with God, many people have found it necessary to approach the Bible warily or even skeptically. This approach began during the **Enlightenment** with a distrust of the "miraculous" dimension of biblical narratives, continued during the rise and heyday of modern biblical criticism with a general distrust of the historical reliability of the Bible, and took on a new form in the late twentieth century as liberation movements accused the Bible of being patriarchal and otherwise oppressive.

This is not the place to examine or critique the "hermeneutic of suspicion" in detail. To be sure, faithful Christians should not deny or gloss over the difficulties in Scripture; that would be either dishonest or naive. Nor should believers be afraid to "wrestle with God" by wrestling with such texts. However, contemporary believers can learn from the examples of their Jewish and Christian forebears that, despite these difficulties, Scripture has been and still is a "revelatory text" (to borrow from the title of Sandra Schneiders's book) that we can approach with a basic "**hermeneutic of trust**" (the words of Richard Hays, in his important article "Salvation by Trust?"). A hermeneutic of trust, however, need not be an anti-intellectual stance.

Readers of Scripture who have come to grips with its difficult dimensions and/or the questions raised by critical study of the Bible may need to embrace what some have called a "**second naïveté**." We may define this as a decision to approach the text, not with the (first) naïveté of an uninformed novice, but with the informed freedom of one who knows the intellectual challenges but nonetheless chooses to open oneself fully to the text as a place for encountering God.[2]

Spirituality, Intellectual Life, and the Bible

There is, therefore, no ultimate conflict between intellectual approaches and spiritual approaches to Scripture. To be sure, doing academic biblical studies and reading Scripture for spiritual growth are different activities, with distinct means and goals. In academic studies, we are primarily interested in the worlds "behind" and "within" the text. This knowledge can guide and assist us as we read the Bible for spiritual growth, but encountering Scripture for spiritual growth is less concerned about the world behind or within the text than it is about the readers or hearers—the person and the world "in front of" the text (see the discussion in ch. 10). In academic biblical studies, we are seeking to make an **exegesis** of the text; in reading Scripture for spiritual growth, we are seeking to allow the Holy Spirit to make us into a **living exegesis** of the texts we read.

Although overall knowledge of the scholarship surrounding a scriptural text might enable the reader to better understand the *what* and *why* of the passage in its original contexts, knowledge of such scholarship is not absolutely necessary for, and may or may not play a role in, an individual's own spiritual growth in reading that passage. Yet reading Scripture for spiritual growth does not mean that "anything goes." All interpretations of a passage are not equally meritorious; some have actually been dangerous, even deadly. It is possible to fool ourselves into thinking that we have "discovered" the meaning of a text. While academic knowledge about the text cannot *force* the meaning of a passage for us, it can *guide* our understanding of it, and it can deter us from pursuing interpretations that do violence to the original sense of the text or to the Christian tradition.

This last point brings us to another aspect of the role of the intellect in reading the Bible for spiritual growth: the importance of the Christian tradition. Although few Bible readers will ever be experts in the history of biblical interpretation or of Christian theology, even the most basic knowledge can be helpful in guiding our reading. For example, if our private interpretation of a passage runs contrary to the main contours of the Christian tradition,

2. The great philosopher-theologian Paul Ricoeur explained the process of interpretation as moving from an innocent, uninformed "first naïveté" through the "critical distance" created by analytical, rational study to the "second naïveté" that is *informed* by criticism but not *enslaved* by it, and through which we can "hear again."

we might very well have to reevaluate that interpretation (e.g., if "Love your neighbor as yourself" were understood to mean loving only members of one's own race or ethnicity while mistreating immigrants, or "zeal for God" were interpreted as a license for violence).

Context Matters

The Jewish and Christian traditions, then, call us to love God with our entire being: heart, soul, mind, and strength. As we strive to grow in this holistic love of God, we become part of the world "in front of the text." Naturally, the person or community in front of the text exists at a certain place and time. Therefore, a particular text might speak to one person eloquently while it fails to touch another person, or it might speak differently to the same person on different occasions. Moreover, that same text may say different things to different people in different social circumstances.

This reality means that a twenty-first-century believer reading Jesus' words "Turn the other cheek" may understand the words in a manner vastly different from the understanding of a first-century person. This is equally true for the understanding of such words by privileged twenty-first-century citizens of North America or Western Europe versus that of oppressed persons in the **Majority World**. The words *within* the text may be the same, but their contextual meaning *in front of the text* often differs unavoidably.

Consider as well the importance of one's developmental stage. Some individuals (regardless of age) understand Scripture in a very literal fashion, while other individuals understand Scripture at a variety of levels. When faced with an opponent, the former group might read "Turn the other cheek" as a literal turning of the head, while the latter group reads it less as a directive for positioning the head and more as a directive for positioning the heart. Some of this is age-related development, of course, but not entirely. Environmental forces and community expectations can also play a large role in determining what is deemed appropriate interpretation.

Necessary Dispositions and Practices for Spiritual Growth through Encountering Scripture

Spiritual growth through reading the Bible does not happen automatically. In addition to adopting a basic hermeneutic of trust, appropriately using our God-given minds, and acknowledging context, certain dispositions and corollary practices are required.

The first disposition in permitting Scripture to foster our spiritual growth is *openness*—to God, to others, and to change itself. If we approach Scripture firmly believing that we already know its meaning, spiritual growth will be impeded, for inherent in any growth is change. Thus, we must approach Scripture with both humility (that we do not yet have all the "answers") and patience (knowing that we will not receive all the answers immediately).

Being open to change means that we must not only read Scripture, but that we must also engage in the practice of *permitting Scripture to read us*—to question and challenge us, even as we read and question Scripture. All too often, people think that reading Scripture is like reading any other book. In some ways, of course, it is. But in a fundamental way, it is not. Reading a novel might be for enjoyment; reading a textbook might be for education; reading and analyzing a poem might be for the purpose of submitting a paper. Reading Scripture *as Scripture* is for relationship, relationship with God and God's people. In all relationships, there is give and take, and frequently a bit of a struggle. For any relationship to succeed, there must be a commitment to the relationship and honesty in dialoging with the other—in this case, with God. There must also be a willingness to invest time and energy in the relationship.

Practically speaking, that means *persistence* in reading Scripture, a second necessary disposition. We cannot expect to have a unique encounter with God or receive a profound spiritual insight every time we read Scripture. For some people, failure to have such an experience makes them weary of daily Scripture reading and even leads them to abandon the habit. "It says nothing to me," they will moan. Yet common human experience tells us that the ability to receive something depends as much on the receiver as it does on the giver. Our mood—how tired, distracted, bored, uncomfortable, preoccupied we are—certainly plays a role in our receptivity to what is being offered. Furthermore, we must recognize that growing in the knowledge of God, as with any person, is a gradual process—not a series of successive mountaintop experiences.

A good way to facilitate this persistence in reading Scripture is to adopt the practice of having a set time (and perhaps a set place) allotted to it each day. A commitment to *regularity* is thus another required disposition for spiritual growth. Having a regular time and place does not leave the practice to chance (though if circumstances dictate, the time or the setting can be changed). If drawing closer to God through Scripture is a priority, then we must treat it as any other priority and make time for it even in the midst of a busy life.

Finally, the only way that spiritual growth with the Bible can come about is through an attitude of *prayer*: prayer for the grace to allow God to work with us through Scripture; prayer for the grace to be patient, persistent, humble, and open; prayer to be able to move forward after discernment and to be transformed by what we have read. When we struggle with Scripture, or when we feel like we are "learning nothing new" or "coming up dry," we must remember that the process of spiritual growth is often an unconscious one, invisible to ourselves, and that God is the one who gives the growth.

The practice that is corollary to a prayerful attitude is not simply the act of prayer itself (though that is needed), but the *living of a Christian life*. Growth, in other words, only comes to those who are growing. To read Scripture rightly, we must practice the virtues (such as compassion, hospitality, and forgiveness) to which Scripture calls us. Otherwise we will likely find the God and the call of God attested in Scripture to be so counterintuitive that we may want to reject them or (worse yet) to re-form them in our own image.

Reading Privately and Reading in Communion

Many Christians are accustomed to reading their own Bibles on their own schedules in the privacy of their own homes. They may refer to this time as their "devotions" or "quiet time." Initially, however, Christians did not encounter Scripture by privately reading and meditating on it, but by hearing it read aloud and then interpreted at community gatherings. This occurred both because there may have been only one copy of the inspired text available and because ancient and even medieval societies were fundamentally oral cultures. After the invention of the printing press, the increased translation and dispersion of the Bible, and the sixteenth-century reformations, individual believers (especially Protestants) began to "read, mark, learn, and inwardly digest" the Scriptures, as the Anglican Book of Common Prayer elegantly put it in 1662.

Each approach to reading Scripture—private and communal—has its advantages and disadvantages, so it is important for believers to practice both kinds of reading. As early as the fourth century, the Eastern Christian writer Evagrius expressed his conviction that every Christian should awake in the morning with a Bible in hand. Nevertheless, especially in individualistic Western culture, it is important for Christians to regain the sense of Scripture as a word addressed to *us*, not just to *me*. This is especially challenging for English speakers, since in the Bible many forms of the pronoun "you," as well as many verbs, are in the plural. But English does not generally distinguish the singular and plural forms of verbs or of "you" (with some colloquial exceptions, such as "y'all").

Reading Scripture in a community of fellow believers—what is sometimes called a covenant discipleship group, small Christian community, house church,

Bible study, life group, or fellowship group—can provide structure, wisdom, and accountability. Returning to Romans 12:1–2, we notice Paul saying that the Roman believers' transformation will come through the power of God's grace as they discern God's will *in community* and as together they become a living exegesis of the gospel. Thus it is spiritually important to understand that Romans, like most of the Bible, was written to a *community of believers* and not as a special message to an individual or a select few. As noted elsewhere in this book (esp. ch. 12), contemporary Christians in the West are increasingly recognizing the necessity of what many Christians elsewhere value instinctively: "reading in communion" (the title of a landmark book by Stephen Fowl and L. Gregory Jones).

Some Ways of Growing Spiritually with Scripture

Over the years, various ways of using Scripture for spiritual growth have been recommended. Three will be described here: meditation, *lectio divina*, and structured questioning. All three can be used privately or in groups.

Meditation

Meditation with a Scripture passage occurs when we read a portion of Scripture and reflect on it or enter into the text imaginatively. For example, we may choose a narrative text and imagine what it might have been like to be a person in the story. This is much more than idle daydreaming; it is an exercise in *disciplined* imagination. We normally identify with a figure in a story for a particular reason. Who was the person we chose, and why were we drawn to this person? What is that character's relationship with God like? What kind of moral and spiritual character does this person seem to have? What might we have done differently if we were that character in the story? What does this imaginative process teach us about our own vocation, gifts, flaws, questions, and concerns?

For example, the story of Jonah is a tale about an unwilling prophet who tries to escape God's call. When that is unsuccessful, Jonah reluctantly goes to Nineveh, as commanded by God, to urge the people to repent. When they do so, Jonah is angry because he believes them to be an evil people who deserve punishment.

Meditating on this story, we might consider how we would have acted in Jonah's place. Would we have possessed a greater willingness to live out the prophetic call? Why or why not? How would we have responded to the Ninevites' repentance? Having asked ourselves such questions, we might then reflect on times we have felt God's promptings in our own life and either ignored them, tried to escape them, or accepted them. Why did we do what we did? What was the impact of our action, or inaction, on our relationship with God?

Such scriptural meditation can be done privately, but it can also be enriching to reflect on a text in this manner as part of a group. This can be a powerful experience as one hears the insights of others, perspectives that might be radically different from one's own.

Lectio Divina

Another method of encountering Scripture for spiritual growth is *lectio divina* (sacred, or holy, reading). This method developed among Christians in the monastic period and reached its height during the Middle Ages. Today, Christians from many traditions are rediscovering its spiritual benefits.

Originally, *lectio* involved reading (aloud) and memorizing Scripture as a means to integrate body and mind, a practice that was adopted from the Jewish tradition. The person then meditated on the text by repeating it inwardly, and prayerfully dwelling on it, in order to evoke personal prayer. In other words, the reader rested in the words, letting them "soak in," so that he or she might grasp their personal significance in that moment. Many people have compared this kind of contemplative reading to *chewing*—a completely unhurried, even prolonged process rather than an act of "gulping down" a few morsels. The process may last for a few minutes or for an hour or more. Sometimes in *lectio divina* nothing seems to come to mind, while at other times a great deal is revealed.

Building on the tradition and stressing that "living out" the text is the ultimate goal of *lectio*, M. Robert Mulholland (*Invitation to a Journey*, 112–15) outlined six steps for contemporary *lectio divina*:

- *Silencio*—silent preparation
- *Lectio*—receptive reading
- *Meditatio*—processing
- *Oratio*—heartfelt, responsive prayer
- *Contemplatio*—self-abandonment to God and God's will
- *Incarnatio*—living the text

The goal in *lectio* is not to read (much less study) a whole chapter at a time; in fact, one might ponder one verse or even one part of a verse, letting it resonate in one's heart and soul. Some people deliberately read, not with a terminus in mind, but until they find a word, phrase, or image that strikes them. Take, for example, the experience of reading Luke's story of the crucifixion and encountering Jesus' prayer from the cross: "Father, forgive them; for they do not know what they are doing" (Luke 23:34). What feelings and other responses to God does Jesus' word of love and compassion generate in me? How many times have I been forgiven by God (or by others) because I didn't really know what I was doing? How often have I forgiven another because it seemed that the other person didn't know the enormity of his or her actions? If I have never forgiven someone this generously, why not? What does my honest encounter with this text mean in terms of my relationship with God and others?

Although *lectio divina* is frequently practiced by individuals, as with meditation, group *lectio* is also possible. A small group follows the pattern outlined above, with everyone engaging the same passage individually and then sharing their various insights about it. This also can be a powerful experience in terms of spiritual growth, as one hears and reflects on the insights of others and how God is operating in their lives.

Structured Questioning

Yet another method of reading Scripture involves *structured questioning* of the text in order to discern how God might be speaking to us through it. In effect, as noted earlier, this means that our questioning the text is a means of allowing the text to question us. Several different question formats have proved to be beneficial. A very simple approach is to ask the text three questions:

- What does this text say?
- What does it mean?
- What does it mean to and for me/us in my/our context?

Another set of questions is based on the fourfold medieval approach to Scripture discussed in chapter 9:

- What did this text say in its original context?
- What does this text urge us to believe (faith)?
- What does this text urge us to anticipate in this life and the life to come (hope)?
- What does this text urge us to do in our context (love)?

Yet again, we may pose the following three-part question: What convictions, comfort, and challenge does God offer us in this text?

This method is perhaps most conducive to group discussion, but it can also be helpful for individual reflection. In both individual and group reflection, it is important to carefully consider each question without any rush or eagerness to get to some "right" answer. Doing so underscores the dignity of the person(s) "in front of" the text.

Conclusion

Whether we use meditation, *lectio divina*, or structured questioning, we can join our forebears in faith, encountering God in Scripture and responding to God in prayer and commitment. For this reason, many people refer to all of the approaches to the Bible described in the preceding section as "praying with Scripture" or just "praying Scripture." Such phrases neatly summarize the trust, openness, and transformation that are both the root and the fruit of spiritual growth through Bible reading.

QUESTIONS FOR REFLECTION AND DISCUSSION

1. Do you sense any tension between academic and spiritual approaches to Bible reading? In what ways has this chapter helped to identify and address that tension?

2. What does it mean for you to read the Bible with a "hermeneutic of trust"? Does trust allow for questioning? doubt? confusion?

3. Engage a text of Scripture using one of the ways of reading for spiritual growth discussed in this chapter that you have not previously used. How would you describe, and possibly commend, the experience to others?

FOR FURTHER READING AND STUDY

Brown, William P. *Sacred Sense: Discovering the Wonder of God's Word and World.* Grand Rapids: Eerdmans, 2015. Texts from Genesis to Revelation that provoke wonder in various forms.

Casey, Michael. *Sacred Reading: The Ancient Art of* Lectio Divina. Liguori, MO: Triumph, 1996. A modern classic.

de Villiers, Pieter G. R., and Lloyd K. Pietersen. *The Spirit That Inspires: Perspectives on Biblical Spirituality*. Acta Theologica Supplementum 15. Bloemfontein, South Africa: University of the Free State Press, 2011. Scholarly essays that attempt to define and/or practice "biblical spirituality."

Gorman, Michael J. *Cruciformity: Paul's Narrative Spirituality of the Cross*. Grand Rapids: Eerdmans, 2001. A serious reading of Paul's Letters that bridges the gap between academic biblical studies and Christian spirituality.

Harrington, Wilfrid J. *Seeking Spiritual Growth through the Bible*. New York: Paulist Press, 2002. Major spiritual themes in both the OT and the NT.

Hays, Richard B. "Salvation by Trust? Reading the Bible Faithfully." *The Christian Century* (February 1997): 218–23. A significant call for the use of a hermeneutic of trust in reading the Bible.

Johnson, Luke Timothy. *Living Jesus: Learning the Heart of the Gospel*. San Francisco: HarperSanFrancisco, 1999. A leading scholar's explanation of how reading the NT can be a means to knowing the living Jesus.

Lincoln, Andrew T., J. Gordon McConville, and Lloyd K. Pietersen, eds. *The Bible and Spirituality: Exploratory Essays in Reading Scripture Spiritually*. Eugene, OR: Cascade, 2013. Studies by noted scholars of both Testaments, relating academic biblical study to spirituality and human flourishing.

McEntyre, Marilyn Chandler. *What's in a Phrase? Pausing Where Scripture Gives You Pause*. Grand Rapids: Eerdmans, 2014. Prayer through meditation on fifty scriptural phrases, such as "Let there be light."

————. *Word by Word: A Daily Spiritual Practice*. Grand Rapids: Eerdmans, 2016. An invitation to pray by dwelling on single biblical words from different angles.

Mulholland, M. Robert, Jr. *Invitation to a Journey: A Road Map for Spiritual Formation*. Downers Grove, IL: InterVarsity, 1993. A guide to various means of spiritual growth, including *lectio divina*, by a Protestant biblical scholar.

————. *Shaped by the Word: The Power of Scripture in Spiritual Formation*. Rev. ed. Nashville: Upper Room Books, 2000. A study of the nature of the Bible and of its role in personal spiritual development.

Pennington, M. Basil. *Lectio Divina: Renewing the Ancient Practice of Praying the Scriptures*. New York: Crossroad / Herder & Herder, 1998. A modern classic from one of the great modern contemplative Christians.

Peterson, Eugene H. *Eat This Book: A Conversation in the Art of Spiritual Reading*. Grand Rapids: Eerdmans, 2006. A spirituality of *lectio divina*, including living the scriptural story.

Reynolds, Alan. *Reading the Bible for the Love of God*. Grand Rapids: Brazos, 2003. A brief but elegant exploration of reading Scripture to deepen a relationship with God.

Schneiders, Sandra M. *The Revelatory Text: Interpreting the New Testament as Sacred Scripture*. 2nd ed. Collegeville, MN: Liturgical Press, 1999. An in-depth serious look at the nature of Scripture and its transformative power.

————.*"Written That You May Believe": Encountering Jesus in the Fourth Gospel.* New York: Crossroad, 2003. A scholar of the NT and of Christian spirituality fusing the two disciplines in a study of the Gospel of John.

Waaijman, Kees. *Spirituality: Forms, Foundations, Methods.* Leuven: Peeters, 2002. A comprehensive and classic study of spirituality, stressing its biblical roots and its goal of transformation.

21

Scripture and Christian Ethics: Embodying Pentecost

Brent Laytham

For Christians, ethics and Scripture are not two separable things. "**Christian ethics**" already implies and requires the two-Testament Christian Bible, while "Christian Scripture" necessarily entails forming and norming the Christian life. This is because Christian ethics is gospel-disciplined reflection on Christian life in its totality, and the "manger" in which that gospel lies is Christian Scripture. It is because Christian Scripture is written to give us Christian life (cf. John 20:31) that is shaped "worthy of the gospel of Christ" (Phil. 1:27). So the "and" in "Scripture and ethics" does not connect two disparate things, but rather invites us to see more clearly how the Christian gospel makes them one. From this perspective, for Christians, *Scripture is ethics*.

But seeing truly has always been hard (see Gen. 3), and it would be even harder in considering the subject of this chapter if we immediately looked at how the academic disciplines of biblical studies and **moral theology** (the older name for Christian ethics, and generally preferred by Roman Catholics) account for the "and" in the phrase "Scripture and Ethics." So before surveying such second-order, conceptual accounts related to academic disciplines, we will first look at the church's primary engagement with Scripture in its own life.

Church Practices: Where Scripture *Is* Ethics

Church is where Scripture and ethics unite as Christian existence from, in, and with God's gospel story. The previous chapter displays some of this, with its focus on encountering God in spiritual practices like meditation, *lectio divina*, or structured questioning. Christians believe that through such practices God authors, directs, and shapes our lives. Similarly, in corporate and personal worship God works through practices of Scripture to author and authorize gospel-shaped lives. We regularly hear Scripture read and preached; we often pray and sing Scripture (psalms, canticles such as the Magnificat, the Lord's Prayer); and we enact Scripture whenever we gather, praise, thank, intercede, baptize, break bread, or wash feet. In these practices, Scripture is God's living and active word as through it God authors Christ's life in us by the power of the Holy Spirit. In other words, the Bible performed faithfully in the life and practices of the church is what we mean by *Scripture*, and understood this way *Scripture already is ethics*.

This truth is hard to see, though, for three reasons, all of which involve *reductive* understandings of Christian ethics.

First, today people think of ethics as only part of life, different from worship, and different also from spirituality, politics, community, and mission (topics of the other chapters in part 3). Scripture does not allow such distinctions, however, as we see in 1 Peter 2:9: "But you are a chosen race, a royal priesthood, a holy nation, God's own people, in order that you may proclaim the mighty acts of him who called you out of darkness into his marvelous light." Worship and politics intertwine in the description "royal priesthood," spirituality and politics are joined in "holy nation," community surfaces in both "chosen race" and "God's own people," and mission resounds in the calling to "proclaim the mighty acts of" the triune God. This statement from 1 Peter about the church's identity and calling already is ethics, even as it sits within four chapters that look more like ethics to us—a discussion of how Christians should "live such good lives" (2:12 NIV as a summary of 1:13–4:19). First Peter shows us that in Christian existence worship, spirituality, politics, community building, mission, and ethics are one interwoven life, rather than being differentiated activities.[1]

The word "activities" hints at the second reason it is hard to see that our scriptural practices already constitute ethics. Today ethics is commonly understood to mean moral decisions about right and wrong actions. Accordingly,

---

1. It is also the assumption of the other authors of chapters here in part 3 that these are dimensions of a single integrated reality.

Christian ethics would be how Christians make their moral choices, guided by various Christian authorities—especially Scripture. This common understanding, while not entirely wrong, is not fully right either: because our choosing comes second, as response to God's first having chosen us (1 Pet. 2:9);[2] because deciding right or wrong is poor pottage compared to the covenant calling to discern God's "good, pleasing and perfect will" (Rom. 12:2 NIV); and because acting well requires seeing truly, a capacity that is equal parts good character (consider the *good* Samaritan in Luke 10) and **eschatological** awareness.[3] In other words, because the gospel itself announces that (1) God has acted (2) to heal and perfect creation, (3) fundamentally changing our "now" from old constraints to new possibilities, Christian ethics is so much more than deciding and doing. As *gospel-disciplined reflection on Christian life in its totality*, Christian ethics includes how the gospel creates, shapes, directs, and perfects Christian identity, character, desire, perception, deliberation, intention, decision, and action.

Finally, it can be extremely difficult in Europe and the United States to see how Scripture already is ethics because the culture of individualism obscures the fact that both Christian Scripture and Christian existence are fundamentally *ecclesial* (from the Greek word for church, *ekklēsia*). The Bible is the church's book, and discipleship is the church's life. Wherever the Bible and discipleship become separated from church, they become attenuated, distorted, and usually separated from each other, too. The African concept of *Ubuntu*, especially as communicated in the life and writings of Archbishop Desmond Tutu, has been a gift to the whole world and a helpful corrective for the church in the West. *Ubuntu* suggests that "our humanity is bound up in one another" and that "interconnectedness is the very root of who we are."[4]

For Christians, Scripture has always had a role in producing, shaping, and perfecting Christian life. Doctrinally, the church has believed that Scripture does so by the power of the Holy Spirit, not only when Christians intentionally

2. The priority of God's choosing us is a common theme across both Testaments. Consider just these selected examples: Abraham (Gen. 12), Moses (Exod. 3), Israel (Deut. 7:6), Ruth (Ruth 4:11–13), David (1 Kings 8:16), various prophets, Mary (Luke 1), disciples (John 15:16), the church (1 Cor. 1:27–28), and quintessentially Jesus (Luke 9:35)!

3. Eschatology is about ultimate matters: God's purposes fully and finally realized in history in the resurrection of the dead, the kingdom of God, and new creation. In 2 Corinthians Paul declares that because of Christ's resurrection (5:14–15) everything has changed (5:17) such that he now sees everyone differently (5:16).

4. Desmond Tutu and Mpho Tutu, *The Book of Forgiving: The Fourfold Path to Healing Ourselves and Our World* (San Francisco: HarperOne, 2015), 8. For an extended discussion of this challenge of living in community, see "Scripture and Christian Community" (ch. 23) in this book.

turn to Scripture for guidance and direction, but especially when they enact scriptural practices in which moral formation and information are more habitual or implicit. Scripture already is ethics for the praying and praising church, long before the church consults Scripture about a difficult moral choice.

But whenever the church teaches new converts how to live, or confronts a question about its own way of life, there is a more explicit moral engagement with Scripture. This often takes a deeply held (and sometimes unexamined) presupposition about the structure of morality and links it with a particular biblical genre or form. For example, where the moral life is construed as universal obligation to keep the law or to obey rules, Scripture is engaged as a collection of rules to be obeyed—usually with special emphasis on the **Decalogue** (the Ten Commandments in Exod. 20 and Deut. 5), the "commands" of Jesus (especially in the Sermon on the Mount, Matt. 5–7), or the *Haustafeln* (the "household codes" that conclude several NT epistles).[5] Where the moral life is construed as responsibility for achieving the best outcomes, Scripture is engaged as a collection of goals or principles—often with special emphasis on doing justice (emphasizing the prophets, as summarized in Mic. 6:8), or on loving neighbor as self (Mark 12:31; Rom. 13:9).

In other words, there are some common correlations between understandings of what the Christian life centrally is and what the Bible focally teaches. But the earlier paragraphs of this chapter already indicate that these understandings leave out as much as they include. For example, neither a divine-law nor a godly-principle approach to the moral meaning of Scripture finds much significance in the daily praying of the Psalms, although an emphasis on the formation of Christian character does. Moreover, just as each approach reduces the fullness of Christian existence to one of its dimensions (rules, principles, character), so each approach inherently distorts or subordinates the unity of Christian Scripture to a single form: law or exhortation or prayer.

All of this leaves us with two challenges. At the primary level of Christian existence, a great challenge is our tendency to settle for reductive accounts of the moral life that concomitantly produce reductive practices of engaging and embodying Scripture. Nonreductively defined, Christian ethics is the discipline of critical inquiry into how best to live the Christian life in particular times and places; its scope includes normative guidance, for both individual disciples and Christian communities, about well-formed character, faithful behavior, and true aspirations that are fully and properly Christian.

5. Much of the church's history of moral theology and of **catechesis** (intentional teaching to form Christian lives) has used the Decalogue and the Beatitudes as primary texts.

Perhaps an even greater challenge, sometimes lamented as "ignorance of Scripture," is disengagement from robust participation in the church's many practices of Scripture. (The greatest challenge has always been the gospel itself, with its total claim and total demand confronting our rebellious, restless hearts.) Scholarship, to which we now turn, will help the church meet these two challenges only to the degree that it does justice to all the ways God the Holy Spirit draws the church into Christ's life in and through its practices of engaging Scripture.

Scholarly Study: Scripture *and* Ethics

Scholarly work often settles for accounts of Scripture *and* ethics, rather than displaying how in the church's lived existence Scripture *is* ethics. This is partly because of three challenges attending scholarly, or secondary, accounts of the Scripture-ethics relationship. These challenges are similar to the three challenges related to the church's primary moral engagement with Scripture discussed above.

First, a holistic scholarly account of how Scripture is ethics is increasingly difficult, given the multiplication of academic subspecialties. Today, ethics and biblical studies are separate academic disciplines so sizeable that few scholars could hope to master both; indeed, biblical scholars typically train in only one Testament and limit their research to a portion of that. So scholarship rarely engages the full scriptural canon, settling instead for an Old Testament or a New Testament ethics.[6] Books connecting Scripture and ethics are understood as "building bridges" not only between separate realities (the Bible as artifact and ethics as activity) but also between distinct scholarly competencies.[7] While at their best academic specializations can serve the unity of the church's various practices of Scripture, at their worst they dismember that unity.

Second, modern ethics has pursued a universal outlook that attempts to construct a morality applicable to all, regardless of who or where they are. At the same time, modern biblical scholarship has attended ever more closely to the specificity of particular texts. The result has been ethicists who are unsure how to account for particularities of moral identity, community, and tradition, and **exegetes** who are unable to imagine the unity

---

6. The best exception to this generalization is Allen Verhey's *Remembering Jesus*.

7. E.g., Harrington and Keenan's *Jesus and Virtue Ethics* is subtitled *Building Bridges between New Testament Studies and Moral Theology*. They use the same subtitle in *Paul and Virtue Ethics* (Lanham, MD: Rowman & Littlefield, 2010).

(and universal significance) of the biblical canon. This situation means that most books on the Bible and ethics begin with the claim that among the biggest challenges the enterprise faces is the diversity of the canon, and the question of its putative unity. For Christian ethicists attempting to put biblical sources in the service of a universal ethic, the most common path has been to read Scripture's legal materials and other commands as forms of **natural law** (moral law inscribed in nature itself). Scholars who took the Bible's audience seriously seemed to be faced with the choice of surrendering universality in favor of a particular ethic for a peculiar people (as in the title of Christopher Wright's work *Old Testament Ethics for the People of God*). However, because this particular people carries the particular story of God's good news for all creation, some scholars now find that attending to Scripture's unity as a narrative of divine mission dissolves the perceived conflict between universal and particular. (This is displayed nicely in the final chapter of this book.)

Third, historical criticism often divides Scripture from ethics, because its focus on what a text of Scripture *originally meant* necessarily demands additional interpretive steps to get to Scripture's *present moral meaning*. Therefore, much of the academic "Scripture and ethics" literature posits that the enterprise's greatest challenge is the historical distance between then and now that requires hermeneutical solutions. Some biblical scholars leave the hermeneutical work to Christian ethicists, contenting themselves exclusively or primarily with descriptive accounts of the ethics of particular biblical texts or communities. Students should be aware, therefore, that titles like *The Ethics of the New Testament*[8] or *Understanding Old Testament Ethics*[9] may present only historical accounts, without any attention to how such "glimpses of a strange land"[10] impact Christian existence here and now.

Locating meaning in the past and application in the present has two effects. First, it can allow for the claim of neutrality: both biblical studies and Christian ethics can be done entirely as description of what texts meant or how and why Christians act, without any commitment to the truth or goodness of what is studied. Second, seeking past meaning hermeneutically mediated for present application hides the reality that the church across time is Scripture's

8. E.g., Wolfgang Schrage, *The Ethics of the New Testament*, trans. David E. Green (Philadelphia: Augsburg Fortress, 1990).

9. E.g., John Barton, *Understanding Old Testament Ethics: Approaches and Explorations* (Louisville: Westminster John Knox, 2003), which—despite having a chapter titled "Reading for Life: The Use of the Bible in Ethics"—focuses so relentlessly on explaining what the text meant that it offers nary a hint at how the OT could or should shape lives today.

10. Cyril S. Rodd, *Glimpses of a Strange Land: Studies in Old Testament Ethics*, Old Testament Studies (Edinburgh: Bloomsbury T&T Clark, 2001).

true audience, called to be interpretation enfleshed, or **living exegesis** (as several chapters in this book put it).

Notice that these three scholarly challenges parallel the ecclesial ones noted above. Just as fragmented thinking tempts us to imagine ethics too narrowly, so scholarly specialization threatens to fragment the Scripture-is-ethics enterprise. Just as transposing our primary focus from God to us takes Christian ethics from the universal gospel of God's act in Christ and dislocates it to particular human acts, so scholarly focus on particularity obscures the unity inherent in Scripture as God's story for Christian witness to all creation. And just as cultural individualism threatens to lose the centrality of the church in Christian ethics (in the West, and in places influenced by the West), so scholarly claims that the Bible is "someone else's mail" threaten to lose the church, too.

Not all is lost, however. One of the best and most sophisticated examples of Scripture and ethics scholarship is still Richard Hays's *The Moral Vision of the New Testament*, published in 1996. Hays's work displays some aspects of all three challenges listed above. First, as the title reveals, Hays focuses not on Scripture as a whole, but on his area of specialization, offering an exceedingly rich reading of the NT, with the hope that "the Old Testament suffuses the entire enterprise" (309).[11] He meets the second challenge head-on, displaying ethics as a particular people's particular way of life embodying a universal vision of new creation. Finally, although Hays posits the hermeneutical necessity of bridging the historical gap, this is for him "an *integrative act of the imagination*" more akin to musical improvising (as in blues) than to applying a theory or following methodological directions (6, emphasis original). Nonetheless, he offers ten proposals to guide our imaginative improvisations, the last of which is "Right reading of the New Testament occurs only where the Word is embodied" (310).

This metaphor of *embodying Scripture* through *imaginative improvisation* may be the best way to encapsulate the full ethical scope of what God is doing in and through Scripture. To display this important claim more fully, the remainder of the chapter reads the event of Pentecost, narrated in Acts 2, as an instance where Scripture-is-ethics finds embodiment.

Pentecost as Scriptural Embodiment

I believe that what is true of Pentecost is also true of Christian ethics as scriptural embodiment. I hope the eight summary claims that follow can both

---

11. Brian Brock, in *Singing the Ethos* (39–42, 49–51), suggests strongly that Hays fails to give the OT its due.

enliven our encounter with this scriptural text and energize our imaginative improvisation of Scripture.

Pentecost begins in communal prayer (Acts 1:14; 2:1). So does Christian ethics, because scriptural embodiment is not produced by ethical effort nor exegetical proficiency, but comes as God's gift, answering the church's prayer. Typically that gift is given in and through the patient work of attending, in community, to the mystery that God is. Embodying God's Word through imaginative improvisation requires that we are deeply engaged with and by God.

Pentecost is an event that begins "suddenly" (2:2), even though "all that Jesus did and taught" (Acts 1:1, referring to the Gospel of Luke) precedes it. In other words, Pentecost is an eschatological event by which time is fundamentally shifted from "nine o'clock in the morning" to "the last days" (2:15–17). Likewise, Christian ethics begins with the good news that in the event of Jesus Christ, God has not intoxicated us with new *wine* (2:13), but with new *time*, opening the future to astonishing possibilities for life. Embodying the Word through imaginative improvisation requires that we understand *when* we are.

Pentecost is narrated as an event in a larger, longer story of "God's deeds of power" (2:11). Peter tells the story (2:14–36) by reading Scripture in a pattern of *this is that*: *this* embodiment you see is God faithfully keeping *Scripture's promises* to Israel (2:16–21), to David (2:23–24, 30–36), and to the whole world (2:38–39). Christian ethics understands our two-Testament canon as a covenant narrative stretching from creation through Christ to a cosmic, comic consummation.[12] Only by indwelling that canonical story can we rightly frame moral identity, desire, perception, intention, and deliberation. Therefore, embodying the Word through imaginative improvisation requires that we know truly *where* we are (meaning which story we live in) so that we can discern rightly *who* we are (what role we have been given to play in the story).

Pentecost's main character is not Peter but God (2:24), the Triune God, who typically acts thus: Jesus doing—that is, embodying—God's will by the Spirit's power (2:22–23). So Pentecost happens because Jesus "received from the Father the promise of the Holy Spirit" (2:33). Christian ethics knows that it is first of all about what the Triune God has done, rather than what we should do. Our improvisation, therefore, will never imagine that making the story end well is our job; God is responsible for the story's happy ending, and in raising Christ by the power of the Spirit, God has already guaranteed that ending.

12. By "comic" I do not mean humorous, but the opposite of tragic: a drama that ends, not with death and disaster, but with the happy ending of joyous life at the marriage supper of the Lamb (Rev. 19:7–9; 21:9).

Yet God's triune action properly leads to the question "What shall we do?" (2:37 NIV), and Christian ethics knows that our answer will have the same triune structure as Jesus' embodiment did: our imaginative improvisations of Scripture must embody the Father's will in Christ-shaped lives by the power of the Holy Spirit. This is why the entirety of the four Gospels, not just the explicitly "ethical" passages, functions to shape Christian communities into people who practice self-giving love, offer hospitality to strangers, show mercy to sinners, renounce violence, practice reconciliation, and so on.

Pentecost is an event in the life of the people of God, part of the long-standing "I-you" conversation[13] between God and Israel (2:22, 36). The twelve apostles (2:14) standing visible to "devout Jews from every nation" (2:5) embody Scripture's promise of covenant renewal: God's regathering Israel's twelve tribes from exile. The 120 disciples "speaking about God's deeds of power" (2:4–11) embody the arrival of God's salvation (2:21, 40, 47) because they are witnesses that God raised Jesus from death (2:32). Christian ethics is ecclesial, not individual. Embodying the Word through imaginative improvisation requires us to recognize that *we* are *Christ's church*, and to act from that identity as a called covenant community entrusted with a promise meant not just for us or our children, but "for all who are far away, everyone whom the Lord our God calls" (2:39).[14]

Jesus is at the center of Pentecost, both as the divine person who "poured out" the Spirit (2:32–33) and as the Jewish man whose action ("deeds of power, wonders, and signs," 2:22) and passion ("handed over . . . crucified and killed," 2:23) make him "Lord and Messiah" (2:36). Christian ethics bears witness to Jesus as this "Holy One" (2:27) who is both God *incarnate*, embodying Scripture's calling to be God's faithful covenant partner in the pattern of crucifixion-resurrection (2:23–24), and God *exalted* (2:33), embodying Scripture by redeeming creation,[15] filling it with gladness.[16] Embodying the Word happens only if the church knows *who Jesus is and what is he doing* (Holmes, *Ethics in the Presence of Christ*, viii), such that our imaginative improvisation conforms to his pattern and his goal; as he did, so we also carry crosses toward the day of salvation.

Pentecost is messy, violently (2:2) upsetting our inadequate categories (2:15), while graciously forgiving (2:38) the mess we have made of God's covenant

---

13. Acts 2:17–21 quotes Joel 2:28–32. In both, God says "I will" and is speaking to a plural "you."

14. What cannot be pursued here is the reality that Jews are the people of God, too.

15. Acts 2:21 quotes Joel 2:32; Acts 2:35 quotes Ps. 110:1.

16. Both filling (2:2, 4, 13, 17) and gladness (2:26, 28, 46) are eschatological signs of redemption.

(2:23). Christian ethics continually works to see everything anew from the perspective of the gospel, even if that requires us to resist worldly powers (cf. Acts 4) or rethink received categories (cf. Acts 10–15). Christian ethics lives by repentance (2:38), trusting so fully in the freedom of forgiveness that we have the courage to attempt scriptural embodiment through wildly imaginative improvisations.

Pentecost cuts to the heart (2:37), transforming desires and dispositions (cf. 2:42–43, 46) by the power of the Spirit. Christian ethics recognizes that the necessary work of forming desire and character is the Spirit working in and through church practices: "the apostles' teaching and fellowship, . . . the breaking of bread and the prayers" (2:42). We engage Scripture not only to be informed but also to be formed, to become good readers capable of good readings, holy performers able to embody the Word because the Spirit is transforming our imaginations.

Imaginative improvisations that faithfully embody Scripture will ever be forms of Pentecost, gifts of the Spirit rather than achievements of a particular ethical theory or hermeneutical strategy. Nonetheless, we are best positioned to receive this gift of faithfully embodying Scripture when we are rooted in practices of Scripture that are prayerfully focused on God, oriented eschatologically by resurrection hope, narratively placed in the scriptural story, ordered by the agency—indeed the victory—of the Triune God, ecclesially situated, christologically centered, repentantly engaged, with a willingness to be transformed in astonishing and gladdening ways. If we read thus, Scripture truly is ethics, because every day is Pentecost.

QUESTIONS FOR REFLECTION AND DISCUSSION

1. Did this chapter challenge any of your preconceived ideas about ethics? What new insights, and possibly also new questions, do you have?

2. Which of the difficulties and challenges discussed in the chapter most affect your ability to see that Scripture already is ethics?

3. How do you think students of Scripture/ethics should handle the scholarly challenges of specialization, particularity, and historical distance?

4. How might some of the claims about Pentecost as scriptural embodiment help your church or other Christian community more faithfully embody the Decalogue, the Sermon on the Mount, Psalm 104, Genesis 1–2, or Ephesians?

▣ FOR FURTHER READING AND STUDY ▣

Blount, Brian K. *Then the Whisper Put on Flesh: New Testament Ethics in an African American Context*. Nashville: Abingdon, 2001. Looks at the ethical contributions of various NT writings from an African American perspective.

Brock, Brian. *Singing the Ethos of God: On the Place of Christian Ethics in Scripture*. Grand Rapids: Eerdmans, 2007. Rethinks biblical ethics by critiquing contemporary authors, commending Augustine's and Luther's exegesis of the Psalms, and interpreting Psalms 104 and 130 as ethics.

Carroll R., M. Daniel, and Jacqueline E. Lapsley, eds. *Character Ethics and the Old Testament: Moral Dimensions of Scripture*. Louisville: Westminster John Knox, 2007. Sixteen women and men write chapters on moral character in particular parts of the Old Testament.

Chan, Yiu Sing Lúcás. *The Ten Commandments and the Beatitudes: Biblical Studies and Ethics for Real Life*. Lanham, MD: Rowman & Littlefield, 2012. A Catholic from Hong Kong offers exegesis and virtue interpretation of two classic moral texts.

Davis, Ellen. *Biblical Prophecy: Perspectives for Christian Theology, Discipleship, and Ministry*. Interpretation: Resources for the Use of Scripture in the Church. Louisville: Westminster John Knox, 2014. A close reading of the "prophetic perspective" in both Testaments, meant to guide the church's prayer, discipleship, and ministry.

Fedler, Kyle D. *Exploring Christian Ethics: Biblical Foundations for Morality*. Louisville: Westminster John Knox, 2006. A beginning text that introduces ethical theory and then surveys key sections of Scripture: creation, covenant, prophets, Jesus' teachings, his life, and Paul's Epistles.

Gill, David W. *Doing Right: Practicing Ethical Principles*. Downers Grove, IL: InterVarsity, 2004. A Christian ethic that interprets the Ten Commandments as "area principles," laws governing specific areas of life.

Green, Joel B., ed. *Dictionary of Scripture and Ethics*. Grand Rapids: Baker Academic, 2011. After three orienting essays to the multiple interrelations of Scripture and ethics, there are significant articles on every biblical book and genre and nearly every ethical theory and moral "issue."

Harrington, Daniel, SJ, and James Keenan, SJ. *Jesus and Virtue Ethics: Building Bridges between New Testament Studies and Moral Theology*. Lanham, MD: Sheed & Ward, 2002. Thirteen ethical topics addressed exegetically (from the Synoptic Gospels) by Harrington and ethically by Keenan.

Hauerwas, Stanley. *Matthew*. Brazos Theological Commentary on the Bible. Grand Rapids: Brazos, 2006. Theological commentary by a leading ecclesial ethicist.

Hays, Richard. *The Moral Vision of the New Testament: Community, Cross, New Creation; A Contemporary Introduction to New Testament Ethics*. San Francisco: HarperCollins, 1996. Offers descriptive exegesis of much of the NT, three focal images to synthesize diversity, and ten hermeneutical guidelines, concluding with five "test cases": violence, divorce, homosexuality, ethnic conflict, and abortion.

Holmes, Christopher R. J. *Ethics in the Presence of Christ*. London: T&T Clark, 2012. A New Zealand ethicist uses close readings of John 5, 18, and 21 to describe the ethical significance of the presence of Jesus' power, truth, and love.

Lapsley, Jacqueline E. *Whispering the Word: Hearing Women's Stories in the Old Testament*. Louisville: Westminster John Knox, 2005. Four stories are case studies to develop three strategies for paying moral attention to God through reading Scripture.

Marshall, Christopher D. *Compassionate Justice: An Interdisciplinary Dialogue with Two Gospel Parables on Law, Crime, and Restorative Justice*. Eugene, OR: Cascade, 2012. A New Zealand exegete reads the stories of the prodigal son and the good Samaritan through the lens of criminal victimization in order to develop an ethic of restorative justice.

Miller, Patrick D. *The Ten Commandments*. Interpretation: Resources for the Use of Scripture in the Church. Louisville: Westminster John Knox, 2009. Though Miller's appendix explicitly treats "the ethics of the commandments," the entire book displays the Decalogue as shaping the life of the people of God.

Pontifical Biblical Commission. *The Bible and Morality: Biblical Roots of Christian Conduct*. Rome: Libreria Editrice Vaticana, 2008. Available online at http://www.vatican.va/roman_curia/congregations/cfaith/pcb_documents/rc_con_cfaith_doc_20080511_bibbia-e-morale_en.html. An official Catholic statement.

Spohn, William. *Go and Do Likewise: Jesus and Ethics*. New York: Continuum, 1999. A Catholic ethicist shows how Jesus shapes moral perception, disposition, and identity when the NT is engaged through spiritual practices and faithful imagination.

Stassen, Glen H., and David P. Gushee. *Kingdom Ethics: Following Jesus in Contemporary Context*. Downers Grove, IL: InterVarsity, 2003. A comprehensive Christian ethic focused by the Sermon on the Mount (Matt. 5–7) but attentive to Scripture more broadly.

Verhey, Allen. *Remembering Jesus*. Grand Rapids: Eerdmans, 2003. Describes how the early church remembered Jesus in moral matters, and then uses that method to develop a biblical (both Testaments) ethic of sickness and health, sex and family, economics, and politics.

Wright, Christopher J. H. *Old Testament Ethics for the People of God*. Downers Grove, IL: InterVarsity, 2004. A descriptive study of the OT, with a final section focused on the literature and theory of contemporary "application."

Wright, N. T. *After You Believe: Why Christian Character Matters*. San Francisco: HarperOne, 2012. Noted British scholar presents a virtue ethic rooted in the NT.

22

The Bible and Politics

Christopher Rowland

The student who is beginning academic study of the Bible may wonder what the Bible has to do with politics. **Politics** is about the organization of society and public affairs. It concerns the nature and power of the state, but it also relates as much to a church, or other religious body, and its operations as to a national or local government. The political dimensions of how people relate to one another and function together are just as much a way of understanding religious groups as any other group.

Basically, then, politics is about how groups of people organize themselves. There are different examples of such organization. So the word "political" can be used to describe organizations and the dynamics of relationships of groups, as well as the power relations in the group and the patterns of authority which emerge. That is an important point. In our modern world it is assumed that in some ways the political is different from the religious. But this is to misunderstand the role of the political, which offers a perspective on human interaction and organization rather than asking questions about the nature of the theological dimensions of such a group. Thus, the political and the religious complement each other in what they offer to anyone seeking to reflect on and analyze what is going on within a body of people. Reading the Bible therefore involves thinking about both theology *and* politics.

Politics and the Bible: Uses and Abuses

The Bible is full of texts from different times and different places reflecting the culture and the political concerns and pressures of each particular age. From the most ancient traditions in the Hebrew Bible, or Christian OT, to the writings of the NT, the texts evince first the world of tribal leadership, including its religion and organization, and eventually, with the growing imperial power which over several centuries dominated the life of the Middle East, the sort of world that culminated in the hegemony of Rome in Judea in the first century CE. We cannot always reconstruct the details of the backgrounds of texts with certainty. Nevertheless, it is clear that from the perspective of modernity there are many practices, beliefs, and cultural arrangements which sit uneasy with our assumptions and prejudices on a variety of issues.

It is tempting to go back to the Bible and suppose that we are going to find values that support our modern prejudices, but it is not as easy as that. On a range of issues the Bible demonstrates not only its cultural and political contextualization but also how different the assumptions are when compared with our own. Take the issues of slavery and race, for example. There are few in the modern world who would argue for slavery. Nevertheless, with the exception of a few verses which may suggest support for the abolition of slavery, the Bible says little about slaves that is anything other than supportive of an institution which is abhorrent to modern sensibilities.

The story of the exodus from Egypt has been used to support the ideology of a powerful group having the right to inhabit land at the expense of the people already dwelling there. The stories of the birth of the Jewish people are tied up not only with belief in God, but also with a promise made to Abraham and his descendants (e.g., Gen. 12) to inherit the land. The account of the conquest of this land, where Abraham was said to sojourn, by the nascent Jewish (Israelite) nation under Joshua, is as much a part of historical and contemporary *Realpolitik* as any item of the Bible.[1] Historically, there have been several examples of construing one's right to travel, like Israel out of Egypt, to displace indigenous peoples before taking possession of their land. For instance, the promise of the land to a group who regarded themselves an elect nation, a "city set on a hill" (cf. Matt. 5:14), fired the European expeditions of exploration, expansion, and colonization by the Boers in South Africa, and before that the journeys to the "New World" that led to the conquest of the Americas. It is important to recognize that contemporary **liberation theology** uses the image of liberation from bondage in Egypt, while avoiding

---

1. *Realpolitik* refers to pragmatic politics with little or no ethical concerns.

the rest of the story and thus the displacement—and indeed slaughter—of the indigenous Canaanites, in espousing its rhetoric of liberation.

The same sort of interpretive challenge is true for issues as diverse as race, gender, and sexuality. That is not to say that we do not find ways in which we can see in the Bible deep-seated support for struggling with received wisdom and the task of finding ways of being more loving, just, and fair in our interpersonal and political arrangements, but there is no blueprint for that which we can read from the pages of the Bible. A glance at history confirms this claim.

A Window on Monarchy, Power, and the Politics of Holiness

Much of the account of the origins of the Jewish nation is a story of their monarchy in the period up to the sixth century BCE, and then narratives of how the people related to the imperial rulers of the world empires of the day. The biblical accounts of kingship are full of ambivalence about monarchy as an institution and its effects, nowhere better exemplified than by 1 Samuel 8 and 10 and the rules for the exercise of kingship in Deuteronomy 17.

The OT accounts of monarchy have provided a blueprint for later political arrangements in different ways. The sixteenth and seventeenth centuries in England are only one example of the way in which opposing sides have appealed to the Bible to endorse their political preferences. Thus, the monarchists could see the way kings like David and Josiah were models of kingship and how the "Lord's anointed" was one whose authority was absolute, since he reigned with the authority of God. The "good king" (for example, Josiah, according to 2 Kings) was a paradigm for the first Protestant monarch in England, Edward VI. Like Josiah, Edward was monarch of a reforming kingdom, which looked back to the law of God to remove the abuses which had built up over the years in the practice of religion. But there were contemporaries of Edward who appealed to the ambivalence toward monarchy found in Deuteronomy 17:14–20 and especially in the dire warning that the prophet Samuel gave to the people about the effects of monarchy (1 Sam. 8:7–9).

There is a critique of monarchy in the portrayals of Jesus in the Gospels, where Jesus (as Messiah/king) contrasts markedly with royal behavior of the conventional kind. In the Gospel of John, the understanding of Jesus as a king is of one crowned with thorns (John 19:5), whose followers do not wage war (John 18:36). Throughout the Gospels, Jesus behaves as one who is lowly and humble (e.g., Matt. 21:1–11). There is a pattern of leadership and an example for others which are based not on superiority or mighty acts of military power, but on service (e.g., Mark 10:42–45). Nowhere is this seen more clearly than in the juxtaposition in Revelation 5:5–6, where the Lion of the tribe of Judah, the descendant of King David, is a slaughtered Lamb, not a warrior king like David (e.g., 2 Sam. 5:25).

Before Constantine, Christianity was a fringe movement which often attracted hostile interests of contemporaries and those in authority. Once Christianity became part of the fabric of political power, biblical imagery provided the ideological justification of the emperor. The image of Christ Pantocrator (Greek *Christos Pantokratōr*, "Ruler of All") enthroned in glory offered a pattern for the imperial rule. Mainstream Christianity was content with an ordered status quo in this life, preferring to worship Jesus as Lord, the guarantor of earthly potentates, rather than the humble Son of Man who had nowhere to lay his head (Matt. 8:20).

Consistently pervasive in Scripture, however, is that tradition of altruism which runs like a thread from the command to love one's neighbor in Leviticus 19 to the ethics of the Pauline communities. Throughout the Bible, priority is given to this ethic, above "burnt offerings and sacrifices" (Matt. 9:13; 12:7; Mark 12:33; cf. Hosea 6:6). For Paul, the exercise of power through the Spirit cannot be the true mark of the nascent community. In the famous passage in 1 Corinthians 13, prophecies and tongues of ecstasy must take second place to that which will always be the hallmark of life in Christ: love. It is this theme which typifies the practical advice Paul gives to the Christians in Corinth as they struggle to find ways of being community.

The authority and demand for exclusive devotion to the God of Israel is a constant theme in the Hebrew Bible, and not unrelated to the love command (Lev. 19:18b; Deut. 6:5). The exclusive devotion demanded of the people of God in the Bible is encapsulated in the word "holiness." God is holy; therefore the people are expected to be holy (Lev. 19:2). That sense of separation and distinctiveness is epitomized by Sabbath observance, which, according to the creation narrative, reflects the rest that the Deity enjoyed after the six days of creation (Gen. 2:1–3; cf. Exod. 20:8–11). The distinctiveness of Jewish life finds its focus in Sabbath observance and the attention it attracted. In lives lived in the middle of other cultures, this kind of practice, matched by obedience to the rest of the law of Moses, is the bedrock of the pattern of life which distinguished the life of a holy nation. The service of God by keeping the divine commands involved a polity which protected the vulnerable and maintained justice. Early Christianity before Constantine paralleled this pattern to a large extent. The politics of holiness in the Bible, which also pervades the language and ideology of the NT (e.g., 1 Pet.1:16; 2:9), cannot be overestimated.

Two Principles of Interpretation

The previous discussion raises questions about an appropriate **hermeneutic**, or interpretive strategy, when it comes to politics. There are two principles of interpretation which I want to stress.

First, there is the christological criterion: how does a political arrangement or practice look in the light of the Jesus story as we find it in the canonical Gospels? As we have seen, a Christian reading of the Apocalypse (Revelation) has its key in the person of Christ, the Lamb in the midst of the divine throne, standing as if it had been slaughtered (Rev. 5). The orientation is toward Christ the faithful witness (Rev. 3:14). The fundamental story which shapes the community's life is of a crucified messiah who refused armed struggle as a way of inaugurating the kingdom of God (Matt. 26:53; John 18:36). This christological criterion is not the reconstruction of scholars, nor does it emerge from noncanonical texts. It evinces a clear preference for the fact that the canonical Gospels witness to Jesus in life and death, and this must pervade interpretations of the Bible and indeed of experience itself. Therein lies a crucial aspect of criticism. The story of the Lamb who is slain offers a critique of human history and of our delusions, of the violence we use to maintain the status quo and the lies with which we disguise the oppression of the victim.

The second principle comes from Latin American **liberationist** biblical hermeneutics. Clodovis Boff contrasts two ways of engaging with the Bible in liberationist hermeneutics (Boff, *Theology and Praxis*). One of these he terms **"correspondence of terms"** and the other **"correspondence of relationships."** Correspondence of terms is a *direct, immediate* engagement in which the modern reader identifies with a biblical story; the person or event depicted in the Bible offers an imaginative frame for viewing the modern world. In this kind of engagement with the Bible, biblical words become the tool for discernment in the present. The Bible functions less as a window onto antiquity and more as a way of understanding oneself that is socially and contextually meaningful.

Correspondence of relationships complements correspondence of terms, according to Boff. In this approach, one looks at the similarities between the biblical text, which bears witness to the life and struggles of the people of God at a particular time and place in the past, and the contemporary situation and experience of a reader or community of readers. The contemporary state of affairs is understood as *analogous* to that to which the Bible bears witness, and it may inform, inspire, and challenge readers of the Bible. This method is not about applying a set of principles from a theological program, however, but offering orientations, models, types, and inspirations to the biblical interpreter.

We return now to the text of Scripture itself, having already briefly noted its political character and considered two basic principles of interpretation: the christological criterion and the principle(s) of correspondence. What are some of the ways in which we see politics at work in each of the Testaments?

Politics in the Bible

Politics in the Hebrew Bible

As noted above, the story of the Hebrew Bible is itself a story of politics, of a nation's culture, its fortunes, and the evolution of its political arrangements over centuries, as well as its relationship with dominant imperial forces in the region. It is a mix of stories of migration, of enslavement and liberation, of settlement and the relationship with indigenous peoples and cultures, and of the consequences of being caught up in wider global forces. Large parts of the Hebrew Bible (the Christian Old Testament) are the product and consequence of one episode of these larger forces, as the Jerusalem elite was transported to exile in Babylon in the sixth century BCE. This crisis, at once religious and political, led to a time of reappraisal and self-understanding, which was as remarkable for its depth and productivity as for its later effects. The memories and legends, the laws and the analysis of what went wrong—all of which led to the debacle of exile—are mirrored in the pages of the Hebrew Bible.

The distinctive sociopolitical arrangements and the consequence of their accommodation to the settled life in and around Jerusalem occupy much of the Hebrew Bible. The politics of identity and of difference, and the ability to offer a critique of the shortcomings of those who were at ease in **Zion**, constitute one of the most remarkable political stories in history. The foundation of it all is a discomfort with ease and complacency, and thus the necessity for the maintenance of a different perspective on social arrangements. During the heyday of King Solomon's reign, the triumph of Judea, its incipient hegemony in the Middle East, and its prestige were the start of a movement of criticism, which resulted in the prophetic writings of the Hebrew Bible. Whether through vision or social isolation or marginality, the prophets forged another perspective on the myths and the confidence of the political settlement in what became a divided state. They catalogued its shortcomings, perhaps inspired by the alternative vision of society which finally saw the light of day in biblical books like Deuteronomy and Exodus.

It is all too easy to be so caught up with the religious texture of these texts (and the way in which they have inspired Judaism, Christianity, and Islam) that we miss the extent of their political character. Throughout, the Hebrew Bible tells a thoroughly political story. Incipient social arrangements were transformed into the monarchy and its attendant cultic arrangements, as the temple in Jerusalem, and also in Samaria on Mount Gerizim, became an institutional vehicle for the politics of identity and offered an ideology for the political arrangements which accompanied them. The genius of the Hebrew Bible, however, was that political critique accompanied these developments. One cannot read Amos or sections of Isaiah without being struck by the way in which a nation's ability to offer a critique of its political and institutional arrangements had emerged, and in the form in which they presented what turned out to be a necessary counterpoint to the story of **settlement** and consolidation. There is grit in the shoe of the political story told. "You were once slaves in Egypt" acts as a constant refrain, bringing a people back to their origins as migrants and as an oppressed people, who needed always to be aware of another dimension to the politics of their day which relativized—and indeed tempered—self-satisfaction about the present.

The Political Character of Early Christianity (The New Testament)

Christianity began life as a thoroughly political movement, in which the relationship with the political is endemic to what it is about. The fact that this should have become attenuated is itself a cause of puzzlement, but it is a dimension of the Gospels which has been recovered in recent years. Christianity had its beginnings in, and was originally confused with, Judaism, because of its countercultural aspects. The ongoing input of Jewish sources into emerging Christianity meant that it inherited the political characteristics of Judaism. Sociological approaches to the Bible (see ch. 10) have been highly illuminating in drawing out the political character of much early Christian identity, with its countercultural attitudes and practice. When Paul set up communities in different places, there was an immediate political impact, in varying ways, both internally within those groups and externally in how they related to the wider society. Paul never set out to write a systematic set of instructions on how these communities should function, but it is significant that the Greek word he used to describe them, *ekklēsia* (assembly), is very political in its character and harks back to the OT's notion of the public assembly of Israel. Similarly, Paul's notion of the body of Christ resembles the ancient understanding of the body politic.

Figure 22.1. Rembrandt's 1635 painting of Christ driving the money changers from the temple (Rijksmuseum, Amsterdam).

John the Baptist and Jesus

This political character of Christianity is built into it from the very start. According to the Gospels, Jesus was linked with John the Baptist, who was executed for subversion by Herod Antipas (Josephus, *Jewish Antiquities* 18.116). John's message of a decisive moment in God's purposes provided the context for Jesus' own activity. Jesus was in conflict with scribal religion, and the volatile atmosphere of Jerusalem at Passover time, a festival particularly linked with political liberation, also led to attempts by the priestly hierarchy in Jerusalem (the local elite which managed the Roman colony) to take action against him. According to the Gospels, Jesus was executed with the connivance of the Roman colonial governor of Judea, Pontius Pilate, yet with the active involvement of the Jerusalem priestly elite. Jesus preached against the temple, something which had attracted intense opposition when Jesus' prophetic predecessors embarked on the same activity (Jer. 7; Matt. 23; Luke 11:42–52). In addition, from the perspective of the authorities (in Jerusalem in particular), this made Jesus a threat to public order. When he neared Jerusalem, his position became untenable. Jesus resembled other prophetic figures described by the first-century Jewish writer Josephus (e.g., *Jewish Antiquities* 20.97–99, 167–72, 185–88), figures who looked back to God's deliverance of old and promised a new era of deliverance. In Jesus we have a nonconformist with eschatological beliefs, which put him in a different position from that of a mere prophet of doom, and made him to be more of a harbinger of the messianic age.

Paul

What about Paul? There is no explicit attempt to confront the might of Rome in the Pauline Letters. Instead there is an attempt to negotiate a modus vivendi (way of life) and wherever possible to keep one's head down (e.g., 1 Thess. 4:10–11), thus offering a better outcome than a deliberate confrontation with the religion of empire. By contrast, the early Christian martyr narratives of the second to fourth centuries present a more heroic, but probably partial, picture of early Christian experience. Such public profession was the exception rather than the rule, however paradigmatic the martyr narratives were intended to be. Many Christians functioned "below the radar," carving out patterns of life which contrasted with the dominant culture, thereby attracting new adherents to what was as much a political as a religious movement. The politics of Paul is to be found in the complex negotiation of community formation, in which the boundaries of a new political entity (the body of Christ), based on convictions about the coming of the Messiah, create ambiguous relationships with those outside it (cf. 1 Cor. 8).

The service of the practical politics of community formation and maintenance is what pervades the Pauline Letters. Paul was actively engaged in shaping and holding together embryonic communities, so that social cohesion takes precedence over human freedom, a theme particularly explored in 1 Corinthians 8–9 (cf. Rom. 14, esp. 14:19). The character of life in the messianic community, waiting for the consummation of the messianic times, emerges as *the* crucial issue in the Pauline corpus, even if Paul paradoxically resorts to law as the means of enabling the social cohesion that he regards as crucial. The messianic impulse and community cohesion are a constant dialectic in the Pauline Letters.

What distinguishes the messianic life is, according to Paul, above all social rather than aesthetic or spiritual. As with Jews, there was the necessity among Christian communities for distance and nonconformity in belief and practice, which Paul also explores in 1 Corinthians 8–10. Messianic life may seem to be socially conservative, but that initial assessment conceals the complex mix of negotiating the time while waiting for the "impending crisis" (1 Cor.

7:26), which required the implementation of certain patterns of living which characterize life as the "temple of the Holy Spirit" (1 Cor. 6:19). Being *in* the world means inhabiting the present age; not being *of* the world indicates that "our citizenship is in heaven, and it is from there that we are expecting a Savior" (Phil. 3:20). It is that pattern of messianic life in this age—a politics of holiness—which is explored in the pages of the NT. The Letters of Paul indicate the difficulties posed by the improvisation necessary for communities living "as if" a new age has come, but recognizing the culture of the old age as still very much something to be reckoned with.

Apocalypticism

Apocalypticism—the term comes from the Greek word *apokalypsis*, meaning "revelation"—was important to early Christianity, *not* because it is a form of cataclysmic **eschatology** (as is often thought), but because it offered a different mode of understanding, based on experience of the divine through vision, audition, or dream, which could bypass conventional channels of authority based on tradition. *The* **apocalyptic** text in the Bible, the book of Revelation (the *apocalypse* [= "revelation"] of Jesus Christ, according to Rev. 1:1), typifies Christian hope and its political outlook. This is nowhere better seen than in its unmasking of the pretensions of the Beast and Babylon (Rev. 13 and 17) and the hope for the transformation of this world and its structures. The book of Revelation offers the most sustained political discourse in the NT. The Apocalypse enables an enhanced vision of the reality that confronts people living in a particular moment of time and does not offer a timetable about the end of the world. Central to early Christian hope was the expectation of a new age *on earth* (see Rev. 21:1–4), a belief which was still widely held, at least to the end of the second century, as is evident in the writings of Justin Martyr, Irenaeus, Hippolytus, and Tertullian (see, e.g., Irenaeus, *Against Heresies* 5.33.3–4).[2] This is the type of belief presupposed in the Matthean version of the Lord's Prayer, where there is an earnest longing for God's kingdom to "come on earth as it is in heaven" (Matt. 6:10).

Conclusion

In Martin Luther's influential **two-kingdoms theology**, the religious and the political are the means of effecting the ordering of the world for human

---

2. This belief appears as well in later writers such as Lactantius (240–320 CE).

flourishing. The divinely appointed rulers were agents of God, leaving the church to attend to spiritual matters. Such a division can seem to be underpinned by Jesus' enigmatic words, "Render to Caesar the things that are Caesar's, and to God the things that are God's" (Mark 12:17 RSV). But in all likelihood, given the context in which the saying is found, this tantalizing comment tells us little about a worked-out political theology and more about the need for circumspection in responding to those who would question. Indeed, the very ambiguity of the saying is suggested by the charge leveled against Jesus, according to Luke's Gospel: "We found this man perverting our nation, forbidding us to pay taxes to the emperor, and saying that he himself is the Messiah, a king" (Luke 23:2). It is a comment which aptly indicates the political character of the stories told in the Bible and the effects of those images on ancient and modern readers alike.

QUESTIONS FOR REFLECTION AND DISCUSSION

1. Before reading this chapter, how did you understand the relationship between religion and politics? How has this chapter affected your thinking?

2. Do you think there is a different understanding of politics in the OT as compared with the NT? Explain your answer.

3. When Jesus went up to Jerusalem and cleansed the temple, to what extent was there a threat to the established order in what he did?

4. "The kings of the Gentiles lord it over them; and those in authority over them are called benefactors. But not so with you . . ." (Luke 22:25–26a). Do you think Jesus expected a different kind of politics from his followers?

FOR FURTHER READING AND STUDY

Barr, James. "The Bible as a Political Document." In *Bible and Interpretation: The Collected Essays of James Barr*, edited by John Barton, 1:198–214. Oxford: Oxford University Press, 2013. A leading Hebrew Bible scholar outlines the pitfalls of seeing the Bible as a political document.

Boff, Clodovis. *Theology and Praxis: Epistemological Foundations*. Maryknoll, NY: Orbis, 1987. An extended theological justification of liberation theology plus a readable and very helpful introduction using the Bible in discussion of contemporary political issues.

Bradstock, Andrew, and Christopher Rowland. *Radical Christian Writings: A Reader*. Oxford: Blackwell, 2002. Some of the texts that give evidence of political appropriations of the Bible.

Porter, Stanley, and Cynthia Westfall, eds. *Empire in the New Testament*. Eugene, OR: Pickwick, 2011. Essays on various NT writings in relation to empire.

Prior, Michael. *The Bible and Colonialism: A Moral Critique*. Sheffield: Sheffield Academic Press, 1997. A perspective on the political dimension of modern biblical scholars' attitudes to the land of Israel.

Rowland, Christopher. "Scripture." In *The Cambridge Companion to Christian Political Theology*, edited by Craig Hovey and Elizabeth Phillips, 157–75. Cambridge: Cambridge University Press, 2015. Aspects of the role of Scripture in Christian political theology.

Walzer, Michael. *In God's Shadow: Politics in the Hebrew Bible*. New Haven: Yale University Press, 2012. Politics in various themes and other aspects of the biblical text.

Wengst, Klaus. *Pax Romana and the Peace of Jesus Christ*. London: SCM, 1987. A searching investigation of the differing political emphases in the NT.

Wink, Walter. *Naming the Powers: The Language of Power in the New Testament*. Philadelphia: Fortress, 1984. Explores the meaning of the language of principalities in the NT and related Jewish sources.

Yoder, John Howard. *The Politics of Jesus*. 2nd ed. Grand Rapids: Eerdmans, 1994. A pioneering study that put the political character of the NT on the map.

23

Scripture and Christian Community

Jonathan Wilson-Hartgrove

I grew up in the church (Southern Baptist), raised by people who loved me and taught me to love Scripture. When we were young, we received rewards for memory verses. When we got older, we were to internalize the value of the Bible, "hiding God's Word in our hearts that we might not sin against God" (cf. Ps. 119:11). I have a distinct memory of a minister asking each of us at a large youth gathering to turn to the inside front cover of our personal Bibles. "I want you to write, 'Dear . . .' and then fill in your name. Now, turn to the back and write, 'From, God.'"

The intent of this exercise was clear and good: we were to internalize our love for Scripture by receiving it personally, like a letter written to each of us. The unintended consequence for far too many of us—not only in that room but also in Western Christianity more broadly—was that by making the Bible personal, we made our reading of it individual. As a letter to *me*, Scripture was about *my* spiritual life and *my* soul's salvation. I don't mean to suggest that this way of reading the Bible was exclusive. It was manifestly clear to me that the Bible was also a personal letter to my friends, my parents, our neighbors, and the families I met on mission trips halfway around the world. The Bible was for each of them as much as it was for me. But it was for each of us *individually*. While teaching and preaching informed our understanding, the Bible was most powerfully present to me in quiet times when I studied God's Word alone.

"Do you not know that your body is a temple of the Holy Spirit?" (1 Cor. 6:19). As an individual reader, I heard a challenge to take care of my body—to eat well, sleep, exercise, and be chaste (when I was young, so much of "the Bible and me" was about sex). Then I took a Greek class in college and learned that the "you" in 1 Corinthians 6:19 was actually "y'all" (plural "you"). Paul wasn't writing only about *my* body being a temple. He was writing to a gathering of believers in first-century Corinth, telling them that their body politic—their collective, shared life as the body of Christ (1 Cor. 12)—was a temple of the Holy Spirit every bit as much as the majestic building in Jerusalem. Their individual bodies-as-temples were part of an even greater, communal temple (see 1 Cor. 3:16).

As a way of reading, "the Bible and me" made it seem like my holy and righteous living was the most important thing God was up to in the world. Learning that almost all the "yous" in the Bible were actually "y'alls" interrupted me. I had to go back and reread everything. "The Bible and community" became a way of understanding that the gathering together of a people is actually God's great work in the world. Though the good news is personal, it is never private. "The Bible and community" taught me that I get to be part of God's cosmic and eternal work by participating as a living member in Christ's body, the church.

Community in the Bible

Community in the Hebrew Bible

In the beginning, the Bible says, God created the heavens and the earth. Genesis imagines a cosmic scene in which the earth is a bubble surrounded by the waters of chaos, a home carved out to make space for life. This home, filled with flora and fauna, fowl and fish, is ultimately and at its heart a garden where God can dwell together with people. "Let us create in our image," God says, speaking in the plural. Christian theology has made much of the trinitarian suggestions in this first-person plural: "Let us . . ." But the theme of community in the Bible helps us to notice that when God speaks in the plural, God also creates in the plural: "Male and female he created them" (Gen. 1:27). From the first chapter of the Bible, God is community, creating community "in our image."

But not all community reflects the image of the true and living God. Refusing the gift of their life with God and each other, Adam and Eve break faith with each other and with God. Using the language of "I" and "me," they forsake the community they were made for. Things fall apart, and community becomes dangerous. Cain kills his brother, then goes on to father a civilization that cooperates to no good end. The tower at Babel rises and falls as a reminder of the danger of human community without God.

Indeed, God's image-bearers have veered so far from their intended course that, by Genesis 7, God is ready to destroy them and their good home. It is only Noah's family that tempers God's righteous anger. Once again we witness the Creator carving out a home—much smaller this time and made of gopher wood. The waters of chaos rush in to wash away all that has been corrupted, but floating atop the waters is the ark, a little home filled with a small community of people and animals.

When Israel is called to be God's people—first as a promise to Abram and Sarai (Gen. 12) and later as a long shot held out to the Hebrew people in bondage (Exodus)—a little ark in a raging sea is the image that captures their vocation. Israel's foundational documents are not a constitution to inspire all people, but rather a peculiar set of commandments to set a small group off from the surrounding peoples. Much of the Torah is filled with foundational stories and legal precedents for this peculiar people. It is hard to believe that a collection of books like this could have ever become a best seller. They read, in truth, more like the dusty archives of an ancient village, cut off from the rest of the world.

Nevertheless, the theme of community in the Bible helps us see how this particular collection of writings and sayings came together to form one corpus. Communities need foundation stories. They need laws. They need history and songs, collected wisdom and prophetic challenge. The Torah, Nevi'im, and Ketuvim would not be published together in any modern-day self-help book. When we pay attention to the story Scripture tells, "the Bible and me" doesn't actually make good sense of the canon as we have it. Community, however, proves to be a theme that holds these disparate writings together. The Hebrew Bible makes much more sense as an archive of a community than it does as a handbook for how to build a better me.

Community in the New Testament

When we turn to the Gospels, this uniting theme of community illuminates what Jesus is up to when he claims the authority of Israel's God, calls twelve disciples (just like the twelve tribes of God's peculiar people), and goes up on a mountain to reinterpret Israel's legal code ("You have heard that it was said . . . but I say to you . . ." [Matt. 5]). Jesus is a teacher and a healer, but he is more than a guru inviting individuals to be enlightened. After working closely with a small group of unlikely friends, articulating and demonstrating God's way in the world, Jesus says to Simon, "You're a rock, and on this firm foundation I'm going to build my *ekklēsia*, and the gates of hell shall not prevail against it" (Matt. 16:18, paraphrased).

In the New Testament as we have it, this is the first occurrence of the Greek word *ekklēsia*, usually translated "church." Its root verb *kaleō*, "to call," is modified by the prefix *ek-*, meaning "out." The community Jesus establishes in the Gospels—the movement of people that he foresees storming the gates of hell itself—is literally "the Called-Out-Ones." Like the people of Israel in the Hebrew Bible, the community of the Called-Out-Ones turns out to be a uniting theme of the story the New Testament tells.[1]

But this is dangerous territory: as soon as we say that Jesus reestablished Israel when he called his church together, we are making a political claim. "**Supersessionism**" is the term scholars use to describe a theology in which the Christian church replaces Israel. It has been part of the ideological justification for persecutions, from the slaughters during the Crusades to the Holocaust of the twentieth century. Such a "replacement theology," however, required so-called Christians in the West to forget the Jewishness of Jesus and his Called-Out-Ones. The historical fact that all Jews did not recognize the teachings of Rabbi Jesus must not obscure the Jewishness of the Called-Out-Ones. Supersessionism is a misreading of the Bible that results in part from failing to recognize the central role that community plays in Scripture.

After all, the Gospels are followed by the Acts of the Apostles—the foundation story of the Called-Out-Ones, who bear the Spirit of their Christ, from whom they take their common name ("It was in [Syrian] Antioch that the disciples were first called 'Christians,'" Acts 11:26). As with every naming story, what happened at Antioch is charged with meaning for all people who will bear the name "Christian." In the synagogue at another Antioch (in Pisidia, now central Turkey), where Paul preached Jesus as the Christ (**Messiah**), the Holy Spirit filled **gentiles** (non-Jews), and they worshiped God just as the children of Israel did (Acts 13:13–52). The Called-Out-Ones were no longer a sect of Judaism in the broader society; they were a strange new mixture of Jew and gentile. What do you call this new peculiar people? Acts says they were called "Christians" for the first time at Antioch.

---

1. Although etymology (word origins and constituent parts) is never a sufficient indicator of meaning by itself, the various uses of the word *ekklēsia* justify focusing on its etymology in order to understand its significance.

In his writings (which make up a great deal of the NT Letters), Paul articulates a theology to make sense of this new community of Called-Out-Ones he first witnessed at Antioch, then helped to share and spread across the known world. Upon close reading, his letters turn out to be as idiosyncratic as the various books of the Hebrew Bible. One minute Paul is greeting old friends, the next he's recalling the story of Abraham. He quotes lyrics from praise hymns, then turns to detailed instruction about money, administration, or even particular people who have had some disagreement with one another. As a single piece of art, the NT is a mosaic of pieces from here and there that have been glued together to form a whole. What unites the various pieces? *Community* emerges as a compelling theme.

The Greek term *allēlōn*—"one another"—occurs one hundred times in the NT. "Love one another," "pray for one another," "accept," "greet," "instruct," and "serve one another." Whether Jesus is teaching the disciples or the apostles are writing to early Christian communities, the New Testament reads like the correspondence of community organizers. The "you's" of the New Testament Letters are plural because they are addressed to the Called-Out-Ones at Rome, at Corinth, at Galatia, Ephesus, Colossae, and Philippi. Even the letters that are addressed to individuals are addressed to community leaders, directing them in a more personal way about matters of leadership that affect the whole. "Now you are the body of Christ," Paul writes to the Corinthians, employing an image that was central to his teaching as a community organizer (1 Cor. 12:27). All that God has been up to since the beginning of time was embodied in Jesus the Christ, Paul says. Now the resurrected body of Christ is the global community of Called-Out-Ones who bear his name by the power of the same Holy Spirit that enlivened Jesus. The Gospels tell the story of Jesus, the Word who "became flesh and made his dwelling among us" (John 1:14 NIV). As Paul understands it, this is also the story of the church. The wisdom of God is present on earth in the community of God's Called-Out-Ones.

The Bible ends with an **apocalypse** (the book of Revelation)—a form of literature meant to unveil the deeper realities of the world that we see and read about in the newspaper. As an art form, it is unfamiliar to those of us who study in universities and trust cable news to tell us what's happening in the world. We find its modern equivalent in the poetry of exiles and the spoken word rhymes of America's inner cities. Apocalypse is "coded" to protect vulnerable people from those in power. It is also subversive, offering images and language to oppressed people who must put their hope in something beyond the present status quo.

What is the hope of the NT's Apocalypse? Its language is never clearer than the line from chapter 11 that Handel sampled in his *Messiah*: "The kingdoms of this world have become the kingdoms of our Lord, and of His Christ, and He shall reign for ever and ever!" (Rev. 11:15 NKJV). This kingdom language is political, but not in any partisan sense. The Apocalypse was written by a seasoned community organizer, rapping from exile on a prison island about how the life that Jesus taught and practiced, and the community that is his body, is the true hope for all people. God's good news to Israel in Egypt is the same as the Apocalypse's message to persecuted Christian communities: "The LORD will fight for you, and you have only to keep still" (Exod. 14:14). This is not a message of resignation, but of communal nonviolence, faithful witness, and hope.

The Bible in Community

To see community as a theme from Genesis to Revelation is to recognize that, as a book, the Bible finds its home in community. For much of its history, this was literally true. The best historical scholarship we have on the Hebrew Bible suggests that much of Torah was not written down until the **Babylonian exile** in the sixth century BCE. As an **oral tradition**, Scripture lived in the telling of God's gathered community. Long before there was an official canon in Judaism or Christianity, scrolls of Torah were kept in synagogues, and single NT letters were read aloud to gatherings in early Christian homes. Community is not simply a theme in the Bible; the Bible is a book for communities.

Another way of saying this is to note that the Bible is a **liturgical** book, a book for gathered prayer and worship. No religion is simply a collection of shared beliefs and stories. The content of faith is always expressed and embodied in shared practices. Fundamental to the Judeo-Christian tradition is the liturgical practice of fixed-hour prayer. "Seven times a day do I praise thee," the Psalmist says (Ps. 119:164 KJV). In the book of Daniel, we witness a son of Israel in exile going to the lions' den for refusing to give up his daily practice of fixed-hour prayer (Dan. 6). This daily liturgy was inherited by the early church as they "spent much time together in the temple each day" (Acts 2:46, slightly altered). All Christian worship is shaped by this liturgical tradition.

Because liturgy is the Bible's native home, a **lectionary** lays out a schedule for how to read Scripture in daily, weekly, and seasonal rhythms of prayer and worship.[2] Because the Christian lectionary is, fundamentally, a Jewish lectionary, Psalms are always at its heart, inviting us to sing our way into God's story.

2. While not every Christian church uses a lectionary, lectionaries go back to the early church and have been used throughout the history of the church and by many Christian communities.

Readings from the First and Second Testaments became an important part of Christian liturgy very early, always culminating in a reading from the Gospels that made clear how central the person of Jesus was to the self-understanding of the Called-Out-Ones. These lectionaries shaped daily worship for early Christian communities and regularly invited those communities into God's story, following an annual rhythm of anticipation in Advent, celebration at Christmas, preparation through Lent, and exultation at Easter: "Christ is risen! He is risen indeed!" If the Called-Out-Ones have a battle cry, this is it. In the liturgical rhythm of the church, each Sunday is a little Easter. While the church reads the Bible liturgically every day, a lectionary of Scripture's most beloved texts was developed for worship gatherings on the day that Jesus rose from the dead. This is the Bible that Christians know best.

While the Bible has always had a home in Christian worship, it also found a home after the fourth century in **monastic communities**. In much the same way that the Levites were "set apart" in Israel to keep the temple and its traditions, monks and nuns became set apart in the Christian tradition as keepers of the liturgy and of Scripture. Long before universities, monasteries were the home for Christian scholars. Here people learned Hebrew and Greek, copied manuscripts by hand before the advent of the printing press, and devoted considerable time to reflection on the Bible and its themes. They did not do this work independently, but as vowed members of a community under a **rule of life**. The most important of those rules in the West is the Rule of Benedict.

A collection of seventy-three short chapters (most of them paragraphs, really), Benedict's Rule addresses two essential elements of a "school for the Lord's service." The first is how to read the Bible. Benedict outlines a lectionary for daily prayers, exhorting members of his community to remember when they are overwhelmed by praying through the Psalms every week that the desert monks prayed the whole Psalter every day! In addition to telling a community what to read when, the Rule also instructs monastics on how to practice a life together that is, in essence, a **living exegesis** of Scripture. Benedict is clear that this is the goal of every Christian life. If monks are set apart, it is only for the purpose of helping everyone see more clearly the "life that is truly life" (1 Tim. 6:19 NIV).

While monasticism is a minority movement in the Christian tradition, both in the East and the West, it has consistently been embraced as a reminder that community is at the heart of our faith, just as our faith finds its meaning in community. For Roman Catholic and Orthodox Christians, the fact that an overwhelming majority of the church's saints were monastics draws our attention to the centrality of communal monasticism for the life of the church.

For Protestants, who have often distanced ourselves from monasticism, the fact that Martin Luther and several other leaders of the Reformation were monks is noteworthy.

The long history of the Bible's home in community helps us see that the modern notion of an individual scholar or church member reading the Bible alone is a novel idea. Of course, the critical reflections of the scholar and the personal piety of the individual Christian can add, and have added, a great deal to the community's understanding of Scripture. At best, however, these practices bring each individual back to the community, encouraging "one another to love and good deeds, not neglecting to meet together, as is the habit of some, but encouraging one another" (Heb. 10:24–25). The Bible is essential to Christian life, but the Bible cannot guide the Called-Out-Ones apart from community. Cyprian of Carthage, a third-century teacher of the church, said it like this: *extra ecclesiam nulla salus* ("Apart from the Called-Out-Ones, there is no salvation").

A Living Exegesis of Ephesians 2

I read the Bible and practice my faith as a member of God's Called-Out-People at a **new monastic community** called Rutba House, in the Walltown section of Durham, North Carolina. While our community is made up of Christians from Roman Catholic, Protestant, Anabaptist, African American, and Holiness traditions, our reading of the Bible is shaped by the monastic lectionary and the practice of *lectio divina* (sacred reading). We read the Bible together in daily, fixed-hour prayer; we try to live the Bible together in daily, shared life. Our life together is an experiment in the lived exegesis that Benedict's Rule aims to inspire. It's messy, but this is where "Bible and community" hits the ground for me.

I know from experience that our reading of Scripture in this place is shaped not only by our personal histories but also by the history of this racially divided Southern town where my neighbors (mostly African American) still call the local university (Duke, all-white until 1963) "the plantation." We are, like all people-called-out, a "community with/in a community." We cannot know who we are in Christ apart from understanding the forces that have shaped this place and our social relations within it.

At the same time, we have learned that we need a story that brings us together and reminds us who we are apart from the divisions we inherit in this place. While we must know and reflect critically on our time and place, self-reflection is not enough. We need something from beyond us to gather and unite us. In so many ways, that's what the Bible does. We read it best when we live into the shared identity it offers in Christ.

"Now in Christ Jesus you who once were far off have been brought near by the blood of Christ," the book of Ephesians tells us (2:13). I look across the circle at morning prayer. Sammie, a black man who is my age, almost to the day, has lived a very different life from me. We both went to public schools in this state and watched the same sitcoms growing up, but Sammie went to prison when I was in college and faced decisions I will never need to face because he was born black in America. Still we "who once were far off have been brought near." We have been eating, praying, meeting, and walking together for years. What do we have in common? What is it that keeps bringing us together, even when we frustrate and disappoint one another? "The blood of Christ," Ephesians says.

Blood, for the biblical writers, is the life of the human body. Sammie knows this in the most visceral way. He has, on the streets of this neighborhood, felt a knife rip into his stomach and watched his blood flow out on the ground. He has watched his life slipping away from him, and I have seen it, too. The proposed answer to this fracture in human community has often been "the law." Sammie's assailant was arrested, as he has been on multiple occasions. But the law, Sammie has shown me, cannot heal our brokenness or repair the breech in our fractured humanity. We need something more.

Which is why, Ephesians says, Christ himself "is our peace; in his flesh he has . . . abolished the law, . . . that he might create in himself one new humanity in place of the two" (Eph. 2:14–15). This is what Jesus was doing on the cross, as he poured out his own blood for the life of the world. And this is what Jesus is doing now, in this place, bringing Sammie and me together in a way of life where we are invited to live into an identity beyond black and white, beyond "respectable citizen" and "ex-con." Why do we do this? Is it some sort of reconciliation ministry, a special calling for people who care about social divisions? Sometimes we're tempted to think so. Sometimes others want to describe this little circle as a niche community—something other than "normal Christianity." But Ephesians insists otherwise. Ephesians says Jesus has brought us together by his blood and in his body so that he "might reconcile both groups to God" (Eph. 2:16).

Sammie and I have been brought together at this time, in this place, so we might have a relationship with God. In the end, this is why the Bible and community matter to me. Because apart from the Called-Out-Ones, there is no salvation. Without life together with Sammie and others, I cannot know the God of the Bible in Jesus Christ.

QUESTIONS FOR REFLECTION AND DISCUSSION

1. How have you experienced the influence of either Western individualism or Christian community—or both—in the reading of Scripture? What have been the effects of such experiences?

2. What is your reaction to the motif of "community" as a key to understanding both Testaments?

3. What is the relationship between the role of Scripture in community and the notion of the community as a "living" or "lived" exegesis of Scripture?

FOR FURTHER READING AND STUDY

Benedict of Nursia. *The Rule of Saint Benedict*. Cambridge, MA: Harvard University Press, 2011. A brief sixth-century guide to life in Christian community, including lectionary guidelines and a way of life; the bedrock of Western monasticism and a foundational document of democratic society. http://www.osb.org/rb/text/toc.html.

Claiborne, Shane, Jonathan Wilson-Hartgrove, and Enuma Okoro. *Common Prayer: A Liturgy for Ordinary Radicals*. Grand Rapids: Zondervan, 2010. A contemporary, ecumenical guide for daily fixed-hour prayer, drawing on ancient practices and blending them with the experience of contemporary new monastic communities.

Davis, Ellen F. *Getting Involved with God: Rediscovering the Old Testament*. Lanham, MD: Cowley, 2001. An accessible, engaging reading of the Hebrew Bible that makes the connection between the biblical story and God's people, past and present.

Lohfink, Gerhard. *Jesus and Community*. Philadelphia: Fortress, 1984. A reading of the Gospels revealing Jesus as a community builder who equips the original and subsequent disciples to become master community builders.

Moore, Charles E., ed. *Called to Community: The Life Jesus Wants for His People*. Walden, NY: Plough, 2016. More than fifty brief selections on the theory and practice of Christian community from diverse writers, including Thomas à Kempis, Søren Kierkegaard, C. S. Lewis, Dorothy Day, Dietrich Bonhoeffer, Elizabeth O'Connor, Jean Vanier, Eugene Peterson, John Perkins, and Jonathan Wilson-Hartgrove.

Oden, Thomas C., ed. Ancient Christian Commentary on Scripture. Downers Grove, IL: InterVarsity, 1998–. A multivolume series of excerpts from sermons, letters, and commentaries of the first five Christian centuries; an invitation to read with the ancient community of faith, liturgically and in community.

Thurman, Howard. *Jesus and the Disinherited*. Boston: Beacon, 1976. The pastor and public theologian who gave us the term "beloved community" connects the social location of the community Jesus organized in first-century Palestine with the plight of African Americans; important for translating the gospel's message into the twenty-first century's global culture, indelibly shaped by America's racism.

Vanier, Jean. *Community and Growth*. Rev. ed. Mahwah, NJ: Paulist Press, 1989. A classic text on Christian community life, filled with the lived exegesis made possible by holding the Bible and community together.

Wilson-Hartgrove, Jonathan. *Living Faithfully in a Fragmented World: From "After Virtue" to a New Monasticism*. 2nd ed. Eugene, OR: Cascade, 2010. A cultural, philosophical, and theological rationale for the contemporary practice of intentional Christian community among the poor.

——. *Strangers at My Door: A True Story of Finding Jesus in Unexpected Guests*. New York: Convergent, 2013. Narratives of community and hospitality from the Rutba House, the intentional community cofounded by the author of this chapter.

Yoder, John Howard. *The Politics of Jesus*. 2nd ed. Grand Rapids: Eerdmans, 1994. A Christian ethicist's reading of the NT, highlighting the political nature of Israel's God and the necessity of community for a full understanding of Jesus' message.

24

The Bible and Christian Mission

N. T. WRIGHT

Introduction

The Christian Bible hinges on Jesus. It looks forward from his richly complex achievement to the ultimate establishment of his universal lordship, and to the tasks for which, in anticipation of that end, he commissions his followers and equips them by his Spirit. It looks back to the biblical narratives of creation and covenant, of Adam and Abraham, of Moses, David and the prophets, seeing there the deep roots both of Jesus' own work, present and future, and of the church's tasks in the interim. The Bible thus constitutes the God-given narrative within which the church discerns its vocation and orders its life. The first Christians did not suppose that their fresh readings of Israel's Scriptures were identical to those on offer among their Jewish contemporaries, though there are similarities and analogies. But they claimed that once they saw the events concerning Jesus as the goal toward which the Scriptures had been tending, they saw not only a deep coherence in the Bible itself but also a fresh vision of how those same Scriptures, with their tantalizing glimpses of a glorious ultimate future, were to be fulfilled.

The events concerning Jesus form a coherent whole, despite modern tendencies to break them up, whether into scattered fragments of early Christian reflection or into the two large (and to modern eyes somewhat contradictory) themes of "kingdom" and "cross." Nevertheless, it will be convenient for

clarity's sake to separate here the different strands of kingdom, cross, resurrection, ascension, second coming, and the gift of the Spirit, concluding
with an all-embracing reflection on the underlying theology of temple and
creation. In each case we will see both how the theme in question informed
and energized the mission of the early church and how the church read the
ancient Scriptures as the narrative of God's mission (the *missio Dei*) to the
world. Doing so will allow us to read Scripture today to help us discern God's
ongoing mission and ours within it; that is the task of **missional hermeneutics.**

Jesus and the Kingdom of God

When the early Christians told the story of Jesus announcing God's kingdom, they were not simply providing historical reminiscences. They were
also consciously reinforcing the foundations of their own work. The slogan
"kingdom of God" was itself specific to the first-century Jewish context (where
it carried overtones of political revolution), and was not always retained. But
when Paul speaks of every knee bowing at the name of Jesus (Phil. 2:6–11),
or when John the Seer glimpses the Lion who is also the Lamb sharing the
divine throne (Rev. 4–5), these different expressions and their underlying theology are best understood as the outworking of Jesus' original proclamation.
When Acts concludes with Paul in Rome announcing God as King and Jesus
as Lord "openly and unhindered" (Acts 28:31 RSV), we are seeing the answer
to the disciples' question in Acts 1:6 as to whether this was the time for the
kingdom to be restored to Israel. Yes, seems to be the answer, but not in the
way you imagine—just as Jesus had corrected the aspirations of James and
John in Mark 10:35–45, reframing the notion of kingdom itself around his
own **cruciform** vocation.

That, indeed, characterizes Jesus' entire public career. Jesus' actions and
teachings have some things in common with the launching of a revolution
(an inner circle, hints of history reaching its climax, a challenge to suffer, and
the promise of victory), enough for some to want to hijack his movement for
that kind of purpose. But his characteristic public work of healing (especially
exorcism) and unorthodox or even scandalous celebration pointed elsewhere:
to a sense of creation healed, of covenant renewed, and above all of forgiveness of sins. In Jesus' world, the individual meaning of forgiveness resonated
with the larger theme of the undoing of Israel's long exile, as in Isaiah 40 or
Daniel 9. Jesus constantly hinted that all this was symptomatic of a revolution
deeper than his contemporaries had thought necessary: the breaking of a dark
power, more dangerous than any political oppressor. His parables, coming at

these themes from many angles, constantly hinted that he was enacting the fulfillment of Israel's hopes, but in a way nobody had previously imagined. The early Christians told and retold these stories to ground their own vocation to be a new sort of kingdom people. We note, for instance, Jesus' redefinition of kingship in his tense dialogue with Pilate (John 18:33–38).

As the early Christians did so, they were retrieving and reexpressing the scriptural hope that God's kingdom would put the world to rights. The biblical notion of God's kingdom went back at least to the Passover victory over Pharaoh, his armies, and his gods (Exod. 15:18). It came to regular expression in psalms such as Psalms 96 and 98; the prophecies of Daniel, especially chapters 2 and 7; and Isaiah, especially the theme of God's return and reign in 52:7–12. Jesus was seen by his first followers to have been claiming that Israel's Scriptures constituted a narrative with a goal in mind. God would at last establish his sovereign and rescuing rule over Israel and the world. Jesus' own work was, he hinted, the way in which this was coming true. The early church saw this Scripture-fulfilling achievement as the foundation of its own mission. They were Passover-people—but of a new sort.

Jesus and His Death

When Jesus wanted to explain to his followers what his approaching death would mean, enabling them not only to understand it but also to share in its effects, he didn't give them a theory. He gave them a meal, rich in reshaped Jewish symbolism, evoking Israel's ancient traditions and pointing them forward in a fresh direction. Paul taught that this meal looked back to Jesus' death and on to his coming, shaping and energizing the church for its work between those events (1 Cor. 11:17–34). The Bible thus dovetails with the sacramental dimension of the church's missional vocation, each interpreting and reinforcing the other. And Jesus' final meal, resonating with Passover symbolism but also incorporating the sin-forgiving new covenant of Jeremiah 31, draws together Israel's scriptural traditions into a fresh focus which the first Christians developed in their own work and writings.

The point of it all could be expressed like this. Israel's history was to be seen as the narrative both of divine promise and of human rebellion. Israel's exile in Babylon, the result of idolatry and sin, was the large-scale acting out of the human rebellion and exile catalogued in Genesis 3–11 (also ending in "Babel"). The call of Abraham's family to reverse and undo this disaster was thus problematic: the people called to bear the promise were themselves radically infected with the disease. The original biblical "mission"—the commissioning of Abraham and his family, the call of Israel to be the "nation of priests" (Exod. 19), the vocation of the Servant-people to be a light to the nations (Isa. 49:6; cf. 42:6; 60:3)—had thus always been paradoxical, as prophets regularly reminded the people and as the Psalms regularly lamented (a classic example is Ps. 89). The Pentateuch itself, announcing this "mission" in Genesis and Exodus, warns near its end that Israel, though about to inherit the land and to celebrate divine blessing there, will remain foolish and unfaithful, with disastrous results (Deut. 32).

John the Baptist announced a similar double message of promise and warning. Jesus himself, the greatest prophet of them all, announced not only the arrival of God's kingdom but also God's judgment on his rebellious people, particularly for their refusal to embrace the way of peace (Luke 19:41–44). Jesus seems to have concluded that Israel's own history, and with it the history of God's entire world, was being funneled down onto one place and one moment in a dark vortex of promise and disaster, of tragedy and triumph. The repeated biblical promises of divine blessing and new creation for the world were to be attained by the obedience of Israel. But, faced with Israel's disobedience, the mission of God could only be accomplished through the single faithful Israelite, the Messiah, coming to the place of rebellion, the place where the world's wickedness would reach its height and the divine love would reach its depth. Jesus saw his forthcoming crucifixion (the four Gospels draw this out in various ways) as his messianic enthronement, his missional victory, the overthrowing of the anticreational powers in the world and hence the revolutionary moment from which the new mission would begin. By dying in the place of sinners, Jesus was robbing the dark powers of their base of operations. Luke especially brings this out: "the power of darkness" had closed in around Jesus (22:53), but by this means Jesus fulfilled Isaiah 53 in taking the place of the wicked (22:37) and acted this out in submitting to the punishment they deserved (23:2, 25, 30–31, 39–43). That is why, from Easter onward, "repentance and forgiveness of sins" could be and would be announced to the nations, not simply as a "religious" option but as the sign that the rule of the powers had been broken (24:47).

The same point comes out forcefully in John 12:20–36. Reflecting on the request of some Greeks for a meeting, Jesus discerns that the moment has come—through his own approaching death!—for the dark power that has ruled the world to be overthrown, so that the nations can be free to come to him, and through him to the Father. "Now is the judgment of this world; now the ruler of this world will be driven out. And I, when I am lifted up from the earth, will draw all people to myself" (12:31–32). The root of the Jesus-focused mission of the church is the Jesus-shaped victory over the powers.

In all this, and much more, the early church was consciously retrieving, and reading in a fresh way, many strands of Israel's Scriptures. Isaiah 40–55 is one obvious source, focusing on the "Servant" songs, particularly the fourth (52:13–53:12). The psalms of suffering, such as Psalms 22 and 69, are another. But it would be a mistake to see these simply as **prooftexts**. They constitute particular strands, already themselves complex, within the larger narrative. And the narrative was the story of Israel, of the Creator's rescue operation in and for his creation. As Jesus' first followers looked back to his death and understood it within its scriptural matrix, they knew that in their own mission they were not simply persuading people to understand and accept a theory. They were summoning them to Jesus himself, the living Lord, whose death had dealt with sins and thereby defeated the powers. They were inviting hearers into the new world which had thereby come into existence.

Jesus and His Resurrection

Jesus' resurrection was a shock. Nobody had expected Israel's Messiah to be killed and then to rise from the dead. "Resurrection," for those (such as the Pharisees) who believed in it, would happen to *all* God's people at the *end* of time, not to one person in the middle (1 Cor. 15:23). But this unexpected gap, between the Messiah's resurrection and everybody else's, was quickly seen to be the time for mission. What Jesus had accomplished, the church must implement. The energy of Jesus' resurrection was released, through the Spirit, into his people, so that they would share in the life of new creation and become its agents in the world (e.g., Eph. 1:15–23).

The first Christians thus saw Jesus' resurrection as the beginning of the new creation. From the first their mission was understood in terms of bringing signs of that new creation to birth through the gospel's work of human rescue and renewal. "We are his *poiēma*," his "poem," his "workmanship," wrote Paul (Eph. 2:10), "created in Christ Jesus for good works"—not simply "good works" of moral behavior, but the fresh creativity whose rich variety reflects the lavish creativity of God himself, thereby offering a sign to the powers of the world that Jesus is Lord and they are not (Eph. 3:10–11). What has been launched in the resurrection is the new Genesis: heaven and earth are freshly joined in the Messiah (Eph. 1:10). All this, with its message of "peace" to those "far off" and those "near" (Eph. 2:13–18), is the context and foundation of the church's mission.

This is well displayed in John 20:19–23. The risen Jesus greets the disciples with the word "Peace!," resonating backward into the hopes of ancient

Israel and forward into the goal and means of their mission. Then he repeats it, making that mission explicit: "Peace be with you. As the Father has sent me, so I send you." That rhythm of "As . . . so . . . ," in the context of the Scripture-fulfilling address "Peace," says it all. *Jesus' own mission to Israel is the foundation and the shaping of the church's mission to the world.* And for this otherwise impossible task, Jesus' followers are given his own Spirit, described here in terms reminiscent of Genesis 2: Jesus breathes on them, as the Creator breathed into human nostrils. The ancient promise of life, shimmering like a mirage throughout Torah, now itself comes to life in new creation.

Jesus' resurrection thus looks onward to the fuller expressions of missional hope throughout the NT, especially in Romans 8, where the whole creation will be rescued from its slavery to corruption and decay; in the "new heavens and new earth" of Revelation 21 and 2 Peter 3:13. Some might misunderstand this hope as an excuse for doing nothing: God will renew the world, so we can only wait. That was never the early Christian conclusion. Different circumstances allowed for different expressions of new-creational mission, but even martyrdom itself was seen as a paradoxical sign of God's victory. The testimony of the early church was that sharing the Messiah's cruciform path would bear fruit as the watching world came to see death itself as a beaten enemy.

Jesus' resurrection thus compelled a fresh, new-creational, and missional reading of Israel's Scriptures. In line with some other early Jewish readers, Paul interpreted the land-focused promise to Abraham in terms of the worldwide extension celebrated in the Psalms (Gen. 15 with Pss. 2; 72; see Rom. 4:13). The whole world is now, in that sense, God's holy land. The notion of a total renewal of heaven and earth looks back to Isaiah 65 and 66, reflecting the growing awareness both that the Creator God has ongoing plans for the entire creation and that those plans must include rescue and healing from decay and death. All these strands of hope, retrieved by the early Christians in terms of their own mission, looked back to the good creation itself, to Genesis 1 and 2, where heaven and earth were designed as a single though differentiated whole—as, in fact, a *temple*, with the human pair as the "image" reflecting God to the world and the world back to God.

The resurrectional renewal of humans in God's image (Col. 3:10, applying the **christological** "image" of 1:15) was the sign and means of the reconciliation and renewal of all creation (Col. 1:18–20). The "renewal of all things" (Acts 3:21, my translation) was the goal, and the life and mission of the church was the path toward that goal. The final overthrow of death itself, and with it the promise that God would be "all in all" (1 Cor. 15:28), remained firmly in God's own hands. In other words, in the present we do not "build the kingdom" by our own work, even by our own Spirit-driven work. We build "*for* the kingdom," as Paul puts it in Colossians 4:11. Paul's last word in his long exposition of resurrection in 1 Corinthians 15 is to insist (v. 58) that "in the Lord your labor is not in vain." This is the assurance of mission: all work done in the Lord and in the power of the Spirit will somehow be taken up, enhanced and transformed no doubt, when God finally renews all things.

Jesus and His Ascension

The ascension of Jesus has sometimes been misunderstood in terms of Jesus' *absence*. By itself, this would either undermine mission ("What shall we do, now that Jesus has gone?") or reduce it to merely human effort ("We'll have to get on with it by ourselves"). This is a mistake. The Bible can use "up" and "down" language for heaven and earth, but this natural metaphor ought not to disguise the underlying biblical cosmology, which is of heaven and earth being made for each other, with "heaven" being in effect the "control room" for "earth." Heaven, God's space, is the sphere from which the whole world is run. The point of the ascension is that Jesus is now in control: "He must reign," writes Paul, "until he has put all his enemies under his feet" (1 Cor. 15:25). That is why Matthew has the risen Jesus declaring, "All authority in heaven and on earth has been given to me" (Matt. 28:18); this is then the context for the disciples' missional task: "Go therefore and make disciples of all nations, baptizing them . . . and teaching them . . ." (28:19–20). This again is consonant with the idea of Jesus' reign in Philippians 2:9–11, and with the victory shout in Revelation 11:15: "The kingdom of the world has become the kingdom of our Lord and of his Messiah, and he will reign for ever and ever." That is the biblical framework for mission.

Like every other aspect of the early church's missional vocation, this too is rooted in Israel's Scriptures. The Psalms speak repeatedly of a coming time when God will be exalted as king and the nations will be brought into his realm: "God is king over the nations; God sits on his holy throne; the princes of the peoples gather as the people of the God of Abraham, for the shields of the earth belong to God; he is highly exalted" (Ps. 47:8–9). Paul, summing up the entire message of Romans with its emphasis on mission and unity (Rom. 15:7–13), quotes the Psalms (18:49; 117:1), the Torah (Deut. 32:43), and the Prophets (Isa. 11:1): "The root of Jesse shall come, the one who rises to rule the Gentiles; in him the Gentiles shall hope" (Rom. 15:12). That Scripture-rooted celebration of Israel's Messiah as lord of the whole world is, then, the basis not only for the ultimate hope but also for the mission in which signs of that future hope are brought forward into the present time.

Jesus and His Spirit

We have already spoken of the Spirit breathed by Jesus on his followers, equipping them so that their peaceful kingdom-mission will be both their own work and that of Jesus himself. The classic statement of this comes in Acts 2, with the wind and fire of Pentecost coming upon the disciples. This is not primarily about a new "religious experience." It is the further joining of heaven and earth: the powerful energy of heaven coming to reside in, and to operate through, Jesus' followers. The church quickly anchored this experience and energy in readings of Scripture, going back to passages like Joel 2:28–32 and Ezekiel 37:9–10 to explain that this was the effective sign of the new creation, happening both in the disciples and through them in the wider world. Here again Romans 8 takes center stage, as Paul unfolds his vision of God's rescuing and restorative justice and love. This is a new exodus; and Paul envisages the Spirit performing the work which, in the first exodus, was done by the divine presence in the pillar of cloud and fire. The Spirit, in other words, is "leading" God's people to their "inheritance"; and in the process the Spirit is enabling them, as the deep heart of their mission, to be intercessors for the world, sharing and bearing the suffering and inarticulate groanings of all creation so that the Father's love may come to birth in the darkest places of the world (Rom. 8:26–27).

This chimes in with the Farewell Discourses in John, where the disciples are commissioned for their own mission and assured that their prayers will be answered. That is the context for the promise that the Spirit will call the world to account: the Spirit "will prove the world to be in the wrong on three counts: sin, justice, and judgment" (16:8).[1] This difficult but important passage offers a blueprint for the church's mission, rooted in Jesus' confrontation with Pontius Pilate in John 18 and 19. This Spirit-led mission will involve speaking the truth to power, holding up a mirror to the ways in which God's world is still rebelling against his rescuing rule. Here too we sense the scriptural rootedness: when the Servant is exalted, "he shall startle many nations; kings shall shut their mouths because of him" (Isa. 52:15). This theme looks back to Abraham's victory over the kings in Genesis 14, and also to the exaltation of the Son of Man and the destruction of the

---

1. My translation in *The Kingdom New Testament: A Contemporary Translation* (New York: HarperCollins, 2011).

"beasts" in Daniel 7. That missional vision of the overthrow of the powers which oppose God's good creation and then restoration of creation requires the church to look to the Spirit for the power, the words, and the effective result (Mark 13:11).

Jesus and His Coming

Properly speaking, the "second coming" (**parousia**) lies beyond the mission of the church. Once Jesus returns, the church's present work will be complete. To be sure, there will be new tasks in God's new world; we are rescued in order to be "kings and priests," and this will be as true in the new Jerusalem as in the present (Rev. 5:9–10; 20:4; 22:5). But from the first the early church understood the promise of Jesus' "coming" or "appearing" (Col. 3:4; 1 John 3:2) as coloring their work in the present time. The glorious future, which every generation must anticipate, is not to mean laziness now (2 Thess. 3:6–13). "Do not be weary in doing what is right" (3:13).

New Temple, New Creation

In and through the whole story of Jesus, the early church discerned the coming true of ancient scriptural promises and hence the renewal of their Scripture-based mission. The powers had been overcome, so that the good news could make its way into the wider world. Heaven and earth had come together. In all this we detect, in repeated patterns, a central feature of the exodus story. The construction of the wilderness tabernacle brings to a preliminary conclusion the story which begins with Genesis 1 and goes horribly wrong in Genesis 3. Heaven and earth are made for each other, with the human pair as the "image" in the original creational "temple": that image-bearing vocation is the foundation of all other missions, human in general and Israel-shaped in particular. The **tabernacle** was designed as a "little world," a symbolic representation of the heaven-and-earth creation. There was, of course, no human-made "image" of the divinity. In the place of the original image-bearing humans there was Aaron the high priest, representing Israel. And there was, above all, the clouded presence of Israel's God himself, coming to dwell with his people.

This was not an end in itself. The Scriptures regularly hint that what was true in the tabernacle, and then in Solomon's Temple, was a long-range signpost to God's intention for creation as a whole. The whole world, in other words, was to be filled with the divine glory, with God's people—represented by the priest, the king, or both, or even a prophet—functioning as the representative of God himself and thus as the image-bearer. That, from one angle or another, is what is said in Numbers 14:21; Psalm 72:19; Isaiah 6:3; 11:9; 35:2; 40:5; Habakkuk 2:14; and elsewhere. In particular, this is the vision of the end held out at the close of Ezekiel, where in chapter 43 the glorious divine presence comes to fill the newly rebuilt temple.

All of this comes to its biblical climax in the arrival of Jesus himself. "The Word became flesh and lived among us; we gazed upon his glory, glory like that of the Father's only Son, full of grace and truth" (John 1:14, my translation). God's project for the world is focused on the incarnate Son, and then on the worldwide, Spirit-led implementation of the Son's work. What John says explicitly, evoking both Genesis and Exodus, the other biblical writers hint at from several angles. The promised divine glory has returned, in the person and work of Jesus; and God will do for the whole creation at the end what he did in Jesus, bringing it through death to a new life, a new world. The picture of the new Jerusalem in Revelation 21 and 22 is of a structure like an enormous version of the holy of holies in the Jerusalem temple; and the redeemed humans are there as the royal priesthood, as a result of the royal and priestly work of Jesus himself. The present life of the church, energized for mission by the Spirit, is thus the anticipation of the eventual filling of all creation: the Messiah "in you [plural], the hope of glory" (Col. 1:27). This is the biblical narrative, from Genesis to Revelation, which sets the terms and the context for the church's mission.

That mission, then, is not about rescuing people *from* the world. It is about rescuing humans *for* the world, for new-creation tasks of every kind in the present, pointing on to the eventual new creation, a fresh gift from the Creator. Mission is not something added on to "biblical theology," as though one first had to discover the content of Scripture and then, by "mission," had to teach or preach that content. The story of Scripture, focused in the Gospel events concerning Jesus, is about mission from start to finish:

- God's mission in creation, with his image-bearing humans charged with bringing creation to full flourishing;
- God's mission in redemption and covenant, calling Abraham and his family to be the means of rescuing and restoring humans and therefore creation;
- God's strange mission in Jesus, coming to the place where Israel and all creation had plunged into the darkness of death, defeating all the powers that had opposed and corrupted humans and the world, and thence launching new creation in resurrection, ascension, and Spirit.

The church's mission is not something other than this story. It *is* this story, seen from the point of view of those who hear Jesus' call, "As the Father has sent me, so I send you" (John 20:21). The Bible provides a real-life, real-time drama. It hands us the script and bids us play our part.

QUESTIONS FOR REFLECTION AND DISCUSSION

1. In what ways does the Christian Bible hinge on Jesus, and what is the significance of this for Christian mission? Why is it important to plot Christian mission in accord with the scriptural story, specifically the story of Jesus?

2. What is the relationship among the mission of Israel, the mission of Jesus, the mission of his disciples and the early church, and the mission of the church today?

3. In what ways, according to this chapter (either explicitly or implicitly), has the church made—and might the church still make—mistakes in its missional practices?

4. This chapter depicts Christians as kingdom people and Servant people. Some of the terms used here to describe Christian mission are "Scripture-based," "Jesus-focused and Jesus-shaped," "Spirit-driven," and "new-creational." How does this presentation, expressed in these terms and in other ways, challenge and/or illumine your understanding of Christians and Christian mission?

FOR FURTHER READING AND STUDY

Bauckham, Richard. *Bible and Mission: Christian Witness in a Postmodern World.* Grand Rapids: Baker Academic, 2003. The missional implications of the biblical story for the contemporary church and world.

———. "Mission as Hermeneutic for Scriptural Interpretation." Lecture presented at Cambridge University, Cambridge, 1999. http://richardbauckham.co.uk/uploads/Accessible/Mission%20as%20Hermeneutic.pdf. Bauckham's missional hermeneutic.

Beale, G. K. *The Temple and the Church's Mission: A Biblical Theology of the Dwelling Place of God.* New Studies in Biblical Theology. Downers Grove, IL: InterVarsity, 2004. Traces the theme of the temple and its implications from Genesis to Revelation.

Bosch, David. *Transforming Mission: Paradigm Shifts in Theology of Mission.* Twentieth anniversary ed. Maryknoll, NY: Orbis, 2011. A classic, field-defining book that includes careful study of the Synoptics and Paul.

Brownson, James V. *Speaking the Truth in Love: New Testament Resources for a Missional Hermeneutic*. Harrisburg, PA: Trinity Press International, 1998. A classic statement of how to read Scripture missionally.

Dunn, James D. G. *Beginning from Jerusalem*. Vol. 2 of *Christianity in the Making*. Grand Rapids: Eerdmans, 2009. A careful, critical history of the early Christian movement, using Acts as its principal source.

Flemming, Dean. *Recovering the Full Mission of God: A Biblical Perspective on Being, Doing, and Telling*. Downers Grove, IL: InterVarsity, 2013. A holistic understanding of the church's mission rooted in that of Israel, Jesus, and the NT writings.

———. *Why Mission?* Reframing New Testament Theology. Nashville: Abingdon, 2015. The witness of several NT writings to the mission of God and the church's participation in it.

Goheen, Michael W. *A Light to the Nations: The Missional Church and the Biblical Story*. Grand Rapids: Baker Academic, 2011. The missional identity of the church in light of the biblical witness in both Testaments.

Gorman, Michael J. *Abide and Go: Missional Theosis in the Gospel of John*. Eugene, OR: Cascade, 2017. Johannine spirituality as participation in the life and the life-giving mission of Father, Son, and Paraclete.

———. *Becoming the Gospel: Paul, Participation, and Mission*. Grand Rapids: Eerdmans, 2015. A reading of Paul's Letters for their witness to God's mission and their implications for the contemporary mission of the church.

———. *Reading Revelation Responsibly: Uncivil Worship and Witness; Following the Lamb into the New Creation*. Eugene, OR: Cascade, 2011. The Apocalypse as a manifesto of hope for, and witness to, the new heaven and new earth.

Hastings, Ross. *Missional God, Missional Church: Hope for Re-evangelizing the West*. Downers Grove, IL: InterVarsity, 2012. Based on John 20:19–23, a study of Christian mission as receiving and disseminating shalom.

Middleton, J. Richard. *A New Heaven and a New Earth: Reclaiming Biblical Eschatology*. Grand Rapids: Baker Academic, 2014. Holistic salvation and human flourishing in eschatological and missional perspective.

Newbigin, Lesslie. *The Open Secret: An Introduction to the Theology of Mission*. Rev. ed. Grand Rapids: Eerdmans, 1995. A classic statement of the church's participation in the mission of the Triune God.

Schnabel, Eckhard J. *Early Christian Mission*. 2 vols. Downers Grove, IL: InterVarsity, 2004. Encyclopedic study of the mission of Jesus and his disciples and of Paul and the early church.

Senior, Donald, and Carroll Stuhlmueller. *The Biblical Foundations for Mission*. Maryknoll, NY: Orbis, 1983. Detailed study of mission according to both Testaments.

Sunquist, Scott W. *Understanding Christian Mission: Participation in Suffering and Glory*. Grand Rapids: Baker Academic, 2013. The history of the Christian mission, the mission of God, and contemporary mission considered within the framework of suffering and glory.

Wright, Christopher J. H. *The Mission of God: Unlocking the Bible's Grand Narrative.* Downers Grove, IL: InterVarsity, 2006. A modern classic on missional hermeneutics and on the God of mission, the people of mission, and the arena of mission according to both OT and NT.

Wright, N. T. "Paul and Missional Hermeneutics." In *The Apostle Paul and the Christian Life: Ethical and Missional Implications of the New Perspective,* edited by Scot McKnight and Joseph B. Modica, 179–92. Grand Rapids: Baker Academic, 2016. Paul's missional reading of Israel's Scriptures and of Jesus, which can serve to refocus the church for its mission.

———. *Scripture and the Authority of God: How to Read the Bible Today.* New York: HarperOne, 2011. Scripture as the authority not merely for ideas but also for transformative action.

———. *Surprised by Hope: Rethinking Heaven, the Resurrection, and the Mission of the Church.* New York: HarperCollins, 2008. The nature of early Christian hope, the biblical witness to God's future plan, and the implications for contemporary Christian mission.

Glossary

Chapters in parentheses indicate the principal chapter(s) in which the term is considered, thus making this glossary a sort of general index, with links to chapters rather than pages. A full subject index begins on page 432.

African American criticism (or hermeneutics): An interpretive approach that (a) highlights the presence of Africa and Africans in the Bible, (b) resists racist and oppressive interpretations, (c) stresses themes such as exodus and liberation, and (d) draws on traditional and contemporary African American resources in interpretation for the preservation and progress of African American churches and communities. (chs. 10, 17)

African hermeneutics: An approach to biblical interpretation in African contexts that (a) includes local sources (**inculturation, indigenization**); (b) emphasizes the oral and community dimensions of the Bible; and (c) involves **distantiation, contextualization**, and **appropriation**. (chs. 10, 16)

Alexandrian school: An early Christian school of biblical interpretation that arose at Alexandria in Egypt and tended to emphasize **allegorical interpretation**,

seen most strikingly in the work of Origen. *See also* **Antiochene school**. (chs. 9, 11, 14)

allegorical interpretation: A method of interpreting texts in which words, numbers, characters (e.g., Melchizedek), objects (e.g., the burning bush), and events (e.g., the conquest of Canaan) are assigned a symbolic significance as representing spiritual realities in addition to, or in place of, their literal meaning. *See also* **Alexandrian school; senses of Scripture**. (chs. 9, 11, 14, 16)

allegory (adj. **allegorical**): A text deemed to have symbolic meaning expressed in its words, numbers, characters, objects, and events. *See also* **allegorical interpretation**. (chs. 9, 11, 14)

American exceptionalism: A belief that the United States holds a special place in the divine plan and is therefore superior to other nations by virtue of its

401

vocation of spreading freedom and democracy. (ch. 12)

Anaginōskomena. *See* Readable Books

anagogical sense. *See* senses of Scripture

Ancestral Period: Also known as the Patriarchal Period, the time from Abraham and Sarah to Moses. (ch. 2)

ancient Near East: The region of the ancient world constituted by Mesopotamia (the land between the Tigris and the Euphrates Rivers), Egypt, Syria, and Israel. (ch. 2)

Antiochene (or Antiochian) school: An early Christian school of biblical interpretation that originated in Syrian Antioch and tended to emphasize both historical and typological exegesis over against allegory. Antiochene scholars include John Chrysostom. *See also* Alexandrian school. (chs. 9, 14)

antitype. *See* typological exegesis

apocalypse: Greek for "revelation"; (1) a genre of Jewish and Christian literature filled with symbolism and visions intended to unveil unseen realities (e.g., heaven and its inhabitants) as well as historical realities (past, present, and future) in order to offer a critique of contemporary political arrangements in light of the coming kingdom of God; (2) a name for the last NT book (Revelation). (chs. 1, 4, 5, 6, 14, 22, 23)

apocalyptic (adj. and n.): Shorthand term (and the subject of much scholarly dispute), used by some for a worldview ("apocalypticism") and by many for a type of literature ("apocalyptic literature") that reflects a belief in good and evil cosmic powers as well as hope in God's coming intervention to transform the present age of evil/sin into the age of justice/peace. (chs. 3, 4, 5, 12, 22)

apocalypticism. *See* apocalyptic

Apocrypha (adj. apocryphal): From the Greek adjective meaning "hidden"; (1) the books of the Greek OT (Septuagint) not included in the Hebrew canon or the Protestant canon but included in the Catholic and Orthodox canons (*see also* deuterocanonical; Readable Books); (2) certain early Christian writings not included in the NT (usually "NT Apocrypha"). (chs. 1, 3, 5, 6)

apology (adj. apologetic): A defense, especially of one's life, beliefs, or practices. (chs. 7, 9)

Apostolic Fathers: A modern designation for a corpus of the earliest preserved noncanonical Christian writings, dating from the late first and second centuries. *See also* postapostolic era. (ch. 5)

appropriation: (1) Generally, the utilization of Scripture for contemporary belief and practice; (2) sometimes (e.g., in certain forms of African hermeneutics) understood as the final step in the interpretive process, following distantiation and contextualization, with the goal of deriving meaning and life transformation. (ch. 16)

Aramaic: A language closely related to Hebrew and the lingua franca of the Persian Empire that gradually replaced spoken Hebrew after the Babylonian exile, and was thus the language of some later parts of the OT and of Jesus. *See also* Targum. (chs. 1, 4, 10)

Asia: (1) In the Roman era, the westernmost Roman province of Asia Minor; (2) in the modern era, the continent that includes China, India, Russia, and so forth. (chs. 2, 4, 19)

Asia Minor: The peninsula (roughly equivalent to modern Turkey) that has as its northern border the Black Sea, on its western side the Aegean Sea, and to the south the Mediterranean Sea; also known as Anatolia. (ch. 2)

authority: A source of truth or practical guidance for a community of interpreters, such as Scripture, the theological tradition, official leaders, reason, human experience, and the leading of the Holy Spirit. *See also* **magisterium; Readable Books; rule of faith; Wesleyan quadrilateral**. (chs. 4, 12)

Authorized Version (AV): The English translation of the Bible published in 1611 in England during the reign of King James I, known popularly as the King James Version (KJV) or King James Bible. (ch. 7)

Babylonian exile: The period (586–539 BCE) during which many of the people of **Judah** were deported to Babylonia. (chs. 1, 2, 3)

BCE: "Before the Common Era," a scholarly alternative to the traditional "BC" ("Before Christ"). *See also* **CE**. (ch. 1)

behind-the-text approaches: Interpretive approaches that view the text as a window through which to access and examine a deposit of meaning, which is thought to be located in the history assumed by the text, that gave rise to the text, or to which the text gives witness; often in contrast to **in-the-text approaches** and **in-front-of-the-text approaches**. (ch. 10)

Bible: From the Greek word for book, *biblion* (pl. *biblia*), derived from the words for the papyrus plant (*byblos, biblos*); the collected sacred writings of Judaism and Christianity. *See also* **canon; Scripture; Tanak**. (chs. 1, 7)

biblical criticism: The application to biblical texts of the standard methods of

investigation and norms for truth used with other historical documents; sometimes, more generally, scholarly study of the Bible. (ch. 10)

biblical theology: A disputed term, sometimes contrasted with **dogmatic theology**, referring to convictions about God and all things in relation to God that are expressed in, or originate with, the biblical texts. (ch. 10)

Book of the Twelve. *See* **Minor Prophets**

Canaan: Biblical name for the geographical area between the Mediterranean Sea and the Jordan River, promised to Abraham in Genesis (the promised land) and settled by the Israelites. *See also* **settlement**. (ch. 3)

canon: From the Greek word *kanōn*, meaning "measuring stick"; (1) a rule, norm, or guide for faith and practice; (2) especially a list, collection, or catalog of **Scriptures** (sacred writings) that the Jewish and/or Christian communities consider inspired and authoritative for their faith and practice. (chs. 1, 3, 4, 5, 6, 13, 14)

canon within the canon: The concept of the existence of books that play a more central role within the formal canon, or of a central, governing theme or principle (such as "justification by faith," "liberation," or "spiritual conflict") that functions as a means of determining the value, meaning, or authority of the biblical canon as a whole or its various parts. (chs. 9, 12, 15, 19)

catechesis: Teaching intended to form Christian individuals and communities. (ch. 21)

catholic: Global in nature; universal. (ch. 19)

Catholic: Referring to the Roman Catholic Church and its members. (ch. 13)

Catholic Epistles (Letters): The non-Pauline letters of the NT, so called because they have often been thought to have a universal or "catholic" audience, sometimes excluding Hebrews and/or 1–3 John; also called the General Epistles (Letters). (ch. 4)

CE: "Common Era" (i.e., the shared Christian and Jewish era), a scholarly alternative to the traditional "AD" (*Anno Domini*, "in the year of our Lord"). *See also* **BCE; Common Era.** (ch. 1)

cessationism: The belief that the supernatural work of the Holy Spirit (seen, e.g., in **glossolalia** and miraculous healing) ended at the conclusion of the apostolic era or soon thereafter; in contrast to **continuationism.** (ch. 15)

charismatic: Referring to those Christians who embrace in practice the reality of all spiritual gifts (Greek *charis*; pl. *charismata*) but may or may not belong to denominationally Pentecostal churches. (ch. 15)

charismatic renewal: The spread of Pentecostalism's lively worship and openness to spiritual gifts to other denominations in the 1960s and 1970s. *See also* **charismatic.** (ch. 15)

Christ: From Greek *Christos*, meaning "anointed one" and hence "Messiah" (from Hebrew *mashiach*, "anointed one"). *See also* **messiah.** (chs. 3, 4, 22)

Christendom: (1) A culture that appears to be dominated by Christians and heavily influenced by Christian values, with or without the support of an established (state) church; (2) the worldwide Christian church(es). (chs. 9, 12, 19)

Christian ethics (sometimes called **moral theology** or theological ethics): Gospel-disciplined, critical reflection on individual and corporate Christian life in its totality in particular times and places, including normative guidance about faithful Christian character, behavior, and aspirations. (ch. 21)

Christology (adj. **christological**): The theological study of and discussion about the person (identity) and work of Jesus. (chs. 4, 9, 14)

church fathers (or **Fathers**): Christian theological writers from the end of the first or early second century CE until about the middle of the eighth century CE who contributed to the development of orthodox Christian scriptural interpretation, doctrine, and practice. *See also* **patristic.** (chs. 7, 8, 9, 13, 14)

coded song: A spiritual whose biblical allusions refer not only to heavenly freedom but also to earthly freedom. (ch. 17)

codex (pl. **codices**): Originally, a writing tablet framed in wood (Latin *caudex*); later, a set of individual sheets of **papyrus** or **parchment** bound together as a "book" and protected by a leather or wooden cover. (chs. 1, 6, 7)

colonialism: The practice of a nation extending its power and control over other, dependent territory, including its people and resources, for the powerful state's own benefit. (chs. 12, 16)

Common Era: The common period and calendar shared by Jews and Christians, beginning with the appearance of Jesus and the early church. *See also* **BCE; CE.** (ch. 1)

concordance: An alphabetical list or index of words that occur in a corpus of literature (esp. the Bible), with their references or textual locations (e.g., Gen. 1:1). (ch. 1)

congregational hermeneutics (or "every-day hermeneutics"): Interpretive strategies of nonspecialists in the local church with the goal of understanding how they might be faithfully formed by and for their reading of Scripture. (ch. 10)

conquest. *See* **settlement**

contextual criticism. *See* **intercultural criticism**

contextualization: The practice of biblical interpretation that entails analysis of the interpreters' contemporary situation to aid in appropriate engagement with the text. (chs. 15, 16, 19)

continuationism / continuationist reading: An approach to reading the biblical text that expects Christians to share in the same spiritual experiences (e.g., spiritual gifts, miracles) attested in Scripture because they are believed to remain part of the present church age; in contrast to **cessationism**. (ch. 15)

conversion of the imagination: A phrase coined by Richard Hays that refers to the ability of Scripture to encourage fresh reflection and insight in new situations. (ch. 12)

Coptic: The name of the last stage of the ancient Egyptian language, written primarily with a modified Greek alphabet; Coptic writings include some of the gnostic **Nag Hammadi** texts, certain NT apocrypha, and some early translations of the NT. (chs. 5, 6)

correspondence of relationships: Clodovis Boff's phrase for an interpretive strategy using analogy in which one looks at the similarities between the biblical text as a witness to the life and struggles of the people of God to which the Bible bears witness and the contemporary situation and experience of the reader(s). (ch. 22)

correspondence of terms: Clodovis Boff's phrase for an interpretive strategy of direct, immediate application of the biblical text to the reader, who finds in the biblical story an imaginative frame for viewing the modern world. (ch. 22)

Council of Trent: A key Roman Catholic counter-Reformational ecumenical council held between 1545 and 1563, whose decisions included adopting the **Vulgate** and the longer OT canon. (chs. 6, 7, 14)

covenant: (1) A formal agreement (originally political) specifying mutual benefits and obligations between the contracting parties; (2) thus, one of the major theological terms for describing the binding relationship of God with Israel and all humankind; (3) occasionally used to refer to the Jewish Scriptures or the NT, as in "Old Covenant" or "New Covenant." *See also* **testament.** (chs. 1, 3, 4)

creed: A formal, authoritative summary of basic Christian beliefs. *See also* **Niceno-Constantinopolitan Creed; rule of faith.** (chs. 4, 6, 9, 11, 14)

criteria of authenticity: A set of scholarly principles for attempting to discern the historical genuineness of sayings and events attributed to Jesus, including, for example, multiple attestation, dissimilarity, and embarrassment. (ch. 10)

critical apparatus: A series of notes in the critical Greek or Hebrew text of the Bible giving evidence from manuscripts and other ancient sources that both (a) supports the biblical text provided and (b) indicates alternative readings for uncertain or disputed portions of the text. *See also* **critical text.** (ch. 7)

critical edition. *See* **critical text.** (ch. 7)

critical text: A scholarly reconstruction of the biblical text based on textual-critical evidence indicating the most original reading of the text (for the OT: the uncorrected **Masoretic Text**, with critical notes; for the NT: a reconstruction based on numerous manuscripts). *See also* **critical apparatus; textual criticism**. (ch. 7)

criticisms: The various modern methods used to study the biblical texts, including historical, source, form, tradition, and social-scientific criticism. (ch. 10)

cruciformity (adj. **cruciform**): Cross-shaped existence, referring to the way of the cross or Christlike self-giving, weakness, and suffering. (chs. 4, 12)

D: Abbreviation for the Deuteronomist source, the proposed **Pentateuch** source dating from the late 600s BCE, in Jerusalem. *See also* **Documentary Hypothesis**. (ch. 10)

dalits: The "oppressed," the "destitute," or the "untouchables": members of the lowest caste in the Hindu society of India. (ch. 19)

Dead Sea Scrolls (DSS): A series of more than 800 ancient Hebrew and Aramaic manuscripts (and some Greek fragments) of biblical and extrabiblical writings, dating from the third century BCE to the first century CE, and discovered in eleven caves at **Qumran**, near the Dead Sea, between 1947 and 1956. (chs. 5, 6, 7)

Decalogue: Greek for "ten words"; the Ten Commandments (Exod. 20; Deut. 5). (chs. 3, 21)

deification. *See* **theosis**

Deism: A belief system in which an impersonal God is understood as involved in the initial creation of the universe but not in its ongoing existence. (ch. 11)

deuterocanonical: Referring to a "second canon," a Roman Catholic designation for the seven books (plus additional portions of Esther and Daniel) from the **Septuagint** that are not found in the Hebrew canon or in Jerome's Latin **Vulgate** but are included in the Catholic (and Orthodox) **canon**. *See also* **Apocrypha; Readable Books**. (chs. 1, 3, 5, 6, 9)

Deutero-Isaiah. *See* **Second Isaiah**

Deuteronomic History: A scholarly term for the account of ancient Israel from the beginning of the conquest to the **Babylonian exile** recorded in Joshua through 2 Kings (omitting Ruth) and sharing in part the theological perspective of the book of Deuteronomy. (ch. 3)

deutero-Pauline letters (abbreviated "the deutero-Paulines"): A term used by some scholars to refer to six of the Pauline Letters to represent the theory that they were written by a later author: Ephesians, Colossians, 2 Thessalonians, 1–2 Timothy, and Titus; known more neutrally as the "**disputed letters**" or "contested letters." (ch. 4)

diaspora: Literally "dispersion"; (1) the early Jewish or Christian communities living outside Palestine; (2) other communities dispersed or displaced from and living outside of their homeland (e.g., the African and Latino/a diaspora). (chs. 2, 17, 18)

dispensationalism: A popular Christian **eschatological** belief system focusing on the book of Revelation and proposing that history is divided into distinct eras called "dispensations." (ch. 12)

disputed letters: Letters attributed to Paul whose authorship is questioned; these include Ephesians, Colossians, 2 Thessalonians, 1–2 Timothy, and Titus. *See also* **deutero-Pauline Letters**. (ch. 4)

distantiation: An interpretive step that encourages appreciation of the sacred text in its own historical, social, cultural, and economic contexts. (ch. 16)

divided monarchy: The period of Israel's history (928–722 BCE) following King Solomon's reign in which a unified nation became two entities, Israel in the north and Judah in the south. (chs. 2, 3)

Documentary Hypothesis: The theory, first espoused by Julius Wellhausen, advocating that the **Pentateuch** was composed of four distinct, independently written sources. *See also* **J; E; D; P**. (ch. 10)

dogmatic theology: Formal reflection on and coherent presentation of Christian beliefs, especially as expressed in **creeds** and by theologians through the centuries; also known as "systematic theology"; sometimes used in contrast to **biblical theology**. (ch. 10)

dynamic-equivalence translation (also functional-equivalence translation or, popularly, thought-for-thought translation): A translation that seeks to reproduce the text's sense (or function) by means of changing the form of the original text, when necessary, for the sake of meaning (communicative intent); in contrast to **formal-equivalence translation**. (ch. 7)

E: Abbreviation for the Elohist source, named for its use of the Hebrew word *Elohim* for God, and understood by proponents of the **Documentary Hypothesis** as one of the four written sources of the **Pentateuch**, dating from the mid-800s BCE in the northern kingdom of Israel. (ch. 10)

early Judaism. *See* **Second Temple Judaism**

ecclesial: From the Greek word for assembly, gathering, or community, *ekklēsia*; of or related to the church and its confessions, interpretive traditions, and **liturgical** (worship) life. (chs. 8, 10, 11, 12, 14, 18, 21)

ecclesiology: From the Greek word for assembly, gathering, or community, *ekklēsia*; the theology of the church. (chs. 4, 17, 19)

ecumenical. *See* **ecumenism**

ecumenical councils: (1) The general councils (Nicaea, 325; Constantinople, 381; Ephesus, 431; Chalcedon, 451; Constantinople II, 553; Constantinople III, 680–681; Nicaea II, 787) attended by representatives of the entire undivided church; (2) also, for Roman Catholics, additional councils up to and including the Second Vatican Council (1962–1965). (chs. 5, 9, 14)

ecumenism (adj. **ecumenical**): From the Greek word *oikoumenē*, signifying the entire inhabited world; cooperative relations and activity among Christian churches to express or further the unity of the Christian church. *See also* **generous orthodoxy**. (chs. 8, 11, 12, 13, 19)

eisegesis: The act of "reading into" the text a meaning that is imposed upon it, in contrast to **exegesis** ("leading out")— though it is generally recognized that no interpretation is without bias. (ch. 13)

ekklēsia: Greek for "political assembly," "public gathering," or "community," signifying in the NT an early Christian community similar to the "assembly of Israel" and often translated as "church"; sometimes interpreted, from its component parts in Greek ("out" + "call") as the "called-out-ones." (chs. 21, 22, 23)

encyclical: In the Roman Catholic Church, a papal circular letter written to address a specific issue. (ch. 13)

Enlightenment, the: The period of European intellectual history (also known as "The Age of Reason") in the late seventeenth and the eighteenth centuries, when human reason was cultivated and applied to traditional teachings, including religious claims, texts, and authoritative teaching. (chs. 8, 9, 10, 11, 20)

Epistle (or Letter) of Barnabas: A second-century document included in the **Apostolic Fathers**, attributed to Barnabas, the companion of the apostle Paul, which uses typology to interpret the OT. (chs. 5, 6, 14)

eschatology (adj. **eschatological**): From Greek *eschatos* ("last"); the theology, doctrine, or study of the "last things" and ultimate matters: God's purposes fully and finally realized in history in the resurrection of the dead, the kingdom of God, and the new creation as the age of universal justice and peace. (chs. 4, 12, 15, 21, 22)

Essenes: A separatist Jewish group that rejected the legitimacy of the temple leadership in Jerusalem and established themselves in various places; it is likely that some moved into the Judean desert during the **Hasmonean** period to form an ascetically oriented community at **Qumran**, which is generally believed to be responsible for copying, composing, and preserving the **Dead Sea Scrolls**. (ch. 5)

Eucharist: From the Greek word *eucharistia*, meaning "thanksgiving"; the act, or sacrament, also known as "(Holy) Communion" or the "Lord's Supper," in which the death of Jesus is remembered and his living presence experienced. (chs. 5, 8, 13)

evangelical: (1) Referring to Christian (usually Protestant) individuals and bodies characterized over the last century by an emphasis on biblical authority, theological orthodoxy, and personal conversion to Christ as well as (a) gradual and cautious acceptance of biblical criticism; (b) a variety of social and political agendas, from conservative to progressive; and (c) interdenominational cooperation primarily with Christians of similar conviction; (2) in some contexts, a form of the word means "Protestant" or "Lutheran." (ch. 12)

evangelist: From the Greek word for "good news," *euangelion*; (1) a Christian preacher or missionary; (2) a writer of a canonical **Gospel** (i.e., those according to Matthew, Mark, Luke, John). (chs. 4, 7)

everyday hermeneutics. *See* **congregational hermeneutics**

exegesis (adj. **exegetical**): The act of "leading out" of the text a meaning based on the careful literary, historical, and/or theological analysis and interpretation of a text; in contrast to **eisegesis** ("reading into"), though it is generally recognized that no interpretation is without bias. *See also* **living exegesis**. (chs. 1, 8, 9, 10, 12, 13, 15, 16, 20)

exegete: One who analyzes or interprets the Bible. (chs. 8, 9, 13, 15, 21)

exegetical reciprocity: The principle, followed by rabbis and **church fathers**, whereby one part of Scripture is used to clarify another, regardless of the chronological sequence of the texts. (ch. 14)

exile. *See* **Babylonian exile**

exodus: The foundational event of the people Israel in which, according to the biblical accounts, Moses led the people out of Egypt, perhaps in the mid-thirteenth century BCE. (chs. 2, 17, 24)

extracanonical. *See* **noncanonical**

Farrer Hypothesis (or Farrer-Goodacre Hypothesis): A theory about the Synoptic Gospels advocated by Austin Farrer (1904–1968) and championed today by Mark Goodacre, according to which Mark was the first Gospel, Matthew used Mark, and then Luke used both Mark and Matthew, thus eliminating the need for the Q hypothesis. *See also* **Q.** (chs. 4, 10)

Fathers. *See* **church fathers**

feminist criticism (or interpretation or hermeneutics): Interpretive strategies that include (a) conducting historical and literary investigations into the portrayal of women and other marginalized groups in biblical texts as well as (b) bringing contemporary concerns of and about women and other marginalized groups into the practice of biblical interpretation. *See also* **ideological interpretation; liberation theology; womanist criticism.** (chs. 8, 10, 11, 17, 18)

Fertile Crescent: The area of arable land stretching from the Nile Valley at the southeast coast of the Mediterranean Sea to the Persian Gulf. (ch. 2)

figural reading (or interpretation): The use of a variety of techniques to advance and extend the literal or conventional (usual or primary) interpretations of biblical texts. (ch. 11)

first deportation: The 597 BCE deportation into exile of the Judean king, along with the upper echelons of Judean society, by the Babylonian king Nebuchadnezzar II. *See also* **Babylonian exile.** (ch. 3)

First Isaiah: A designation for Isaiah 1–39, largely the work of the eighth-century prophet Isaiah of Jerusalem. *See also* **Isaiah; Second Isaiah; Third Isaiah.** (ch. 3)

First Jewish Revolt: A Jewish uprising against the Romans, beginning in 66 CE, that resulted in the destruction of the temple in Jerusalem in 70 CE and ended with the fall of Masada in 74 CE. (chs. 2, 5)

First Testament: An alternative name for the Christian Old Testament. (ch. 1)

formal-equivalence translation (or, popularly, word-for-word translation): A translation that emphasizes close agreement between the translation and the form and wording of the original text; in contrast to **dynamic-equivalence translation.** (ch. 7)

form criticism: The method of analysis that (a) classifies units of the biblical text according to literary patterns, or forms, and then (b) seeks to identify the relationship between the forms of those units and their functions in the sociohistorical settings of the communities in which they were orally transmitted. See also *Sitz im Leben.* (ch. 10)

Former Prophets: The first writings in the division of the Hebrew Bible known as the **Nevi'im** ("Prophets"), including Joshua, Judges, (1–2) Samuel, and (1–2) Kings; known in Christian tradition as part of the "historical books." *See also* **Latter Prophets; Prophets.** (ch. 3)

Four Document Hypothesis (or Four Source Hypothesis): A theory about the origins of the Synoptic Gospels according to which Mark's Gospel was written first and the authors of Matthew and Luke each used two main sources,

Mark and **Q** (variously understood as written and/or oral material), to which each added unique material, labeled **M** (Matthew's special written and/or oral material) and **L** (Luke's special written and/or oral material). *See also* **Q**; **Two Document Hypothesis**. (chs. 4, 10)

fourfold exegesis. *See* **senses of Scripture**

Four Source Hypothesis. *See* **Four Document Hypothesis**

Fourth Gospel: A common designation for the Gospel of John. (ch. 4)

functional-equivalence translation. *See* **dynamic-equivalence translation**

fundamentalism (adj. **fundamentalist**): Referring to individuals and churches (usually Protestant) characterized by (1) adherence to the so-called fundamentals of Christian doctrine (the virgin birth, the verbal inspiration and inerrancy of the Bible, and so forth); (2) general rejection of biblical criticism and espousal of very "literal" interpretations of the biblical text; (3) support for very conservative theological, social, and political agendas; and (4) a separatist approach to interchurch cooperation. (chs. 12, 13)

Gemara: Jewish rabbinic commentaries on the **Mishnah** produced after about 200 CE and included with the Mishnah in the two versions of the **Talmud**. (ch. 9)

General Epistles. *See* **Catholic Epistles (Letters)**

generous orthodoxy: An approach to Christian faith and life that affirms the historic **creeds** and practices of Christianity with a spirit of openness to others and to differences of interpretation within the large Christian family. *See also* **ecumenism**. (ch. 12)

genre: Literary type, form, or classification (e.g., historical narrative, collection of prophetic oracles, letter, apocalypse). (chs. 1, 3, 4, 5, 9, 10)

gentile(s): Any non-Jewish person or people, or all non-Jewish peoples as a whole ("the nations"). (ch. 3)

global pentecostalism: The body of Christians worldwide, estimated beyond 600 million, who subscribe to some form of **pentecostal** or **charismatic** Christian faith. (ch. 15)

glocal: Referring to the world and to one's interpretive context as being both "global" and "local." (ch. 19)

glory of the LORD, the: In the OT, a way of speaking about the manifestation of God's presence. (ch. 3)

gloss: An interpretive comment, written between the lines or in the margins of biblical texts and sometimes, in the early medieval period, extracted and compiled into books. (ch. 9)

glossolalia: A form of prayer or prophecy in ecstatic utterances or a language unknown to the speaker and often unintelligible to the hearers, mentioned as a spiritual gift in 1 Cor. 12–14; often referred to as speaking or praying in tongues, or simply "tongues." (ch. 15)

gnosticism (n. and adj. **gnostic**): A term referring to diverse religious movements of the second and third centuries that were generally dualist, stressed gaining special knowledge as the means to salvation, and often reread the Scriptures as esoteric documents. *See also* **Manichaeism**; **Nag Hammadi library**; **Valentinian**. (chs. 5, 6, 9, 14)

gospel/Gospel: "Good news"; (1) the salvific message about Jesus preached by his followers ("the gospel"); (2) a genre of early Christian writing that includes accounts of Jesus' activity and/or teachings, whether canonical or not (e.g., "early Christian gospels"; "the Gospel of Thomas"); (3) one of four such accounts included in the NT canon, usually indicated by an uppercase *G* (e.g., "the Gospel of Luke"; "the Gospels" as the collection of four). (chs. 1, 2, 4, 5, 6)

Greco-Roman (adj.): Relating to or influenced by the cultures of both ancient Greece and ancient Rome during the Roman Period. (chs. 2, 4)

Greek: The **lingua franca** (common tongue) of the Mediterranean basin following the conquests of Alexander the Great, and hence the language of both the LXX and the NT. *See also* **Hellenism; Hellenistic Period**. (chs. 1, 2, 3, 4, 7)

Griesbach Hypothesis (or Griesbach-Farmer Hypothesis): A theory about the origin of the Synoptic Gospels proposed by Johann Jakob Griesbach (1745–1812), who thought that the first NT Gospel was Matthew, that Luke made use of Matthew, and that Mark used both Luke and Matthew; advocated more recently by William Farmer (d. 2000). (chs. 4, 10)

haggadah ("tale" or "telling," related to the Hebrew verb "tell"): A Jewish method of detailed interpretation of biblical narratives, usually drawing a moral from the story. (ch. 9)

halakah (related to the Hebrew verb "walk"): A Jewish interpretive practice of deriving concrete regulations governing individual behavior and social practices from Scripture. (ch. 9)

Hasmonean (or Maccabean): Referring to the second-century BCE family of the Jewish priest Mattathias, who revolted against Antiochus IV, and the subsequent dynasty and period of independence in Jewish history until Rome conquered Judea in 63 BCE. (ch. 2)

Haustafeln: "Household codes," or ancient guidelines for relationships within the household, adapted by some early Christians and found in several NT letters. (chs. 4, 21)

Hebrew: The primary language of the **Tanak**, or **Old Testament**. (chs. 1, 3, 7)

Hebrew Bible (HB): An alternative designation for the Scriptures of Israel (**Tanak**; the Christian **Old Testament**), written primarily in **Hebrew**. *See also* **Masoretic Text**. (chs. 1, 3)

Hebrews: (1) The ancestors of the Israelite nation (from Abraham and Sarah until the time of Moses); (2) an anonymous Jewish-Christian NT writing usually understood as a homily in letter form. (chs. 1, 4, 6)

Hellenism: Greek culture, especially as it was spread beyond Greece by Alexander the Great and his heirs. (ch. 2)

Hellenistic Period: The period of Greek cultural influence throughout the Mediterranean basin, beginning with Alexander the Great ca. 333 BCE. (ch. 2)

heresy: Religious belief understood to be outside the pale of orthodoxy, or acceptable beliefs. Also called **heterodoxy**. (ch. 4)

hermeneutic: A general interpretive philosophy, theory, approach, or strategy; **hermeneutics**: the art and principles of interpretation; adj. **hermeneutical**. (chs. 6, 8–19)

hermeneutic(s) of suspicion: A sort of "guilty-until-proven-innocent" approach to the biblical text because of its alleged patriarchal, oppressive, or otherwise problematic nature or influence; in contrast to a **hermeneutic of trust**. (chs. 11, 12, 14, 18, 20)

hermeneutic of trust: An approach to the Bible characterized by trust in its ability to be a place of encountering God and the divine word; in contrast to a **hermeneutic of suspicion**. (chs. 12, 14, 15, 20)

Herodian Period: The years 37 BCE–66 CE, during the Roman Period in Palestine, when the rulers from Herod the Great to his great-grandson (Herod) Agrippa II reigned. (ch. 2)

hesychasts: Monks, championed by St. Gregory Palamas (d. 1359), who meditated in quietude and claimed to see God with their physical eyes. (ch. 14)

heterodoxy: "Different belief," in contrast to "**orthodoxy**" (right belief) and normally meaning "**heresy**." (ch. 4)

historical-critical method: The modern approach to biblical texts, birthed in the **Enlightenment** and eschewing any reference to God or faith, that uses certain historical criteria to attempt to (a) trace a text's historical origins and development and (b) discern its original meaning; sometimes used interchangeably with **biblical criticism** and **historical criticism**. (chs. 8, 10)

historical criticism: The method by which historians draw on whatever ancient sources are available to them in order to reconstruct past events for the purpose of narrating the story of the past; the interpretive practice of making judgments about texts on the basis of their historical setting and the meanings possible in that setting; sometimes used interchangeably with **historical-critical method**. (chs. 10, 11)

holiness: (1) God's inherent differentness from humanity; (2) the quality of being set apart for divine service. (ch. 3)

Holy Tradition: In Orthodox Christianity, the body of tradition that guides the church, including both Scripture as its core and the subsequent teachings and practices of the church. (ch. 14)

homily: A short, liturgically centered sermon. (chs. 4, 13)

hypostatic union (from Greek *hypostasis*, "individual reality"): The doctrine of the union of the divine and human natures in the one person of Jesus Christ, the second person/individual reality of the Trinity. (ch. 9)

icons (adj. **iconic**): Sacred images of Jesus, biblical figures and events, and saints that are especially significant in Orthodox liturgy and spirituality as "windows into heaven." (chs. 9, 14)

ideological interpretation: Sometimes known as political interpretation, an interpretive approach that includes both (a) uncovering the ideological interests of those who composed and edited biblical materials and (b) bringing one's own ideological interests and agendas (e.g., Marxist, liberationist, feminist) to the task of biblical interpretation. (ch. 11)

inculturation (or indigenization method): An approach to biblical interpretation that deliberately interacts with the text's original context and with the contemporary cultural context in which the text is being engaged. *See also* **African hermeneutics**. (ch. 16)

indigenization method. *See* **inculturation**

inerrancy: The quality of being without error, commonly used to signify either Scripture's alleged lack of any sort of error, including historical and scientific error (sometimes called "verbal inerrancy"), or its lack of religious/theological error alone. (chs. 12, 13)

in-front-of-the-text approaches: Interpretive approaches that focus on (a) the perspectives of various readers and communities of interpretation and (b) the effects that texts have on their readers as they bring their interests and questions to the text and actively produce textual meaning. *See also* **behind-the-text approaches; in-the-text approaches.** (ch. 10)

intercultural criticism (or **contextual criticism**): An interpretive approach that stresses (a) the distinctive context and questions of the reader/interpreter and (b) his or her interaction with interpreters from other cultural contexts. (ch. 10)

intertextuality (adj. **intertextual**): (1) The phenomenon of a text using and reshaping other texts as resources, especially through quotation and allusion; (2) especially the use of the OT by NT writers; (3) occasionally, referring to the relationship between text and reader. (chs. 4, 8, 19)

in-the-text approaches: Interpretive methods that focus on the qualities of the text itself (e.g., structure, narrative elements) and locate meaning therein. *See also* **behind-the-text approaches; in-front-of-the-text approaches.** (ch. 10)

Isaiah: (1) The eighth-century BCE prophet (Isaiah of Jerusalem) whose oracles are found primarily in chs. 1–39 of the prophetic book bearing his name; (2) also, the prophetic book itself as a whole. *See also* **First Isaiah; Second Isaiah; Third Isaiah.** (ch. 3)

Israel: (1) The nation/people descended from the ancestors Abraham, Isaac, and Jacob (renamed Israel); (2) the land promised to Abraham and his descendents, referring to a geographical region (originally **Canaan**), with the precise contours varying from era to era; (3) the northern kingdom during the **divided monarchy.** *See also* **Judah.** (chs. 2, 3)

Israelis / Palestinians: The modern peoples living within the region of ancient Palestine. (ch. 2)

Israelites: The term used to describe the people of God from the time of Moses to the **Babylonian exile.** (chs. 2, 3)

J: Abbreviation for the Yahwist (German "Jahwist") source, named for its use of the Hebrew word **YHWH** for God, and understood by proponents of the **Documentary Hypothesis** to be one of the four written sources of the **Pentateuch**, originating in the southern kingdom of Judah in the mid-900s BCE. (ch. 10)

Jews: Derived from the Hebrew and Greek words for **Judah** and **Judea/Judean;** the term for the people of Israel after the **Babylonian exile,** replacing "Israelites." *See also* **Judaism; Second Temple Judaism.** (chs. 1, 2)

Judah: (1) One of the tribes of Israel; (2) the name of the southern kingdom during the period of the **divided monarchy.** *See also* **Judea.** (chs. 2, 3)

Judaism: The beliefs and practices of **Jews** ("Judahites," or people of **Judah**) during and after the period of the Second Temple. *See also* **Second Temple Judaism.** (chs. 2, 3, 6)

Judea: The Roman province and territory in Palestine roughly equivalent to the former southern kingdom of **Judah.** *See also* **Second Temple Judaism.** (chs. 2, 3, 6)

Ketuvim (also transliterated as Ketubim, Kethuvim, and Kethubim): Hebrew for

"Writings," the third major division of the Tanak, the Jewish Scriptures. (chs. 1, 3)

kosher laws: From Hebrew *kashrut*, meaning "fit, proper, correct," the instructions concerning which foods are and are not allowed to be consumed by the Israelites, and later by Jews. (ch. 3)

L: The scholarly abbreviation for the special material from written and/or oral sources that is unique to the Gospel of Luke. *See also* Synoptic Problem. (ch. 4)

latinamente: A Spanish adverb ("-mente" = "-ly" in English) referring to the reading of the Bible from a Latino/a perspective, recognizing and embracing the distinct realities of Latino/a history and experience. *See also* Latino/Latina criticism. (ch. 18)

latinidad: Spanish for shared Latino/a identity across races and ethnicities. (ch. 18)

Latino/Latina criticism (or hermeneutics): An interpretive approach that foregrounds the Latino/a American experience, recognizing both the hybridity and the diversity of that experience for the many national, ethnic, and language groups from Latin America and the Caribbean. *See also mujerista* theology. (chs. 10, 18)

Latter Prophets: In the Jewish Scriptures, the three major prophetic books of Isaiah, Jeremiah, and Ezekiel, plus the Book of the Twelve. *See also* Former Prophets; Prophets. (ch. 3)

la vida cotidiana. See *lo cotidiano*

lectio divina: Prayerful meditation on Scripture, often compared to "chewing," usually consisting of several steps, including slow reading of a passage, meditation on it, prayer, and action in response. (chs. 13, 15, 20, 23)

lectionary: A collection of passages from all parts of the Bible, organized around a liturgical calendar for use in public liturgy/worship. (chs. 7, 12, 13, 23)

liberationist interpretation (or hermeneutics): A cluster of approaches to biblical interpretation that focus on themes of liberation in the Bible (e.g., the exodus) and their contemporary significance. *See also* African American criticism; feminist criticism; liberation theology. (chs. 11, 22)

liberation theology: A movement that began in late twentieth-century Latin America in which ordinary people and scholars read the Bible to better understand their experience and as a tool of liberation and human betterment, including freedom from economic, racial, and patriarchal oppression. *See also* liberationist interpretation. (chs. 15, 17, 18, 22)

lingua franca: Common tongue or language (Greek, at the time of the NT). (ch. 4)

literal sense: The usual or primary meaning of a text based on applying ordinary rules of language and on which all other interpretations are normally based. *See also* senses of Scripture. (chs. 9, 11, 13)

literary criticism (or approach): The analysis of a text with respect to its literary aspects, including characterization, plot, and so forth. *See also* narrative criticism. (chs. 8, 10)

liturgical: Having to do with gathered prayer and worship. (ch. 23)

Liturgy of the Hours: A prayer form that includes psalms and other biblical texts for each part of the day, reflecting the various liturgical seasons. (ch. 13)

living exegesis: An idiom signifying the ultimate goal of biblical interpretation as the person's or community's embodying the Scripture in daily life. (chs. 12, 20, 21, 23)

lo cotidiano: Spanish for the communal realities of everyday life, including familial, social, and religious relationships, that provide the concrete context for Latino/a biblical interpretation. (ch. 18)

locus theologicus: Latin for a formal context for theological study and reflection. (ch. 18)

Lord/LORD: The English translation of "Adonai," the word Jews substitute for the divine name, **YHWH**, which is sacred and not uttered aloud; usually written in small capitals ("LORD") in English translations to designate it as the divine name. (ch. 3)

LXX: Abbreviation for **Septuagint.**

M: The scholarly abbreviation for the special material from written and/or oral sources that is unique to the Gospel of Matthew. *See also* **Synoptic Problem.** (ch. 4)

Maccabees: (1) The **Hasmoneans**; (2) one or more of the four writings (1–4 Maccabees) from the OT Apocrypha and Pseudepigrapha concerned with the Hasmonean era. (chs. 1, 2, 3, 6)

macrostory: A central biblical theme that witnesses to God's activity and shapes the identity of God's people. (ch. 17)

magisterium: The official teaching authority of the Roman Catholic Church. (ch. 13)

mainline churches: Protestant churches and traditions characterized by (1) general acceptance of biblical criticism; (2) moderate to liberal theological, social, and political agendas; and (3) ecumenical dialogue and cooperation with similar bodies and with mainstream Roman Catholicism and Orthodoxy. (ch. 12)

Majority World: The non-Western nations of Africa, Asia, and Latin America that make up the majority of the world's population; replaces the older nomenclature of "second world," "third world," and "two-thirds world." (chs. 12, 15, 19, 20)

Manichaeism: A third-century CE dualistic, gnostic religious movement that believed matter is evil. *See also* **gnosticism.** (ch. 14)

Marcion (adj. **Marcionite**; n. **Marcionism**): Second-century Christian presbyter in Rome who rejected the Scriptures of Israel (the OT) as the work of a lesser god and who also rejected most of the emerging NT canonical texts as a result of his convictions. (chs. 6, 14)

Markan priority: The view, held by most NT scholars, that Mark was the first canonical Gospel written. *See also* **Synoptic Problem.** (chs. 4, 10)

Marxist interpretation: Interpretive practices that (a) do historical work on the biblical texts from a Marxist, materialist perspective and (b) bring contemporary Marxist, materialist interpretive strategies and agendas to bear on the biblical texts with an eye toward the contemporary world. *See also* **ideological interpretation; liberationist interpretation.** (ch. 11)

Masoretes. *See* **Masoretic Text**

Masoretic Text (MT): From the Hebrew root *msr*, meaning "hand down, deliver"; the standard edition of the **Hebrew** text of Israel's Scriptures (**Tanak**) that is used today, the result of the work of rabbinic scholars (the "Masoretes") in the sixth to ninth centuries CE. (chs. 6, 7, 9)

matriarchs (adj. **matriarchal**): Israel's female ancestors who appear in Genesis: Sarah, Rebekah, Rachel, and Leah. (chs. 2, 3)

Mediterranean Basin: The lands surrounding the Mediterranean Sea—parts of Asia (including Asia Minor and Palestine), Africa, and Europe—where Greco-Roman cultures thrived in antiquity. (ch. 2)

messiah: From the Hebrew *mashiach*, or "anointed one" (Greek *christos*), a term originally designating the Israelite king, who was anointed with oil for that role, and later used as a term for a hoped-for divine agent of salvation; applied in the NT to Jesus as the fulfillment of that hope. (chs. 3, 4, 22, 23, 24)

Middle Passage: The voyage from Africa to the Americas of enslaved persons who were sold into further slavery. (ch. 17)

midrash: From the Hebrew for "search, inquire"; a form of Jewish (especially rabbinic) interpretation of texts, of which there were two main types, **halakah** and **haggadah**. (ch. 9)

minjung: Korean for "populace" or the "common people"; related to theology and biblical interpretation that gives voice to the powerless and poor. (ch. 19)

Minor Prophets (also called the Book of the Twelve): The twelve prophetic writings from Hosea to Malachi. *See also* **Latter Prophets**. (ch. 3)

Mishnah: The written compilation of oral proto-rabbinic teachings prepared near the end of the **Tannaitic** period, ca. 200 CE, and later included in the two versions of the **Talmud**. (chs. 5, 9)

missio Dei: Latin for "the mission of God." *See also* **missional hermeneutics**. (chs. 1, 10, 24)

missional hermeneutics: An interpretive approach that emphasizes engaging Scripture to discern and participate in the *missio Dei*. (chs. 10, 12, 15, 24)

modernism: A general term for the cultural and philosophical aftermath of the **Enlightenment** in Western culture, in which human reason, the pursuit of objectivity, and the notion of universal values were elevated above the values of the premodern era, including the role of faith. *See also* **postmodernism**. (chs. 9, 10)

Modernist crisis: A period of time in the late nineteenth and early twentieth centuries when the Roman Catholic Church perceived that "modern influences" were attempting to destroy its authority. (ch. 13)

monastic community: A group of monks, nuns, or other Christians who voluntarily set themselves apart for prayer and work, and as keepers of the liturgy and Scripture. *See also* **new monasticism**. (ch. 23)

moral sense. *See* **senses of Scripture**

moral theology: Usually a synonym for **Christian ethics**; an older term still typically preferred among Roman Catholics. (ch. 21)

Mount Horeb. *See* **Mount Sinai**

Mount Sinai: The mountain where, according to Exodus, Moses received the Ten Commandments from God; also known in some biblical texts as Mount Horeb. (ch. 3)

MT: Abbreviation for **Masoretic Text**

mujerista **theology**: The doing of theology and biblical interpretation by, or on behalf of, Latinas. *See also* **Latino/Latina criticism**. (ch. 18)

Nag Hammadi: A town in Upper Egypt near which scrolls written by various **gnostic** authors were discovered in 1945. *See also* **Nag Hammadi library.** (chs. 5, 14)

Nag Hammadi library: The collection of mostly **gnostic** ancient **Coptic** texts dating from the mid-second to the mid-fourth centuries CE and found near Nag Hammadi in 1945. (ch. 5)

narrative criticism: An interpretive approach that focuses directly on the biblical texts themselves, which may include attention to both (a) the various literary elements of biblical narratives (e.g., sequence, characterization) and (b) the rhetorical power of stories to draw readers into their plots. (ch. 10)

nations, the: A designation for non-Israelites; also **gentile(s).** (ch. 3)

natural law: The moral law inscribed in nature itself. (ch. 21)

neo-patristic synthesis: A phrase used by some Orthodox Christians to indicate a creative but faithful gathering of the insights of the **church fathers** to address contemporary issues. *See also* **patristic.** (ch. 14)

Nestorians (n., adj. Nestorian; n. Nestorianism): Also called the Church of the East, Christians in Persia who used **Syriac** liturgical rites and, in the seventh century, sent missionaries to China; their **Christology** affirming the independence of Jesus' humanity and his divinity was deemed **heresy.** (chs. 14, 19)

Nevi'im: Hebrew for "Prophets," the second major division of the **Tanak,** the Jewish Scriptures. (chs. 1, 3)

new monasticism: A varied network of present-day churches and other Christian communities that intentionally relocate to live and serve in economically and socially challenged places. (ch. 23)

New Testament (NT): The second part of the Christian Bible, containing writings that present the new covenant (Latin *testamentum*) inaugurated by the coming, life, death, and resurrection of Jesus Christ. (chs. 1, 4)

Nicene Creed. *See* **Niceno-Constantinopolitan Creed**

Niceno-Constantinopolitan Creed: A Christian creed formulated at the First Ecumenical Council at Nicaea (325 CE; the Nicene Creed) and the Second Ecumenical Council at Constantinople (381 CE) to combat various **christological** and other heresies. *See also* **ecumenical councils.** (chs. 6, 14)

noncanonical: Referring to important religious texts in early Judaism and Christianity that are not included in their scriptural collections (canons); also called parabiblical—literally, "surrounding the Bible"—or extracanonical. *See also* **canon.** (chs. 5, 6)

Old Testament (OT): The first part of the Christian Bible, containing the Jewish Scriptures (the **Tanak,** or **Hebrew Bible**) and, except in Protestantism, several additional writings from the Greek Old Testament (the **Septuagint**). (chs. 1, 3)

oral tradition: Stories and other significant aspects of religious or cultural heritage passed on orally instead of, or prior to, being written down. (chs. 3, 4, 6, 10, 16)

orthodox, orthodoxy, Orthodoxy (from Greek *ortho,* "straight" or "correct"): (1) Beliefs that conform to the tradition and accepted as authoritative, as opposed to **heresy** or **heterodoxy;** (2) when capitalized, a branch of Christendom. *See also* **ecumenical councils; generous**

orthodoxy; proto-orthodox; rule of faith. (chs. 5, 6, 11, 14)

P: The Priestly source for, or material in, the **Pentateuch**, probably reflecting a postexilic period and attentive to matters such as liturgy, ritual, and sacrifice. *See also* **Documentary Hypothesis.** (chs. 3, 10)

Palestine: From the Hebrew for "land of the Philistines"; the territory from the Mediterranean Sea to the Jordan Valley and from Galilee to the Negev. (ch. 2)

papyrus: A marshland plant found in Egypt, Galilee, and other wetlands that could be cut into strips, woven, and dried to form a writing surface; papyrus sheets could be glued or sewn together to form a **scroll** or **codex.** (chs. 1, 7)

parabiblical. *See* **noncanonical**

parallelism: The "thought rhyme" typical of ancient Hebrew and Jewish poetry, of which one main form is the pairing of similar ideas or images, rather than similar-sounding words. (ch. 1)

parchment: Writing material prepared from animal skins, which could be used to provide more durable manuscripts than those made from **papyrus;** parchment sheets were attached to form a **scroll** or **codex.** (chs. 1, 7)

parousia: Greek for "coming" or "appearance"; the eschatological appearance, or "second coming," of Jesus. (chs. 4, 5)

passion: The suffering and death of Jesus Christ. (ch. 4)

Pastoral Epistles: Three of the Pauline letters, 1–2 Timothy and Titus, addressed to two of Paul's younger colleagues but whose authorship is disputed. (ch. 4)

Patriarchal Period. *See* **Ancestral Period**

patriarchs (adj. patriarchal): Israel's male ancestors who appear in Genesis: Abraham, Isaac, and Jacob. *See also* **Ancestral Period; matriarchs.** (chs. 2, 3)

patristic: From Latin *pater*, "father"; of or related to the writings of the **church fathers,** theological writers from the end of the first or early second century CE until about the middle of the eighth century CE. (chs. 8, 9, 10, 13, 14)

Pax Romana: Latin for the period of relative peace and stability established by the **Roman Empire** by means that included conquest and repression. (chs. 2, 4)

Pentateuch: "Five scrolls"; the first five books of the Bible (Genesis–Deuteronomy), also referred to as **Torah.** (chs. 3, 6, 10)

pentecostal hermeneutics: An interpretive approach that emphasizes the interrelationship of the church, Scripture, and the Holy Spirit, with emphasis on continuity between God's activity attested in Scripture and God's activity today. (chs. 10, 15)

Pentecostalism: From "Pentecost" (see Acts 2); an evangelical Protestant movement that began in the early twentieth century and emphasizes holiness, divine healing, eschatological anticipation, the gifts of the Spirit (including **glossolalia**), postconversion experiences of empowerment by the Spirit, and mission. *See also* **global pentecostalism.** (ch. 15)

pericope: From Greek *peri*, "around," and *koptein*, "to cut"; a small unit of the biblical text, especially in a historical narrative, particularly in a NT Gospel. (ch. 10)

pesher: Hebrew for "interpretation"; an ancient Jewish method of commenting on the contemporary age by means of a line-by-line exposition of Scripture. (ch. 9)

Peshitta: From the **Syriac** word for "simple"; the authorized Bible of the Syrian Orthodox Church dating from the fourth or fifth century CE. (chs. 6, 9)

politics: The organization of society and public affairs; concerns the nature and power of the state but also relates to a religious body and its operations. (ch. 22)

polyvalence: The quality of possessing multiple meanings or possible interpretations. See also *sensus plenior*; **surplus of meaning**. (ch. 12)

postapostolic era: The period of early Christian history (ca. 70–150 CE) after the presumed death of the original apostles, during which some of the later NT and the earliest non–New Testament Christian writings were composed. *See also* **Apostolic Fathers**. (ch. 5)

postcolonial criticism (or **hermeneutics**): An interpretive approach that attempts (a) to expose and critique colonialism and power structures more generally, as well as (b) to identify and critique the use of the Bible to support or challenge imperial power and other forms of abusive power. (chs. 8, 10, 18)

postexilic: Referring to the period after the return of the exiles from Babylon to Judah. (ch. 3)

postmodernism: The cultural and philosophical reaction to modernism, with its claims of objectivity, universal values, and "metanarratives," that stresses both the impossibility of value-free judgments and the participatory processes in knowing and making meaning. (ch. 10)

precritical: A term sometimes used to refer to exegetical practices used prior to the formation of the historical-critical

methods during and after the **Enlightenment**. *See* **premodern interpretation**. (ch. 14)

premodern interpretation: The interpretive approach to Scripture of the pre-**Enlightenment** era that was governed by theological convictions (e.g., that God speaks through an essentially unified Scripture), the aim of which was to help Christians think and live more faithfully. (chs. 9, 11)

prima Scriptura: An understanding of the role of Scripture that puts it first, but not alone, as an authority for the church; in contrast to *sola Scriptura*, "Scripture alone." (ch. 14)

primeval history: The biblical account in Gen. 1–11 of creation and of human life to the time of Abraham. (ch. 3)

primus inter pares: Literally, "first among equals," referring to the special honor given to a preeminent church leader, such as **Orthodoxy**'s Ecumenical Patriarch of Constantinople, who does not possess jurisdictional rule over other leaders. (ch. 14)

promised land. *See* **Canaan; Israel**

prooftext: A scriptural text used to attempt to justify a belief, usually without consideration of the text's context and in isolation from other texts. (chs. 13, 14, 24)

Prophets: *Nevi'im* in Hebrew, the second division of the Jewish Scriptures, which includes the **Former Prophets** and the **Latter Prophets**. (ch. 3)

prosperity gospel: A popular theology that claims God will grant material blessings to those who follow the divine plan articulated by those offering the message, which often includes generous giving to the messenger's ministry. (ch. 12)

proto-orthodox: Signifying those strands of Christianity that foreshadowed the later orthodox convictions articulated in the **Niceno-Constantinopolitan Creed.** (ch. 6)

proto-rabbinic: Referring to a form of Jewish scholarship contemporary with Jesus and the earliest Christians that anticipated later rabbinic Judaism (after 70 CE). (ch. 5)

Psalter: The Psalms as a collection, known as the "prayer book" of Israel. (ch. 3)

pseudepigrapha (sing. **pseudepigraphon**): From Greek *pseud-* ("false") and *graphai* ("writings"); (1) falsely attributed, **pseudonymous** writings; (2) a collection (the OT Pseudepigrapha) of noncanonical ancient Jewish and Jewish-Christian writings from ca. 200 BCE to 200 CE that purport to originate with a biblical character. (chs. 1, 5)

pseudonymous: From Greek *pseud-*, "false," and *onoma*, "name"; referring to a writing attributed to an authoritative person from an earlier era who is not the actual author. *See also* **pseudepigrapha.** (ch. 4)

purity, ritual. *See* **ritual purity**

Q: Often understood as an abbreviation for the German word *Quelle*, "source," and used to designate a hypothetical written source of sayings of Jesus common to Matthew and Luke but absent from Mark. *See also* **Synoptic Problem.** (chs. 4, 10)

Qumran: A site near the northwest shore of the Dead Sea that was home to a community of sectarian Jews (likely Essenes), where, beginning in 1947, hundreds of ancient scrolls and fragments were found in nearby caves. *See also* **Dead Sea Scrolls.** (chs. 5, 6)

rabbinic: Referring to Jewish teachers (rabbis), especially the era of Jewish teachers following the destruction of the second temple in 70 CE ("rabbinic Judaism"). (chs. 1, 2, 3, 9)

rabbinic Judaism. *See* **rabbinic**

rapture: A modern **dispensationalist** Christian term for the escape of believers to heaven, an idea allegedly found in the **Synoptic Gospels,** 1 Thessalonians, and Revelation. (chs. 4, 12)

Readable Books (*Anaginōskomena*): In early Christianity and in **Orthodoxy,** noncanonical books considered orthodox and thus normally suitable for reading by the faithful. (ch. 14)

reader-response criticism: An in-front-of-the text approach to interpretation that focuses on the text's real or anticipated impact on readers. (chs. 10, 13)

reception history: The history of how biblical texts have been interpreted across the centuries in diverse contexts and media. See also *Wirkungsgeschichte*. (ch. 8)

redaction criticism: An interpretive method that focuses on (a) the redacting, or editing, of earlier sources for the preparation of a new text and (b) the literary and theological contributions of the redactor(s) and of the resulting text. *See also* **redactor.** (ch. 10)

redactor: In the process of producing biblical texts, someone who edited or adapted an existing source. *See also* **redaction criticism.** (ch. 10)

regula fidei: Latin for **rule of faith.** (chs. 5, 6, 9, 11, 12)

relevance theory: A theory of communication stressing that all communicators take for granted, rather than articulate, some information that their audience already shares. (ch. 15)

Renaissance: "Rebirth"; a period that began in fourteenth-century Italy and spread to northwestern Europe, consisting of a humanistic revival of interest in classical (ancient Greek and Roman) art and literature. (chs. 7, 9)

restorationism: A movement that seeks to restore to the contemporary church forms of church life from the earliest, foundational days in the apostolic period. (ch. 15)

rhetoric: The art of persuasive speech. (chs. 4, 9)

rhetorical criticism: The analysis of rhetorical forms and strategies in biblical texts, and of the ways texts exercise power and persuade audiences. (ch. 10)

righteousness (Hebrew *tsedaqah*): The quality of maintaining right relations with God and with other people, often paired with the term "justice." (chs. 3, 4)

ritual impurity: Usually a temporary state that would prevent a person from coming into contact with sacred things, rectified by ritual purification. (ch. 3)

ritual purity: A state in which there are no hindrances to a person coming into contact with sacred things. (chs. 3, 5)

Roman Empire: The military, political, and legislative entity that grew out of the Roman Republic and formally began with the establishment of the first emperor, Octavian (Augustus), in 27 BCE. (ch. 2)

rule of faith (Latin *regula fidei*): A summary account of basic Christian teachings eventually represented in the Apostles' Creed (and similar texts) that serves as a standard of **orthodoxy** and a theological framework for scriptural interpretation. (chs. 5, 6, 9, 11, 12, 14)

rule of life: A collection of the principles and guidelines for life together in a Christian community. (ch. 23)

saga: A short, easily memorized folk story, common in Genesis, that was handed down from generation to generation as **oral tradition.** (ch. 7)

Scripture(s): From the Latin *scriptura*, "writings"; sacred writings, especially those of Judaism and Christianity. *See also* **Bible; canon.** (chs. 1, 3, 5, 6)

scroll: A roll of **papyrus** sheets glued together, or of **parchment** sewn together, to form a roll containing written texts. (chs. 1, 7)

Second Isaiah (or **Deutero-Isaiah**): A designation for the part of the book of Isaiah beginning at ch. 40 (probably through ch. 55, or possibly ch. 66), and generally believed to have been written during the **Babylonian exile,** not by Isaiah of Jerusalem. *See also* **First Isaiah; Isaiah; Third Isaiah.** (ch. 3)

second naïveté: A phrase coined by Paul Ricoeur to indicate the interpretive stance of those who have moved from the "first naïveté" of the uninformed interpreter of Scripture through a time of critical distancing from the text to a place of renewed, informed openness to the text. (ch. 20)

Second Temple: The temple reconstructed from the ruins of Solomon's temple after the Babylonian exile beginning ca. 520 BCE and destroyed by the Romans in 70 CE. *See also* **Second Temple Judaism.** (chs. 2, 3, 6)

Second Temple Judaism: The richly varied Judaism(s) of the Second Temple period, ca. 536 BCE–70 CE, also known as "early Judaism." *See also* **Judaism.** (chs. 2, 3, 6)

Second Testament: An alternate name for the **New Testament**. (ch. 1)

Seleucid: Pertaining to the rule of Seleucus I Nicator and his descendants (312–63 BCE) after the division of the Greek empire of Alexander the Great. (chs. 2, 3)

senses of Scripture: The levels or aspects of meaning in a biblical text first posited by early Christian writers and incorporated into an interpretive approach called fourfold exegesis: (1) the historical (or literal) sense; (2) the tropological (or moral) sense; (3) the spiritual or allegorical (doctrinal) sense; and (4) the anagogical sense (referring to mysteries seen by *theōria* [spiritual vision], or to the afterlife). (chs. 9, 10, 11, 13, 14)

sensus plenior: Latin for "fuller sense" or "deeper sense"; a modern term used especially by some Catholic scholars to describe the multiple meanings of the words of Scripture beyond the literal and spiritual senses. *See also* **polyvalence; surplus of meaning**. (ch. 13)

Septuagint (**LXX**): Traditional name for the most influential Greek translation of the Hebrew Scriptures, which probably began at Alexandria in Egypt in the third century BCE and was used by both Jews and Christians. (chs. 1, 3, 6, 7)

settlement: The arrival of Israelites in the land of Canaan beginning toward the end of the thirteenth century BCE; sometimes known as the conquest. (chs. 2, 3)

Sheol: Hebrew for the place of the dead. (ch. 5)

Sitz im Leben: German for "setting in life," a technical term used especially in **form criticism** to refer to the social and religious context in which a literary type (e.g., miracle story) took shape and was utilized. (ch. 10)

social memory: The shared knowledge and memories of a social group. (chs. 4, 7, 10)

social-science (or **social-scientific**) **criticism**: The application of methods of social history and analysis to the study of biblical texts and the communities that produced and received them, including both (a) social description and (b) interpretation based on other cultures or on theoretical models. (ch. 10)

sola Scriptura: The Protestant Reformation principle of "Scripture alone" as the authority for Christian faith and practice. (chs. 9, 12, 13, 14)

source criticism: The identification and analysis of possible written or oral sources upon which a biblical text is based. *See also* **Documentary Hypothesis; Synoptic Problem**. (chs. 3, 4, 10)

spiritual sense. *See* **senses of Scripture**

supersessionism: A theology in which the Christian church replaces Israel as the people of God. (ch. 23)

surplus of meaning: The quality of a text's having meaning(s) beyond that intended by the author or understood by the original audience. *See also* **polyvalence;** *sensus plenior*. (ch. 12)

synopsis: From Greek meaning "seeing together" or "seen together"; a document that places narratives, such as those found in the Gospel accounts, in parallel with one another. (ch. 10)

Synoptic Gospels: Also called the "Synoptics," the three canonical Gospels (Matthew, Mark, and Luke) that share a similar or common perspective on Jesus' life and teaching (synoptic: "seeing together" or "seen together"). (chs. 4, 10)

Synoptic Problem: The scholarly conundrum of accounting for the similarities and differences among the Synoptic Gospels, including which Gospel was written first and how the Gospels and their supposed sources are interrelated. *See also* **Four Document Hypothesis; Markan priority; Two Document Hypothesis.** (chs. 4, 10)

Syriac: A language closely related to **Aramaic** used by a large group of ancient Christian churches in the East. *See also* **Peshitta.** (chs. 6, 9)

systematic theology: The careful interpretation, articulation, and organization of Christian doctrines, sometimes known as **dogmatic theology.** (ch. 10)

tabernacle: The portable tent shrine that Moses and the Israelites were instructed to build, for their journey in the wilderness to the promised land, to serve as the locus of the divine presence. (ch. 3)

Talmud: The compilation of the Jewish **Mishnah** and the **Gemara,** which appeared in two editions: the Palestinian (ca. 450 CE) and the Babylonian (ca. 550 CE). (chs. 6, 9)

Tanak (also Tanakh): Referring to the Jewish Scriptures, an acronym formed from the first Hebrew letter of each of its three divisions (**Torah, Nevi'im, Ketuvim**). (chs. 1, 3)

Tannaim (adj. **Tannaitic**): The Jewish rabbinical scholars active before 200 CE. *See also* **rabbinic.** (ch. 9)

Targum (pl. Targums or Targumim): An Aramaic translation/interpretation of Scripture, dating from ca. 250 BCE to ca. 300 CE. (ch. 9)

Ten Commandments, the. *See* **Decalogue**

testament: From a Latin word (*testamentum*) that can mean "covenant," referring to the two divisions (**Old Testament, New Testament**) of the Christian Bible. (chs. 1, 3, 4)

textual criticism: The scholarly discipline that seeks to reconstruct the earliest form(s) of a text and to trace the history of its transmission. (ch. 7)

theandric (or **theanthropic**): A patristic term used for Jesus, who is both divine (*theos*) and man/human (*anēr/anthrōpos*), and by extension for the Scriptures as both divine and human. (ch. 14)

theocracy: "Rule by God": (1) the condition of divine rule; (2) a religiously based government. (ch. 9)

theological interpretation: The interpretive approach that emphasizes (a) the interpreters' **ecclesial** location; (b) commitment to the church's confessions, traditions, and liturgical life; and (c) the prioritizing of theological concerns over other concerns—all with the goal of enhancing faithful living and worshiping before God by bringing theological concerns to bear on scriptural interpretation, and vice versa. (chs. 8, 10, 11, 12)

theology: The study of God and all things in relation to God. *See also* **dogmatic theology**

theophany: A manifestation or appearance of God, such as at the burning bush (Exod. 3) or on **Mount Sinai** (Exod. 19–20). (ch. 3)

theōria: Spiritual "sight" by which divine mysteries, and God the Son, may be seen, sometimes in this present life, but certainly by those who are glorified. (ch. 14)

theosis (or *theōsis*): From Greek *theos*, "god"; a term, especially common in Orthodoxy, signifying the destiny of humankind—to share in such divine traits as holiness and immortality and thus become "gods" (i.e., godlike) by grace; sometimes referred to as divinization or deification. (chs. 14, 20)

Theotokos: Title for Mary, mother of Jesus, meaning "God-bearer" and used especially in **Orthodoxy.** (ch. 14)

Third Isaiah (or Trito-Isaiah): A designation for Isa. 56–66, generally believed to be written after the **Babylonian exile,** rather than by the author of chs. 40–55 (**Second Isaiah**) or by Isaiah of Jerusalem. *See also* **First Isaiah; Isaiah.** (ch. 3)

tongues. *See* **glossolalia**

torah, **Torah:** (1) Hebrew for "tradition" or "instruction"; (2) when capitalized, the Jewish designation for the first five books of the Bible, Genesis–Deuteronomy, the first division of **Tanak;** (3) sometimes translated as "law/the Law." *See also* **Pentateuch.** (chs. 1, 3)

tradition criticism: Analysis of the process by which historical events came to be recounted, shaped into oral and written traditions, and included in the Bible's historical narratives. (ch. 10)

transliteration: Transcription of the symbols (letters and characters) of a source language (e.g., Greek or Hebrew) into corresponding letters in another, target language (e.g., English) to facilitate pronunciation of the words of the source language. (ch. 5)

Trito-Isaiah. *See* **Third Isaiah**

tropological sense. *See* **senses of Scripture**

Two Document Hypothesis (sometimes known as the Two Source Hypothesis): A theory about the origin of the **Synoptic Gospels** according to which Mark's Gospel was written first and the authors of Matthew and Luke each used

and adapted two main sources, Mark and Q, but also knew and used other oral traditions. *See also* **Four Document Hypothesis; Synoptic Problem.** (chs. 4, 10)

two-kingdoms theology: Martin Luther's understanding of the divinely intended separation between the political and the spiritual realms as the means of effecting the ordering of the world for human flourishing. (ch. 22)

Two Source Hypothesis. *See* **Two Document Hypothesis**

type: A symbolic precursor within a text. *See also* **typological exegesis.** (chs. 9, 14)

typological exegesis: An interpretive approach that views the text as a narrative in which ancient events and figures (the "**type**") are understood to foreshadow later or contemporary events and figures (the "antitype"). (chs. 8, 9, 14)

typology. *See* **typological exegesis**

Ubuntu: An African concept, especially made known in the West through the life and writings of Archbishop Desmond Tutu, stressing humanity's interconnectedness. (ch. 21)

undisputed letters: The seven Pauline letters whose authorship by Paul is not in question: Romans, 1–2 Corinthians, Galatians, Philippians, 1 Thessalonians, and Philemon. (ch. 4)

united monarchy: The period of Israel's national unity between North and South under the kings Saul, David, and Solomon (1025–928 BCE). *See also* **divided monarchy.** (chs. 2, 3)

Valentinian (Valentinus): Referring to the teaching (or the person) of a late second-century **gnostic** teacher from Egypt and to his adherents. (chs. 6, 11, 14)

verbal inerrancy. *See* **inerrancy**

version: A translation of the Bible. (ch. 7)

Vulgate: The Latin translation of the Bible prepared in the late fourth and early fifth centuries, most of which was the work of Jerome of Bethlehem (d. 420 CE), and which became the official Bible of the Roman Catholic Church. (chs. 1, 7, 9)

Wesleyan quadrilateral: An image summarizing the four-dimensional theological method ascribed to the successors of John Wesley that views Scripture, tradition, reason, and experience as the four guides for doing theology. (ch. 12)

Wirkungsgeschichte: German word often translated as "effective history" or "history of influence," and derived from the philosophy of Hans-Georg Gadamer, referring to the subsequent impact of a text as it is engaged by interpreters. *See also* **reception history**. (ch. 8)

wisdom literature: Books within the Writings of the **Tanak** / **Old Testament**—Job, Psalms, and Proverbs—that emphasize practical wisdom; in the NT, James is often considered to be wisdom literature. (chs. 3, 4)

womanist criticism (or **hermeneutics** / **theology**): An expression of feminist and African American theology and engagement with the Bible that includes a wide range of interpretive practices in the service of concerns for the flourishing of African American women, their communities, and other oppressed communities. (chs. 10, 17)

Writings: Designated **Ketuvim** in Hebrew, the third division of **Tanak**, including Psalms, Proverbs, Job, Song of Songs, Ruth, Lamentations, Ecclesiastes, Esther, Daniel, Ezra, Nehemiah, and (1–2) Chronicles. (chs. 1, 3)

YHWH: The personal name of Israel's God, possibly related to the Hebrew verb "to be"; in Jewish tradition, this name is holy and never uttered aloud, though it is sometimes pronounced and spelled as "Yahweh" by Christians. *See also* **Lord/Lord**. (chs. 2, 3)

yin-yang: Literally, in Chinese, a "shaded area" (yin) and a "brightly lit area" (yang) that are in constant flux; a term used by Asian biblical interpreters in reference to the marginality and in-betweenness of interpretation. (ch. 19)

Zion: Jerusalem: the locus of God's presence among the Israelites, used particularly in the Psalms and Prophets, and sometimes designated "Mount Zion." (ch. 3)

Scripture Index

Subject and Author Index